The
Coming
of the
Book

D0145273

**Titles in the
Verso Modern Classics
Series:**

**Karl Kautsky and the
Socialist Revolution
1880–1938**
Massimo Salvadori

The Coming of the Book
The Impact of Printing 1450–1800
Lucien Febvre and
Henri-Jean Martin

Antonio Gramsci
Life of a Revolutionary
Giuseppe Fiori

For Marx
Louis Althusser

The

The Impact

Coming

of Printing

of the

Translated by

1450–1800

Book

David Gerard

Lucien

Febvre

and

Henri-Jean

Martin

VERSO

London · New York

Edited by Geoffrey Nowell-Smith and David Wootton

First published as *L'Apparition du Livre* by Éditions Albin Michel, Paris 1958
First published in English 1976
This edition published by Verso 1990
© Éditions Albin Michel 1958
Translation © New Left Books 1976

Verso
UK: 6 Meard Street, London W1V 3HR
USA: 29 West 35th Street, New York, NY 10001-2291

Verso is the imprint of New Left Books

ISBN 0-86091-797-5

Typeset in Monophoto Garamond by Servis Filmsetting Ltd
Printed in Great Britain by Biddles Ltd, Guildford

Foreword

H. J. Martin

In 1953 Lucien Febvre invited me to edit this book. He let me have his plan of work and the text of the Preface as it appears here. We agreed that I should send him my first draft which he would amend and expand. In October, 1955 I sent him the manuscript of chapters 1, 2, and 4, and the two first sections of chapter 5, which he was able to revise and put into shape. In January, 1956 I handed over chapter 3, the conclusion to chapter 5, and chapters 6 and 7. He looked them over and gave his verbal approval. At that time he intended to revise the book *in toto*. Because of his untimely death it has been my task to complete the book without his precious help. If I am therefore more or less solely responsible for the work as it stands, I would still like Lucien Febvre's name to stand at the head of a book which was his in conception and inspiration. It is my way of dedicating it to him in recognition and with affection.

October 1957

Preface

Lucien Febvre

About the year 1450 some rather unusual 'manuscripts' made their appearance in the northern regions of Western Europe. Although not very different in appearance from traditional manuscripts, they were 'impressed' on paper, sometimes on vellum, with the mechanical aid of a printing press which used moveable type. The process was simple. But it was the object of considerable curiosity and fascination. In fact, these new books were to cause profound changes not only in the habits of thought but also in the working conditions of secular and religious scholars, the great readers of the time. The changes (we won't say revolution) soon broke the bounds of this original audience and made considerable impact on the world outside. The object of the present work is to study those changes, their causes and effects, and show just how the printed book became something the manuscript neither could nor did become, for reasons we will have to analyse in detail. If this book had not already been titled *The Coming of the Book*, it could easily have been called without pretension *The Book in the Service of History*.

Let there be no mistake; do not take this book for something it is not. It was never our intention to write or rewrite a history of printing: there would be no point in doing again what has already been done by such basic works on the subject as Mortet's *Les Origines et débuts de l'imprimerie*. It can safely be assumed that the authors know the history of the book – at least, as much as is known about it at present – and that they are fully aware of all the work done on printing history since Mortet, necessarily tentative though it is, especially for the early period, and sometimes quite inadequate. There will be no lengthy account of the discovery of printing. Nor will there be any repetition of the hoary old arguments about the primacy of this or that country or about such-and-such a master-printer's significance compared with another's, over the assigning of the honour for printing's discovery to this or that individual, or over the provenance of the oldest incunabula. Perfectly good books are available to keep anyone interested up to date on such questions. It was not part of our purpose to publish another work of that kind.

The book is a relative newcomer in western society. It began its career in the mid-15th century, and its future is no longer certain, threatened as it is by new inventions based on different principles. What needs did it satisfy? What role did it assume? What causes did it serve or fail? It was born in one of those creative periods of change and transition, which all lasting civilisations go through. It was conceived and created a little after the commotion caused by the invention of gunpowder and portable firearms, instruments which men in the 15th century enjoyed contrasting to the peaceable printing-press. It came into being several decades before the enlargement of a world whose boundaries were no greater in the time of Aquinas than they had been in the time of Ptolemy: before, that is, the great sea voyages after 1492 led to the seizure of great continents previously unknown to Europeans. Printing began achieving results before the progressive development of a new perception of space gave western man a system of perspective which has conformed to his needs over the past 500 years, and before the calculations of an astronomer-monk in the Baltic led to the first of the many humiliations to which this Earth of ours was to be subjected in the succeeding centuries. Thus the printed book played its part in a whole range of basic changes which were taking place at the time, though not all at once, nor in such a manner that their effects were cumulative from the very beginning. Yet how can we understand what all this meant to men of the late 15th and early 16th centuries unless we grasp the great variety of innovations of which printing was a part?

To repeat: we hope to establish how and why the printed book was something more than a triumph of technical ingenuity, but was also one of the most potent agents at the disposal of western civilisation in bringing together the scattered ideas of representative thinkers. It rendered vital service to research by immediately transmitting results from one researcher to another; and speedily and conveniently, without laborious effort or unsupportable cost, it assembled petmanently the works of the most sublime creative spirits in all fields – a service which Michelet has described in unforgettable terms. By so doing, it gave their ideas a new lease of life and endowed them with unparalleled strength and vigour. They came to have a new kind of coherence and, by the same token, an incomparable power for both transformation and propagation. Fresh concepts crossed whole regions of the globe in the very shortest time, wherever language did not deny them access. The book created new habits of thought not only within the small circle of the learned, but far beyond, in the intellectual life of all who used their minds. In short we are hoping to prove that the printed book was one of the most effective means of mastery over the whole world. That is the goal of the present work and, we hope, its novelty.

As usual there is an important preliminary problem: how to arrange the book and where to set limits to the subject. We will not use those quite puerile subdivisions based on the artificial distinctions of dates, the kind of thing that is fed to schoolchildren to keep them happy: 'On what day, month, and year did the Middle Ages end?' (We would translate such a question thus: 'What date, in the mind of its inventors, marked the birth and the death of that intellectual abstraction, with no claim to existence other than pedagogic convenience?') We propose, without wasting any time on such controversies, to examine the influence and the practical significance of the printed book during the first 300 years of its existence, from the mid-15th century to the end of the 18th, that is, the period between two changes of climate. At the beginning stands an epoch of intellectual, social and economic upheaval which was to make a lasting mark on the minds, the attitudes, and the actions of Europeans, and which Michelet in a happy phrase called the Renaissance. Then, at the other end of the period, we deal with the second great epoch, another age of confusion, in which political revolution occurs amid a succession of radical economic and social changes leading in the cultural field to that literary and artistic revolution which, under the name of Romanticism, was to unleash further new ideas and feelings. And finally, despite those rechargings of sensibility which found expression through a remarkable upsurge of Christianity and through a passionate search for emotional satisfaction linked to the promise of social reform, let us not forget that modern industry produced, among those whom contemporaries began to call the proletariat, a class consciousness oriented towards action and the fulfilment of its demands.

The end of one epoch is the beginning of another. An elite society gave way to a mass society. Printing found itself inevitably drawn to a further profound transformation. New needs and a new clientele. Therefore mechanisation replaced the old hand press. Therefore, the antagonism developed between craftsman and mechanic, between old-style printing shop and modern mass production. A series of new inventions quickly followed which did much to increase what we might call the virulence of the press. Slowly the machine found its way into what was soon to become the book industry. The printing press sought out and found a form of motive power different from muscle-power. Between 1803 and 1814 Koenig built three types of machine which were the prototypes of modern printing plant: the power-driven platen press, the stop-cylinder press and the two-revolution press. As early as 1791 an Englishman, Nicholson, had worked out the principle of the cylinder steam press with self-inking rollers. Inventions like these of course greatly accelerated the output of books and prepared the ground for the newspaper, the most recent newcomer yet to the world of print. The newspaper! It characterises the grip printing had on readers in the late 19th and early 20th centuries. All such inventions were the result of great social transformations, but in turn gave further impetus to their development.

The whole period is thus of about 400 years duration, from the Renaissance to the Industrial Revolution. How should we subdivide this stretch of time? What criteria should we apply?

If it were a matter of writing a history of printing during the first three centuries of its existence we would be forced to divide the work according to the stages of development of printing technology. Even then I do not know if this would produce the best results, for the methods used in 1787 (when François Ambroise-Didot I, learning from earlier attempts, devised a press which permitted a whole sheet to be printed at once) were very much those which Gutenberg would have recognised as being employed in his own shop, had he been able to reappear and visit a printing press in the France of Louis XVI. But as we have said, the story is about something other than the history of a technique. It has to do with the effect on European culture of a new means of communicating ideas within a society that was essentially aristocratic, a society that accepted and was long to accept a culture and a tradition of learning which was restricted to certain social groups. We will re-use the word we have just used, despite its ambiguities and equivocations, and speak of a relatively restricted elite. An elite which, apart from the aristocracy of blood, included those who had moneyed wealth, political position or prestigious intellectual reputations. How did the printed book facilitate the rule and the activity of these men? How did it preserve the moral, religious and literary heritage accumulated by their predecessors from the 11th to the 15th century? How did it ensure the continuity of a tradition which linked Gutenberg's contemporaries with the three ancient cultures of Greece, Rome and Early Christianity? Conversely, how successful was the book as an agent for the propagation of the new ideas which we classify sometimes under the name Renaissance, sometimes under that of Humanism? How were the two major religious denominations, Catholic and Protestant, served by the press, not to mention other sects? And how did it help the counterattack by unbelievers, firstly Freethinkers, then Deists, then Atheists, and finally Materialists, against revealed religion? Then, again, what literary forms might it claim responsibility for spreading? What others did it resist? How did the physical format of the book help Latin survive its long struggle with the vernacular, or the vernacular languages against old established Latin? I need not continue. A book like this one does not recognise any divisions (within the basic framework of the social structure) other than those which are created by the problems it deals with, and which it aims to help the reader understand.

It was necessary to say all this briefly before embarking on a journey in which no previous guide, so far as we know, has ever pointed out the hazards or come up with the results we are looking for. At least we will try to produce something not too unpleasant to read, and once the book is read the reader may at least have the confidence that he has found in it results born of trustworthy statistics and of enquiry which no-one has yet generalised or assessed.

Manuscripts

Marcel Thomas*

At the beginning of a book dealing with the evolution of printing in the West, perhaps it is worth briefly recalling the historical role of the manuscript, for so many centuries the sole written medium through which ideas found expression. It is not our intention to offer a history of the manuscript book, which would require a whole volume to itself, but rather to show how the production of manuscripts was organised from about the middle of the 13th century to the late 15th in response to growing demand, and to point out what needs the manuscript tried to fulfil up to the time when the printed book appeared and took things a stage further.

Historians have long divided the evolution of the manuscript in western Europe into two main periods, the 'Monastic Age', and the 'Secular Age'. These terms, long current in the field, and familiar to anyone who knows something of the subject, may be somewhat lacking in precision, but nevertheless they do express an undoubted reality. In the 700 years between the Fall of Rome and the 12th century, it was the monasteries and other ecclesiastical establishments associated with them which enjoyed an almost complete monopoly of book production and so of book culture. It is also true that from the end of the 12th century a profound transformation took place. The social and intellectual changes which are particularly clearly reflected in the founding of the universities and the development of learning among the laity, and which occurred at the same time as the bourgeoisie emerges as a class, had profound repercussions on the ways in which books came to be written, copied and distributed.

In this short survey we will ignore the Monastic Age which has been the subject of many recent and excellent studies.[1] Our intention is to

* Keeper in the Department of Manuscripts, Bibliothèque Nationale.

show (in so far as the surviving evidence makes it possible, for many of the problems relating to our subject are still far from being solved) how, from the 13th century onwards, new organisational structures made it possible to satisfy, more or less, the new requirements for books expressed by a steadily growing number of clients.

Although it is impossible to draw up an accurate list of centres of manuscript book production or furnish details of the output of a particular region at a particular time, we can at least give a reasonably accurate impression of the conditions under which books were made and disseminated in the 13th, 14th and 15th centuries. We will not summarise here even the most important features in the evolution of the manuscript book, we will only describe the situation that had developed at the time when printers placed their new techniques of manufacture at the disposal of book producers.

In the Secular Period, if we leave aside changes in the presentation and decoration of books, only small technical improvements can be said to have taken place. But one innovation must be mentioned because it had important effects both upon their manufacture and upon their price, namely the introduction of paper. It did not replace parchment, but supplemented it and made possible the production of less expensive books alongside the traditional luxury manuscripts, though the difference in price was not as great as is sometimes thought. It also made possible the production of books in greater numbers than before.

Later in this volume there is a brief account of paper and its introduction into Europe, and we shall see how papermaking made printing possible. As far as the manuscript goes, paper did not offer advantages over parchment apart from its lower price and the possibility of producing it in unlimited quantity, in theory at least. Medieval paper was more fragile than parchment, had a rougher surface, and was less impervious to ink and less amenable to the pigments used by the illuminators. On the other hand it was lighter in weight. But less than might be imagined, since parchment of great delicacy was being produced in the 13th century, even thinner than the paper of the same period. For example many small Bibles of that date were, thanks to the joint skills of parchmenter and copyist, actually less bulky than the two-volume modern translation by Lemaistre de Sac. Admittedly it requires keen eyesight to read them now, and the eyes need to be accustomed to the handwriting. But there is no doubt that these small Bibles were less cumbersome than the more famous early printed Bibles, and in fact portable printed Bibles were not produced until the 16th century.

Although the main advantage of paper was its low cost and, by the 15th century, its relative abundance, it is not easy to make exact comparisons with parchment or vellum. While we possess many manuscripts which mention the price of vellum, and accounts (usually royal accounts) which record the purchase of vellum and paper,[2] the significance of the terms used is not always clear. Vellum was generally bought by the bundle (usually a dozen and a half whole skins), or by the dozen skins, or by the individual whole skin, or by the *cahier*, that is, already cut and folded into booklets of six or eight leaves. When *cahiers* are mentioned in accounts we have no way of knowing their dimensions or even the number of pages, and so we can draw no firm conclusions about costs.

At the end of the 14th century the price of skins varied between 12 and 20 deniers in Paris. The average area of a skin being about $\frac{1}{2}$ a square metre, ten to twelve were needed to make a volume of 150 leaves measuring 24 cm × 16 cm, typical dimensions of a manuscript book in the 14th–15th centuries. The raw material from which such a book was made could thus be worth anything from 10 to 20 sous in its crude state, and to this we would have to add 4 to 6 deniers for preparing it, i.e. clearing the surface of the remaining bristles and of other blemishes to render it fit to write on. Even these figures are only an indication, since prices varied so much depending on the quality of the skin, the supplies available, and the region in which it was sold. At Paris, the Lendit Fair was an important centre for the sale of vellum.

A simple calculation will be sufficient to demolish the stories so often told about the fabulous numbers of sheep and calves required to make a single book. Even modern works of scholarship continue to repeat these old errors. Thompson, for example,[3] quotes an order by the Countess of Clare in England in 1324 for a copy of the *Vitae Patrum*, for which no fewer than 1,000 skins were allegedly required. At the current price of 2 pennies per skin, the vellum alone would have cost the fabulous sum of £6. In fact an examination of the *Vitae Patrum*, whether in Latin or in one of the contemporary French versions, quickly shows that when written in two columns the text generally fills about 150–160 leaves of 25 cm × 16 cm, or a total area amounting to no more than 6 square metres – a dozen skins at the most.

At about the same time Treasury accounts[4] show that the price of paper was 2 sols 6 deniers for a quire of 'petite forme' (i.e. about 50 cm × 30 cm), which would be a denier and a half for a leaf measuring 0.15

metres square, while vellum, as we have seen, was worth a maximum of 24–26 deniers for a skin measuring o.5–0.6 metres square, including the cost of shaving and preparation. While the difference is certainly appreciable, it is far from attaining the importance once assigned to it. In fact, until the 15th century paper did not seem to possess sufficient advantages, or perhaps was not marketed in large enough quantities, to supplant parchment.

But was there an abundant supply of parchment? In France as in England its price remained reasonably stable from the second half of the 14th to the first half of the 15th century, when book production was increasing rapidly, and this seems to prove that it was not such a rare commodity. It would be interesting to study the number of livestock, and of sheep in particular, to see if there was a corresponding increase over the same period. We do know that 300 years later, when vellum was no longer in general use, except in the copying of legal documents and for some industrial purposes, more than 100,000 bundles a year, each containing 40 skins, were sold in France.

All of which does not mean, of course, that printing could have developed the way it did without paper. Even if a leaf of vellum would have passed through the press easily, the smallest edition of a work would have consumed several hundred skins, even for a book of small format. For larger sizes, thousands of skins would have been required. Aloys Ruppel[6] calculated that each volume of the Gutenberg Bible that was printed on vellum must have required 170 skins (340 leaves measuring 42 cm × 62 cm). The 30 or so copies produced in this way, therefore, would have needed 5,000 skins. For the 100 copies printed on paper the equivalent on vellum would have used up 15,000 skins. Under such circumstances we can only wonder that so many luxury editions were printed on vellum in the 15th and 16th centuries, even though many were Books of Hours of small size.

Monasteries in the Secular Period continued to copy the manuscripts they needed for their own use, just as they had done in the 'monastic' period. The rules of the monastic orders prescribed a certain number of hours each day for intellectual work, and copying was an important part of this. Organised on traditional lines, the scriptoria[7] produced works of learning and service books, and went on doing so until printing finally relegated the manuscript to the past – and indeed beyond, for, as much from tradition as necessity, monasteries still continued to copy missals, antiphonaries and breviaries until well into the 16th century. The predominant feature of the new period which began at the beginning of the 13th century was that the monasteries were no longer the sole producers of books of all kinds and thenceforth scarcely produced more than were needed for their own use.

Intellectual life was now centred outside the monasteries, and it was in the universities that scholars, teachers and students, working in cooperation with artisans and craftsmen, organised an active book trade.

Occasionally, and up until a later date in England than in France, a monastery where the art of calligraphy or illumination was particularly well preserved would still be approached by a monarch or nobleman with a request for a de luxe manuscript. The sale of these was a source of income to the abbeys, but the practice grew rarer and rarer. John Lydgate, poet and monk of Bury St. Edmunds, who composed and copied texts in English which he sold to laymen until his death in 1446, was an exceptional case.[8]

From the early 13th century, and even from the end of the 12th, the foundation of the new universities gave rise to a new reading public. The new readers were, it is true, still chiefly clerics; but for as long as they were at university they were closely attached only to their college, their *alma mater*, and not to any other religious community.

The professors needed texts for their courses, along with works of reference, and commentaries. In medieval education the gloss or commentary on well established authorities was all important in every field of learning. It was therefore indispensable for them to have these works conveniently to hand, and the university would have to provide a library where they could consult them. But it was not always possible to secure texts already in existence, and so the need arose for the establishment of workshops where professional craftsmen, employed by the university, could copy essential texts expeditiously and cheaply.

This did not exclude the use of libraries which existed outside the university, where many rare and useful works could often be found. The loan of books had long been an established practice in the Middle Ages, and various church foundations, such as monasteries and chapters, loaned out works which they would not have agreed definitively to relinquish by selling them to the new university libraries.

Despite the importance of oral instruction, the students too required a few essential books. Even if, for much of the time, they took notes at lectures and trusted to their memory, which medieval methods of education must have served to develop considerably, they still needed some basic books. If they had no time to copy them for themselves and were rich enough to have it done for them, they could order them from professional copyists, who appeared in increasing numbers around the universities. In each university town a Guild of Scriveners or Stationers came to be formed, consisting of clerks in holy orders and also often of laymen: the booksellers were laymen, while the scriveners were usually clerks. Both were assimilated into the university as a clerical branch and enjoyed certain privileges: in particular exemption from some taxes and from duties of watch and ward, together with the right to be tried by the university courts (this being the privilege of *committimus* which goes back in their case to the beginning of the 13th century).[9]

As the price for their privileges, the booksellers, copyists and 'stationers' (the term dates back to classical antiquity and was first revived in the Italian universities) had to accept strict control by the university. As the servants of a body of scholars which extended its protection over them, they were not free, as ordinary craftsmen were, to work for themselves. The way their work was organised was a constant reminder that they were carrying out what we should call a 'service'.

Numerous documents,[10] the chief ones dated 1275, 1302, 1316, 1323 and 1342, give us a fairly precise idea of their duties. They were appointed after a preliminary enquiry to confirm their good standing and professional ability, and they had to furnish guarantees and take an oath in the presence of the university authorities. Once installed, their duties were strictly laid down and their activities controlled. The booksellers were not so much retailers as custodians of books. Because of their scarcity, manuscripts were sold and resold through successive generations of students and teachers. This second-hand market employed the bookseller, who was usually no more than an agent for the vendor, as an intermediary. The security he had to pledge to get his appointment guaranteed his solvency. He could buy and sell only under certain conditions. He had to advertise publicly the titles he held in stock to prevent his making a profit out of an artificial scarcity. And he was remunerated for his labours according to a fixed rate of commission, not being allowed to charge more than 4 deniers for the sale of a volume if the purchaser was a student or teacher at the university, 6 deniers if he was not.

Alongside the booksellers who simply sold books or acted as intermediaries in the sale of books, there were the 'stationers', whose role was more complicated and whose functions have recently been made clearer by the remarkable work of Father Destrez. Thanks to him we now know in some detail the mechanism of the 'taxation' of copies and of the circulation of the 'exemplaria' and, in general, of the institution of the *pecia* or the loan of sections of books.[11]

To keep proper intellectual as well as economic control over the use of books, the authorities required all essential works to be scrupulously checked for textual correctness so that no errors might slip in, distorting the sense. To assure the reproduction of copies under the best conditions, so that the text would be unaltered and the copyists could not make unjustified profits, the universities devised an ingenious system. Manuscripts were loaned which had been carefully checked and revised. From them copies could be made and charged for according to a fixed tariff or 'tax'. The original text (the 'exemplar') was returned to the stationer after copying, and he could hire it out again. This method prevented the corruption of the text, which could otherwise become worse with every copy made, since by this method each copy was made from the same original. Anyone who has had to study the transmission of ancient texts will understand what a good idea this was.

The stationers, apart from multiplying copies themselves, loaned the copy-text or exemplar to students who either wished to copy it or have it copied by the authorised copyists. It did not go out as one book, but in quires (*peciae*), so that several copyists could be making copies from the same manuscript simultaneously. The hiring charge for each quire was determined by the university, and stationers were forbidden to increase it. Moreover they had to loan them to anyone wanting to copy them. If an exemplar was known to be imperfect it was withdrawn from circulation. A number of exemplars have come down to us, often written in a large hand and very worn because of constant use. Since they were made to a consistent standard they had the added advantage of providing a reliable measurement of the quantity of text that a copyist had transcribed, and so made it easier for clients and authorised copyists to agree on a price.

The system thus established for the multiplication of texts lasted until the close of the Middle Ages. In Paris, for example, it was within the framework of such an organisation that printing was introduced, under the auspices of the university. As far as the authorities were concerned, the printing press simply represented a handy means of multiplying indispensable texts even more rapidly and accurately than was possible under the *pecia* system.

The first Paris presses, as we shall see, were set up not so much to turn out the basic university texts of the Schoolmen as to produce a plentiful supply of the classical authors, and the examples of a pure Latin prose style which were particularly in demand. The *pecia* system seems to have answered most normal requirements quite easily. Even before scribal workshops were fully developed in the late 12th and early 13th centuries, Latin texts of Aristotle had spread across Europe:[12] more than 2,000 copies of Aristotle's works have come down to us from the 13th and 14th centuries. If we include those that have disappeared, it is evident that the works of an author of his standing were widely known and that, if the spread of ideas was slow, it was nonetheless effective. The role of memory must not be underestimated in all this. Teaching was conceived in such a way that it could not but develop the memory. Remember that even now a Muslim child of 12 is supposed to be able to recite the whole of the Koran by heart, surprising though it might seem to us.

Still, it was difficult to assemble all the books needed for research. While Raoul de Presles was preparing his translation of *The City of God*, he collated no fewer than 30 manuscripts and 200 different works to compose his commentaries, in order to make his edition as 'critical' as possible.[13] But a note found in a manuscript of the 14th century testifies to the difficulties encountered in the search for a given text: 'I have handed over 14 sols to the scribe who wrote this and 10 deniers to the inn-keeper, and to the person who found the exemplar for me in the inn, 2 sols'. This tip for the person who told him of a copy to be found in an unexpected place recalls the book expeditions of Richard de Bury, author of the *Philobiblion*. We need not exaggerate, however, the difficulties of scholars in the 14th or 15th century; it was simply that texts were much scarcer than they were to be after printing took over. The information we have about libraries in the 15th and 16th centuries (discussed below, p. 263 ff.) gives us an idea of how the situation improved.

While new methods were being used in the universities to supply as many of the required 'learned' works as possible, there remained the problem of producing popular or recreational literature. A new reading public emerged in the late 13th century, with the slow and gradual change from feudalism. A bourgeois class was appearing alongside the nobility and the clergy, equally capable of developing a literary culture. Lawyers, lay advisers at Court, state officials and, later on, rich merchants and town citizens – all needed books, not only in their own subjects like law, politics or science, but also works of literature, edifying moral treatises, romances and translations. This kind of material was not intended for clerics, although they were sometimes the authors, and usually it was in the vernacular. Original works, at first in verse, then prose, adaptations of out-dated works and translations of Latin or medieval classics were soon produced. To distribute them, and satisfy the demands of a growing reading public, required a reorganisation of the book trade.

Any history of French literature will confirm that writings in the French language were already extant by the 12th century. But the means of dissemination were a different matter. The literature of the day was meant above all to be recited or read aloud to an audience, since the reading public was not large enough to warrant any other form of publication. It may seem surprising that a large body of traditional literature could develop in such conditions. We are so permeated by our written culture that it is not easy to make the effort of imagination needed to understand the manner in which oral culture perpetuates itself, despite the fact that we have evidence on the subject from many contemporary cultures. Perhaps the new media of our age, broadcasting and the cinema, may help us grasp how ideas and works can be transmitted without passing through the medium of print.

In the 11th and 12th centuries little was read in the vernacular but many texts were composed in it. M. Faral[14] has shown convincingly how the *jongleurs* on their travels from château to château singing and reciting their poems, romances and lives of the saints – in verse because it was easier to memorise – often composed their own material. The names 'trouvères' and 'troubadours' give us an indication of their roles as creators of literature; the minstrel, on the other hand, attached to a great household, worked only for the lord and his household, to whom he addressed the poems which he either recited from stock or composed himself. The circumstances in which the early men of letters were constrained to practise their craft posed some delicate problems. It was impossible for these writers to retain any literary rights in their work unless they jealously kept the text of their compositions to themselves. But if they did that it was impossible for them to enjoy the satisfaction every artist seeks by broadcasting his work to as large an audience as possible. The two conflicting demands had to be reconciled according to the author's material needs. The best solution was to find a patron, as writers had done in ancient Rome. To him the author could offer his work, in which he included, if need be, flattery of the benefactor and his family. Failing that he could teach the words of his poems and songs to other *jongleurs* for a fee, or sell them copies.

By the late 13th and early 14th centuries we become aware of a more specialised audience, of the emergence of a large public of readers as well as listeners. Henceforward authors could write (or compile) their works without worrying about how they would be communicated to their public. The surest way to success was still through the patron. By getting a king, prince or great nobleman to accept a dedication, and presenting him with a de luxe edition, the writer secured not only the virtual certainty of material reward for his pains, but a good chance of seeing his composition becoming a popular success. Fashion is set at the top and snobbery is a feature of every age. If the public knows a translation has not only been accepted but requested by the king of France, it is almost inevitable that the translation will be widely in demand and that more copies will be requested from the author. He can then have another copy made by a scribe from his own master copy and thus become his own publisher. Boccaccio, for example,[15] in a letter to his friend Maghinardo dei Cavalcanti, which accompanied his gift of a de luxe copy of his latest works, explains how it stayed in his hands a long time after completion because he did not know to whom he might offer it. Finally, he sends it to his friend so that he may let his relations have the pleasure of reading it after him, and after that may 'publish' it abroad (*emittat in publicum*). In fact, this seems to have been one of the tacitly understood functions of the patron, because in the dedication of his *De claris mulieribus* (*On Famous Women*) to Andreina Acciajuoli, Boccaccio writes: 'If you think it good to give my book courage enough to appear in public (*procedendi in publicum*) then, once it is spread abroad (*emissus*) under your auspices, it will, I believe, rise above all the insults of ill-wishers.'

For authors more concerned about material benefits, there was always the possibility of keeping a copy-text of their book and selling further copies made from it, and sometimes we hear of authors running what amounts to their own publishing concern, as did Jean Wauquelin of Mons.[16] Sometimes they used an agent or bookseller, as when Jean Golein sent a copy-text of his translation of Guillaume Durand's *Rational* to the bookseller Henri de Trévou, who sold it in 1395 to the Duke of Orleans' valet for his master 'in his name and on behalf of M. Jean Golein'. This translation had been made by Jean Golein for Charles V twenty years earlier.[17]

The system of patronage was widespread in the 14th and 15th centuries, at least as a method of launching a new work. This explains the difference between the sometimes considerable sum paid out by a king or prince to an author for a first edition or presentation copy of a recent work, and the much lower price which later copies fetched, even if de luxe. From the economic viewpoint the author's rights may be considered to be vested in that first edition, even if it only consisted of a single copy, since thereafter he had no rights in his work. Hence to some extent the patronage system allowed literary men to live by the pen; the price paid by the author was his obligation not to say anything displeasing to his patron, while at the same time trying to write to please a growing public.[18] Books were even quite frequently produced by express command. Charles V, for example, rewarded a number of translators. When, in the hope of encouraging certain political reforms, he wanted to have his advisers and state officials read Aristotle's *Politics*, *Economics* and *Ethics*, he had them translated for that purpose by Nicole Oresme between 1369 and 1372.[19]

Once the work had been completed and offered in its 'first edition' to the patron who had ordered it, or at least accepted it as a gift, later publication was arranged through the copyists and booksellers. The author participated in the process at least in the early stages, though under conditions that are still rather obscure. He appears to have had no greater financial interest in ensuring the speedy circulation of his work than the troubadours had in the previous century, because once it had left him it was out of his hands. Yet he had no desire to remain in total obscurity. He had to find a balance between these two opposing interests.

We are ill-informed about the organisation of the book trade outside the universities, but we know that book dealers who were appointed by the university could do business with private individuals, and that they were not then subject to the same regulations (this we deduce from the regulations' silence on the subject). It is quite certain that, from the end of the 12th century in France and the early 14th century in England,[20] workshops were in existence employing copyists to produce books in the vernacular to be sold just as printed books are today.

Even members of the aristocracy who maintained their own scriptoria were willing to make use of such sources. The Duc de Berry, for example, who frequently ordered de luxe editions from the artists domiciled with him and in his pay, also purchased equally fine copies of manuscripts from booksellers. We know for example that in 1403 he acquired a manuscript of the Arthurian tales in prose from a bookseller called Raoul du Montet.[21] The surviving records reveal that the book was bought from a bookseller and not executed by command: proof that the clientele with a taste for de luxe editions was large enough for a stationer to order a manuscript to be prepared at considerable expense (it was sold for 300 gold écus) without a definite buyer in view. With an increase in this kind of clientele producing an increase in demand, copyists and associated craftsmen concerned in the making of books were prompted to rationalise their production methods to improve productivity.

Long before this, a degree of specialisation had developed in the monastic scriptoria. Some monks specialised in copying, others in illumination, according to their talents. But scribe and illuminator still worked side by side in constant collaboration. In the secular age, however, it became more and more common for separate workshops to be set up, with copyists in one shop, rubricators perhaps in another, and illuminators in another. Thus quite recognisable production lines slowly came into being, involving a large number of artisans, each of whom had his specific task.

By then, the raw material on which everything else depended was rarely prepared in the workshops of the copyists. Treasury accounts show that the vellum, which was usually bought in the crude state (*parchemin froutin*), passed through the hands of specialist craftsmen whose job was to thin it, shave it and bleach it. The payment of each is usually listed separately. When one artisan had written the text, another (the rubricator) added the initial letters or the chapter headings. A further specialist would do any fine capitals that might be required, whether they were coloured, illuminated or historiated. He would not even read the text, and so, in order to avoid any delay or doubt, the copyist would inscribe a small guide letter in the blank space reserved for the initial, a letter known as the *lettre d'attente* (literally the 'waiting letter'). Thus we have proof that the work was done in stages. The illumination, if it was required, came next. This art has been studied in some depth and thanks to the work of Henri Martin we have long had considerable knowledge of its craft organisation;[22] but here we will confine our account to a demonstration of how, in this field as well, attempts were made to introduce serial production.

The illuminator's atelier was separate from the copyist's, though the latter supplied the artist with an indication of the illustrations he wanted. The instructions he placed in the margin have generally disappeared in our surviving manuscripts, though Léopold Delisle[23] has tracked down numerous examples. They seem to have been very brief – for example: 'a Pope on his throne'; 'two monks'; 'a lady on horseback'. The chief artist would first take charge and decide in greater detail what scenes and portraits were to be drawn.[24] If the manuscript was not too expensive he would be content to do a rapid sketch in pencil to help his pupils compose their pictures, according to rules which were well understood and which they had put into practice a thousand times before. Thus an illuminator's atelier at the beginning of the 15th century could produce both a masterpiece like the great Book of Hours known as the 'de Rohan' and mass-produced works in which the general style of the master is recognisable but which are obviously hack copies. And, once the main work was completed, still more specialists might be required to do the backgrounds if the style employed demanded the use of special techniques – if, for example, it called for backgrounds of burnished gold, with or without scrollwork or stippling, or of chequerboard patterns.

Given this multiplicity and complexity of operations, it has frequently been emphasised that the production of a single book involved a colossal amount of work. Such a view is justified, but we must not generalise too readily. The supreme luxury article, a work of art in itself, designed for admiration rather than use – like the sumptuous books belonging to the Duc de Berry, the greatest bibliophile of his day – took months if not years of work and cost a fortune. But many other books were also being turned out (editions of the Book of Hours, for example, whose use spread everywhere in Europe in the 14th and 15th centuries) which were within reach of clients of modest means, and yet were illuminated and decorated. The trade in these Books of Hours was the virtual monopoly of certain specialist workshops, and in these, above all, an ingenious division of labour allowed time to be saved and made possible proper mass production. Ateliers of this kind existed in Flanders, and M. Delaisse has shown how illuminators would produce identical stock scenes for each of the main religious festivals (the Nativity, the Annunciation, etc.), while scribes copied out the different calendars of the various dioceses, so that they could then be joined on to those sections of the Book of Hours which did not vary from diocese to diocese.

   Illuminators even perfected a process which permitted them to make several copies from one original. As Henri Martin has shown, a kind of tracing paper (*carta lustra*) with a resin base was in use from the 14th century which allowed identical copies to be made of a single 'cartoon' or design. There were frequent cases of quarrels and even brawls between illuminators accusing each other of stealing the original cartoon, a priceless resource. Nor were methods like this confined to Books of Hours. Manuscript 117/120 in the Bibliothèque Nationale, which contains tales from the Arthurian cycle, is an exact replica of a manuscript in the Library of the Arsenal. Foliation, the subjects of the illustrations, the breaks in the text to leave space for illustrations are all identical. A discovery made in Holland by M. Lieftinck and announced at the *Congrès des Sciences Historiques* by M. Samaran in 1955[25] gives us an idea of the productive capacity of the workshops using methods like this. In a manuscript at the University of Leyden (B.P.L. 138), which contains a collection of texts known as the *Auctores Octo* and was written in 1437, there is a reference in Flemish to an order from someone who was almost certainly a wholesale bookseller to the chief copyist in a workshop. The order is for a large number of copies of different texts which went to make up a little manual used in the Faculty of Arts: 200 copies of the Seven Penitential Psalms, 200 copies of Cato's *Disticha* in Flemish, 400 copies of a small prayerbook. Figures as large as this amount to true editions.

So, from the mid-13th century, copyists were forced to improve their methods to meet the growing demand, and this in turn led in some workshops to something very like standardised mass production. By using the *pecia* system they succeeded in multiplying university textbooks while avoiding the dangers of reproducing copying mistakes in manuscript after manuscript. Through the rationalisation of work in the large ateliers they were able to produce great quantities of manuals, elementary textbooks and literary works (translations, prose adaptations of the chivalric epics, courtly romances). Most frequent of all were those devotional works without which no bourgeois household was complete, since they were commonly offered as a marriage gift. Even before it was printed in so many editions, the *Travels of Sir John Mandeville*, completed in 1356, was widely reproduced in manuscript. 250 copies survive to this day in many languages: 73 in German and Dutch, 37 in French, 40 in English, 50 in Latin, not to speak of Spanish, Italian, Danish, Czech and Irish translations. All were circulating in the early 15th century.[26]

All things considered, the work of copyists and scriveners paved the way for the printers. On the eve of the appearance of the first printed texts a growing demand for books was obvious, particularly among the emergent social classes, the merchants and the bourgeoisie, who were themselves, in the first half of the 15th century, the inventors and the beneficiaries of many radical new techniques (for example, the blast furnace). Printing, which was essentially a technical development, was to have repercussions which could not have been foreseen in its early stages. The aim of the pages that follow is to show how printing came into being and what were its effects, both immediate and unforeseen.

Preliminaries: The Introduction of Paper into Europe

1

Why did the first printed books appear when they did, about the middle of the 15th century? Why was it that everywhere, from Avignon to Mainz, from Haarlem to Strasbourg, men were exercising their ingenuity on the problem of producing multiple copies of manuscripts by mechanical means? Were the reasons purely intellectual? Certainly the scholars of the day, those great readers we call humanists, were constantly in pursuit of the few and scattered copies of ancient texts which lay in the libraries. Surely they dreamt of some new technique which would enable them to publish large numbers of copies at low cost. Without such a pressing motive no one might have begun searching for the solution that came with printing. Certainly, at the beginning of the 15th century, a period when so many changes were in gestation, men were forced more and more to think about improving the supply of manuscripts to meet the rising level of demand. From the time of the creation of universities in the 13th century there had developed a growing need to own more and more manuscripts. Yet, despite the revival of scholarship and education, there had only been minor improvements in the manuscript industry, like the *pecia* system which reduced the time the precious master copy was taken out of circulation, and the use of abbreviations to increase the speed of writing. Books, however, still depended on the human hand.

The necessary resources to make mechanical reproduction possible were not yet available. Perhaps what was essentially lacking was the technique of making moveable type. An individual letter (a 'sort') requires a metal punch which is used to strike a matrix with great precision in a block of less hard metal. Individual letters are then cast from the matrices, and have to be made from the proper alloy – all of which indicates why the new art was developed by goldsmiths. But there was nothing to prevent it having been developed in the 14th century. Similarly, all the processes covered by the term presswork, i.e. the composing of the type, the inking, and the operation of the press (if, that is, a press was really necessary) could well have been developed before Gutenberg if there had been an absolute need for them. But the important thing was missing.

What we call the printing 'industry', a term used since the introduction of mechanised printing in the early 19th century, was in origin an artisan's trade dependent on one primary material without which it would have been impossible, namely paper. What use would it have been to be able to print with moveable type if the only medium was skin, which takes ink poorly, and when only the costliest skin, that of the calf, was flat and supple enough to be used under the press? It would have been impossible to invent printing had it not been for the impetus given by paper, which had arrived in Europe from China via the Arabs two centuries earlier and came into general use by the late 14th century.

I
The Progress of Paper

It was in the 12th century that a new kind of 'parchment' made its appearance in Italy, introduced by merchants trading with Arab countries. Paper did not have the same surface qualities as parchment. It was more fragile and had a rag base, reminiscent of cotton in appearance (for a long time it was thought to be made of cotton), and it tore easily. At first it was thought of as an ersatz product, but it finally won acceptance and was even thought to have advantages for some purposes : when a document was not intended for preservation or for letters, rough drafts or documents being minuted for later engrossment. So the notaries of Genoa, where paper first made its appearance from Arab Spain, used it for their accounts and would sometimes use old Arabic manuscripts for scribbling things in the margins; soon whole bales of paper were arriving in Italian ports. Occasionally the new material was in use at the Chancelleries of various European states. But fear of its fragility and the risk of it perishing made rulers proscribe its use for the making of charters. Roger of Sicily in 1145 ordered that all charters on *carta cuttanea* made in the time of his predecessors were to be recopied on parchment and then destroyed, and in 1231 the Emperor Frederick II forbade the .se of paper to record public Acts.[28] Despite such edicts paper gained ground and paper mills were started in Italy. There were several papermakers near Fabriano in the early 14th century. Two factors assisted in the development of the industry in that area, the same factors which were to aid the spread of papermaking in the whole of western Europe. The first was technical. As early as the 11th century, if not before, there had existed a device to transform the rotary action of a mill into a reciprocal movement by means of levers. This technical improvement revolutionised a number of early industries. At Fabriano it allowed the papermakers to replace by mallets the old grindstones which the Arabs used to pulverise rags and so to increase output, reduce costs, and produce paper of superior quality.[29] The second factor was the extended cultivation of flax and hemp at the close of the Middle Ages, and the substitution of linen for wool in the making of underwear. This made for a rag base in paper that was less costly and more plentiful just at the time when paper was coming into general use.

With such factors in its favour, the Fabriano trade enjoyed increased prosperity and in 1354 Bartolus the jurist commented on 'the famous town' near Ancona where the best paper was made. The drive to improve quality and quantity made the manufacturers seek better methods, and not only were they the first to use mallets instead of the old grindstone, but they now improved the adhesive properties of their pulp by sub-stituting animal glue and gelatine for the vegetable glues used by the Arabs, which had hitherto given paper its cotton-like finish. Great care was taken over the finish, a job for specialist workmen, and each manu-factory used its own watermark, a conventional and often symbolic sign, to identify its products. This device marked the adaptation of the new medium so that it conformed with European conventions.[30]

In the second half of the fourteenth century, papermakers began to feel restricted at Fabriano and spread to Voltri, Padua, Treviso and Genoa. They soon established two other major centres of production, in the region of Liguria around Genoa, and around Lake Garda, then part of the Venetian Republic. Italian merchants, and particularly the Lombards, were the prime promoters of paper throughout Europe. Briquet in his masterly work *Les Filigranes* shows that the watermark of a winged eagle was common not only in Italy but also in Spain, Holland and Belgium between 1362 and 1386,[31] and about 1365 the journal kept by Lodovico di Ambrogio, a papermaker of Fabriano, tells us that he was selling his product in Fano and Perugia. His travels took him by way of a small port on the Tuscan coast called Talamona to Venice and, by way of Aigues-Mortes, to Montpellier. On the 23rd November, 1365, we learn that he exported 20 bales of paper weighing 1,333 kilos to Montpellier. In three and a half years he shipped 240 bales, or 14,175 kilos, through the port of Talamona.[32]

By this time paper was beginning to replace parchment everywhere. In the late 13th century it was already in use for official purposes in the south of France. It was in use in 1248 by the notaries of Marseilles and in the same year by the commissioners of Languedoc. From 1243–8 the commissioners of Alphonse of Poitiers used it, and in Toulouse the records of the royal commissioners were kept on paper from 1272 to 1274. Shortly afterwards it was to be found in general use in Switzerland and it was gradually adopted in northern France. There, the secretaries at the Chancellery in 1340 used a minute book made of paper, which is still preserved in the Public Record Office in Paris.[33] Its use was spreading through the Low Countries and Germany, while in Venice its use by the business community already went back a long time.

Furthermore, papermaking was established outside Italy when Italian merchants abroad, anxious to expand their trade, encouraged skilled craftsmen to leave Italy to teach their trade elsewhere in anticipation of increased demand. In the Troyes region, at Comtat Venaissin, and around Paris at Corbeil, Essones and St. Cloud we know that primitive papermaking plants appeared in the 14th century, and by the mid-15th France was self-supporting, while the Champagne region actually developed an export business.[34] Italy continued to be the main supplier of Spain, England, the Low Countries, Austria and Germany, even though mills were already in existence in Germany, as they were in Switzerland. Only a few mills were working in Germany at the time of the invention of printing. But warehouses were storing Italian paper in all the great commercial centres, and the last lingering prejudice against paper had disappeared nearly half a century earlier, even if manuscripts were, for a long time, still inscribed on vellum. Was this habit? Probably, but also preference for a tried and tested material, when permanence was the prime requirement. It was this that influenced Gerson when he advised against copying texts on paper in 1415 because it was less durable than vellum.[35] By that time, however, such advice was little more than an expression of nostalgia, since paper had already won the day. One of the indispensable preconditions of the printed book had now been realised.

2

Preconditions of the Growth of Paper-Making: Natural and Industrial

Before examining the characteristics of those areas which became centres for the manufacture of paper to supply the printing press, the influence which the location of paper mills had on the location of printing shops and the impetus that the new invention of printing gave the paper trade, let us first determine what preconditions were necessary to the setting up of a paper mill.

Firstly, how exactly is paper made? The process scarcely changed from the 14th to the 18th century – the replacement of the mallets by cylinders, which took place at the end of the 17th century, being the only major development.[36] The raw material used, old rags, was obtained from specialised dealers, who collected it and brought it to the mill, where it was then sorted. For the best quality paper, printing paper particularly, a flimsy white rag was essential and it had to be separated from the tougher fabrics. After the sorting came the steeping of the rags, which were chopped into small pieces and left in selected places, usually cellars, to ferment. In this process the fatty substances were forced out and the cellulose gradually separated. The raw stuff was then brought to the mill, usually a water mill which had been used to grind corn before its conversion for papermaking. In the milling machine the main shaft had little levers which brought the small wooden mallets into operation, pounding up and down in the beating troughs which contained the treated rags. The mallets employed in the preliminary, reducing, stages of this process were fitted with nails or tiny knives.

The rags were finally reduced in water containing a carefully measured quantity of soap, to produce a paste of determinate thickness which ended as pulp. This was fed into a vat of warm water of a fixed temperature. Into this vat there was then inserted a form – a wooden frame encasing a lattice of brass wires which allowed the water to drip away while retaining a layer of pulp. The form was shaken to distribute the pulp evenly before drying. After they had begun to dry, the sheets which resulted were pulled away by a workman called a *coucheur* who spread them on felt that absorbed more water. Next, the sheets of paper and felt were repeatedly squeezed under a tight press and then the sheets were again taken to the 'little' hanging room where they dried in the air. However, sheets used in this state would drink up ink and so they needed coating with a size, which gave a smooth finish. Lastly, the sheets were dried in a 'great' hanging room, and were sent for final texturing, and finishing with flint. The paper was gathered into reams of 25 sheets, and into bundles of 20 reams, after which it was ready for delivery to market.

To make paper, water was essential, and pure water at that. It was needed to turn the beaters, and to make the pulp. According to Briquet one kilo of paper would need some 2,000 litres of water. Janot, another expert, says that even today to make 300 kilos of paper an hour 200,000 litres of water are required, or 700 litres an hour per kilo.[37]

Such water must fulfil certain requirements. Some rivers never made it easy for the mills along their banks to make paper because their water is often stained brown if it has a high iron content, is muddy, or is full of organic impurities. The water has to be limpid and pure. So manufacturers erected their mills upstream rather than downstream from towns, to eliminate various kinds of detritus. For the same reason they were often situated on the higher reaches of the large rivers or on the middle reaches of their tributaries. Such sites could also be ideal sites for water propulsion; the upper reaches of a river, being narrow and winding, make it easier to cut a secondary channel (generally a chord subtending a curve) or to channel the river directly to drive the mill. It is noticeable that the first papermakers settled in limestone regions, while today such water is not favoured for papermaking. Evidently the disadvantages were less important then than now and were more than compensated for by the abundance of clear water.

In fact many rivers combined the characteristics required for the establishment of paper mills. In France the important centres we find are on the edge of mountain regions: in the Auvergne, at Thiers, Ambert and Chamalières; in the Vosges, around St. Dié and Epinal; and in Angoumois and on the plains of Champagne.

Still more important, and more of a worry to the first papermakers, was the supply of rags. To make a decent paper a great quantity of old rags or rope was needed. Hence the search for fabrics naturally led to mills being established near towns – sometimes near the sea to facilitate exports, but in that case at a port, like Genoa, where rag collection was also easy. Again, it was no coincidence that mills were started in centres of

linen manufacture, such as the Vosges, where there were other favourable conditions, and in Champagne and the Dauphiné, where the extension of the cultivation of hemp encouraged papermaking in the 18th
century at Bourgoin, St.-Jean-en-Royans, Tullins, Domène and Peyrus.[39]

As the trade grew, so rags became scarcer and had to be found farther
afield. Hence the increasing importance of the rag and bone men – the
collection of old clothes became lucrative business from the 15th to the
18th centuries. In the Vosges collectors paid for old rags either with
money, or with pins (1588), and later with crockery. They worked for
second-hand dealers with businesses near the mills who did a rough
sorting of the rags before selling them. At first rags would be gathered
from the immediate neighbourhood of the mill, but by the end of the
16th century ragmen from the Vosges were at work at Metz and Pont-à-
Mousson and in Burgundy. In another papermaking region, that of
Toulouse, Antoine de Laugerière made his fortune in the first third of
the 16th century selling rags by the ton. Many carters were also rag
collectors.[40]

The Vosges and Toulouse were, however, relatively minor industrial
centres. At Troyes, merchants came to the fairs in Champagne with
wagon loads of rags. Once the Auvergne centre developed, the best rags
– from Burgundy – were sent up the River Saône to Lyons where carts
waited to transport them. Auvergne carriers, especially the Forez
carriers, were carting loads from as far afield as Velay and Nivernais.[41]

To ensure supplies and prevent the rag collectors demanding exorbitant
prices, papermakers appealed to the State to grant them monopolies in
rag collection. In 1366 they obtained at Treviso a privilege of this type
from the Venetian Senate, and in 1424 a manufacturer, originally from
Fabriano and working in Genoa, secured a monopoly on the collection
of old rope. In the 1450's, the papermakers of Genoa complained they
were under the thumb of the rag merchants and sought to prosecute
them. In Switzerland, where mills sprang up in the Basel region, similar
steps had to be taken to protect the local industry and the authorities
decided that for 24 hours after rags were put on sale only customers from
Basel should be allowed to buy them. When the industry started in
Germany it was customary to mark out a zone around each town and
grant the right of rag collecting to the local papermakers. In 1622, for
example, all rags collected in the Bremen area were reserved for the mills
of Bremervörde and Altkloster.[42]

The shortage of basic raw materials was probably felt later in France than elsewhere, but it was felt there more acutely. The decline of the industry at Troyes in the 16th and 17th centuries appears to have been caused initially by a critical shortage of rags. In 1674 Colbert, although aware of the problem and concerned at the decline in the industry, could find no solution beyond stipulating that papermakers must keep their vats filled with rags! In the 18th century, reading and writing increased sharply and so there was a new crisis of supply and demand. So great was the dearth of materials in the Auvergne in 1732 and 1733 that the export of rags from that region was forbidden. Moreover, in 1754, the ban was reinforced by refusing to allow the establishment of collecting depots near the ports or frontiers.

Eventually it was clear that only new solutions would prevent chronic crises. In 1719 Réaumur had suggested to the *Académie des Sciences* that it must be possible to make paper from wood. The German, Bruckmann, between 1727 and 1730 had copies of his *Magnalia Dei in locis sub-terraneis* printed on paper made from wood. In 1741 Jean-Etienne Guet-tard, a member of the *Académie des Sciences*, began experimenting with many different kinds of material – palm leaves, esparto grass, aloes, nettles, even mulberries and seaweed; while John Strange in England and Schäffer in Saxony were carrying out experiments on similar lines. In 1786, Léorier Delisle of Langlée published the works of the Marquis de Villette on paper made from marsh weed, and in England between 1801 and 1804 attempts were made to commercialise similar processes; but all these were pioneer efforts. During the French Revolution paper was consumed on a vast scale (one of the reasons for the disappearance of so many early French archives). But it was only in 1844 that the idea of mixing wood pulp with rag pulp was conceived by the bookbinder, Gottlieb Keller. In 1847 Woelter took out a patent for this process. And it was only towards 1860 that straw was definitively and universally applied as a substitute for rags in the manufacture of newspaper.

So as long as rag remained the essential raw material of papermaking – from the 14th to the 19th centuries – the expansion of the papermaking industry appeared forever threatened by lack of raw materials. At Troyes and perhaps Venice in the 16th century, in the Auvergne and Angoumois in the 17th and 18th centuries, papermakers were forced to sacrifice quality to quantity in face of the increasing demand. They had to use poor quality rag and consequently produced worse paper; customers complained and went elsewhere. New mills began in places where they had not so far been found, near to centres of consumption. The story, in brief, of the papermaking industry is that its development was always conditional on the supply of its raw materials.

3
Commercial Factors

From the 14th to the 17th centuries, in response to a growing demand, while shortage of raw material cramped development of the large centres, new establishments were repeatedly founded in regions which until then had had nothing to do with paper making. In order to enable production to flow more easily, new centres were almost always situated at the cross-roads of commercial routes, and if possible near large centres of consumption.

Here again at the beginning, the Italians, because of their resources of capital and technical expertise, played an important part. By the late 15th century Italian production was no longer enough for European needs, and transport added considerably to the cost of such heavy goods: before delivery to French or German customers paper had to pass through three or four hands. Moreover Lombard merchants abroad were willing to finance the conversion of corn mills to make paper near the profitable markets of France, Switzerland and Germany, and they encouraged skilled craftsmen to leave Italy to teach the new art. So we see a Florentine setting up a small mill at Carpentras (1374) and we hear of Italian merchants persuading workmen from the Pignerol region to come and start mills around Avignon at the beginning of the 15th century.[45] Local merchants sometimes invited Italians to do the job. In 1391, for example, Ulman Stroemer of Nuremberg converted a corn mill in Gleismühl and entrusted the instruction of the German workmen to three Italians, Francesco di Marchio, his brother Marco, and a servant. The Church was interested in the new industry and in 1466 Jean de Jouffroy, abbot of Luxeuil, permitted two Piedmontese to start a mill on the Breuchin, a tributary of the Lanterne, in return for annual dues of four reams of paper. Before 1455, the chapter of St. Hilaire d'Angoulême had had its corn mill converted to make paper.[46] The universities naturally wanted to obtain supplies at the lowest possible cost and encouraged the setting up of mills. The construction of mills in Corbeil, Essones, St. Cloud and, especially, around Troyes was greatly encouraged by the University of Paris.

The history of the paper mills supplying Paris is well known thanks to the works of Stein and Le Clert[47] which prove that the growth of a major industry was made possible by the proximity of an important centre of consumption, like Paris, to the cross-roads of a number of trade-routes, like Troyes. Let us take this as a typical example. The University of Paris from the mid-14th century wished to lay in stocks of paper at the best available rates and assigned the right to start factories at Essones and Troyes to Jean le Bon, their owners being exempted from taxes and certain duties in their capacity as agents for the University. Nearer still to the capital, at St. Cloud, two citizens of Paris, papermakers, took the bishop's mill on a long lease in 1376 to make at the said mill: 'paper and other commodities such as may be profitable, except that they may not at any future time grind corn or cause to have ground any corn what-soever'.

But the paper used at Paris came largely from Troyes. By way of the Rhône and Saône rivers, Italians had brought paper to the fairs of Champagne from an early date, and via the Seine and its tributaries it could quickly be carried to Paris, the coastal towns and on to England. There was regular communication between Troyes and Flanders, and Picardy like Champagne was renowned for its hemp. In these conditions, it is hardly surprising to hear of mills starting up along the Seine and its tributaries with the help of Italian money. From the end of the 15th century, Champagne was supplying part of northern Europe, and it was there that Ulrich Gering bought his paper some 75 years later on – the paper with the anchor watermark which was used in the earliest incun-abula published in Paris. The same watermark is found in books printed in the Low Countries at Louvain and Delft and in Germany at Mainz and Cologne.[48]

In Paris the *paupeleurs* or papermakers formed their own Guild in 1398, and the papermakers of Troyes and Paris, who found that competitive new mills were in business all round them, asked the Sorbonne in 1415 to intervene to maintain their preferential status. Letters Patent of King Charles VIII dated 1489, confirming the rights of the University of Paris, list those persons other than Masters, scholars and regents who are entitled to enjoy them: they include 24 booksellers, 4 parchment makers, 11 papermakers (4 from Paris, 7 from Troyes, Corbeil and Essones), 2 illuminators, 2 scribes and 2 binders. For a long time the title 'Official Papermaker to the University' was greatly coveted by makers from

Paris and Troyes, since it was a kind of noble title which conferred exemption from taxation and other substantial privileges which were jealously guarded by the University.

Everywhere, the presence of a large town encouraged the establishment of paper mills, and if Lyons had not happened to be close, with its numberless printing presses, there would probably have been few paper mills in Beaujolais and probably none in the Auvergne. But often the paper was used far from its place of manufacture. For example, Champagne paper was used in Flanders, the Low Countries and north Germany from the 15th to the beginning of the 18th century, and Angoulême paper was used in Spain, England, Holland and the Baltic States in the 16th and 17th centuries. In addition the great production centres were to be found at commercial cross-roads. Despite their proximity to Paris and Lyons, the Troyes papermakers would not have been so numerous but for the fairs of Champagne, nor those of Auvergne without the fairs of Lyons. Paper was a heavy commodity and so access to river transport favoured the development of a centre of production, and proximity to a port was even more valuable. In the 14th century, Italian papermakers set up in the Venice and Genoa districts. In the 16th and 17th centuries, the case of Angoulême is even more striking. During the English occupation of France in the early 15th century Italian paper had been exported to England via Bordeaux. Then a local industry developed whose products were exported by way of La Rochelle and Bordeaux. As a consequence, at the end of the 17th century, when Angoulême paper was famous for its quality, Paris stationers complained that they were obliged to import it overland and so had to pay more for it than their Dutch competitors who received it by sea.[49]

4
The Coming of Printing and the Development of the Paper Industry

Aside from the introduction of the printed book, the demand for paper was felt in many new fields: teaching spread, business transactions became more complex, writing multiplied and there was a growing need for paper for non-literary uses, by tradesmen, haberdashers, grocers, chandlers. A whole new species of trades was created which depended on paper: carriers, box-makers, playing-card makers, bill-posters and related trades whose precise duties were never exactly demarcated, despite endless lawsuits between the rival Guilds.

Yet the main customer was still the printer, the newest arrival. The press was a huge consumer of paper, using 3 reams a day per press. In the 16th century (figures are impossible for the earliest period because there is little documentary evidence) there were at a conservative estimate between 500 and 1,000 presses at work in France, so that paper mills had to supply anything from 1,500 to 3,000 reams a day to keep them in production, which means 450,000 to 900,000 reams a year, if they were working at full capacity.[50] It is not surprising to find that one of Gutenberg's associates owned a paper mill[51] and that the richest men among the papermakers were those who supplied the booksellers, nor was it so surprising that their children were attracted to a career in books and took to printing. They reinvested in the printing of books the money they had made out of the production or sale of paper. Thus the development of papermaking centres favoured the development of printing centres. The entry of Charles VIII into his city of Troyes was celebrated in a verse – albeit a bad one – in which the papermaking trade has a prominent place : –

> Aussi furent de Troyes les papetiers
> En très grand pompe, habillez de migraine
> Et si bien montez sur beaux puissants destriers
> De bordure couvert très belle et saine.
> Pour y venir laissèrent courir Seine,
> Levèrent vanne, délaissant leurs moulins.

According to some, the author of the verse, a papermaker or relation of a papermaker, was one of the Le Bé family. The career of this family was typical in that a family famous for its paper also produced some of the most skilled punch-cutters and letter founders of the 16th and 17th centuries.[52]

In 1405 one Guyot Le Ber (or Le Bé) the elder, a papermaker, was tenant of a mill at St. Quentin near Troyes. Gradually the family expanded the business and soon possessed several mills. The family were appointed Official Papermakers to the University of Paris while also continuing to sell their own products for profit. From 1470 to 1490 their paper was to be found from Paris to Dortmund, from Troyes to Canterbury, from Heidelberg to Dijon, from Mainz to Utrecht and from Bruges to Cologne, all of it bearing the watermark *B*. Already rich in the 16th century, in the 17th they were ennobled. Nevertheless one of the famous Le Bé sons, Guillaume, took up typography and punch-cutting, working with Robert Estienne from 1545 to 1550. Though knowing no Hebrew, he soon mastered enough to cut an alphabet; then he left for Paris and Venice where he worked with the celebrated Aldus firm and perfected his art. On his return to Paris he set up his letter foundry at the corner of Rue St.-Jean-de-Latran and St.-Jean-de-Beauvais at the sign of the *Grosse écritoire*. There he engraved Hebrew letters for Estienne, and musical notation for Le Roy and Ballard. He founded the most distinguished dynasty of type founders in Paris and his son Guillaume II was also a papermaker, type founder, bookseller and printer in the early 17th century.

Nor is Le Bé an isolated example of such inter-connections between the trades involved in book production, for in many places papermakers invested money in publishing. In the early days books sold slowly and often the paper they were printed on could only be paid for as and when they were sold, so that papermakers often acted as bankers to printers and booksellers, while conversely publisher-booksellers would sometimes rent a mill whose product they used. Such was the case, for example, in Strasbourg where Andreas Heilmann, Gutenberg's associate, owned a mill which was rented later, in 1526, to the printer Kopfel and then, in 1550, to another printer, Wendelin.[53] Towards 1535, Eustache Froschauer, whose brother was the printer Christoph Froschauer of Zurich, took a lease of a mill in Zurich. When he died in 1549, Christoph took over the place in his name.[54] Eusebius Episcopus, the famous Basel printer, rented the Courcelles mill in the neighbouring county of Montbéliard between 1575 and 1587. In the later 17th century some Toulouse printers, the Boudes, operated a mill near the city,[55] and later still Beaumarchais acquired mills at Arches and Archettes while he was publishing Voltaire. Finally, in 1789, the Didots bought the Essones mills where the first continuous-process papermaking machinery was to be operated ten years later, as we shall see.

Contact between the papermaking industry and the book trade was always close; the prosperity of either trade depended upon that of the other. To prove this, we have only to compare the distribution of paper mills and printing shops in Europe at different periods. When printing was first making its victorious way in the period from 1475 to 1560 Europe was becoming covered with paper mills.

To demonstrate this, it is worth comparing the distribution of mills in 1475 and 1560, especially in France.[56] In 1475, before printing had made any real impact, a few mills were at work in Lorraine, in Franche-Comté, and at Ambert, Périgueux and Toulouse. There were only two important centres: at Troyes and at Avignon. By 1560, despite a slight decline from the beginning of the century, the Champagne region was still three times more important than it had been in 1475. The mills in the Vosges region also tripled and there were new ones in Brittany and Normandy. In the Angoulême area, which was to be so important in the 17th century, there was also a rapid expansion. Proximity to Lyons with its innumerable printing shops and its fairs had encouraged the growth of paper mills in the Beaujolais and especially the Auvergne. Gradually France eclipsed Italy as Europe's papermaker and most of the Strasbourg incunabula bear French watermarks, especially those of Champagne. For a long time the field remained open to the papermakers of Troyes and their imitators, for there was little competition from Germany, the Low Countries or England. Even a small place like Bar-le-Duc sent its paper along the Meuse as far as Brussels, Louvain, Utrecht and Zwolle where its paper figures in the earliest printed version of the *Ars moriendi*, the *Speculum humanae salvationis* and the *Fasciculus temporum*; it even went as far as Oxford where it was employed in printing the *Canterbury Tales*.[57]

However, paper mills did spread through the rest of Europe, even if not so rapidly as in France. In Switzerland, they appeared in the neighbourhood of Freiburg and, especially, of Basel, where the Italian family of Galliziani settled. Around Basel in 1570 there were seven paper mills supplying the town's printing presses.

In Germany the first mill, at Gleismühl, began work in 1391. By 1420 there was one at Lübeck and some time later at Gennep near Cleves (1428). In 1431 we hear of one at Lüneburg, in 1460 at Augsburg, in 1469 at Ulm: and there were others elsewhere. Between 1480 and 1490 a mill opened in Leipzig, in 1482 one opened in Ettlingen, in 1489 at Landshut, in 1490 at Breslau, in 1496 at Reutlingen. Yet in general progress was slow and not until the mid-16th century was Germany self-sufficient. In 1516 Nordlingen, Augsburg and Nuremberg were still applying for help to Milanese financiers to help set up an industry, while in the West of Germany they had recourse to France for their supplies.[58] Thus even the Rhineland towns, where printing enjoyed such a spectacular career, continued for a long time to import their paper.

Curious as that may seem, the situation was even stranger in the Low

Countries, where papermaking took still longer to grow. Plantin, for instance, used to send to Champagne for his paper[59] and in the mid-17th century the Moretus firm were still buying paper from France; the Elzeviers feared they might have to shut down their publishing house following the end of business relations with France.[60] They adopted their famous small format just to keep their presses working, and began producing these 12mos in the teeth of many complaints from their learned customers. Dutch businessmen did nonetheless invest money in Charenton mills and sold the product throughout Europe from England to the Baltic and from Spain to the Low Countries. Near Angoulême a high-quality paper marked with the arms of Amsterdam was produced. In Louis XIV's reign, this paper, which left the kingdom as blank sheets and therefore free of tax, returned to France in the form of books and pamphlets whose contents often displeased the King.

But the need to manufacture paper on the spot eventually made itself felt in Holland, as elsewhere. When the States General forbade the importation of French paper in 1671, the Dutch set up their own mills. The need to improve quality and to adapt the methods of production to the caprices of their national form of motive power, the wind, led to a new invention – the use of cylinders instead of mallets. This enabled higher output and better quality. The new method soon spread to Germany. But it was not adopted in France until the end of the 18th century, and this, for a long time, ensured Dutch supremacy.

Despite suffering a great crisis whose effects were felt as late as 1725, the French trade did recover and mills began to appear in Brittany, Dauphiné and Champagne, and in the South-West and the North. But the large papermaking centres in the Auvergne and Charenton never recovered the place they had once held in the European markets. Each country had its own industry by this time and in Germany about 500 mills were producing 2½ million reams a year by the late 18th century. The Italian trade was still active at this time, and in England, where a very small number of mills were in operation in the 16th century, 100 were at work in 1696, many begun by Huguenot refugees. In 1722, 300,000 reams were made in England, and it was an Englishman, John Baskerville, who first had the idea of making wove paper without wires or chain lines, in 1750.

So the great increase in the numbers of paper mills coincided with the increased consumption of paper and the use of more and more printing presses. Technical research played an important role in the period when modern industry was in gestation, while France, keeping to traditional methods longer than other countries, fell behind in the early 18th century. Then it attempted to catch up. Desmarestz, a factory inspector, enlisted the aid of a Dutch-trained engineer called Ecrevisse in encouraging selected entrepreneurs to adopt new methods. Some did, for example the Réveillons at Courtalin-Faremoutiers in Brie, the Johannots, and the Montgolfiers (the first aeronauts). On 26th March 1789, on the eve of the French Revolution, the celebrated printing firm of Didot, who were already trying to improve technology, bought the mills at Essones. Here ten years later, while research was proceeding in England and Germany to discover a way to replace the old hand press by modern machinery, a book-keeper back from America called Louis-Nicolas Robert constructed the first papermaking machine. The time was ripe. At the beginning of the 19th century, in order to satisfy the new needs for information and education, more books, administrative publications and, soon, newspapers were required, and consequently more paper had to be produced. Here lay the reason behind the mechanisation of the book and paper trades.

The Technical Problems and their Solution   2

How, in the middle of the 15th century, did Gutenberg and his contemporaries succeed in mastering the many technical difficulties which the invention of printing must have posed? Through what stages did they have to pass (as far as we can ever know or guess) before reaching the final solution? What improvements were introduced into printing between 1450 and 1800? How did these improvements help to strengthen printing and increase the diffusion of the book? These are the questions we would like to consider in the present chapter. For the early period they are particularly hard to answer, although we are able to depend on so many meticulous scholars, historians and specialists in the tradition of Hain, Haebler and Proctor. To repeat: we are not concerned here with problems of attribution, of the paternity of printing and its improvement, so to speak. What we want to do, in so far as it is possible, is to show by what techniques the first incunabula were printed and how these techniques were gradually perfected in the 15th and 16th centuries so that more books could be printed more rapidly. In other words we wish to show how books were first printed on the hand press from the 16th to the 18th centuries and then how a technical revolution was necessary in the late 18th and early 19th century to keep pace with the demand for books and magazines.

I
The Wood-Cut, Ancestor of the Book?

By the mid-14th century paper was in use throughout Europe and before the end of that century had become a common commodity. This offered new possibilities, not because of its price, which in fact dropped only slowly, but because it was possible to manufacture large quantities of the new material possessing a perfectly plane surface; hence it was an ideal medium for mass production of pictures and texts.

A standardised method of making pictures was well known by the 14th century and it was used to decorate bindings with designs impressed into leather by means of an engraved (*intaglio*) plate. In manuscripts the great ornamental capitals which filled the space left by the copyist at the head of each chapter and paragraph were occasionally made with small embossed stamps made of wood or metal. The technique of block printing of patterns on cloth had come from the East and was used to impress designs on silk or linen fabrics and to produce simple devotional pictures and religious scenes using coloured inks.[61] Paper was well suited to this process. Compared with fabric printing, printing on paper with embossed (relief) stamps gave a cleaner and more exact line, whether in black and white or in colour. The earliest examples of xylography, or woodcut printing, known to us are pulls taken on paper of designs intended for cloth: they appeared only a short time after paper had come into common use in Europe, that is, about 70 years before the printed book. They pointed towards a method which might be appropriate for the printing of script.

The first block prints go back to the end of the 14th century and perhaps earlier; we know there was a thriving trade in them along the Rhine and in Burgundy.[62] The new process made possible a multiplication of religious pictures and needed only simple equipment, a block of wood and a knife. It proved enormously successful at a time when religious observance was at the centre of spiritual and intellectual life, the Church in a dominant position, and culture still essentially oral. In such circumstances a graphic technique for the multiplication of devotional images was bound to appear as more of a necessity than printing. The woodcut picture could depict legends or saints (until then only visible on church columns, portals, or windows) vividly enough to arrest the imagination. Because they were portable, people could take them home and contemplate them at leisure; they could see the miracles of Christ or scenes from the Passion, feel that Biblical characters came to life in their hands, be reminded of the ever-present fact of death or see the fight between angels and demons for the soul of a dying man. It is not surprising that the need for this kind of simple visual resource was felt long before the need for printed literary, theological and scientific texts, interest in which was restricted to a small group of clerics and scholars. Even if the reproduction of such texts had been as easy as that of block prints – and this was not the case – it would still have been natural and logical for the block print to precede the printed book. But in fact the technique of the wood-cut did not in any sense inspire printing, which was the result of a quite different technique.[63]

At the beginning of the 15th century popular religious iconography developed, and it seems probable that the first workshops producing cuts were in or near monasteries, and that the great monastic orders helped to promote the widespread use of pictures.[64] The trade in block prints developed quickly and pictures like the Virgin of Brussels (1423), St. Sebastian of Vienna (1437), St. Roch and St. Apollina were available everywhere, adorning the houses of ordinary citizens, and also protecting them against misfortune. St. Christopher, patron saint of travellers, protected one from sudden death, St. Sebastian from injury, St. Roch from the plague, St. Apollina from toothache. Possibly indulgences were attached to the possession of other prints; they were sold in their thousands on pilgrimages, at church doors and at fairs.

The first wood-cuts were without a text but soon it was found effective if a short legend was added, either in a streamer cut out for the purpose, or between the white spaces separating the figures. At first the legends were inscribed by hand, but later they were engraved in the wood with the picture. At the same time the pictures became more secular in character, and consisted for instance of fantastic alphabets in the shape of men and animals, or legendary histories such as that of the Nine Champions of Christendom. The most spectacular development was in the making of playing cards, which was soon to become a large and prosperous industry. The cards were printed from blocks and then coloured, no longer drawn by hand and then illuminated as they had been before. Parallel developments could be detected in the trade in satirical posters, in commercial prospectuses and, finally, in calendars, where text naturally took precedence over picture.[65]

Soon a simple sheet was not enough and small quarto wood-cut booklets appeared. A whole literature came into being, consisting of the most popular moral and religious stories of the day: figures from the Apocalypse, the *Biblia pauperum*, Lives of the Virgin, the *Speculum salvationis*, the Passion, Lives of the Saints, the *Ars moriendi*, etc. By this stage the text was of equal importance to the illustrations, and provided poor clergy in isolated places with models for their sermons and religious instruction. Above all, because of their price and format, these were the first books that were within the reach of the mass of people. Those who could not read could at least grasp the sense of a sequence of pictures, and those who had some rudimentary knowledge of reading – and the popularity of block-books in which the text figured prominently tends to prove the existence of large numbers of such readers – could follow the texts much more easily because they were in the vernacular.

It is with these works, many of which postdated printing, that the story of the block-book ends after it had scarcely begun. Xylography as a technique, however, is not abandoned. The pictures cut for the block-books are exactly the same as the wood-cuts used in the earliest printed books, and the first illustrated books are often adorned with pictures which have already had an independent life as prints. And indeed, for several hundred years, right until the invention of photography, the trade in prints continued to flourish alongside that of the printed book.

No relics have been scrutinised so closely or interrogated so keenly as the block-books which have come down to us, scarce vestiges of a trade that was once extensive. Their very scarcity is a proof of their popularity with a huge public which hardly bothered to preserve them. Most of those which survive have done so because they were inserted in the bindings of books or in the lining of chests. We have no wish to revive old arguments about which country can rightly claim priority in this art, or the correct dating of this or that print, or the origins and types of occupation of the cutters. We must ask a different question, one which bears directly on the origins of printing. If the first block-books appeared before the invention of printing, can we then establish a filiation between xylography and the printed book? Could not the wood cutters, tired of repeatedly engraving new letters for every page, have thought up the idea of cutting the individual letters they had to carve out of the old block? Or of cutting individual letters which could be placed side by side just as a text is composed for printing? After which all that would remain would be to go on to substitute metal for wood.

This seductive theory was in vogue among historians of printing in the last century. But no simple version of this theory will stand up to close scrutiny. For one thing many of the cuts, particularly those with a written text, date from the *second* half of the 15th century. They therefore date from a period in which printing had already been invented, and in which they were competing with it in the realm of popular literature. But the chief objection is the sheer difficulty of cutting letters in wood with sufficient precision for the letter to register cleanly; to compose them properly would be very difficult since wood warps in dry or humid conditions. Wooden letters wear out quickly, and so it would have been necessary to go to the trouble of repeatedly cutting huge quantities of them one at a time. Nor can the theory be sustained if we are supposed to think of the craftsmen as simply substituting metal for wood, since the wood engraver was quite ignorant of the techniques of casting and making fonts from type metal. Besides, the surviving documents prove clearly that the first printed books did not emerge from wood engravers' workshops somehow re-adapted to a new process. Gutenberg, traditionally, and perhaps rightly, seen as the inventor of printing, was a goldsmith; so was Waldvogel of Prague, who was carrying out his own experiments at the same time; so were many other printers of the first generation, especially at Basel, where they were members of the Guild of Goldsmiths.

Thus the printed book cannot be thought of as a refinement introduced by wood engravers. There are further reasons to support this view. Thick, black printing ink only replaced the older ink used in block printing (which was made from lamp black and was brown and watery) after the appearance of the printed book. Similarly, it was not until after the coming of printing that the press was used in xylography in place of the old method of rubbing used in the production of block-books, which allowed printing on one side of the sheet only.[66]

This is not to say that the printed book owed nothing to xylography. The very existence of texts and pictures printed with wood-blocks may have made the possibility of using paper for the mass-production of texts more evident, and quite probably the success of block prints and books made it possible to foresee the kind of success that a more perfect process might enjoy. In short, it is possible that the widespread use of block-books spurred Gutenberg's own initial enthusiasm and persuaded Fust to help finance him. Perhaps letters were originally cast in earthen moulds, in which wooden types had left their impression; perhaps someone experimented at first with a metallographic process to produce block-books. But it is necessary to reiterate that such experiments could only have been undertaken and carried to a successful conclusion by specialists in metal-working, and particularly in the art of metal founding. It is to the activity of these metal founders that we must now turn.

2
The 'Discovery' of Printing

Just what problems faced the men who were experimenting in the first half of the 15th century, trying to find a method for reproducing books by mechanical means? First we must recall some of the essential aspects of the printing process and then, briefly, describe the details of the technique eventually adopted, which was to remain the basis for printing right up to the Industrial Revolution in the 19th century.

The technique of printing by hand can be reduced to three essentials: moveable type cast in metal; a fatty based ink; and the press.[67] The problems of producing an ink thicker than that in common use, and of devising a printing press which would do away with the rubbing technique of the wood engravers, were relatively easy to solve, and we shall not dwell on them here. They were in any case secondary to the really essential problem on which the whole secret of the art of printing, at least as developed in the West, depends – namely the making up of a page of print from separate, moveable types.

Let us recall what the process involves. For each letter or sign a punch must be made from hard metal at the end of which the letter is engraved in relief. The punch is used to strike a die in a softer metal which holds the intaglio (impression). Held in a mould, the die can then cast as many 'sorts' as desired, the letters being made from a metal which fuses at a low temperature, tin for instance or lead. The letters appear in relief as on the original punch.

The pioneers benefited from the experience of goldsmiths and engravers of medallions as well as the moneyers, who were often, anyway, recruited from the ranks of the goldsmiths. They knew already how to make the blind stamps which were used to ornament the leather covers of books. From the 13th century metal founders had known how to employ punches engraved in relief to produce the clay moulds from whose hollow matrices they made the relief inscriptions on crests. Pewter makers were using brass die-stamps from the 14th century, and for a long time die-stamps had been used to strike coins, medals and seals. Although coins and medals were normally made by inserting a thin strip of metal between dies struck by a hammer, they also knew how to obtain this effect by casting metal in a mould, and this latter method, favoured in antiquity, came back into favour at the end of the 14th century in Italy.[65]

So, from the beginning of the 15th century, the techniques of casting from moulds, whether metal, or a mixture of fine sand and clay, and that of die stamping were both known. It was also known how to combine the two techniques by first punching out a matrix and then casting metal in it, in order to obtain figures in relief – the principle involved in letter founding. All that was lacking was the idea of adapting the technique to printing, which would merely demand solving the problems of detail involved in such an adaptation. Probably the inventors tried various devices, only gradually arriving at the final solution. Recent work tends to suggest that the first experimenters, finding that a page made up of so many moveable letters was unstable, and that it was incredibly difficult to hold the characters together firmly to form a level surface suitable for inking, probably tried to overcome the difficulties by casting whole pages en bloc from a single mould.[69]

If we keep these facts in mind (and we have given the details at the beginning to help the reader understand what follows) we may proceed to the documentary evidence which gives us a glimpse of the experiments which led eventually to success. Unfortunately we possess very little evidence. Archival material is rare and such documentary evidence as has survived is difficult to interpret. So long as the technique was still in its infancy, the early pioneers (reasonably enough) did not possess an appropriate vocabulary in which to describe the instruments and materials with which they were beginning to work. Almost as sparse, though slightly more explicit, are the hints to be gleaned from contemporary chroniclers. As for the examination of the earliest printed books which have come down to us, although this may support some hypotheses, it can tell us nothing definite about production processes. Most such books, in any case, seem to have been printed when the invention had already been perfected, and was being applied on a commercial scale.

Firstly the archives. Pride of place must go to a number of cryptic documents relating to the famous lawsuit which took place at Strasbourg in 1439.[70] A citizen of Mainz, one Johann Gensfleisch, known also as Gutenberg, a goldsmith descended from a family of moneyers, had settled in Strasbourg by 1434, and probably a few years earlier. From 1436 to 1439 he was in partnership with three others, Hans Riff, Andreas Dritzehn and Andreas Heilmann, to improve a number of secret processes which he had communicated to them in return for their investment of money and which was intended for the fair at Aix-la-Chapelle.[71] Andreas Dritzehn died and his heirs demanded that they succeed him as partners. This gave rise to a lawsuit and the documents relating to it have survived. We learn that there were three secret processes which Gutenberg was developing: the polishing of precious stones, the manufacture of mirrors (if we can so interpret the word *Spiegel*) and a new art which involved the use of a press, some 'pieces' (*Stücke*) either separate or cast en bloc, some 'forms' (*Formen*) made of lead, and finally 'things related to the action of the press' (*der zu dem Trucken gehöret*). These texts, though susceptible of many and contradictory interpretations, appear to indicate that Gutenberg was then engaged on experiments in printing. But nothing in them helps to elucidate the real import of his researches, how far they were advanced or what process they employed, although it is conceivable that he was already printing with some skill. But we need not labour the point. He was not the only one making such experiments. Documents discovered in Avignon reveal that another goldsmith, Procopius Waldvogel of Prague, entered into agreements with the citizens of Avignon[72] between 1444 and 1446, undertaking to teach some the art of the silversmith (*ars argenteria*) and others the art of 'artificial writing' (*ars artificialiter scribendi*). In a contract dated 1444 there is a reference to *duo abecedaria calibis, et duas formas ferreas, unum instrumentum calibis vocatum vitis, quadraginta octo formas stangni, necnon diversas formas ad artem scribendi pertinentes*. In 1446 there is a reference to *nonnulla instrumenta sive artificia, causa artificialiter scribendi, tam de ferro, de callibe, de cupro, de lethono, de plumbo, de stangno et de fuste*. In the same year Waldvogel supplied or promised to supply equipment for reproducing Hebrew and Latin texts to Davin of Caderousse, a Jew: *viginti septem litteras ebreaycare formatas, s(c)isas in ferro bene et debite juxta scientiam et practicam scribendi . . . una cum ingeniis de fuste, de stagno et de ferro . . . ingenia et instrumenta ad scribendum artificialiter in littera latina.*

What exactly was the process Waldvogel was perfecting? Since the texts are not couched in an appropriate technical vocabulary this question poses such problems of interpretation that it is impossible to give a final answer. It has been argued that he is referring to a kind of primitive printing press or even a writing machine. But that seems improbable. The two alphabets of steel mentioned in the lawsuit of 1444, the 48 letters engraved in iron and the 27 Hebrew letters in the 1446 lawsuit could well be punches but equally well matrices. The 'pieces of tin' (*formas de stangno*) could be castings, but how do we interpret that word *forma*, already used in the Strasbourg documents? Does it refer to individual letters or to a whole page of letters cast at one time? In that case was it not some kind of block printing? Do the *formas ferreas* in the 1444 lawsuit refer to a block matrix made by using the punches successively? These are the questions raised by Maurice Audin.[73]

From the archives let us pass on to the narrative sources. First the famous mention in the Cologne Chronicle of 1499, particularly interesting because the writer says he received his information from Ulrich

Zell, the first printer in Cologne, who was in contact with Schoeffer, one of Gutenberg's partners. This is the translation: 'The noble art of printing was first invented at Mainz in Germany. It came to us in the Year of Our Lord 1440 and from then until 1450 the art and all that is connected with it was being continually improved . . . Although the art was discovered in Mainz, as we have said, the first trials (*vurbyldung*) were carried out in Holland in a Donatus printed there (*gedruckt syn*) before that time. The commencement of the art dates from these books; actually it is now much more authoritative and delicate than it was in its first manner. With the passage of time it has been perfected still more (*mehr künstlicher wurden*).'[74]

This is the source of the great controversy about the 'first manner' employed in Holland, the subject of so much hypothesis.[75] Since Holland was a great centre of xylography, it could be assumed that what are being referred to are wood-cuts; but then that technique was also well known in Germany, the Rhineland and France. Other sources, though later, testify to the persistence of the story and appear to confirm the theory that impressions were obtained in Holland by some process or other, which attempts have often been made to reconstruct. In 1561 two Humanists, Jan Van Zuren and Dirk Volkertroon Coornhert of Haarlem, claimed for that city the glory of having been the cradle of printing and Adrian de Jonghe records in his *Chronicles of Holland*, printed after his death, a local tradition according to which an inhabitant of the place, one Laurens Janszoon, surnamed Coster, before 1441 invented the art of assembling moveable type cast in metal with a view to reproducing texts by mechanical means. Besides other books, Coster allegedly printed a *Speculum humanae salvationis* and a Donatus. His secret was divulged in Amsterdam in 1442, then at Cologne and at Mainz by a workman who had left him.[76]

Some references have been found which mention the purchase at Bruges of copies of a Doctrinale 'cast from mould' and they have sometimes been associated with these accounts. They may be found in the *Mémoriaux* of Jean le Robert, abbot of St. Aubert de Cambrai, under the dates 1445 and 1451. But here again there is a problem of interpretation: is the phrase used, *jeté en moule*, synonymous with *taillé en moule* ('cast' as opposed to 'cut')? If so, then ordinary wood-cuts are being referred to. (Playing card makers were qualified as *tailleurs de moules*.) Or does the phrase *jeté en moule* allude to a technique of metal casting by which the page was cast in a single block from a matrix prepared beforehand? There have been some attempts to interpret it in this way.

In the face of such vagueness and difficulties of interpretation we are reduced to what are sometimes very tenuous hypotheses about early attempts at printing in Holland. We get no nearer to a solution by looking at the books since no evidence of actual techniques used can be found by examining them. One fact, however, deserves to be noted: there exists a whole series of undated printed books, very probably of Dutch origin, among which are two leaves of an ABC and four of a Donatus, preserved in the library at Haarlem. Some experts believe these to have been cast from earthen moulds and not metal matrices, and perhaps made with wooden punches. These texts are probably later than the first books printed at Mainz, but it is still possible that the method used derived from an earlier one than that employed at Mainz.[77]

Others, better qualified than us, are still trying to throw light on these problems. We may confine ourselves here to saying that it will probably never be possible to establish with any confidence how the early pioneers achieved their results. The crucial question relates to the actual making of the letters. What kind of punches did they use in their first trials? Were the matrices always of metal or did they use clay and fine sand to make their moulds at the beginning? If so, did they use wooden punches? Did they not make moulds of lead by melting lead around a metal or wooden punch, and would they not end up with letters of lead or some metal if the medium used was a lead mould? Did they turn out the matrices and printing-blocks for whole pages at a time? One thing is sure about the early craftsmen: that they were feeling their way forward by slow degrees for a long time before they found the answer. And another fact seems certain: that the men at work on this were numerous – Coster (if he did exist) in Holland, Gutenberg, Fust and Schoeffer in Mainz, Waldvogel at Avignon, all were trying to perfect the process, to reproduce texts by mechanical means. Lack of documentary evidence is probably all that prevents us from adding the names of other pioneers who must have been struggling with the same problems in the years between 1430 and 1450 when the success of the xylographs had demonstrated the utility and prospects of such an invention.

Be that as it may, if they had not already done so between 1445 and 1450 the various experimenters were on the point of achieving a breakthrough, and the fifteen years after that marked a decisive step in the history of printing, when the invention once perfected began to be applied commercially and industrially, and spread throughout Europe.

Mainz was without any doubt the cradle of the first printing industry and its evolution is linked with three names: Gutenberg, the man named in the Strasbourg legal suit, Johann Fust, a rich citizen who was his financier, and Peter Schoeffer, a former student of the University of Paris who was probably a copyist and a calligrapher before turning printer. After remaining in Strasbourg until at least 1444, Gutenberg returned to his native city before October, 1448. But to continue his experiments he had to have more capital and he found a backer in the person of Fust who loaned him 800 florins at 5 per cent interest in 1450, to pay for certain implements (*Geczuge*). Later he promised to let Gutenberg have another 300 florins for his 'book work' (*Werk der Bücher*) under another agreement by which the expenses incurred in buying paper, parchment and ink were guaranteed. All this suggests that Gutenberg was on the brink of success in his work, if he had not already succeeded. But in 1455 there was a dramatic turn of events. Fust accused Gutenberg of not keeping to his agreement, and took him to court, where he was ordered to pay the interest due and return the capital not yet spent.[78] Two years later, on the 14th October 1457, the first work which can be dated came from the press, the Mainz Psalter, the work of Fust and his new associate, Schoeffer. Subsequently, Schoeffer developed the business, and his firm, which continued in existence until the beginning of the 16th century, remained for a long time one of the most important printing houses in Europe.

Many mysteries remain. The perfect execution of the Psalter proves that it was no first attempt. Some early copies of Donatus, and some German astronomical calendars, suggest that printing had already been going on as a trade since 1450 at the latest, and it is possible that Gutenberg had produced some printing before his return to Mainz, particularly during his partnership with Fust. Was it when Gutenberg's experiments had finally come to something that Fust took the opportunity of ridding himself of an inventor who had become an embarrassment and whom he could replace with one of his assistants, Peter Schoeffer, who knew his master's secrets but was perhaps more amenable and possessed more business acumen? If so, Gutenberg appears to be the typical genius, stripped of the secret to which he had devoted years of his life. Did he continue to work after his rupture with Fust? What happened to him? Did he go on with his experiments at Bamberg as some suppose, without convincing proof? We know very little about him after 1455. It is thought he may have lived in penury because from 1457 until his death he was unable to pay the chapter of St. Thomas at Strasbourg the sum of 4 livres he owed as interest on a loan made in 1442. In 1465 the Archbishop Elector of Mainz ennobled him for personal services and attached him to his palace at Eltville where one cannot help wondering if he installed a printing press. At all events, despite the many contemporary references to his role in the invention of printing, the name of Gutenberg does not appear on the imprint of any book.[79]

It is generally agreed that several workshops were simultaneously in operation between 1450 and 1455 in Mainz producing a great number of books on a commercial scale: Donatus' Latin grammar for beginners, calendars in the vernacular, 'letters of indulgence' (receipts given to those who bought the indulgences granted by Pope Nicholas V in 1451 in order to assist the King of Cyprus, Guy de Lusignan, against the Turks). Then there were more important works, like the celebrated 42-line Bible in three volumes, traditionally regarded as the first printed book, the 36-line in three volumes, printed before 1461, the Mainz Psalter, the Constance Missal, the *Catholicon* of Giovanni Balbi (1460) and many others. All these came from Mainz presses and have been the subject of intense study and grouped into categories according to the design of their letters;[80] some scholars have even tried to assign them to actual workshops. Without following them into this specialised territory, we can at least be certain that during the first period of the commercial application of the press, printers were becoming more confident of their powers as their methods improved and their production techniques became more efficient. In the first years they restricted themselves to printing posters and pamphlets. Then they became bolder and published great works. When Pfister of Bamberg first combined letterpress with illustrations engraved on wood the book assumed its final and definitive form. At the same time, pupils of the first printers began to spread across Europe, teaching wherever they went the most effective method for the diffusion of ideas known until the present day.

3
The Making of the Type

Despite the crudity of their methods, the first printers often succeeded in producing masterpieces. The 42-line Bible ascribed to Gutenberg has compelled the admiration of experts. But we can only imagine the problems and anxieties he had, and guess at how much time it took him. There were, after all, many technical improvements that had yet to be introduced and which were needed to increase the productivity of the new industry. Experts and historians have hardly begun to reconstruct the many trials and errors which must have been necessary to overcome the problems faced by the first printers.

To begin with, there was the problem of making type sorts. Not only did the printer need a foolproof method of making them with the aid of punches and moulds, but he had to find metals and alloys tough enough not to damage the punch when struck, and a matrix that would not melt when the alloy was in the fluid state and on the point of fusion. It was vital, too, that the alloy-produced characters should accept ink and not quickly wear out with use. It seems that the first punches were of brass or bronze, metals less durable than the steel later used, and that they initially used matrix moulds which were made by pouring lead round the punches. The next stage was to use lead matrices and finally to switch to copper. Some have credited Schoeffer with the use of steel and copper for making punches and matrices. But others think that steel punches date only from the last quarter of the 15th century, and lead matrices are still to be found in the first decades of the 16th century.[81] In such conditions, where several metals with different properties were involved, it is easier to explain the diversity of types used in the 15th century: for they were made from punches and matrices which often wore out very quickly. An even greater drawback was the use of so many typographic signs imitated from the handwriting employed in writing manuscripts. The first printers cast letters joined by ligatures and used standard abbreviations ($\bar{a}$ for *an* or *am*; *q* for *quia*) so that there were many more typographic signs than there are today. It makes us wonder whether the gradual abandonment of the ligatures and abbreviations so common in the 15th and 16th centuries was not partly due to a wish to reduce the number of punches and matrices needed, one aspect of the tendency toward uniformity and simplification so characteristic of the evolution of the book.

The letters themselves present similar problems. Did the inventors immediately hit upon an alloy tough enough not to wear out quickly? The problem can best be appreciated if it is realised that the actual letters were cast from a composition of three different metals, lead, tin and antimony, combined in strict proportions to secure maximum strength. If made only of lead they oxidised, while letters made of lead plus tin alone were not hard enough. Letters cast in the 15th century were certainly strong, and so were those of the next 300 years, though probably less so than those of today. Ambroise Firmin-Didot has studied the Greek letters used by Aldus and concluded they must have deteriorated rapidly. In 1570 Paulus Manutius came up against this difficulty and found that he needed new characters cast for each new book he printed. Otherwise, he claimed, they would be worn out after four months when he was still only in the middle of the work.[82] Largely on the basis of evidence found in colophons, where the impression is often said to have been carried out *staneis typis*, it has been argued that the first letters were made of an alloy with a tin base. Did they hesitate to add too much lead to avoid having to cast leaden letters in lead matrices (a feasible but tricky operation) and so damaging the matrices? Antimony must have come in later because antimony mines were not in operation until the 16th century. The only objection to this theory, which must at least modify it, is that the oldest types surviving, which were made in Lyons at the end of 15th or early in the 16th century, and have been studied by M. Audin, prove under spectrographic analysis to contain tin, lead and antimony, with sometimes a speck of silver or iron.[83] If an alloy of this sort wore more quickly it could only be because of variations in the proportions of the various metals in the compound, which is difficult to mix accurately in any case. In fact the proportion seems to vary with each individual letter. Moreover it is quite possible that other printers, who were not so skilled or who did not have access to the necessary metals, used alloys of inferior quality. Indeed, nearly 300 years later in 1764, Fournier, the type founder, suggested how difficult and delicate a task it was to achieve the right combination of elements. He said that for a long time printers had used a mixture of lead, crude copper called *potin*, antimony, and sometimes iron, which yielded a metal too thick and viscous; only in the last thirty years had they simplified the process and improved the quality of the metal by using lead and an alloy of antimony.[84] Which goes to show that even in the 18th century they had not attained an entirely satisfactory alloy.

So type tended to wear quickly. Printers were forced to replace letters frequently and in this area were beset for a long time by many difficulties.[85] To understand just what these were it must be remembered that punch cutting, striking and casting moulds were all long and delicate operations which only specialised craftsmen could perform. A punch cutter, for instance, needed to be a very experienced man with years of practice behind him. At the beginning of printing, an industry created out of nothing, the earliest printers had to cut their own punches, make their own matrices, and cast their own type: each of which tasks would have taken up a great deal of time and money, and probably had to be carried out with the help of only the most rudimentary equipment. If they met with any success it was only because so many of them had formerly been goldsmiths.

Soon specialists began to emerge in the new crafts associated with printing. They travelled from workshop to workshop, hiring their services out to masters who wanted to top up their stocks of letters or to refurbish them. But punches and matrices remained the property of each workshop and this explains the rich diversity of type founts found in incunabula. The designing and cutting of type took up a great deal of time, so that printers would use the new letters as they were cast and mix them with older characters which were only gradually replaced. Furthermore the production of new type cost a lot of money and when the chance came printers would buy material which came on to the market after a death or a bankruptcy. This happened only rarely. But they could ask a richer fellow tradesman to sell them some founts, or better still to let them have matrices from which they could turn out their own type. From the last quarter of the 15th century printers seem to have been ready to engage in this kind of deal, though at first perhaps only reluctantly, altering some of the capitals each time, which they had re-engraved so as to differentiate between the work of each establishment.

It is in this way that there began to be a measure of specialisation. The type founding business expanded in the early 16th century. In Germany it passed into the hands of the great printers; in France it was the speciality of a small number of engravers, one or two of whom were celebrated, like Garamond and Granjon. At the same time the number of punches increased. The abandonment of gothic type and the adoption of roman favoured rationalisation. Since it made much old stock unusable, gradually, during the 16th century, the manufacture and sale of individual alphabets was concentrated in a small number of enterprises whose proprietors diligently collected the best punches they could find. By the 17th and 18th centuries a few dozen wealthy establishments had the monopoly of type founding in Europe, but the market was now rationally organised since printers could obtain the type they needed without having to cast it themselves.[86] Founts cost a great deal and that is one reason why printers continued for a long time to buy founts that lacked a sufficient number of letters. At the close of the 16th century, they usually bought from 60,000 to 100,000 sorts, only enough to set up a few dozen pages at a time. They therefore were forced to use the same letters over and over again, which caused them to wear out all the more quickly. Moreover they would have to print off each 'forme' as soon as it was composed in order to recover the type for immediate use. Thus the conscientious author could only correct his text in the course of printing, and this meant that there were often innumerable variants in a single edition.

If the market in type took a long time to become organised, any kind of uniformity or standardisation of type dimensions took even longer. Lack of a consistent standard of measurement proved a constant source of trouble to the early printers. The 'height to paper' (i.e. the total height of each sort), which is today fixed by official regulations, was variable; each region, indeed each shop, had its own convention. Sometimes founts cast in the same foundry were not even all cast to the same dimensions; at least that seems a fair conclusion when we find that a series of 222 type sorts surviving from the 15th and 16th centuries in Lyons contains 14 variations of height. When the characters in each fount had their own peculiar height it was impossible to use two founts together without having to file all the letters of one of the founts to make them the same height as the others: a delicate chore, and one which must have held up book production. But once type casting became the prerogative of the great type founders the move towards uniformity began, even though each founder produced type of a particular height since this prevented his clients from taking their custom elsewhere. In the 18th century, when Louis XV ruled that type heights were to be set at $10\frac{1}{2}$ 'lines', Fournier[87] tells us that the printers and founders at Lyons were using characters of up to $11\frac{1}{2}$.

There was an identical lack of uniformity when it came to the shape of the letters themselves. There was no standard of measurement, only a traditional and picturesque nomenclature. Gros Oeil, Paragon, Cicero, Gros Romain, Augustin were all purely arbitrary names without general agreement as to their meaning. Thus, there was much room for confusion. It was not until the 18th century that the efforts of Fournier and Didot forced the adoption of a definite standard of measurement, the points system, the 'point' being 144th the size of the king's foot. This is the unit of measurement used in typography to this day.[88]

4
Composition and Impression

Now let us look at the work of the printer himself, after having discussed the work of the punch cutter and of the type founder. His craft may be divided into two parts, composition and printing. Composition is the process by which type is assembled into pages and groups of pages in the 'forme', which is then placed in the press itself ready for the next stage, the actual printing process.

The technique of hand composition, used less and less today since the invention of machines like the linotype and monotype, has hardly changed since the beginning of printing. The equipment used is much the same: the compositor stands in front of a 'case', a large wooden cabinet subdivided into a series of pigeon holes each containing a different letter or sign. He takes out the letters one at a time and places them in his composing 'stick', a small slotted receptacle, formerly wooden, now metal. When a line of type has been assembled in the stick (i.e. 'composed') the compositor places it in a 'galley', a small tray in which the lines of type are held, with a 'lead' between each line (the leads are small lead pieces which do not register and which keep the lines apart). He then groups the lines into pages and assembles the pages in the forme where they are secured with wooden wedges and firmly tied together.

The compositor has to master a series of movements, carrying them out adroitly and with such speed and accuracy that each of his movements becomes automatic. This type of manual rhythm had not previously been required in the manufacturing processes of the 15th century. It prompts the question, how far did the need to increase output impel printers between the 15th and 18th centuries to find methods which would enable these operations to be carried out as efficiently as possible?[89]

Two observations should quickly be made. Firstly, the earliest compositors were undoubtedly less comfortable than their modern counterparts. When hand composing is done today the compositor stands before a sloping case with his freedom to move unimpeded. In the 15th century (and even in the 16th) this was not so, as a picture in the *Printers' Dance of Death* (Matthew Husz, Lyons, 1499) shows: the compositor sits at a very low case, which is only slightly tilted and is mounted on a trestle. In the early 16th century a series of prints – generally, printers' marks – show a case which is placed a little higher, tilted rather more to allow access to letters in the upper half of the case, and placed on a desk to facilitate handling: but the compositor still works sitting down. It is only in the second half of the century that the case assumed its present position and the compositor stood, as he does today.

Secondly, the work of early compositors often entailed work of great delicacy. Today, for example, a compositor can tell by touch which way up a letter is as he takes it from the pigeon hole by feeling for the notch cut in its shank, and so can insert it in the composing stick without having to glance at it. Old types which have survived and traces left by type which had become embedded in the pages of certain early printed books at the moment of impression prove that 15th-century types were not normally notched so the compositor must have had to use his eyes to check the letters before placing them in the stick.

But the critical problem in the technique of composing is that of the distribution of the sorts inside the case. To work really fast a compositor has to handle the letters without pausing or looking: he has to become an automaton, just like a modern typist at the keyboard. To acquire dexterity the printer has to work at cases in which the letters are always 'dissed' (distributed) in the same order. Cases have to be arranged uniformly in all the establishments where he might be called on to work: otherwise he would have to restrain his reflexes every time he changed his place of work (something that happened much more frequently in the 15th–17th centuries than today).

Nowadays in any one country the same case, with no more than minor variations, is always used. In the upper compartment ('upper case') two sub-compartments contain large and small capital letters. In the lower compartment nearer to the compositor are the lower case letters. Cases used in different countries will vary according to the language of the country, just as the letters on typewriters do.

How were the sorts distributed? Were the letters arranged in a different way in each country as happens today? Or did Latin favour uniformity, and, if so, when did the differentiation between the cases of different countries begin? Unfortunately such questions are almost impossible to answer, since no documents containing precise information on this subject survive from before the end of the 17th century. If we recall that, owing to the habit of engraving letters ligatured together and founded in the same type, and owing to the many abbreviations used in the 15th and early 16th centuries, the number of typographic signs was itself variable, then it is clear that the case could not have been uniform. All the evidence suggests that type was dissed in a different way in each area according to local practice, for at a time when local traditions were strong it is easy to tell the origin of a wood-cut of the 15th or 16th centuries by its style, or a 15th-century character by its shape; even the presses varied from district to district. On the other hand the travels of journeymen printers, which were so frequent in the period, must have served to transplant trade practices far from their place of origin, and this in turn must have led to a general acceptance of the practices which were felt to be best. Hence principles which seem to us to be self-evident, like the separation of upper and lower case letters, must sooner or later have been adopted. Yet no strict rules seem to have come into being for several centuries; although such rules would have served to make the compositor's work easier and to help him acquire those automatic reflexes whose necessity we have stressed.

In a work entitled *Science pratique de l'imprimerie*,[90] Fertel, a printer from Amiens, tells us that the dissing of type still varied in France from workshop to workshop as late as 1723. It appears that master printers made changes as they saw fit, usually in the upper case, so that when journeymen changed their place of work they had to 'relearn the layout' each time. Fertel advised two dispositions of type which he judged most convenient and wished to see in general use. One involved the placing of the large and small capitals in alphabetic order, as they are today. The letters J and U, which were not in general use in the earliest days, were displaced, and this seems to point to a very old tradition. In the bottom left hand side of the upper case and in the lower case, the lower case letters were stored, as they are today, in pigeon holes of varying size depending on how frequently the letters they contained were used. This layout, with a few notable exceptions, is like the one given in Momoro's *Traité elémentaire de l'imprimerie* (1793) and in the *Encyclopédie*[91] (where, however, the plan of a case and the elevated drawing which accompanies it do not agree in their representation of the lower case). It seems therefore that even by the end of the 18th century in France the location of the letters in the case did not yet accord with any absolutely agreed pattern. It was only at the beginning of the 19th century that a layout like Momoro's or that shown in the *Encyclopédie* became general (without even then being absolutely settled) and since then it has remained part of normal trade practice.[92]

The essential equipment for making the impression of type on paper was of course the press. Solid and rustic, this hardly changed from the mid-16th to the late 18th century. The principle was simple.[93] The forme – a set of several pages of type held together so that the characters could not get out of position – was placed on the bed or press stone, originally made of smooth and polished marble but replaced in the 18th century by a steel plate. Thus positioned, the forme was then inked with two ink dabbers, the sheet of paper was placed over the standing type, and then the press was brought into play. A sharp pull on the press bar activated a screw, connected at one end to a flat platen poised above the marble slab. The paper, pressed hard against the forme by the action of the platen, took the imprint of the type.

Thus summarised, the whole principle seems easy. But in practice three crucial problems had to be solved before the instrument could be applied industrially. Firstly, it was almost impossible to ink the forme when it lay between the bed and the platen, since it was impossible to raise the platen high enough to make this operation feasible. Hence, somehow, the forme had to be moved when it was to be inked. To achieve this, the first printers placed it and the stone beneath it on a small carriage mounted on rails which moved back and forward by means of a crank (the 'guide') and a simple system of pullies.

The second problem or series of problems involved the actual printing. It was important that the paper – particularly the margins – was not splashed with ink at the moment of printing. There was a risk that the ink would spread beyond the inked areas on the forme. So a protecting sheet of paper or parchment was used which exposed only those parts of the forme which held the type. Further, whatever the quality of the characters or the care spent on their precise justification (i.e. the alignment of each line of type) the letters would not all stand at exactly the same height. If the sheet were placed directly in contact with the platen, letters which were slightly below the others would be badly printed, and others would leave either too much or too little impression on the paper. To overcome this and to introduce a bit of give into the surface of the platen, either a sheet of felt or several sheets of paper needed to be inserted between the sheet to be printed and the platen.

These different problems led the printers to use the system of the frisket and tympan. The 'tympan' is a double frame (large and small tympan) secured to the press by hinges. The bed and the forme are placed within it. Each of the two frames has a sheet of parchment stretched across it, and the smaller one is covered with a sheet of thick flannel to ease the pressure. The 'frisket' is another frame hinged to the large tympan on the side opposite the one which attaches it to the press. It consists of a taut sheet of parchment or strong paper cut away in those places where the sheet meets the type, which prevents the sheet being marked during the printing. When a sheet is being printed the frisket folds back on the tympan, trapping the paper, which, in addition, cannot be displaced because it is attached to the tympan by two spikes.

The final problem was the most difficult, and concerned the size of the platen, which was necessarily restricted. To achieve a proper result the press bar must be pulled in such a way as to apply pressure evenly over the type. Consequently the surface of the platen has to be exactly parallel with the top surface of the type. As a result for a long time it was impossible to print as large an area as a whole sheet at once: half a sheet was printed, the carriage was moved, and the second half printed. Two pulls, therefore, were required to print one sheet.

This was the method used in most European countries from the mid-16th to the 18th century. The press was a relatively efficient instrument, yet simple enough in its construction to be made without difficulty by a joiner or simple carpenter, and so in France, at least, there were no specialised printing-press makers until the 18th century.

Did the earliest experimenters in printing begin by using the rubbing technique, used to print the block-books, before they realised how a press could create typographical impressions? Possibly; but they must very soon have used the press in the accepted way since it is inconceivable that the 42-line Bible could have been printed by any other method. But how then did the first presses come into being? How was a suitable press first built? Did they first try out methods different from that finally adopted? Did some printers – in particular itinerant printers – turn out impressions without using a press, or using only some very light and simple form of press?

On the basis of what we know of it, the technique of presswork in the earliest days appears in many respects to have been rather peculiar and it may have been quite different from what we would naturally suppose, especially as regards the method used to assemble the letters in the forme. If one examines the oldest types that have survived, or the traces left by 15th-century types which got embedded in the pages of certain copies, the results are disturbing; most of them are pierced with a tiny hole or chink and the base is often either bevel-edged or arrow-shaped.

There are hypotheses which attempt to explain this. It has been argued that the holes drilled through many types were made to hold a thin cord or metal shank which kept the type in line and ensured that the page would be level at a time when the device for tightening up the forme was not yet perfected. That seems unlikely. But when it is realised that the holes were made by a sharp instrument and a file *after* the letter was cast, we can appreciate how much time this must have taken for each letter. It gives us an idea of the almost insurmountable difficulties that the first printers had to resolve to exercise their craft at a time when the technique of typography was still primitive.[95]

The custom of cutting a bevel or arrow shape at the base of the characters is still more mysterious. It is certainly possible that it was intended to make it easier to achieve the same height to paper for all types. For the bevelled shape would enable easier and more exact work. But a rectangular base would surely have been better than a bevel or an arrowhead. Types placed out of true by the latter methods will tend to fall over even when held together, especially when the technique of securing absolute register by the rigid tightening of the forme was unknown. In conditions like these, hampered by unstable type, defective founts, and a precarious method of clamping the forme, how is it that books of the 15th century were so meticulously printed? The technical experts who have asked this question have proposed an extremely bold hypothesis to answer it. They think the impression was taken in the reverse way from that which we regard as normal, the reversed forme being placed on top of the sheet of paper. For this we need to imagine a press different – and probably simpler – from the one eventually used. From here we need only make a short step to consider that a press was not indispensable, especially for the production of small books, and to wonder whether the itinerant printers, so numerous in the 15th century, can always have carried a press with them. It is to be hoped that the technical research now in progress will one day enable us to resolve these questions.[96]

Whatever the truth, the first presses must have been primitive. The first books were printed a page at a time, even in quarto, and the formes were always page size.[97] Despite all the care bestowed on them, the lines of print on the pages which were printed in succession on one side of the sheet could not be at exactly the same height from one page to another and the appearance of the books often suffers as a result. After 1470 this inconvenience tends to disappear. It seems that the technique of the double pull on the press bar started at this time. The forme is from then on composed of several pages and could now sometimes be of the same size as the sheet. But for this to be possible the forme, now mounted on a mobile carriage, had to be capable of rapid and precise movement. Very quickly, before the end of the 15th century, a system of cranks and pullies was used to bring about this horizontal movement. For a long time printers were content to slide the carriage over the level surface of a wooden table; eventually it was mounted on two rails to make the operation easier and more accurate.

These were not the only improvements made between the 15th and 18th centuries.[98] Printers did not seek to modify the basic principle of the press but simply improved on detail. In the 16th century they replaced the wooden screw thread with a metal one and reinforced the parts subjected to pressure in order to make the press sturdier. These improvements are visible in wood-cuts of the period and in printers' marks which depict presses. We can distinguish three types of press: one made at Lyons, one in North Germany and the third Flemish. The German press, slender and rather fragile in appearance, at first gave way quite rapidly in many workshops to the Flemish. The Lyons press was quickly adopted in Paris, then throughout France, Switzerland and England, and finally in the Low Countries and Spain. It appears to have been in general use by the end of the 16th century.

However, when the printing industry developed in Holland in the early 17th century, a great map printer, Willem Janszoon Blaeu, who had worked with Tycho Brahe the astronomer and had made mathematical instruments before he came into publishing, introduced many modifications to the press. To make it stronger he reinforced some features of its construction and put in a spring called the 'yoke' to make the platen give a more even impression. The 'Dutch' press gradually spread in the Low Countries, which quickly earned a reputation for high quality work, and then in England, but was never adopted in France, which continued to use the old classic Lyons press. Thus between the 16th and 18th centuries the traditional double action press was only modified in minor ways. For nearly 300 years printers were quite happy with this solid instrument on which they printed at a speed that astonishes us. Each day, 16th and 17th-century workmen, who laboured 12 to 16 hours, turned out 2500–3500 sheets (printed on one side only, it is true). This means they printed one sheet every 20 seconds, a staggering rate of work.[99]

It was not until the end of the 18th century at the time of the Encyclopaedia that the increase in the output of the press and the interest in technical questions led master printers to search for a way of increasing the speed of the press and of making the labour required of workmen less exhausting. Between 1782 and 1785, two great printers, Didot and Anisson, separately perfected a press which required only one pull, by a modification to the screw thread – but their invention was not generally taken up. It was only the increase in the size of editions (already responsible for the revolution in papermaking we discussed earlier) which led to the adoption of a completely new machine, quite different from the hand press. Around 1795 Lord Stanhope in London, helped by a mechanic, Walker, devised a press made almost entirely of metal, still used today by many printers to take proofs. After this the mechanical revolution of the 19th century had its effect. On the 29th November, 1814, John Walker, director of *The Times*, one of the first of the large circulation newspapers, showed printers who were preparing to start work on hand presses the forthcoming issue of his newspaper, printed overnight on a mechanised press adapted for commercial use. It was with some pride that he wrote in that issue of the newspaper, 'Our paper today presents to the public the practical results of the greatest advance in printing since its invention.' He added, 'In one hour no less than 1100 sheets can be printed'.[100]

5
Imposition[101]

The problems so far discussed were not the only ones printers had to face. To ensure a decent print run they had to use paper of good quality, which was not always easy to obtain. Once obtained, the paper had to be prepared. Moreover several pages had to be printed on one sheet, and this was, as we shall see, a complicated process.

To take an impression and accept ink the paper had to be very resistant and carefully sized, factors that could not always be taken for granted in the early days. That is why papermakers from the 15th century took good care over the grades of paper intended for printing. Italian papermakers, in particular, at that time made a paper from fine rags which was of great strength and delicacy and sufficient thickness. It was of a greyish white colour and uniform in quality. It seems, indeed, to have been entirely satisfactory.

But the press is a great devourer of paper and the mills were hard put to it to produce enough. In the 15th and early 16th century printers would often have to use several types of paper of different origin to print a single volume; and, in the 16th century, as the number of presses multiplied, the paper industry in some places could not provide printers with sufficient quantities of suitable paper. The lack of sufficient quantities of good rags and the desire to work faster to make a higher profit encouraged papermakers to produce paper of mediocre quality. For a long time the correspondence of printers throughout Europe is filled with recriminations and complaints against those supplying them with poor quality paper described as 'greasy', 'brittle', 'fragile', 'badly sized'. This was reflected in the quality of the book, especially because the need to make economies made it necessary for printers to buy paper in the vicinity of their press so as to reduce transport costs. Consequently, printers often had to be satisfied with low-grade paper from their own district, and only began to be able to afford to transport paper from elsewhere in the 18th century.

But the most intractable problems were those which concerned the disposition of the pages within the forme. To make this clear we should just recall the basic principles determining the format of a book. The folio book is made by folding the sheets of paper once, and so four pages are printed on each sheet, two on each side. In a quarto book the sheets are folded twice and consist of eight pages, four on each side; in an octavo book the sheets are folded three times and contain 16 pages, eight on each side, and so on. When folded the sheets should comprise a quire which would be made up of four pages in a folio, eight in a quarto, sixteen in an octavo. But often the need to give greater strength to the quires (sections) of folios and quartos make it necessary to insert two sheets at once, so doubling the bulk (and at the same time the number of pages) of each quire. On the other hand in the smaller formats (16mo, 24mo, 32mo) quires made from a single sheet would be too thick and so printers make several quires from the pages printed on a single sheet: for 16mos they cut the sheet in two and make two quires of 8 leaves, that is 16 pages. For 24mos they cut off a third of the sheet and make two quires, one of 8 leaves (16 pages), the other of 4 leaves (8 pages), known in French as the *gros cahier* and the *feuilleton*.

To be able to fold the sheet in this way printers had to be careful to give each page its proper place in the forme. For a folio, pages 1 and 4 had to be set on one side, side by side, and pages 2 and 3 on the other, and likewise for other formats. It seems a complicated method, but it ensured that each quire was of a convenient thickness and the bound volume of maximum strength. It also greatly facilitated the work of the binder because he could fold the sheets which made up a volume mechanically without risk of error in the pagination, which was frequent before this system of imposition (i.e. arrangement of pages in the forme) was adopted.

Recent research[102] has shown that manuscript scribes already knew and practised such a system of imposition, particularly for manuscripts of small or medium format intended for teaching, like manuals and abstracts, and for books of practical religion (breviaries, Books of Hours, works relating to diocesan administration) which were commonly produced in large numbers. Printers, however, were slow to adopt the technique because of the custom of printing books page by page on a small forme (smaller than the sheet of paper) which at first encouraged them to cut the sheet before printing, although this made the whole operation longer. Moreover paper varied, coming generally in two sizes – *regalis* (about 70 cm × 50 cm) and *median* (about 50 cm × 30 cm) and printers often used half sheets of *regalis* along with whole sheets of *median* so that in the same work some sheets would be printed as if for a folio volume, others as if for a quarto volume. Finally, the quires generally included as many sheets as were judged capable of taking a solid binding and the number of pages in each quire would vary in the same volume. Quires in quarto-size incunabula, for instance, rarely consist of a single sheet folded twice, but of two or three sheets folded together. At the end of the 15th century, the custom of making the quire of a quarto from two sheets, or 8 leaves, was established. The disadvantages of such methods are clear: the mistakes which could be made during printing, the calculations printers would have to make to ensure that each page ended up in its right place in the volume, and the difficulties the binder encountered when he was collating the sheets. This serves to show just how complicated the task of the early printers was, in this as in so many other facets of printing, up to the time when, in the light of experience, standard practices came to be adopted in the course of the 16th century. The uniform conventions and tricks of the trade developed at that time often continued in use up to the 19th century and sometimes to our own day.

6
The Chinese Precedent*

We know that by inventing paper the Chinese indirectly contributed to the discovery of printing in Europe.[103] Nothing discovered so far suggests that we owe China any more than that, despite the fact that for nearly five hundred years before Gutenberg the Chinese knew how to print with moveable characters.

A country in which scholars have had a uniquely influential role in society, China more than anywhere else venerated learning as a well-spring of life, and her vast literature has grown richer from age to age. The most ancient written records indicate that the book was in existence as early as the Chang dynasty (1765–1123 B.C.). On fragments of bone and on the scales of tortoise shells, which were split with red-hot pokers for purposes of divination, nearly 2,500 different characters have been made out, the ancestors of the 80,000 characters of today. At that date we quite often find the pictogram which still today signifies the thin sections of a Chinese book. Consisting of four vertical lines crossed horizontally with a large loop, it represents, in fact, the book in its most ancient form, made out of wooden or bamboo tablets inscribed vertically with a pointed stylus dipped in a kind of varnish, the whole bound and held together by leather thongs or silk cords. These books made of wooden slats were used for hundreds of years. Confucius used this type of book to study the *I-Ching* and we are told that his study was so intensive that the thongs snapped three times. The most ancient Chinese books to survive were excavated at the beginning of this century from the deserts of Central Asia – strips of wood and bamboo on which are to be found vocabularies, calendars, medical prescriptions and official documents relating to the daily life of the Chinese garrisons guarding the Silk Route, most of them bearing dates from 98 to 137 A.D.[104] They reflect a degree of technical progress, for they are written in ink brush. Such books however were cumbersome, and the strips had to be laboriously re-corded everytime the cord was broken. They were soon replaced by silk, which was supple, light in weight and yet strong. Woven silk, about 30 cm in width, was rolled round a wooden rod, which was decorated at either end, and the Chinese name for a book meant 'roll' (as did the Latin *volumen*).[105]

* This section is by Mme M. R. Guignard, Keeper in the Department of Manuscripts of the *Bibliothèque Nationale*.

With silk so costly they sought cheaper substitutes. By a process of trial and error, using first silk waste, and then materials which were even more readily available – old linen rags, fish nets, hemp, mulberry bark, they succeeded in making a paste which, when dry, would take writing. A powerful Chinese tradition maintained that all benefits emanated from the Emperor's Court and so the invention of paper was ascribed to the Director of the Imperial Workshops, the eunuch Tsai Lun (died 121 A.D.) but it appears certain that paper was used for writing long before Tsai Lun. It was he who reported on the subject to the Emperor (105 A.D.) and this report has survived, so his name is remembered while the efforts of many anonymous craftsmen have been forgotten.

The most ancient paper that has survived also comes from Central Asia: seven letters written in Sogdian on sheets carefully folded and bearing the address to which they were to be sent. Sir Aurel Stein discovered them in the ruins of a tower on the Great Wall abandoned by the Chinese army in the mid-2nd century A.D.[106] Microscopic analysis by Professor J. von Wiesner has revealed that the paste was made solely from cloth of hemp, bits of which are still intact.[107] We know for certain that the paper was made in China and, as it was used by foreigners far from the centres of production, this proves that the new discovery must have spread rapidly. Paper thus replaced silk, except for luxury manuscripts. Sheets of small size, about 25 cm × 45 cm, were glued end to end to form long strips which could be rolled or unrolled and were attached to a supporting rod. The walled-in library in the caves of Tuen Huang was the source of nearly 15,000 manuscripts dating from the 5th century to the end of the 10th, now divided between the British Museum, the *Bibliothèque Nationale* and the Peking National Library. For the most part they are rolls of paper but there are also to be found among them the different forms of book which the invention of printing was destined to modify.

It was probably the need to find a particular passage in a text straightaway, without having to unroll yards of paper, combined with a pious wish to emulate the sacred books of India which are written on long, narrow palm leaves bound together with fine twine, as well as the task of combining sheets which had been printed separately, which eventually transformed the appearance of the book. Among the manuscripts from Tuen Huang are texts written on leaves of paper pierced with holes through which a fine cord passed. Instead of being separate, the leaves are sometimes stuck together along the outer edges, making an oblong book which opens like an accordion and which the Chinese call a 'whirling book' to describe the rapidity with which the pages could be turned backward or forward at will. So quickly was this type of book adopted into general use that the Arab writer Mohammed Ibn Ishaq remarked in 989: 'The Chinese write their religious books and their works of scholarship on sheets of paper which open like a fan'. This type of book, in form half Indian, half Chinese, has continued to be used for Buddhist and Taoist texts, for collections of prints, paintings, and examples of calligraphy. But, unsupported, the paper tore easily, and the next advance was to fold each sheet in half down the centre, the leaves being bound together along the fold yet remaining free to flutter like wings, hence the name 'butterfly book'. This type of book, the equivalent of our own, was perfect for carrying a manuscript text, but it was only possible to print a text, using the technique of rubbing the sheet on a block which had been engraved in relief and inked, on one side of the leaf. So, to hide the blank verso they began to fold the leaves in two and to sew them together, not along the folds, but along the edges. The fine pliable paper used in China, Korea and Japan was well adapted to this method of binding which has hardly changed even today. A paper or silk cover protected each quire which often corresponded to a chapter. These were assembled six or eight at a time and secured between thin sheets of precious wood or in boxes covered with a rich fabric. The books lay horizontally on shelves and, as each quire carried the title of the text it contained on its spine, the reader had an outline of the contents before his eyes.

The Chinese were not only concerned with the convenience of readers in libraries and were soon looking for practicable and economical ways of multiplying texts. About the beginning of our era they had attained a remarkable mastery of the art of engraving, producing both huge marble steles, on which were engraved classical texts, and talismans, which were used by Buddhist and Taoist monks to provide copies of magic formulae or devotional pictures.

Printing direct from engraved stones was an excellent method for the reproduction of texts and pictures, and, since the steles were intended to preserve the integrity of a text, to commemorate an event or to pay tribute to an individual, this process could be used to make souvenirs for pilgrims. This technique of making prints has never changed and has never lost favour as a rapid and cheap means of text reproduction. The tough yet pliable paper of China can be moulded to the engraved surface by rubbing and hammering it. When damp, the paper penetrates deep into the incisions in the stone and the surface is then ink-stamped in black or colour. Only the sunken portions escape contact with the ink and, when the paper separates itself from the stone as it dries, they stand out in white on a black or coloured background.

It was however the development of the seal engraved in relief and in reverse which led most directly to the printing of books. By the beginning of our era, seals engraved in relief were common, and the pious had them engraved with lengthy religious texts; soon such prayers were added to the large portraits of Buddha or the bodhisattvas which were produced to adorn monks' cells or the rooms of pious laymen. The engravers' skill became greater and greater; moreover impressions of high quality could be made on paper while this technique was of no use on silk. As in the West, so in China, once a suitable medium had been found experiments multiplied, and the engravers tried bolder enterprises. Tracts were soon being produced as well as prayers, and they were in turn followed by short devotional works and by popular texts: calendars or dictionaries.

The earliest evidence we have of such wood-blocks engraved in relief is a small portrait of the Buddha discovered by Paul Pelliot, near Kuche in Sinkiang, which he dates from the mid-8th century A.D. The Tuen Huang Collection in the *Bibliothèque Nationale* includes a great number of devotional prints with prayers attached (9th century), but it is the British Museum which has the privilege of preserving the oldest dated printed book in the world, a long roll printed by a xylographic process in the year 868. The Buddhist text is preceded by a frontispiece, which is both sophisticated in composition and delicately engraved, proof that the art was already well advanced. It required a century, at least, to overcome the opposition of the scholars who thought it sacrilegious to use such a process for printing classical texts and who seem to have feared that their trade as copyists would be threatened.

Originally a craft confined to the upper and lower reaches of the Yellow River, block-printing was eventually adopted by the scholars to preserve and disseminate the canonical writings. As such it was recommended officially by a government minister, Feng Tao, in a report to the Emperor. Like Tsai Lun's, this report has survived. These two men are still credited with the honour of inventions which they did no more than bring to the notice of the Court. Feng Tao proposed, in 932 A.D., to preserve the classical texts by block-printing as a last resort because the dynasty in power did not have the financial means to undertake the engraving of a series of 'Classics On Stone', such as would have been possible in more prosperous times. The success of this project, which took from 932 to 953, sanctified the new art, and little by little all the existing literature was put into print. Attempts were quickly made to improve on the newly adopted method, but copper engraving and experiments with moveable letters were not successful.

The first attempts to print in moveable type (1041–1048) are attributed to a blacksmith and alchemist, Pi Sheng, who used clay and a liquid paste to make letters which he hardened in fire. The composing was done on an iron plate coated with a mixture of paper ash, wax and resin, and the letters were held in place by an iron frame. By gently heating the mixture and then letting it grow cold he made the characters adhere perfectly to the plate, and they could be recovered by reheating them once the page had been printed.[108] By engraving the very hard wood of the juniper tree, or casting lead and copper, attempts were made to make founts of moveable characters, but this was always an exceptional technique in China. It was however used in some grandiose imperial projects in the 18th century like the Ku Chin Tu Chou Tsi Cheng encyclopaedia of 10,000 chapters, for which copper characters were engraved, not cast. A new scheme for arranging the characters by 214 key symbols which was adopted for the great dictionary printed by Emperor Kang Hsi gave some hope of a practical system of locating, and of distributing after use, the tens of thousands of characters, but the cost of such a fount and the manpower needed to carry out the printing was so high that only the government could attempt it. These enormous publications were offered to civil servants ar.[1] mandarins as working books, and their cost was comparatively unimportant. No individual could have financed such an enterprise, or engaged such a work force, or kept such a vast number of characters in a usable order. Further, the fluid quality of the ink used in China hardly lent itself to printing in metal; and, lastly, the printed book was unattractive on aesthetic and sentimental grounds, since it deprived the reader of the pleasure of fine calligraphy and of the style of such and such a calligrapher working in harmony with his text. Wood-block engraving and block-printing, by contrast, make possible a faithful reflection of the calligrapher's style. Only in the 20th century was moveable type again adopted, and then only for newspapers and popular editions.

While publication in China was often subsidised by private individuals who insisted on traditional wood-block methods, in Korea the public authorities took over responsibility for the diffusion of texts, and printing by means of moveable type found its fullest development there.

The technique was first used in Korea in the first half of the 13th century and acquired extraordinary importance in the 15th century through the encouragement of the local King Sejong. His decree of 1403 gives a clear indication of his enlightened policies: 'To govern it is necessary to spread knowledge of the laws and the books so as to satisfy reason and to reform men's evil nature; in this way peace and order may be maintained. Our country is in the East beyond the sea and books from China are scarce. Wood-blocks wear out easily and besides it is difficult to engrave all the books in the world. I want letters to be made from copper to be used for printing so that more books will be made available. This would produce benefits too extensive to measure. It is not fitting that the people should bear the cost of such work, which will be borne by the Treasury.' The fount of 100,000 sorts cast at the instigation of this decree was the first of several. In the course of a century ten founts were made and kept in the official government printing shops.[109] The first three founts (1403, 1420 and 1434) thus preceded the date of the invention of printing in Europe.

Another of China's neighbours, the Uighurs, a Turkic people, also appear to have used this technique which was suited to their writing, for they had an alphabet. A collection of Uighur characters engraved about 1300 on small cubes of wood was discovered by P. Pelliot in Tuen Huang. It is unlikely that these Turkic nomads, though in contact with the West, introduced printing to Europe.

If we except the testimony of Rashi ed-Din, physician to the Mongol rulers of Iran in the early 14th century, no traveller ever mentioned the use of printing in Asia. European interest does not even appear to have been aroused by the first xylographs to arrive from the East, some bright red seals printed on messages from the Mongol emperors of Persia to the kings of France and England, and to the Pope; two examples, dated 1289 and 1305, are preserved in the national archives in Paris. Marco Polo, usually so curious about everything, marvelled at the banknotes he saw in China, but did not perceive that they had been printed from engraved blocks. So the possibilities inherent in this technique, which proved so essential to the evolution of humanity, seem to have escaped the notice of travellers, or at least nobody thought it worth recording anything about it in writing.

The Book: Its 3
Visual Appearance

Let us open the books and see how they changed their appearance in the course of time, and for what reasons.

The earliest incunabula looked exactly like manuscripts. The first printers, far from being innovators, took extreme care to produce exact imitations.[110] The 42-line Bible for example was printed in a letter-type which faithfully reproduced the handwriting of the Rhenish missals. For a long time printers did not merely use the same individual characters but also groups of letters linked by the same ligatures as those used in manuscripts. For an even longer time initials in printed books were rubricated by the same calligraphers and illuminated by the same artists who worked on manuscripts. So much is this the case that the layman sometimes has to examine a book very carefully before deciding whether or not it is printed or handwritten. Many theories have been advanced to explain this. It has been suggested, for example, that it was to deceive the buyer who might distrust the new mechanical process or that it was intended to pass off printed books as manuscripts in order not to offend the susceptibilities, or even arouse the unwelcome attention, of copyists and their 'Guilds', which were jealous of their monopolies.[111]

Such theories do not stand up to examination. A desire to deceive the buyer? Any such deceit would be easily spotted because a 15th-century eye would be more acute in detecting such things than our eyes and would have quickly distinguished a manuscript from a printed book despite all the resemblances. Besides, people soon came to prefer printed texts which were more readable and accurate than the older manuscripts. Resistance from copyists and stationers? Certainly. But we must not forget that most of them were subject to strict university control and were not strictly speaking members of an autonomous corporate body. Consequently they were under university authority which was favourably disposed to printing in its early days, so that the scribes' complaints were in fact ineffectual. Besides, printers and stationers sometimes seem to have collaborated. If copyists undoubtedly complained about the rivalry of those newcomers, the printers, the booksellers who specialised in the sale and trade of manuscripts did not necessarily take the same view. In many cases, in Paris or Avignon for example, they were quite prepared to sell printed books and manuscripts alongside each other. Many of them, sensing the obvious importance of the new method of reproducing texts, went into printing themselves or helped finance the establishment of printing shops. Antoine Vérard, for example, produced printed books which were often on vellum and illuminated, and were faithful copies of the de luxe manuscripts he had previously had written and painted when he directed a scribal workshop.

That the earliest printers scrupulously copied, and often indeed slavishly reproduced, the manuscripts in front of them, should hardly be a matter of surprise. Nor does it require fanciful theories to account for it; it could not have been otherwise. How could they have imagined a printed book other than in the form of the manuscripts on which they were in fact modelled? And would not the identity of book and manuscript be the most obvious proof of their technical triumph, as well as the guarantee of their commercial success? The advent of the printing press did not mean a sudden change in the appearance of the book. It was the first phase in an evolution which we must now try to trace, so as to isolate the various stages by which the printed book moved by degrees away from its original model, the manuscript. We must also explain why and to what extent its appearance varied in the first hundred years of its existence, before it assumed, in the mid 16th century, an appearance which is essentially the same as the one it has today.

I

Type Founts

Around 1450, when printing was invented, texts were being written, according to their contents or their intended recipients, in very different hands. In fact four main styles of script were current, each with its own specific purpose.[112] Firstly, the gothic of scholastic texts, the traditional 'black letter' beloved of theologians and university professors. Then the larger size gothic, less rounded, with straight uprights and fractured letters: the missal letter used for ecclesiastical books. Next a script derived from that used in the Chancelleries (each of which had its own tradition): the 'bastard' gothic, a hand current in luxury manuscripts in the vernacular and in some Latin texts, generally narratives. Finally, the last to emerge, but that with the greatest future which became the normal script for printed books: the 'littera antiqua', the humanist, or roman script. Inspired by the Carolingian minuscule, this script was made fashionable by Petrarch and his disciples but in 1480 was used only by a few exclusive groups of humanists, or by aristocratic book collectors who wanted their classical texts to have a look of antiquity and authenticity about them (or at least of what was taken to represent antiquity and authenticity) to contrast them not only in content but also in appearance with the medieval texts. With this roman script there can be associated a cursive script, the *Cancelleresca*, based on the handwriting used by the Vatican Chancellery about the middle of the 15th century, and used afterwards in the Chancelleries of Florence, Ferrara and Venice; this was the origin of italic.

This rapid summary of what was in reality a much more complex set of overlapping styles, defying rigid classification, must not mislead the reader. Intermediate styles of all kinds are extant between the four ideal types just enumerated; the gothic used by the scribes of Bologna, for example, was influenced by the humanist script; and there existed considerable regional variations within each type of script. The Parisian bastarda type, which was born in the Royal Chancellery and was used in vernacular manuscripts, and which was to inspire the type of Vérard and of Le Noir, differed from the bastarda used in the Low Countries to reproduce the texts of John of Bruges, which was in turn the model for the type produced by the Bruges printer, Colard Mansion. In fact, regional characteristics were so marked a feature that the experienced eye can assign a manuscript to a particular locality with ease.

Such were the different models that were available to early printers; and this diversity explains the extraordinary variety of the letters used in the first incunabula and even in early 16th-century books. There was a conventional type for each class of book and reader, just as there had been in the manuscript period: for the clerk or scholar, scholastic books or manuals of canon law printed in black letter; for the layman, vernacular narratives printed in bastarda type; for the admirer of a polished style, editions of the Latin classics and of their humanist emulators, printed in roman. A typical instance is provided by Gering and his partners, who first brought printing to Paris. They were summoned to the Sorbonne by humanist men of letters, and so naturally they used roman in the printing shop they set up under university patronage. But later, when they left the university and set up shop in the Rue St. Jacques, producing law texts and the Schoolmen for a larger reading public of students and lawyers, they used gothic. Some printers went further in imitating manuscript handwriting, as did Le Talleur, a printer of Rouen, who published two treatises on Anglo-Norman law for Richard Pynson, the English bookseller of Norman extraction. To do this work he cast a type quite different from his normal model, and tried to copy the cursive script used peculiarly by English scribes for this class of work.[113]

Gradually, printing became more uniform for quite material reasons. When the trade of letter founding had not yet started, printers had to make their own punches, and even a single fount cost a small fortune. As each printer could afford to possess only a small number of founts it was difficult if not impossible to cut or acquire one identical with the script of a particular manuscript he wished to print. The sale of copies of the same edition in different towns and countries and, even more important, the nomadic careers of the first printers, inevitably led to the development of uniform types, especially as the scripts of the different regions often varied only slightly between each other. It is true that the first German printers who left the Rhineland to teach Europe the new art attempted at first to imitate the local scripts. In Italy they copied the humanist script, and, even more often, the round script of the scribes of Bologna. But many of them, particularly those with limited means, could not work like this. Having set out from home and with no capital other than a little equipment, a few matrices and some punches, they used founts already cut although far from their own locality. Hence we can follow the journey of a black letter from Basel, for example, to Lyons, to Toulouse, and on as far as Spain.[114] Similarly, the letters in the first books printed at Lyons, which were printed by Le Roy, were cut in Germany.[115] In England for quite a long time they used letters which came from Rouen and Paris.[116]

Regional styles were the first to disappear. Then, more slowly, the major forms of script were standardised until eventually the new roman type triumphed in the greater part of Europe – in Italy, France, parts of Switzerland, Spain and England. The distinctive story of roman was a triumph of the humanist spirit, the story of a victory which deserves telling.

Roman script was made fashionable by small groups of Italian humanists, notably Petrarch and Niccolò de'Niccoli who were passionate calligraphers like many contemporary literati. They wished to impart to classical texts a physical appearance closer to their original look, and

certainly different from the medieval texts which they derided as 'gothic'
– the term also used contemptuously by Alberti to describe the ornamen-
tation of traditional architecture.

Soon, roman spread through Italy as copyists used it in the scriptoria
of Naples, Rome and, in particular, Florence. Collectors who included
princes, bishops, abbots, cardinals, bankers and rich merchants bought
manuscripts in the new style. The richest of them, Mathias Corvinus,
King of Hungary, the Kings of Naples, the Dukes of Ferrara, all of whom
had their own scriptoria, ordered their scribes to use the new script to
copy Latin texts of the classics and even the works of the Fathers of the
Church. Outside Italy, Humphrey, Duke of Gloucester, and, later,
George d'Amboise, Archbishop of Rouen, owned 'humanist' manuscripts in their private libraries. Thus when printing first appeared certain small groups, lovers of *belles lettres* (let us not say humanists),
appreciated and knew how to read the new script, but of course the vast
majority at that time were faithful to the traditional gothic.

Wishing to reach the widest possible clientele printers naturally began
by using traditional types. But already in Italy roman was in regular
use and there were many book lovers who wanted to possess texts in the
alphabet inspired by antiquity, which were still relatively rare in manuscripts. Many of these 'amateurs' financed or encouraged the establishment of printing shops so that printing very quickly publicised the
script which Petrarch and his like had made fashionable. Sweynheym
and Pannartz, who worked at Subiaco and then in Rome and were the
first printers to set up in Italy, began with a semi-roman letter and later
a more characteristic roman (1465–1467). From around this time Adolf
Rusch, a Strasbourg printer, also possessed a roman script which he had
used for his edition of Rabanus Maurus's Encyclopaedia before 1467. In
1469 the German Johannes da Spira in Venice employed a similar script
for an edition of Cicero's *Epistolae ad familiares*, and, while Gering used
a type like that of Sweynheym and Pannartz, Nicolas Jenson in Venice
printed Cicero's *Epistolae ad Atticum* in a roman still regarded as a
masterpiece today.[119]

But only a few books before 1480 were in roman, and in Germany for
example only ten roman founts are known before that date. Amateurs
desiring that type were few and the market quickly saturated. While
printers who catered for it (mainly publishers of classics) were in financial
difficulties by 1472 because of overproduction. Gering and his associates
in Paris, as we have seen, abandoned the Sorbonne for the Rue St. Jacques,

and switched from roman to the traditional black letter. In Spain the Fleming Lambert Palmart began by printing the works of Fenollar in Valencia in roman script, but his example was scarcely followed. Most workshops equipped themselves with gothic – the bastarda form was the favourite – to print for example Villon's *Grant Testament*, the *Farce de Pathelin*, romances of chivalry, chronicles and popular tales in French, Shepherds' Calendars, and the *Ars Moriendi*. The large form of gothic also came in, for the works of Ockham, Nicholas de Lyra and the many commentaries of Peter Lombard.

Gradually, the fashion for humanist scripts, and the wide diffusion of Italian editions in which roman was used, made its victory inevitable, soon followed by that of its associated fount, italic. Venice played a big part in the eventual domination of roman and italic. There Aldus had his roman cut which exercised an enormous influence over 16th-century type founders, while his italic, cut in 1501 by Francesco Griffo after a *cancelleresca* script, permitted a lengthy text to be printed in a short space.[120] Following the Venetian example, Amerbach (who was trained in Venice) and, after him, Froben increasingly adopted roman and italic, spreading their use into Germany and encouraging it in France. In Lyons, the Venetian type was quickly copied, and Balthasar de Gabiano and Barthélemy Trot made imitations of Aldine italic. In Paris, Joost Bade and Henri Estienne spread the use of roman, and between 1530 and 1540 a whole series of romans were used by Robert Estienne, Simon de Colines, Wechel and Antoine Augereau, some being attributed traditionally to the famous Garamond, though it is not possible to say which. These scripts, more perfect than those which had inspired them, rapidly became standard throughout Europe. It was these scripts which were sought and copied by Paulus Manutius and Plantin and which were bought at Frankfurt by Egenolff. Punches cut at this period were acquired by foundries being set up at the time and continuously used until the 18th century.

Roman grew constantly in importance as humanism spread. It began to be used to print vernacular texts, until then traditionally printed in gothic bastarda. Thus in 1529 Galiot Du Pré 'rejuvenated' the presentation of the *Roman de la Rose* and the works of Alain Chartier; he did the same for Villon's *Grant Testament* in 1532 because the public for these works had come to prefer roman[121] which thenceforth was used each year in an increasing number of editions. But the new letter did not enjoy complete acceptance. For some time, university professors continued to prefer the black letter; it only disappeared in the following decades, first from law manuals and then from theology, and it continued even longer in liturgical works. In particular the huge numbers of bourgeois and townsmen, accustomed to decipher manuscript, remained attached to gothic bastarda which resembled it more than roman or italic. Rabelais' *Gargantua*, to be bought by a huge public at the Lyons fair and elsewhere, was printed in black letter. For a long time, therefore, gothic bastarda was used to print popular books, almanacs and 'gothic booklets'. The poorer printers ran off thousands of these, wearing out their founts in the process and buying cast-offs from their richer colleagues who no longer wanted them. Only later, in the second half of the 16th century, when obliged to restock with new types, did they acquire the roman which the public had grown to expect.

Thus the roman script was being used throughout Europe within a century after printing. This triumph of a design artificially made for the lovers of Latin classical texts is less surprising when we remember that Latin was the international language and that the Latin book trade was also international. The extraordinary variety in letter forms must frequently have been a hindrance to the sale of editions abroad, with the result that roman eventually took on the character of a sort of international alphabet. But if it was quickly adopted for the publication of vernacular texts in Italy, and then, after much resistance, in France and Spain, and eventually in England, it never completely won over readers in the Germanic countries. Certainly, Latin texts were printed in roman in Germany, Austria and the Low Countries, but most vernacular texts continued to be printed in black letter. In the 16th century two kinds of gothic made their appearance which have lasted to the present day: *Umlaut* and *Schwabach*.[122] They were easier for most readers and were taken up in the trade. So Luther, whose first works were printed in roman, reverted to the national type face when he wanted to reach the mass of his compatriots. Thus on the one side we have the Latin world and England, and on the other side the Germanic world where for a long time the majority of works were printed in a different script. At the same time in the Slav countries, printers adopted a different script entirely: Cyrillic, adapted from ancient Greek script.

2
Inside the Book: Title Page, Colophon and Printer's Mark

The reader today knows that when he opens a new book he will find on the title page the basic information necessary to decide whether to read the book or not: author, title, place of publication, publisher and date. In theory the law insists on this, at least in France.

But in the 15th and even the 16th century this was not the case. There was no title page in the first books; men had to turn the pages to see what the book contained, and just what it was. As in manuscripts, the text began on the recto of the first leaf, immediately after a brief form of words giving the subject of the work and occasionally the author's name. At least until the beginning of the 16th century, the reader would find most of his information at the end of the book in the 'colophon', a residue from the manuscript: it was there that he could expect to find the name of the printer, place of publication, perhaps the title and the name of the author.

However, from the 15th century another element appeared, an identifying sign called the printer's mark made with a wood-cut and included with either incipit or colophon. At first it was often simply an outline of the mark printers placed on consignments of books they were sending to customers, originally intended for the convenience of carters. Appearing on a blank page at the end of the last gathering or directly above the colophon, it became a species of pictorial publicity not only telling the book's origin but adorning it and affirming its quality. Booksellers and printers had their house sign reproduced as their device and, when the fashion for allegories and emblems inspired by antiquity developed with the triumph of humanism, a complicated symbolism grew up. Aldus used an anchor, Kerver a unicorn, Estienne an olive tree, Galiot Du Pré a ship (a galley, after his first name). The mark once relegated to the last page commonly appears on the title page, which became general usage from the end of the 15th century.

The story of the title page – its purpose to indicate to the reader the 'civil status' of a book – is a curious one and typical of the evolution of the book as a whole. It is instructive inasmuch as it shows us how new ideas emerged which led to new ways of making books easier to use. Since the recto of the first leaf always had a tendency to soil, printers conceived the idea of starting the text on the verso, leaving the recto blank. Then, from a quite natural desire to fill in the blank, they printed a short title on it and this helped to identify the book.[124]

It was in this way that the title page made its debut between 1475 and 1480, and its utility soon became obvious. In France, publishers particularly concerned with the appearance of their books, Vérard, for example, began to decorate the page with large initials often adorned with grotesque figures. Others put their mark in the blank space beneath the title, or perhaps a wood-cut like the one in Alexandre Villedieu's *Doctrinal*, a study book for beginners, showing a teacher and pupils. In other popular booklets, a master key would be shown.

At the end of the 15th century nearly all books had title pages, but they were not quite like those of today. Beginning brief, they soon grew to inordinate length, and in the first third of the 16th century, in a desire to fill the entire page, publishers tended to embed the title in a long formula, often adding an indication of the principal parts of the book, and some verses of the author and his friends. Publishers also, in their desire for publicity, quickly adopted the habit of printing their name and address at the foot of the page. But it was still necessary to turn to the back of the book and look at the colophon to find more precise information – the name of the printer for example and the precise date of printing. At the same time, more and more care was taken to decorate the title page. The fashion for engraved frames spread. Baldung-Grien was using them in Strasbourg from 1510, for Knobloch, Schott and then for Grüninger. A little later Holbein designed a large number of frames for Froben in Basel. Then the new style spread to Nuremberg, Augsburg and to Paris, where Joost Bade reproduced it in a decorative architectural style.[125]

In the German countries and England this fashion for frames persisted for a long time, with the title often drowned in a long formula and surrounded by multiple signs. But the Aldi in Italy, and humanist publishers in France, like Simon de Colines, and the Estienne and de Tournes houses, attempted to clarify the presentation of the title page. From around 1530, the time of the triumph of humanism, more and more new books were to be found with short titles accompanied by only the name of the author and, at the bottom of the page, the publisher's address. Thus, at the same time as roman and italic script began to prevail, the title page gradually assumed its current form.

The replacement of the wood-cut by copper engraving brought new changes in the title page at the end of the 16th century. The title pages of most books looked the same, but it became noticeable, first of all in the large and carefully prepared folio editions, and subsequently in volumes of all kinds, that the technique of the framed title page was coming back into favour. Originally the title was often placed in the centre of an engraved frame. But this method called for a delicate technique, that of double imposition. In contrast to wood-cuts, typeset words of the title could not be printed at the same time as the copper engraving. Besides, the thick black look of the type did not harmonise happily with the elegant thin lines of the engraving. So a technique was soon devised whereby both title and decoration were engraved on the same plate. From then on, the title page became the concern of artists alone, and they were quite naturally inclined to develop the decorative aspect at the expense of the written text. Gradually illustration came to occupy the whole of the page's surface, and the address of the publisher and the date of publication were relegated to a single line at the bottom of the page, while the title was inscribed in the open pages of a book, or on a plinth or draped hangings placed in the centre of the page. The engravings after Rubens which Moretus used in his books were like this, as were many others in the first half of the 17th century.[127] They seem excessive to our modern eyes, accustomed as we are to more simplicity, and certainly in no other area was the baroque style so excessive as in book decoration. In particular, the design of religious works too often became the pretext for an artist of as great a talent as Rubens to create compositions containing multiple figures, each with allegoric meaning so complicated as to impair the vitality of the ensemble.

Simpler work was that of Thomas de Leu in France, or Léonard Gautier, who put the title within the centre of an architectural portico. Michel Lasne, who had worked in Antwerp, imitated Rubens but avoided allegories and overembellished compositions. Soon, in 1640, Poussin, asked to design the publications of the Imprimerie Royale, brought a new approach which caught on immediately and revolutionised design.[128] He went for clarity of outline with just a few figures clothed in antique drapery in a design of wholly classical simplicity. But, as a painter, like Rubens, his first concern was for the unity of his composition and he relegated the title far from the centre of the page. In his work, the purely ornamental engraved title became the frontispiece, an illustration at the front of the book – which meant publishers had to concentrate bibliographic information on a purely typographical page following the frontispiece. From then on, the title page, whose utility was proving indispensable, more or less assumed the form it still has today.

3
The Text and Format of the Book

The move towards a simpler, more uniform product was equally apparent in the appearance of the text. But evolution here, as in every other feature of book production, was a gradual process. To understand what happened, first consider the difficulties confronting scholars and students during the manuscript age. It was impossible to cite page references as we habitually do nowadays, because the leaf signature or the page on which the passage was to be found would vary with each manuscript; hence the chapter number or its heading had to be quoted and even the paragraph, and the text often had to be arranged by subparagraphs for ease of reference. Again, books were written in a crabbed hand, full of contractions because of the need to economise with expensive vellum, so that as much as possible was crammed on to a page, with no space between paragraphs or chapters, no headings or page layout. It is easy to see therefore why manuscripts were difficult both to decipher and to consult.

The first printed books were, as we have seen, exactly like manuscripts, with the same general arrangement, the same abbreviations and the same crabbed writing. Gradually, the lines became more spacious, the script became bigger and the abbreviations less numerous. But the presentation remained almost the same. There is hardly any difference between a manuscript of Aristotle or of *Lancelot* produced between 1480 and 1490 and the same works printed in, say, 1520. Only when public taste gave rise to a new form of literature and roman script came into general use, was the presentation of the text modified.

It is characteristic that signatures were first printed in books not for the convenience of readers but to guide the work of artisans in preparing a book, particularly in binding, which was a very delicate task in a period when each section to be bound might have an unequal number of leaves, and each sheet be inset in a different way. So, to help the binder, printers imitated scribes and added a table on which was listed the first word of each gathering or of each double leaf. This table was called the *register*. With the same aim in view they began designating each section with a letter of the alphabet usually printed at the bottom and to the right of the sheet. The letters were followed by a number, to show the sequence of the leaves (the 'signature'). Probably for the same reason they began numbering the leaves (it is noteworthy that the earliest pagination has no signatures and vice versa). Be that as it may, the practice of showing the sequence of the leaves was slow to develop. Many books were not paginated as late as the beginning of the 16th century and what pagination there was was often faulty. It took even longer before books were no longer numbered by the leaf but, as today, by the page. Perhaps the first example of pagination is Aldus' edition of the *Cornucopia* of Perotti (1499); but it became common only in the second quarter of the 16th century, thanks mainly to humanist printers.

From then on, the book began to have a contemporary look. A triumphant humanism had imposed the use of roman type, which was usually larger and so more readable than gothic script. More and more texts were set across the page in one long line, not in double columns. At the same time, lines became more spacious, attempts were made to achieve greater clarity and chapter headings were more clearly demarcated through use of white space. Gradually the book assumed its modern appearance.

As printed texts multiplied the book ceased to be a precious object consulted in a library. People wished to take a book with them and to be able to transport it easily, to read or consult at any time; hence the growing success of the 'portable format' which also dates from the first half of the 16th century. In addition to the more traditional readers drawn from the clergy, students and the upper classes, the bourgeoisie began to form their own libraries. Quarto and octavo books, though common enough in the 15th century, were only for short texts too slight to publish in folio. Books intended for the pulpit were of large format. In fact the main books which systematically used small formats in this period were devotional works, especially Books of Hours. For these books, which were in constant use and already intended for a large market, had to be easily transportable. Another literature produced in small format and intended for an even larger market, was that of popular tales, known from their shape as 'plaquettes gothiques'.

But from the end of the 15th century, anxious to ease the reading of classical authors, the Aldi launched their famous 'portable' collection. Taken up by the small humanist readership, this format was adopted increasingly at the beginning of the 16th century. In Paris, for example, Simon de Colines started a series like the Aldines, which found many imitators, particularly at Lyons where Venetian models were regularly copied. Soon new literary works were systematically published in small format, easy to handle and consult. If the old romances of chivalry continued to appear in folio and quarto, the Latin poems of the humanists, the works of Marot, of Rabelais and of Marguerite of Navarre and the groups of poets known as the Pléiade all came out in small format. It was in this form that Erasmus' *Adages* spread through Europe, and this too was the form used for the innumerable pamphlets in which Luther and the reformers diffused their ideas. Books with illustrations were often like this as well. Holbein in 1540 drew little vignettes for a 4° and 8vo edition of *Images de la Bible* and *Simulacres de la Mort* which had an enormous success.[129] De Tournes at Lyons and Denis Janot in Paris and printers elsewhere published editions of *Figures de la Bible* and the *Emblems* of Alciat or Ovid's *Metamorphoses*.[130] For students and scholars however the folio was still preferred, since although it was more difficult to handle, it was more legible and it was an easier form in which to trace references.

Thus the book trade in this period was, more than anything, characterised by the division between ponderous, learned tomes intended for use in libraries, and small size literary or polemical works for a larger public. Such a contrast continued to dominate the history of the book in the 17th century. The period 1600 to 1650, the age of the Counter-Reformation, was one in which France was covered with monasteries which were also libraries, in which Protestant theologians fought a battle of erudition with the Jesuits, and in which lawyers, imitating the ecclesiastics, collected great libraries of religious works. The bourgeois classes, apparently, lost the taste for reading they had possessed in the 16th century. Great editions of the sacred texts, and of the Church Fathers, official records of the Great Councils and treatises on canon law enjoyed a revival and large editions in folio multiplied. But for short works in French, quarto was preferred because it was more readable, although less portable, than octavo editions. The trend was clear. When, for example, the Elzeviers, cut off from their main suppliers of paper by the Wars, adopted for their editions of classical authors a small format, the famous 12mos, of minute type to conserve stocks, their scholarly readership began to complain. In the second half of the 17th century by contrast, a public for imaginative literature was growing again. Novels and works of popularisation multiplied and economic conditions did not favour the publication of costly works of reference. These were the reasons for the renewed success of the small format. Similarly, in the 18th century the folio was hardly used at all except for works of permanent value like dictionaries and encyclopaedias. The types of book which were customarily published in quarto or octavo – novels, literary works, popular science and polemic and editions of Latin and Greek authors – now represented the great bulk of book production.

4
Illustration

Manuscripts were often decorated with miniatures; they would be found for example in Books of Hours, missals, devotional works, romances of chivalry and treatises on hunting. But, even more than ordinary manuscripts, illuminated manuscripts, copied by the cleverest calligraphers and illuminated sometimes by famous painters, were only within the reach of the privileged – nobles, both lay and spiritual, and rich merchants.

Here again, the invention of printing did not cause any immediate transformation. Illuminators and miniaturists continued to work after printing began – think, for example, of the *Hours* of Anne of Brittany, of Bourdichon, who died in 1521, or again of Columba. Editors who specialised in the luxury book trade, like Vérard, when they wished to sell a book capable of rivalling luxury manuscripts, had the text illustrated by the same painters who illuminated the manuscripts.

But the method was too costly and time-consuming, except perhaps for a few dedicatory copies printed on vellum for important people. When the need came to supply illustrations for the hundreds of copies of the same book – when books became 'democratised' as it were – other means were essential. Mechanical reproduction of texts meant a corresponding method of reproducing pictures.

One method, xylography, had been in common use and applied in standardised production before printed books had appeared. From the end of the 14th century block-prints began to multiply and the xylographic industry was fully developed by the time that the printing industry began. A wood-cut was easily inserted in a forme alongside the text, and simultaneous printing of picture and text presented no difficulties, so the convention was quickly adopted. In 1461 Albrecht Pfister of Bamberg conceived the idea of illustrating several books in this way; one of them was a small collection of popular fables by Ulrich

Boner, the *Edelstein* (precious stone). In this first illustrated book, the simple figures in line without shadow, afterwards quickly coloured in wash, primitive though they might be, were not without charm, and would have seemed quite natural to a public used to seeing block-prints. Soon Gunther Zainer was turning out illustrated books at Augsburg, popular works and devotional books, while Pfister continued to print stories illustrated with cuts, such as the so-called *Four Stories* (the tales of Daniel, Joseph, Judith and Esther). The same process was used by Ulrich Zell at Ulm and many other printers in other German towns. As in block-printing itself, the purpose of the cuts was always to amplify the text and make it concretely real, not to produce a work of art.[131]

Thus in Germany, where the block-printing industry was flourishing, printers quickly began to illustrate popular books with wood-cuts and, once the technique was perfected, books of all kinds. Printers from the Rhine Valley also took blocks with them when they left home to work elsewhere, or cut new blocks themselves for the books they printed. Thus, the first illustrated books printed all over Europe had a clearly Germanic stamp. In 1467, for example, two years after the appearance of the first printed book in Italy, two German printers in Rome, Sweynheym and Pannartz, published an illustrated edition of Torquemada's *Meditationes* with wood-cuts by a German artist, and the first illustrated book from Naples, a Boccaccio (1478), was printed by a German called Riessinger with wood-cut illustrations that again appear to be by one of his compatriots. Germanic influence also made itself strongly felt at Venice where so many German printers were in business. The first illustrated book in France that we know of was the *Mirouer de la Rédemption de l'humain lignaige*, printed in Lyons. It was the work of a German, one Matthew Husz, using cuts already used at Cologne in 1474 and at Basel in 1476. At Louvain, Brussels, Bruges, Gouda and Antwerp the style of illustration was again inspired by the Cologne school. Later on German influence is evident in the first illustrated English and Spanish books.[132]

Everywhere, then, at the beginning, the German influence was predominant, but soon local trends began to emerge and with them the first regional schools. In a few rare instances the cuts may have been made by local artists, possibly playing-card makers not particularly influenced by German models. There is nothing specifically German about the pictures in the first book from Verona, the *De re militari* of Valturius

(1472), or in the *Missel de Verdun*, printed by Jean Du Pré at Paris in 1481. The borders of foliage, animals and grotesques which appear here for the first time derive straight from the manuscript tradition. From its beginning this style was more flexible than that in Germany in the same period. It developed in Paris and from there made itself felt in Rouen and in England. Vérard, the great specialist in illustrated books at the end of the 15th century, had an agency in London where he published translations of certain of his French works.[133] In Italy however, in Rome, Naples and Venice, where the first illustrated books had been produced by German printers, local schools came into being, more influenced than elsewhere by fresco painting. Accustomed to a more sophisticated art, the Italian public showed little interest in book illustrations, until they were adapted to their own tastes. Very quickly, to satisfy this public, German artists and their Italian pupils adopted the Italian style – the artist who cut the blocks for Torquemada's *Meditationes* may have copied the designs of a Roman artist influenced by the frescoes of Santa Maria sopra Minerva. A taste for almost oriental richness shows up in the work of an unknown artist who cut the headpieces for an Aesop, printed in 1485 in Naples by a German working for the Neapolitan humanist Tuppo.[134]

Thus, in the great publishing centres, schools of illustrators began to grow up, often influenced by local styles of painting and illumination, and by the monumental architecture under their eyes. Each regional school acquired its own manner, its personal language, and began to specialise. In Florence, for example, printers above all illustrated popular books designed for a local clientele. In the big commercial cities like Venice and Lyons on the other hand, printing was largely for export, and printers concentrated on illustrated Bibles and Church books. Lyons also issued popular books and moral tracts, devotional works, and, for a smaller public, translations of the Latin authors best known to the readers of the time, Terence and Ovid, with pictures of the characters. In Paris illustrated books to suit all tastes were published: Books of Hours, devotional works, Villon's poetry, farces like those of Pathelin, Church books, histories and chivalric romances. At Gouda, Gerard de Leeu, the premier publisher of illustrated books in the Low Countries, also produced devotional works and romances for the rich merchants of that country. At Nuremberg, Anton Koberger, primarily a publisher of learned works, produced outstanding illustrated books and employed Wolgemut, the wood engraver, to illustrate the *Schatzebehalter* with 91 full-page pictures representing scenes from the Bible and allegories (1491). He also had 2,000 cuts made for the illustrations to Hartmann Schedel's *Liber Chronicarum* (1493), better known as the Nuremberg Chronicle, which was brought out simultaneously in German and Latin editions,[135] and was sold in France, Italy, Cracow and Buda. Some years later Koberger illustrated the *Revelations of St. Brigid* with blocks by Dürer (1500), and the plays of the 11th-century dramatist Hroswita (1501).

While each school had a manner and language of its own, external influences continued to be felt. Every illustrated book, even the less important ones, was known throughout Europe and often imitated. Koberger's Nuremberg Chronicle, already mentioned, was copied by Schönsperger at Augsburg in 1496, 1497 and 1500. The blocks for the Basel edition of Sebastian Brandt's *Ship of Fools* (1494) served as a model for Parisian engravers (1497) and Lyonnese (1498).[136] The artists who copied them did try to bring off original versions. For instance one of the most famous Parisian illustrated books in the Renaissance, the *Hypnerotomachia Poliphili*, was only an adaptation of an edition by Aldus which had appeared fifty years earlier at Venice. But the blocks for the Paris book were cut in a very different spirit from those of the Italian model: the adaptation to French taste comes out in a search for affectation. Often, however, in the hands of less skilled or practised cutters, or perhaps simply under pressure, the copy became a simple plagiarism. If Venetian engravers of the 15th century could assimilate the twofold influence of France and Germany, this was no longer the case in the 16th century when they were busy with orders from printers for the export market and contented themselves with hackneyed copies of foreign models without any effort at originality.

In each centre the styles of other, foreign, cities were evident and quite often the blocks used in one place came from another. Often publishers with shops in a number of different towns would proceed in this way. Conrad Resch, with branches in Basel and Paris, used blocks cut in Basel to illustrate books he published in Paris. Likewise some publishers would often ask their foreign colleagues to have the blocks they needed cut by a local artist of repute. Urs Graf, for example, the famous Basel artist working as an illustrator for Froben, occasionally worked for Matthias Schürer and Hupfuff of Strasbourg, and for Anshelm of Haguenau, Pierre Vidoue and Conrad Resch of Paris.[137]

Given these circumstances it is easily seen how complex the study of illustrations can be. Even though a minor art, book illustration must be seen as part of the great artistic, intellectual and social movements of its age. But that is not our object, for such a study would require a full volume on its own. One thing that is clear is the importance of illustrations, whether in xylographs or printed books, in the diffusion of iconographic themes. In this context, Émile Mâle has demonstrated the influence of the *Biblia pauperum* and the *Speculum humanae salvationis*. Already the miniaturist who illuminated the *Très riches heures* of the Duc de Berry used a manuscript of the *Speculum humanae salvationis*. Van Eyck in 1440 and Van der Weyden in 1460 owned copies of this manuscript work or perhaps a block-book version, and were influenced by it. But it is particularly when the *Biblia pauperum* and the *Speculum* were reproduced in block-book form that they became popular and were adopted as models by artists. The tapestries of Chaise-Dieu and those in the cathedral at Rheims were influenced by the same two works, as was a tapestry in the cathedral at Sens and another in Chalon-sur-Saône. The two great stained glass windows in the Sainte Chapelle of Vic-le-Comte are also copied from the *Biblia pauperum* and the *Speculum*. Likewise some sculptures in the main doorway in the church of St. Maurice at Vienne in Dauphiné, and the great doorway of the cathedral of Troyes. The same influence can be detected in Limousin enamels and ivory coffers. Similar examples are by no means rare: scenes from Books of Hours often influenced the makers of tapestry and glass. Shepherds' Calendars and the Dance of Death (*Danse macabre*) together with the Books of Hours were also models for mural painters; hence the murals at La Ferté-Loupière and Meslay-le-Grenet, inspired by the Dance of Death printed by Guy Marchant and by Coustiau and Ménard. On the other hand Marchant's Dance of Death was probably a copy of one in the Cimetière des Innocents. Later still, in the 16th century, several enamelists appear to have copied illustrations from books, for example Grüninger's *Aeneid* of 1501, and the *Histoire de la conquête de la Toison d'or* of Jean de Meauregard, and pictures in the *Illustration des Gaules* of Jean Le Maire de Belges are known to have inspired tapestry work.

Perhaps the most striking examples of the role of book illustration in the diffusion of art are the Bible and the *Metamorphoses* of Ovid printed by Jean de Tournes in 1553 and 1557 with vignettes by Bernard Salomon, two works which enjoyed great success, the latter being used as Protestant propaganda. Salomon's illustrations were the inspiration behind many tapestries, silks, enamels, faience pieces, and woodcarvings.

Many series of pictures were inspired by the same vignettes, either directly or via other wood-cuts, and the page borders in the *Metamorphoses* served as models in lace pattern books.[138]

But let us limit ourselves to a few works taken from the most famous books of the 16th century and to a few artists whom we shall often have occasion to mention.

At this period of ostentatious display, picture books spread across Germany and France.[139] It is impossible to ignore the great series of Dürer's (though strictly speaking they were wood engravings), the *Apocalypse* (1498), the *Great Passion* (1498–1501), the *Life of the Virgin* (1502–1510) which came out first as prints, then in book form with letterpress accompaniment. From 1512, Dürer was at Augsburg working with Schönsperger, official printer to the Emperor Maximilian, and to celebrate the Emperor's glory he worked on the *Triumphal Arch*, then on the *Triumphs of Maximilian*. Hans Burgkmair cut Dürer's designs and later collaborated with Schäufelin and Leonard Beck, illustrating the *Teuerdank*, an allegorical description of the Imperial marriage.

Meanwhile the Strasbourg printers, especially Grüninger, were turning out picture books. The Strasbourger, Hans Weiditz the Younger, a pupil of Burgkmair, was perhaps the best painter-engraver of his day and he illustrated the German Bible for Knobloch (1524), and perhaps the *Glücksbuch* of Petrarch published by Steyner at Augsburg in 1532. But his best work without any doubt is the *Eicones vivae herbarum* by Otto Brunfels (Schotten, 1530–1536). While in the other works he was merely seeking to be picturesque, here Weiditz's sole aim was accuracy and he knew just how to render animals and plants with perfect naturalness. In a genre at once more coarse and vulgar another Alsatian, Hans Baldung-Grien, produced 43 blocks for the *Hortulus animae* of Flach (1511–12) as well as many blocks for Grüninger. Finally, two great engravers of Nuremberg, Joost Amman and Virgil Solis designed many blocks for the publisher Feyerabend.

Remember, too, that the Cranachs worked at that time for Luther at Wittenberg (see pp. 287ff.), while at Basel Froben collaborated with Urs Graf, whom we have already mentioned, and more particularly with Hans and Ambrosius Holbein. Holbein did not himself engrave, but his compositions were rendered very skilfully by engravers like Lützelburger, and it was Lützelburger without doubt who produced the small vignettes in the *Figures de la Bible* published by Trechsel at Lyons in 1538 from Holbein's original designs which are now in the museum at Basel.

French book illustration yielded nothing to German. Simon Vostre, the Hardouyns, and later Pierre Vidoue, besides many others, turned out editions of Books of Hours. They blended German and Italian influences and sometimes made them into one. The former came via booksellers of German origin (like Kerver and Wechel) and through the ascendancy of the great German masters, Dürer, Holbein and Schongauer. The French at this time made contact with the Renaissance through the mediation of Germany, especially Basel. This was the case with Oronce Finé, a mathematician from the Dauphiné, who cut blocks and borders. The influence was naturally strong at Lyons where Trechsel, as we have seen, used Holbein's designs. At the same time, Italian influence sometimes came in directly, as for instance in the designs of Geoffroy Tory.

Gradually, the French book escaped from foreign influence and attained its apogee about the 1550's. Among masterpieces produced then were the *Hypnerotomachia Poliphili*, some of whose blocks have been attributed to Jean Goujon. It is more probable that the illustrations in an edition of Vitruvius printed by Gazeau in 1547 were made by that sculptor, as were those in the *Entrée de Henri II*, published in Roffet in 1549. It was Jean Cousin the Elder who published his *Treatise on Perspective* (1560). At Lyons Jean de Tournes hired the best painter-engraver in the city, Bernard Salomon, who did some very lively engravings, both expressive and versatile, with backgrounds of the countryside and classic temples. The pictures he created for the story *La Coche* in *La Marguerite des Marguerites des princesses* (1547) and especially the illustrations to *Quadrins historiques de la Bible* of Paradin as well as the illustrated *Metamorphoses* of Ovid should all be mentioned. We shall see later on the success enjoyed by books of this sort.

These examples may help to emphasise the importance and high quality of the illustrated book in the 16th century, a period of great brilliance in that field. Without going further into that aspect of the subject, let us just recall the kinds of books illustrated between the 15th and the 18th centuries, what needs they fulfilled and the public they were intended for.

Originally we saw that the illustrated book, successor to the block book, had the same aim and the same clientele. It was intended to edify a huge public that could hardly read, to explain the text through the medium of pictures, to make real and comprehensible the different episodes in the life of Christ, the prophets and the saints, and to give some reality to the demons and angels who disputed for the souls of sinners, and also to the mythical and legendary personalities familiar to the men in that age. Such was the aim of xylographs and such was the aim of the first illustrated books. It was not surprising therefore that the most popular illustrated books in the 15th century were works of devotion, pious and moralising, usually in the vernacular. To judge by the catalogues of incunabula the most frequently reprinted illustrated books of the 15th century in France and Germany were stories of the Passion and Life of Christ, stories of Satan like the *Bélial* of Jacques de Théramo, the *Mirror of the Redemption* and others like the *Speculum humanae vitae*, the *Art de bien mourir et celui de bien vivre*, the *Golden Legend* of Jacques de Voragine, the *Story of the Bible*, the *Shepherds' Calendar* and the innumerable popular and moralising fables attributed to Aesop, Bidpay and Cato. Book illustration answered a practical rather than an artistic need: to make graphic and visible what people of the time constantly heard evoked. There is no subtle variation of light and shade, or of tone; just a few simple figures cut with clear and obvious features.

After the introduction of printing the number of Books of Hours and romances of chivalry in private hands grew incessantly, and so, soon, did illustrated editions of the Latin authors which people had been accustomed for a long time to read in the vernacular, Virgil, for instance. There was, however, no longer any question of decorating these by hand, as had been done in illuminated manuscripts. So, with some hesitation, and often with regret, hand illumination was abandoned in their case too. At Venice, for example, they tried an intermediate process using printed borders which could serve as a picture frame for the painter, and in Germany complete illustrations were later finished in colour and only the outline printed. Until the beginning of the 16th century a blank space was often retained at the head of chapters for a coloured initial, although the painters could only finish a small number of the copies printed.

To satisfy a public which knew, even if it did not possess, painted manuscripts treating the same themes, publishers like Vérard lavished great care on their printed books' illustrations, so that they acquired the sumptuous look of a manuscript. In France Books of Hours, which were in such great vogue, were decorated with masses of small wood-cuts assembled as borders, and more and more attention was devoted to conveying light and shade. In Italy engravings were produced by artists who were competing with painters, and so were done more subtly. From about 1500 hatching becomes common in Venice, often somewhat impairing the purity of the wood-cut and robbing it of part of its essential feel.

Soon Renaissance influence and the prestige of Italian art made itself
felt in the Germanic countries as well as in France. Certainly, the first
humanists, especially those of the late 15th and early 16th centuries,
scholars before all else, showed as much disdain for illustrated books as
the theologians of the Sorbonne. Wasn't an illustration merely a simple
way to instruct those who were too ignorant to read the text? Thus
scenes intended to illustrate the translations of Terence and Ovid –
intended, that is, for a public they scorned – could only cause them pain,
especially as they were drawn by artists with little concern for archaeo-
logy, and for readers who knew nothing about Antiquity, who would
be quite happy if the characters of Terence were depicted wearing 15th
century dress. Even when Aldus published his *Hypnerotomachia Poliphili*,
which was more in line with classical feeling, the humanists seemed to
have held aloof from this magnificent edition and it was not reprinted in
Venice.

In France, however, the plain decorative frames taken from Italian
models by Geoffroy Tory enjoyed a great vogue and were imitated
everywhere. Soon Kerver at Paris re-edited the *Hypnerotomachia Poliphili*, illustrated by plates inspired by Italian wood-cuts, and this work
which had had only a limited success in Venice in 1500, caught on in
Paris from 1549. But it was the mathematician, Oronce Finé, whose work
had led him to take an interest in book illustration, who established the
fashion for geometrical frames placed around subjects which were often
allegorical and true to the spirit of the German Renaissance. For an even
larger public had been won over to the new spirit – the children of those
who, in the 15th century, read Aesop's *Fables*, *Scenes from the Bible*, the
Roman de la Rose, the *History of Troy* or *Lancelot*. This new readership
was accustomed to illustrations and it now desired a form of illustration
more appropriate to its tastes. Soon, Holbein and the Basel publishers
who employed him were using finely cut small vignettes to illustrate
popular books, like *the Story of the Old and the New Testament* or the
Illustrated Metamorphoses of Ovid. Very quickly, these books were copied
and imitated everywhere, at Lyons by de Tournes, at Paris by Janot or
Groulleau. In this way, the illustration of texts which had enjoyed such
a vogue in the 15th century, enjoyed an even greater one in the 16th. At
the same time, vignettes of this kind were used to illustrate emblem
books which, from the middle of the 16th century, began to enjoy a
huge success.

However, one whole section of the public, merchants, and humbler groups who scarcely knew how to read, seem, for a long time afterwards, to have remained faithful to the old form of illustration. This public, whose taste scarcely changed, was served by the poorer printers and the smaller publishers who for a long time stayed loyal to the old gothic types and, for an even longer time, to 15th and early 16th-century wood-cuts which they re-bought, used until they wore out and then had re-engraved without any modification. It was undoubtedly because of the importance of this public that from around 1570 there was a noticeable renewal in the fashion for collections and series of popular wood-cut scenes. It was a period when the wood-cutters of the Rue Montorgueil in Paris brought out mass editions of the Stories of the Bible, that descendant of the *Biblia pauperum* with a large block on every page and a few simple lines by way of caption (the ancestor of our strip cartoon). More topical were pictures of the Wars of Religion which had an immense sale. With them there began a new kind of popular literature, the pedlar's stock-in-trade. In France, a small number of printers and booksellers continued in Paris and especially at Troyes to publish *Amadis de Gaule*, and *Mélusine*, along with *Scenes from the Bible* and the standard Shepherds' Calendars which hawkers sold in the country, small towns and even Paris right into the 17th and even 18th centuries. So widespread had this been that in the 19th century, when everyone could read, chapmen's literature enjoyed an astonishing revival, and everywhere there reappeared texts which had been fashionable in the 15th century, and which Erasmus, Rabelais, La Fontaine and Voltaire had not been able to replace.

By 1550 the book trade was beginning to feel the effect of the rise in prices affecting the European economy: the crisis which was to characterise the second half of the 16th century was under way. From that time on the illustrated book made little advance. The work of the engravers seems careless and hurried, and they tend more and more just to turn out poor copies of earlier illustrations. Fewer pictures were published and when publishing revived at the end of the century wood is no longer the medium, but copper. This was a change in technique which represented a new intellectual climate and we must consider its implications.

Copperplate engraving was already well known since the 15th century and had been perfected (like printing) by goldsmiths. It allowed a more faithful rendering of light and shade, lines of greater subtlety were possible, and it had always been preferred by painters. From the end of the 15th century Italians like d'Andrea and Germans like Schongauer had brought the technique to perfection.[140] Attempts had also sometimes been made to apply the technique to printed books; but they had not been too successful, because of a technical obstacle. In the case of wood-cuts it was possible both to place the cut and the typographic composition in the forme, to ink them in the same way and to print both text and illustration at the same time, but engraving meant separate printing of the copper plate, a costly and delicate matter if it was to harmonise with type.

For a long time, as long as the public only wanted pictures which helped its efforts at imagination, wood-cuts, however worn and lifeless, were preferred to copper engraving. But things were changing by about 1600. It must be remembered that the 16th century had been an age of painters. The taste for painting had spread across Europe. Rich merchants in Paris and Lyons, patrician families in Venice and Antwerp had their portraits done, and ordered from a growing number of painters canvasses no longer intended to decorate the walls of churches, but those of their own homes. At the same time, painters became engravers and less wealthy people kept copper engravings as their 'poor man's picture gallery'. Mantegna in Italy and Dürer in Germany made plates that were an immediate success and have remained famous. In France, copper engravers were most often originally goldsmiths and worked in isolation until the Italians, Primaticcio and Il Rosso, came to decorate the chateau of Fontainebleau. A school of copper engravers formed around Fontainebleau and their aim was to spread the new Italian style of decoration in France. The traditional wood-cut seemed coarse compared with these copper engravings. Copper already seemed perfect for rendering architecture, classical monuments, or an exact likeness of the face. Soon, despite the technical difficulties, copper was increasingly used in book illustration. At first it was used only in exceptional cases to illustrate technical works or volumes studded with portraits, but gradually it extended to books of all kinds.[141]

The decisive impetus came from Antwerp, a town with a great many painters, where Hieronymus Cock, a successful printseller, controlled a workshop in which the young Bruegel learnt the use of the burin. Plantin was in daily contact with Cock and his workers and began to have some of his books illustrated with copper plate engravings by the artists in Cock's workshop.

He employed the best copper engravers of the Antwerp School,

Pierre Van der Borcht, the Huys and the brothers Wiericx. In 1566 he published the *Vivae imagines partium corporis* of Vesalius and Valverda illustrated with 42 plates, the *Humanae salutis monumenta* of Arias Montanus in 1571, and in 1574 the *Icones veterum aliquot et novorum medicorum philosophorumque* of Sambuca, in which there were 67 engraved portraits by Van der Borcht. These works spread through Europe and were much appreciated. Soon the consequences of Plantin's work were everywhere to be seen. In 1574, for example, Jean Thevet in Paris published his *Portraicts des hommes illustres* decorated with plates engraved in Flanders. Flemish printsellers and engravers flocked to Paris around this time and French publishers henceforth found more than enough artists ready to furnish what was required.[142]

From the end of the 16th century onwards the wood-cut declined and almost disappeared as a form of book illustration, outside of hawkers' literature. In fact it practically disappeared altogether. Copper began its long reign of more than 200 years, and this was no merely technical change. The technique triumphed because of its powers of minutely accurate representation. As a means of communication conveying a realistic image and a permanent record it was unrivalled. The print became increasingly analogous in its diffusion of pictorial fact to the book in its diffusion of typographic fact. Thus the adoption of copper and the international trade in prints at the end of the 16th and beginning of the 17th centuries helped to widen men's horizons. We need only mention as an example the monumental collection of travels by Thomas de Bry in the early 17th century which imparted a sometimes erroneous but always precise idea of the world, from Lapland to Brazil, through the medium of copper engravings. And we should not forget the enormous work accomplished in one particular domain – mapmaking – by the Dutch publishers of the 17th century.

Books of engravings became collectors' pieces, and, increasingly, merchants and even humbler people, too poor to possess paintings, adorned the walls of their houses with prints: no longer crude wood-cuts, but copper engravings which depicted, faithfully and in detail – and therefore with a greater appearance of reality – religious or historical subjects or different aspects of everyday life.

If there was a call to commemorate an important event which had captured the imagination, a victorious battle for example, the coronation of a king, or fêtes, ballets and spectacles given by a prince; if one wished to know the likeness of a great man; if a man of letters or a rich merchant wished to circulate his portrait to friends or correspondents; if one wished to preserve the memory of a picturesque scene in the street – the engraver was there to do it. Much more so than the painter, since prints could be reproduced. He was the photographer of his day. Thus Callot made known to everyone the principal episodes of the siege of Breda or of La Rochelle; he conveyed the vitality of the fairground, the horrors of war, or the roaming life of Bohemians, and even engraved for theatre lovers portraits of the characters of the Comédie Italienne. Abraham Bosse provided a precise portrayal of the life of the Parisian bourgeoisie, and Nanteuil and his competitors produced numerous portraits of princes and of merchants in the second half of the 17th century. In the 18th century the engravers of the French school set out to portray manners and morals, illustrating the daily life of the aristocracy and the bourgeoisie, and the street-life of Paris.

The print also played its critical part in the diffusion of works of art. From the 17th century, thanks to the engraving, most people were acquainted with the masterpieces of art scattered throughout Europe. A host of engravers from every country devoted themselves to reproducing the paintings, monuments, and ruins of Italy. Engravers were often also commissioned to reproduce the paintings of the great masters of their native country in their own day. Nanteuil and Morin, for example, produced prints after the portraits of Philippe de Champaigne and that portrait painter owed much of his contemporary fame to them.[143] Rubens was well aware of the value of having his works made more widely known through this medium and established an atelier for engravers to turn out prints of his pictures. Henceforth, living in the neighbourhood of the shops of the big printsellers like Mariette of Paris, engravers reproduced the works of the great Italian, Flemish, French or German masters. Everyone could examine them and compare them at their leisure. From then on, it was engravers who made known and diffused ornamental styles.

The engraving was thus an essential medium of information in the 17th century. In the midst of these transformations, the illustrated book lost some of its interest. Forced as they were by economic difficulties to cut costs, publishers confined illustrations to a few plates which could be separated from the text, or to a frontispiece, to avoid the extra expense of double imposition necessary to secure an impression from a copper engraving and letterpress on the same page. Engravers charged high prices for their work, and only exceptional luxury works with assured sales, like Chapelain's *La Pucelle*, a big favourite impatiently awaited by the literary world, would merit adequate illustration. In such cases there was no hesitation in asking even the greatest painters to furnish designs for engravers. Rubens, Vignon, Poussin, Philippe de Champaigne and Le Brun collaborated in this way in book illustration. With them the divorce between text and image became so marked that by the end of the 17th century it was enough to call a book 'illustrated' if a picture of the author was inside. In the classical period there were very few real book illustrators.

In the 18th century circumstances were different again.[144] Economic conditions evolved further, publishers were once more concerned about the quality of their products and vignettes reappeared in the midst of printed pages. Once more, there was a public keenly interested in illustrated books. But times had changed since the 15th and 16th centuries when illustrated books had been destined for a vast public. The new 18th century demand was in the luxury market and came from the aristocracy of wealth, bankers and financiers who, proud of their recently acquired fortunes, wished to start a library of their own. Having no inclination for serious works which bored them, they turned bibliophiles with a taste for sumptuously decorated books. It was an age when rich tax farmers had magnificently illustrated editions made of the *Fables* and *Contes* of La Fontaine, when the most celebrated illustrated book was of the insipid *Chansons* of Laborde, or more indicative still, the *Temple of Cnidus*, a youthful aberration of Montesquieu's. In France at least, there was a dazzling renaissance of the illustrated book. Boucher and Fragonard entrusted their work to the excellent engravers of the French school. But the illustrated book represented only an insignificant proportion of printed output and reached only a small part of the public, one comparable to the contemporary market for bibliophile productions and limited editions of art books. At this period, therefore, the illustrated book would be of small interest to this study had it not been for the great technical skill applied by engravers to the scïentific and technical works of the period in providing illustrations essential to the comprehension of the text. In the age of the 'philosophes' these books were numerous and of particular importance. Buffon's work, and of course the huge enterprise of the *Encyclopédie*, could not have been conceived without the aid of detailed and precise copper engraving which brought to life the many technical articles. Nor could the accounts of explorations, which became increasingly numerous in the time of Cook and La Pérouse and which were accompanied by prints, faithfully reproducing sketches made on the expeditions.

5
Clothing the Book: The Binding

When we examine the old bindings preserved, often in pristine condition, on manuscripts and books printed in any period up to the 19th century one thing strikes us right away: the bindings which cover even quite ordinary books are strong and infinitely better in quality than those which do service today. To take an actual example – the books in the old Bibliothèque Royale, now the Bibliothèque Nationale, were bound in the 17th century with red morocco using gold tooling, and emblazoned with the royal arms. Today most books received by the Bibliothèque Nationale are only bound in cloth.

There is no reason to be surprised by this care for solidity, and the quality of materials used in binding, which arouses admiration in the trade today. At that time a manuscript or its successor, a printed book, was so comparatively rare and costly an item of merchandise that it merited care in its preservation and adornment. From the invention of printing right up to the 18th century, although the readership increased, the book was still the preserve of a small and favoured elite. In days when paper was made by hand and books printed on hand presses, the book was still seen as a precious object, which it was important to preserve, and therefore had to be bound carefully.

What were the distinctive features of bindings between the 15th and 18th centuries? That is, commercial bindings: it is not our intention to discuss luxury bindings, art objects destined for a small circle of princes and bibliophiles. How did binders, between the 15th and 18th centuries, adapt their technique to cope with growing numbers of books? What consequences did increased output have on the quality and the appearance of bindings? These are the main questions we want to answer here.

Again, the coming of printing produced no sudden revolutionary upheaval. The same craftsmen who bound manuscripts applied their skill in the same way to books. They continued to cover the back and the boards, made of solid wood, with precious fabrics like velvet, silk, cloth of gold, if binding luxury editions destined for important people. Otherwise they used leather – tanned calf, sheepskin, and in Germany also pigskin. Then with their finishing tools they impressed designs often in repeated patterns made with fillets or roulettes, sometimes 'blind' (i.e. without gold leaf) and sometimes 'tooled' (with gold leaf). Styles varied from area to area and subjects and motifs were of infinite variety: *fleurs de lys*, eagles with one or two heads, animals of all kinds, real or imaginary, lions and griffins, dragons and greyhounds, coats of arms, the four evangelists, streamers and inscriptions, sometimes just the simple monograph IHS, the pascal lamb, a picture of a saint, the cross, or the head of Christ.[145]

There is no immediate change in appearance between the manuscript books of the early 15th century and the first incunabula up to about the year 1480. They continued to be bound in heavy, solid bindings with metal clasps, their covers studded with nails for protection (books were stored flat or kept on desks). Many were bound in monasteries, in binding workshops, situated in the proximity of the copyists. Others were the products of private workshops, whose binders worked in liaison with copyists serving the secular market, in particular the stationers near the universities.

From around 1480 the consequences of printing began to be felt. The printed book multiplied and its use became more common. Private individuals developed libraries of their own and books ceased to be a purely monastic possession. Monastic binderies diminished in importance while the private binders grew more affluent, especially in university towns where they were assured of finding a clientele. Most often they set up near stationers, or were stationers themselves as well as publishers. Big publishers like the Kobergers owned binderies equipped to carry out mass production. But it must be stressed that books were not bound as part of the normal publishing process as they are now. Only a few copies of a work could expect to be sold in any one town, and many printers had agents in all parts of Europe selling books for them. Since binding was heavy and expensive and transport costs were high, books were sent in unbound sheets from one town to the next in barrels. A few were bound as they were bought, but inventories show that only a small number of copies were bound in the shop, most of the edition being stored in sheets since the buyer preferred to buy it thus and have it bound to his taste later. Unaware of this situation, historians of binding have until recently tended to assume that books were generally bound in the towns where they had been printed.

When, however, the press began to turn out many more books, binders had to adapt their methods to respond to new demands. Work had to be done more rapidly, and serial production was necessary to make bindings of suitable but less ponderous quality to satisfy a larger and less wealthy clientele. Printing encouraged the growth of the paper trade and this increased the number of waste sheets; so began the habit of using 'cardboard' for covers in place of wooden boards. It was cheaper and not as heavy, made by pasting several sheets together which toughened them. Paper of all kinds was used – old proof sheets, old books used as scrap, letters, business files, archives. The dismantling of old bindings often brings interesting finds to light.

The decoration of covers, too, had to be done more quickly and at less cost. By using ornamental plates instead of decorating the whole surface with tiny fillets repeated over and over again, which was laborious and demanded great care, they achieved an impressive effect and saved time. A whole scene could be impressed at once on to the cover with the iron. In France, for example, these plates reproduced scenes from the Old and New Testament, preferably those which figured in the Book of Hours or the images of saints. Most of the subjects chosen had a pious intention, even if the content of the book was not religious. Otherwise, plates were used to impress personal devices of booksellers, or, lastly, for pure decoration.[147] In Flanders, the plates showed a taste for animals and miniatures, and in the Germanic countries, somewhat later, allegorical and mythological subjects inspired by the Renaissance were often used.

In the first years of the 16th century, there was another change. Confronted by the incessant increase of books, binders, always on the lookout for a more rapid method which would economise labour and reduce the cost of their products, developed a different technique, that of the roulette. The roulette was a tiny metal wheel, on which was engraved a simple, repeatable motif. By this means it became possible to decorate bindings with a series of rapidly executed headbands. Sometimes the plate system and the roulette system were used simultaneously. This meant that the centrepiece of a cover could be decorated with a figure and the surrounds run off with the roulette.

Such was the appearance of commercial bindings in the first third of the 16th century. Meanwhile, new processes were introduced into the making of luxury bindings. Copies made for princes had traditionally been bound in cloth, because skins could not be prepared finely enough for the purpose so long as only the 'cold' process of stamping was known. The situation changed, however, when morocco leather and the technique of gold tooling were introduced into Europe from the Islamic world. From the close of the 15th century morocco from Cordova was imported into Naples via the Balearics, and Levant morocco came to Venice via Constantinople. From about that time, Aldus used it in Venice but it was not used in France until the middle of the 16th century.[148] Meanwhile, gold tooling, which had long been known in the East, was also adopted by the Italians. It was in use at Naples in 1475 to decorate bindings for King Ferdinand of Aragon, by applying heated irons to thin gold or silver leaf. By 1500 the Venetians were following this example. Aldus, who had just founded a workshop specialising in Greek typography, did more than anyone to promote the fashion for gold tooling in Eastern motifs which spread to Northern Italy, so that when the French invaded Italy they too developed a taste for gorgeous decoration. The Kings of France, and also the famous Grolier, who was treasurer of Milan, had work carried out for them in Italian binderies and brought the new technique to France. In the second third of the 16th century, French artists surpassed their Italian masters, using polychrome mosaics, interlacings and fleurons painted with resins, or, for more sombre bindings, pure geometric designs in Renaissance style. These bindings are unequalled in the perfection of their technique, but we shall not discuss them further since they were confined to Kings and to a small number of very rich bibliophiles.

At the same time, the semi-luxury binding appeared, the technique of hot-stamping being applied to commercial bindings. From 1520 it was used for plate work as in Geoffroy Tory's famous 'pot cassé' or broken urn. Plates decorated with filets and interlacing were sometimes used to make more economical bindings in imitation of the roulette method. Sometimes a motif – the mark of a bookseller or the bust of a character – is placed in the centre. Finally, until the end of the 16th century, particularly in religious books, an oval-shaped central motif was impressed with a die stamp. But all such methods were costly and time consuming and gradually simple calf bindings appear without decoration. When worsening economic conditions led to a demand for the lowest possible prices less valuable books began to be bound in vellum and even prelates like Cardinal Charles de Bourbon were satisfied with bindings of morocco decorated only with borders of gold fillets.[149]

During the 17th and 18th centuries calf binding was the norm, with a plain gold-filleted border. Morocco was used for more elegant books. When books belonged to a great nobleman or private collector he would often have his arms struck on the centre of the covers. Bibliophiles however continued to have gold decorated bindings 'au petit fer' made in the 17th century. Then, when bibliophile tastes developed in the 18th century, luxury binding in France received a new impulse: mosaic designs were made for Philippe d'Orléans the Regent and his court around 1720; decorated polychrome bindings inspired by Chinese art came into fashion, and especially popular were bindings 'à la dentelle', the surrounds of the plates being gilded by the application of a hot iron frame decorated in a lacework motif. This was the age when Pasdeloup, Monnier and Derôme worked on illustrated luxury orders, vied for by the public. But, once again, these bindings, like the books they covered, were destined for a small and privileged market. The average mass-produced binding was a perfunctory product. From the end of the 17th century, simple marbled paper was sometimes used for small books and for the increasing number of journals.

So if we compare bindings on ordinary books from the 15th to the 18th centuries we find that when the clientele was small (in the 15th and early 16th centuries) binders still decorated even 'trade' books. But as in the course of the 16th century book production increased, editions proliferated and the book reached a larger public, binders sought techniques which would enable them to bind suitably decorated books more rapidly. Soon they had to stop decorating the covers of commercial bindings. While the art of luxury binding enjoyed a boom in the middle of the 16th century and then again in the 18th century, the average book, although durably bound, no longer had any cover decoration. Since books were now stored upright and pushed up closely against one another to save space, only the spine which was to be seen on the shelves of libraries bore any tooling: usually some decorative motifs and a stamped title. With the steam press and papermaking machinery of the 19th century, books were printed more cheaply and quickly in larger editions, and binding was often abandoned in favour of a simple stitched cover. In a word, with the growth in production of books and the increase in the reading public, the average binding gradually shed first its beauty and then its solidity.

The Book as a Commodity

From its earliest days printing existed as an industry, governed by the same rules as any other industry; the book was a piece of merchandise which men produced before anything else to earn a living, even when they were (as with Aldus and the Estiennes) scholars and humanists at the same time. Thus it was vitally necessary from the outset to find enough capital to start work and then to print only those titles which would satisfy a clientele, and that at a price which would withstand competition. The marketing of books was similar to that of other products. To the manufacturers who created the books – the printers – and to the business men who sold them – the booksellers and publishers – finance and costing were the key problems. Those problems need to be studied if we are to understand how they determined the structure of the whole trade.

I
Costs

Firstly, the items which make up the cost of a book. Which part of the cost of a print run is greater – the labour or the raw materials (paper, in particular)? Did the relationship between these different elements vary in course of time, so far as can be ascertained? It is hard to find an answer to such questions. Accounts and day books of printers which have survived up to the present time are rare and those of the 15th and 16th centuries are especially rare. If contracts have survived in greater numbers, we still do not have documents from the same region, in a consecutive sequence, containing data of the kind we require.

Let us take Paris, for example, a city about which there exists quite a lot of information, much of it in some detail thanks to the work of Ernest Coyecque.[150] Firstly, let us look at the printer's equipment in a typical workshop belonging to a small printer, Jacques Ferrebouc, according to an inventory of 1513.[151] The equipment is poor, consisting of one press valued at 10 livres (13 livres with its 2 tympans); various pieces valued at under 8 livres; 5 founts of type, more or less worn, amounting to 40 livres. The whole outfit was worth about 60 livres.

A more important workshop, belonging to Didier Maheu, was valued thus according to an inventory of 1520:[152] three presses equipped with an iron screw thread, platens, nuts and bolts, valued at 60 livres; dies of a gothic fount, decorated with engraved figures, with two moulds, 24 livres; dies for casting a type called 'Bourgeois',[153] 12 livres; the same for a 'Lettre de Somme', 8 livres, and a 'Somme angélique', 7 livres 8 sols; 8 founts, more or less worn, valued at 122 livres. To this we would have to add some engravings and some brass alphabets (i.e. punches) valued at 16 livres. The type cases and the remainder of the stock are estimated at 102 livres. The total value of this printing house is therefore 351 livres.

Last example: a workshop of the highest class which belonged to the celebrated printer Wolfgang Hopyl[154] who printed a number of theological works and school textbooks. The inventory made at his death in 1523 includes 5 presses valued at 24 livres (46 livres with the tympans); ten founts in good condition valued around 360 livres; a great quantity of punches and particularly of dies valued at more than 200 livres; some ornamental letters, devices, wooden and copper engravings amounting to more than 75 livres. In all the equipment is valued at above 700 livres.

According to this evidence the cost of printing presses in Paris between 1520 and 1523 varied (according to their condition) from 9 livres to 20 livres, a comparatively small sum. Nevertheless printers who wished to set up in business could escape even that outlay by renting a press. Hire of a press in 1515 cost 40 sols per year, and between 1540 and 1550, 6 or 8 livres. During this last period a press in good condition was valued at 23 to 30 livres.[155]

So the press itself was relatively inexpensive. The purchase of type, which had, moreover, to be frequently renewed, was more of a burden. The price of founts varied in the inventories mentioned above from 10 to 70 livres according to the wear on the type face and variety and importance of the fount. A deal concluded in 1515 by Nicolas Le Rouge, a bookseller of Troyes, with Symphorien Barbier, a printer from Paris, is evidence that a fount of 'bourgeois' type for printing breviaries, consisting of about 80,000 letter sorts, cost 5 sols per thousand, material included. Thus this fount cost 20 livres,[156] roughly the same price that Didier Maheu's founts of large and small bourgeois fetched in 1520. In 1543, finally, Jacques Regnault delivered to Pierre Gromors a semi-roman fount (cicero) of 60,000 letter sorts costing 6 sols per thousand, plus 2 sols per thousand for the material (lead) – a total of 18 livres for manufacture, 12 sols for materials. We learn that some months later, the dies having been delivered at the same time as the letters, Gromors paid 47 livres, which would be about 28 livres for the dies, an amount which agrees well with the figure in the inventories of Maheu and Hopyl.[157]

This evidence allows us to form an idea of the considerable resources a printer needed in order to get established, although once his plant was acquired it could be used indefinitely. But if he was also the publisher of the books he was printing, then his investment in his business was considerable. Surviving agreements testify to the amount that the financing of some publications could attain. In 1524 François Regnault undertook to print 600 primers according to the form approved in the diocese of Toul for a merchant of that town at a cost of 55 livres.[158] The same year Didier Maheu printed 400 missals for the Bishop of Senlis for 350 livres.[159] In August 1523 a Paris edition of 600 breviaries of the form approved in the diocese of Nevers cost 300 livres.[160] Joost Bade's edition of 1,225 copies (folio) of Claude de Seyssel's *Thucydides* demanded an outlay of 612 livres.[161]

To tender for work on a major publication the printer had to have at his disposal considerable assets. Especially when we take into account his need to renew type frequently, it can be seen that while it was not necessary for him to expend much money to buy a press, type, cases, and even some founts in order to launch himself as a printer, he had on the other hand to have a lot of capital at his disposal to keep his presses employed continuously. An edition of a single title required, on the basis of the above figures, more money than the initial equipping of a printing shop. In addition, as long as a printer was also his own publisher the capital invested in his bookselling business was more than that represented by his workshop. This was true both of Didier Maheu and of Ferrebouc. In fact among all the apparatus of a printing shop the only items of really high value were the ornamental initials engraved on wood, and later on the 'grey' (i.e. copper) letters and the engraved plates found only in the biggest workshops which usually specialised in a particular product – Books of Hours for instance. It is therefore understandable why the majority of printers appear most frequently to be in the employ of wealthy publisher-booksellers who owned alphabets of ornamental letters, plates and sometimes founts which they loaned or hired out to printers employed by them.

Printing costs proper, however, were only a part of the total outlay. Paper also had to be paid for, and was expensive.

We have some figures for the cost of printing alone. In 1518 the Paris printer Jean Vignon undertook to print daily one sheet of the Nantes breviary in 1,300 copies at a cost of 20 sols a day.[162] In 1524 another Paris printer, Jean Kerbriant, undertook to print 650 Nantes breviaries using three formes, at a cost of 60 sols a day,[163] and in the same year Nicolas Higman agreed to print 750 copies of the synodal decrees of the diocese of Sens using 3 formes, for 30 sols.[164] In 1526 Jean Kerbriant charged 65 sols a day for printing an impression of 1,200 copies of the Bourges breviary.[165] All the prices quoted seem small enough if one takes into account the fact that the Master printer had to board and lodge two pressmen and two compositors. The wages of a compositor in Lyons in 1539 amounted to 6 sols 6 deniers a day.[166] A scrutiny of these figures helps us to understand why printers strove for a big output from their journeymen and why they employed numerous apprentices whom they did not pay.

What at that time was the relative importance of the costs of printing generally, in comparison with the purchase price of paper? Some idea may be gained from the following indications. In 1539 the printer Bonnemère asked 14 sols a ream for paper supplied to print the *Collège de Sapience* by Pierre Doré.[167] In 1543 Gromors asked Jacques Regnault for 18 sols a ream for the printing of a book of Bible stories.[168] The price of a ream of paper varied at this time, according to quality, between 10 and 30 sols.

Thus the purchase of a stock of paper sufficient for printing one impression represented a large part of the total expenditure, a fact which does not depend for confirmation solely on the example given (a Paris printing house at the beginning of the 16th century), because in 1478 the printer Leonard Wild of Ratisbon, working in Venice, received 5 ducats for each section of an edition of the Bible of 930 copies, making a total of 243 ducats.[169] The price of common paper in Venice varied from $2\frac{1}{2}$ lira to 4 lira the ream, approximately 200 to 300 ducats in all.[170] Another example comes from the workshops of the printer Ripoli who in 1483 contracted to print a Latin translation of Plato by Marsilio Ficino, charging 3 florins for printing each of the 30 sections, 90 florins in all. Since the whole work was limited to 1,025 copies, each section comprising 4 sheets, the cost price of the paper must have come to between

120–160 florins, dearer than the actual printing costs.[171]

The ratio between the cost of paper and the total cost remained very high – with perhaps a tendency to diminish – up to the 18th century. In 1571 the printer Pierre Roux, before printing the 500 copies of the Statutes of Avignon, received 18 sols to cover the cost of each ream of paper, and 37 sols for the printing.[172] Other clues reveal the connection between the various expenditures on one edition of a book, this time at the end of the 16th century. They concern agreements drawn up for the printing of the Poitiers missal revised in accordance with the decisions of the Council of Trent. Two consortia were formed to undertake the work: one negotiated with a printer at Lyons, the other with a Poitiers printer, and under a final agreement they joined forces to finance the two impressions at common expense. The two groups legally bound themselves to guarantee the cost of their respective commitments.

1,300 breviaries each consisting of $72\frac{1}{2}$ sheets were printed at Lyons at a cost of 578 écus 58 sols 10 deniers, with the breakdown as follows: – printing, 264 écus; paper, 137 écus 58 sols; transport from Lyons to Poitiers, 110 écus. The 1,250 copies printed at Poitiers came to a total of 592 écus 11 sols. Of these 100 écus were for the purchase and transport of necessary founts of type, 204 écus for the printing, and 264 écus for the paper – an exceptionally large sum because the town was suffering at this time under a blockade. It will be noticed that transport raises the price of the Lyons edition by nearly one fifth.[173]

If we examine costs in the 17th and 18th centuries we come to similar conclusions. After the death of a Paris printer, Michel Brunet, in 1648, his inventory shows that he possessed two presses worth 90 and 60 livres. His plant comprised – apart from the presses – fifteen founts, ornaments, copper letters and various tools, estimated total: 746 livres 10 sols. An agreement made a few years earlier, in 1637, between the printer-bookseller Camusat and the letter founder Jean de La Forge, shows that a complete fount of small romans, comprising 150,000 letters, 25,000 quoins and 5,000 quadrats and roman letters and some letters of 2-point size, cost a little less than 30 livres plus the material for making the sorts, the spaces between letters, the quadrats and the romans. In 1644 another Paris printer, Joseph Bouillerot, printing a book entitled *Judith* for its author Nicolas Lescalopier in an edition of 1,000 copies, each copy requiring 50 octavo leaves in a type called St. Augustin, asked 6 livres per sheet. At this period good quality paper fetched 63 sols per ream, or 3 livres 3 sols. We may conclude therefore that, in an 8vo edition, the price of the paper roughly equalled the cost of the printing. Furthermore it can be reckoned, on the basis of these same figures, that the cost price of a contemporary book of 240 pages in 8vo for an edition of 1,000 copies on good paper was about 190 livres: 100 livres for the paper, 90 for the printing.

Here now are some costs incurred in printing a school textbook, 1,000 copies of a 4vo edition of the *Apparatus elegantiarum* under the direction of Guillaume Bénard and Jean Jullien on a paper called 'Joseph' at 50 sols a ream. Printing cost 10 livres a sheet (the work needed very careful press correcting). The price of the paper was therefore half that of printing. And now, another person appears whom we have not yet encountered – the author. He received 30 sols per sheet.[174]

Almost exactly the same conclusions can be drawn about 18th-century printing. According to a memorandum of 1771, a sheet of cicero, interlined and limited to 1,000 copies, breaks down into the following costs: for 2 reams of paper, 16 livres; composing, proof sheets and proof correction by a third party, 12 livres; printing off, 6 livres; redemption of stock and general costs, 50 per cent of the expenses of the edition, say 9 livres. Total: 43 livres.[175]

One last example. This time it concerns a famous work, the *Encyclopédie*.[176] According to Luneau de Boisgermain the expenses for each sheet in an edition of 4,250 copies may be divided thus:

Printing	24 L. 1; so.
Printers' profit and redemption of stock	12 L. 7 sols 6 deniers
Paper	68 L.
Total	105 L. 2 sols 6 deniers

What general conclusions can be drawn from these examples?

Firstly, from the 15th to the 18th century the purchase price of good quality paper is higher than the cost of printing a reasonable run, hence it is not surprising that in periods of deflation or even of stable prices, printers had recourse to paper of poor quality in order to achieve a reduction in the cost price of books.

Secondly, it was a simple matter to gather together the necessary capital to open a printing workshop. The basic equipment did not cost very much and a printer could easily acquire a press, cases, galleys and a number of founts. The real problem was the work itself, since much more capital was required to bring out an actual book, and one important ingredient needed to be constantly renewed, namely the type. Nor should we forget that at a time when booksellers' customers were few, books sold slowly, and to dispose of an edition the printer had to send copies out in small consignments to all the main European centres. So it was difficult to recoup quickly any capital locked up in the business. Could a printer survive a crisis? At such times the book, a 'luxury article', ceased to sell almost completely, and printers had no other way of surviving than printing pamphlets expressing the public discontent. Books are always a hazardous enterprise to their publishers because their reception by the public is so unpredictable, hence the anxiety to find a line for which demand would be fairly constant, church books, for example – the only item which would be sure of sale at a time of crisis. Hence also, the necessity of putting out a number of titles simultaneously to avoid the risks resulting from the poor sale of one particular volume. But that meant a larger capital investment and thus a new problem: finance.

2
The Problem of Finance

Capital is the one resource printers did not have, since they were usually simple craftsmen, and countless documents testify to the chronic impecuniosity of printers from the earliest times. In the 15th century the master printers of Basel, wishing to publish a book themselves, usually had to arrange a loan on the security of their equipment. Often the venture was a failure and many of them ended up losing the punches and moulds which they had made themselves or acquired with great effort. The luckiest of them succeeded in saving some part of their materials and disappeared without paying their debts, setting themselves up in another country, France for instance.[177] In the 16th century, many printers were even more impoverished and, to find work, wandered from town to town entirely dependent on the orders which local municipal authorities, parliaments or the church might give them for printing. In the 17th century, particularly in the provincial towns, printers dragged out a miserable existence, living from day to day executing orders from some township or some individual. Was this inefficiency? Rather it was lack of capital. The only printers who succeeded in setting up an adequate printing outfit were those who managed to find a backer.

The history of printing at Haguenau is of some significance in this respect. This little Alsatian town without a university hardly seemed likely to become an important printing centre. But it occupied a strategic geographical position as a 'staging post', close to Strasbourg and Basel where there was a profusion of printers, and not far from the great German publishing centres of Nuremberg and Frankfurt. Booksellers and printers were continually passing through the town on their travels and books produced there were transported without too much expense to a variety of places. Moreover, at a time when transport costs were high, paper made in the mills of Lorraine and Burgundy could easily be shipped to Haguenau, and labour could be expected to cost less in a little town. Even so, when the printer Gran established himself in Haguenau in 1489 he merely vegetated at first, his business being very limited until 1496. He produced only a few grammars and sermons, perhaps two to four titles a year. The fact was that he was working on a fragile financial base and had little ready capital.

At the beginning of 1497 the situation changed. By then there were enough printers in Haguenau to form their own fraternal association. What had happened? Quite simply Gran had begun a business connection with Rynman, an Augsburg trader, who sold books 'and other items' (possibly printing accessories and type). Gran's printing shop then came to life. He carried out a lot of work for Rynman and contracted with him for supplies of paper, type and other material and was soon working for other big booksellers who followed Rynman's example: Lochner, Hyst and particularly Knobloch of Strasbourg. From that time, Gran printed a dozen folio or large quarto books each year, and by the end had produced nearly 290 books in all, of which 240 were for Rynman and 20 or so for Knobloch. The printers of Haguenau grew more prosperous. While Angst helped Rynman as his corrector from 1511 to 1515 and again after 1519, Thomas Anshelm of Baden Baden, a former student of the University of Basel, left Tübingen, where his printing office was not prospering, to come to Haguenau where he worked for Koberger, Birckx of Cologne, and Knobloch. After him there were many others, like J. Setzer, Melanchthon's printer. Thus the backer, the capitalist, intervened to play an essential role. He was the one who took the risks, the one who took a chance on the sale of the product, and very often it was he who chose the texts for publication. Sometimes he even started a workshop on a big scale, more like an industrial plant than the old craftsman's shop. There were many capitalists ready to finance such operations. It is worth sketching the characteristics of some of these men.

Let us transport ourselves back in time to the House of Barthélemy Buyer[179] in the Lyons of the second half of the 15th century, the age when printing was spreading across Europe after its invention in the Rhine valley. Lyons is brimming with prosperity and its Fair is the rendezvous of the world. Merchants come there from Milan, Florence, Venice and Lucca, and from Germany, four times a year to do business. German and Italian bankers maintain permanent establishments there. Conversely, Lyonnese merchants have connections in all the big European cities and make their way there regularly. The commerce of the city of Lyons was already benefiting from favourable economic circumstances which were to assure its fortune. Situated close to Germany and Italy, on the main route between the major crossroads of the Ile-de-France and the Mediterranean coast, Lyons was in a privileged geographical position. Coming from the towns along the Rhine, from Basel and even from Italy, printers grew prosperous there and were soon selling their books at the Fair.

Lyons was also an intellectual and cultural centre. It is true that it was without a university despite its efforts to found one. But humanism had penetrated its archiepiscopal court and Jean de Bourbon, regent for his nephew, Charles, appointed archbishop at the age of ten, was a man of formidable intelligence and sound judgement. Brought up in Avignon, he was devoted to the life of the mind and applied himself to the restoration of the library of the abbey of Cluny, pillaged by order of the Duke of Burgundy. In his own bishopric of Le Puy he inaugurated a magnificent episcopal library. All the members of this branch of the Bourbon line were scholars and several of them actively encouraged the foundation of printing workshops. The youthful archbishop Charles de Bourbon, who showed the same interest in arts and letters as other members of the family, was to receive a copy of Guillaume Fichet's *Rhétorique* from the author, one of the first books printed in Paris, decorated with the cardinal's arms.

The chapter of St. Jean was also at the height of its reputation at that time and was famous both for its aristocratic membership and its high level of culture. The canons were certainly very often absent from Lyons, but these absences were often occasioned by their studies in French and foreign universities: their names appear on the rolls of the universities of Paris, Toulouse, Orléans, Avignon, Turin, Florence, Pisa, Bologna, Pavia and Ferrara. The same zeal for learning is equally apparent among the bourgeoisie who often succeeded to seigneurial status after the fall of a noble family, and their children were to be found as students in the best universities, notably Orléans where they studied law. They were enthusiastic readers – to such an extent that Louis Garin, a merchant of the old school, more concerned with business and the commercial habits of his kind, was at pains to warn his son about excessive reading:

> Reading nice stories and other fine books
> So long as it doesn't quite ruin your looks
> Is a pastime of head-turning dizziness.
> But if this practice makes you an unhappy man
> Then to love books obsessively's not the best plan
> For hard-headed sound men of business.

This was the social environment in which Barthélemy Buyer grew up. Pierre Buyer, his father, far from being the simple merchant he was once believed to have been, was in fact already a rich local notable, important enough to be regularly consulted by the town council of which he was anyway a member. He seems to have been passionately devoted to law studies; a student in 1426, he secured his degree before 1437, and his doctorate in 1458 just a few months before his death. From Pierre Buyer, Doctor of Laws, it was a short step to becoming Messire Pierre, a higher rank on the road to further honours. Meanwhile Barthélemy's mother, Marie Buatier, belonged to a family of rich haberdashers, some of whose members were of consular rank. These facts deserve notice because Buyer appears to have launched into business through a love of literature (a legacy from his father?) and to have continued through love of money (his commercial background?). By a happy conjunction of circumstances he was able to extend his business. Just after his father's death, in 1460, he was a student in the Faculty of Arts in Paris. There, he must have met two scholars whose names are intimately bound up with the introduction of printing at the Sorbonne, Guillaume Fichet and Johann Heynlin who had developed an interest in the art of printing after Peter Schoeffer's visit to Paris. It is possible that Buyer had also established a connection with Nicolas Jenson, the French printer who worked in Venice, for later on he was in contact with him, and with his son who was in Lyons in 1480. At all events it is obvious that Buyer well understood the twin possibilities latent in the new art – as an agency for the diffusion of culture and a means of earning a return on capital. We next see him lodging an itinerant printer called Guillaume Le Roy who had come from Liège by way of Basel and Switzerland, and directing him to take charge of a printing office which then went into active production. The first fruits of this association appeared on the 17th September, 1473, the *Compendium breve* of Cardinal Lothaire, the first known book from Lyons.

What part did each play in the collaboration? Was Buyer's role simply that of backer, or did he play an active part in the organisation? It has been much debated and it would be profitless to pursue it here. One thing is almost certain: Buyer himself chose the texts for printing and in so doing gave a lead to a type of publishing which was to remain characteristic of Lyons – books in French for merchants and the bourgeoisie, and legal collections. But he was above all prominent as a financier and not content to be a local bookseller retailing only his own publications. Other printers were obliged to entrust the sale of some of their works to him, and both French and foreign booksellers came to him to help sell off their stocks. As local booksellers began to expand their trade through contacts made at the Lyons Fair, Buyer was assured of still more trade outlets. Not even content with this, he opened branches in various French towns wherever there was felt to be a demand for reading matter, chiefly in the main centres of university life like Paris, Avignon and Toulouse.

One example of his enterprise was at Avignon. He made his way there in 1481 and gave some business to two of the most successful local businessmen, Alain and Joachim de Rome. They were to have responsibility for selling a consignment of 78 books, partly from his own printing shop – largely religious works in French – and partly from others – law books in Latin for which there was recognised need in that town. If he seems there to have come up against stubborn competition from German as well as Lyons booksellers, he was more fortunate in Toulouse, the great staging post on the way to Spain. There he accredited his 'servant and clerk', Jean Claret, in 1482 before making contact with Georges de Bogne from Savoy, a bookbinder and seller to whom Jacques Buyer, brother of Barthélemy, was a little later to send a consignment of books. By the beginning of the 16th century the Buyer family was doing considerable business in Toulouse.

Barthélemy also owned a large warehouse in Paris, managed from the time of his death by one Nicolas Guillebaud. He made enough money from the business there to enable him to lend the great sums which Lyons needed for the legal defence of its rights in Paris. In addition, Barthélemy Buyer was important enough to be enrolled in the *Syndicat* with the eminent persons empowered to direct the local administration in the two following years. On his death in 1488 he was rich enough to bequeath 2,000 livres to the canons of the collegiate church and left behind an ample fortune for his heirs.

Such then was Barthélemy Buyer, one of the earliest of the wealthy capitalists to show an interest in printing. He is a figure of great interest because at the beginnings of printing we find a man with a large fortune at his disposal willing to get involved in the new art and assist in its early evolution. Though the records are unfortunately scanty, we do gain some idea of the extent of his trade: this stretched from Lyons to Avignon, from Toulouse to Paris and undoubtedly from Toulouse as far as Spain, perhaps into Germany and probably Italy as well (since we can be fairly certain that Buyer had business contacts in Venice).

Earlier we saw how Buyer had to lodge a printer, Le Roy, in his home and maintain him, using his skills and his printing press for his own purposes, a quite common practice at the time. But when printing itself became common those who invested capital (the publishers, as we should say) no longer had to resort to this procedure and preferred to deal with printers already established in their own business. They would advance a loan or help those whose skills they respected to set up on their own and give them orders, although they would not claim any special monopoly over their services. But – and this was important – they possessed type faces, ornamental letters, embossed plates and other equipment which they only allowed for use in the books they had a special interest in financing.

The famous publisher Vérard operated in this way.[180] While the art was still in its infancy in Paris he appears to have organised a workshop which specialised in the illumination and copying of luxury manuscripts for royalty. He quickly saw the possibilities of the new craft and when Jean Du Pré and Pasquier Bonhomme had published the first illustrated books in Paris he decided to put their press to work on his own behalf. After commissioning Du Pré to print the *Decameron* in 1485 he became the recognised publisher of illustrated books in French. They were aimed at a larger public than that which had previously bought manuscripts. But, for his older customers with old-fashioned tastes, he printed on vellum and had miniatures painted in by hand instead of wood-cuts. All his productions were of the highest quality, his blocks made by chosen craftsmen and the type founts (which he owned) chosen by himself. He did not print himself; he assigned it to some of the finest craftsmen in Paris – Jean Du Pré, Pierre Le Rouge, Pierre Levet, Pierre Laurent,

Jean Maubanel, Gillet Coustiau, Pierre Le Caron, Jean Ménard and Trepperel.

Like Buyer, Vérard did not confine himself to one shop from which to sell his books. He owned two shops in Paris, one in the Palais, the other one first on the bridge of Notre-Dame (1485–1489), then in the Rue St. Jacques near the Petit Pont, and finally in the Rue Neuve-Notre-Dame near the Hôtel-Dieu. He also had a warehouse in Tours, where he had complete control over the trade, and carried on a business with England, had a branch in London and even published some books in English.

Several other big publishers followed Vérard's example and defrayed the costs of publishing, offering plant and materials to the printer, hiring presses or advancing money. Michel Le Noir, a celebrated publisher of chivalric romances, had Pierre Levet working for him. Durant Gerlier collaborated with Hopyl, Le Gier and Simon Vostre, the expert in Books of Hours, and engaged Pigouchet's presses almost exclusively for his own publishing programme. But no publisher in Paris could compare with Jean Petit for the sheer scale of this sort of enterprise.[181] He was a capitalist who without any question was at the head of the Paris book trade at the end of the 15th century and in the early 16th century. From 1493 to 1530 he published more than a thousand books, most of them of major importance, amounting to one tenth of the entire output of the Paris trade. Even more than Buyer he was the archetypal early bookseller/financier. Almost symbolically he came from a family of wealthy butchers. But this trade was no impediment to their acquiring culture and enjoying the best contacts with the scholars of the day. His wealth, and that of his son who succeeded him, was enormous: father and son owned property in Paris and estates at Clamart, Issy, Meudon, Bièvres and Poissy.

This butcher's son who became one of the four great official publishers of the University of Paris was the main publisher for its students and one of the main sources of the diffusion of humanism in Paris. No one put out as many first editions as he did, often sharing the costs with other booksellers and printers. He was the dominant figure in enterprises involving the leading Parisian booksellers and the most skillful printers of the period. He had close contacts with Kerver, Marnef, Berthold Rembolt, Bocard, John of Coblenz and occasionally with Henri Estienne. He employed scores of printers, none of them less than the best: Guy Marchant, Gaspard Philippe, Ulrich Gering, Pierre Le Dru, Félix Baligault, Nicolas des Préz. Besides all this he was the patron of Geoffroy Tory and Joost Bade. His relations with Bade deserve a full account because they reveal how a great capitalist bookseller was able to encourage certain new intellectual movements.[182]

In 1499 Joost Bade, a young printer already widely known among Paris humanists, arrived from Lyons where he had worked for Trechsel. Jean Petit, who seems to have had an eye for talent, tried to attract him into his organisation, giving him particular responsibility for correcting texts. Bade complained that he was wasting time travelling to and from the various printers and Petit hit upon the idea of letting Bade have his own printing office. So was born the great printing establishment of Joost Bade.

Henceforth Petit did much business with Joost Bade, especially when it came to issuing editions demanding care and scrutiny. But the collaboration was never an exclusive arrangement. Joost often worked on his own account, usually when costs were modest, and sometimes he carried out work for other booksellers. Petit for his part went on doing business with many other printers, as we have already mentioned. Barbier, Bonnemère, Gromors, Vidoue, Coustiau and others were also sometimes employed by him. He was in constant contact with Normandy and published some books at Rouen under his own name. In one decree of the Rouen Parlement it is recorded that 'he printed more books than a thousand other publishers together'. He was in business at Clermont where he had a shop, and at Limoges where he had books printed and seems to have had a branch. At Lyons, Petit even had presses working for him and he owned a bookshop in the city. As a result of his operations over a wide area we see him securing power of attorney to recover debts incurred by his associates in Troyes, Orléans, Blois, Tours, L'Ile Bouchard and many other places.

A business empire of this kind was by no means exceptional. Throughout Europe the book trade was in similar hands. In Germany, for instance, a few booksellers employed many printers in a large number of towns. Rynman, whom we mentioned above, did not only employ Gran at Haguenau but also Jean Otmar, Oeglin and Sylvan Otmar at Augsburg, George Stuchs and Jerome Holtzer in Nuremberg, Pierre Liechtenstein in Venice, Pforzheim and Adam Petri at Basel and Knobloch in Strasbourg. Occasionally also, members of bookselling families founded shops in various cities and so increased their sales outlets; in this way a veritable 'international' of publishing houses which ignored national frontiers was created.

In Italy the Giunta family expanded its interests in this way.[183] Filippo, son of a rich Florentine wool merchant, was the most influential publisher and printer in early 16th century Florence. Aided and guided by a cultivated circle of literati and humanists he commissioned the publication of a large number of books on his own and others' account, and his son Bernardo took over at his death, ending up as a Count. Another brother, Lucantonio, after working in Florence set up a business in Venice in 1489. There, working in liaison with the largest booksellers in the town, he commissioned a number of different printers to work for him and then set up his own typographical workshop, which rivalled that of Torresani and the Elder Aldus. His son, Tommaso, carried on the business after his father's death. His two headquarters, in Venice and Florence, remained in close contact. The Giuntas were republicans. Thus Lucantonio's office in Venice became the headquarters of the Florentine republican emigrés in Venice, and Cosimo dei Medici tried to hinder Filippo's activities by encouraging Anton Francesco Doni to set up a strong rival publishing house in Venice.

Yet another member of the Giuntas, Jacques, son of Francesco, born in Florence in 1486, after learning his trade at Venice at his uncle Lucantonio's, set up business in Lyons where he founded a publishing house out of his own capital and also probably with the help of Lucantonio. For 27 years, from 1520 till his death in 1547, he published a great number of books in theology, law and medicine. He employed more than 30 different printers and was head of the Booksellers' Company of Lyons; he worked sometimes in collaboration with Lucantonio or with the booksellers of Lucca. He was rich enough to lend 50,000 livres to Cardinal Tournon in 1537 for the king's disposal and his business covered Europe. He had depots and shops in Frankfurt, Antwerp, Medina del Campo, Salamanca, Saragossa and Paris where his nephew, François Barthélemy looked after his affairs. Other Giuntas copied him, and bookselling establishments bearing the name are found not only in Florence, Venice and Lyons, but also in Burgos, Salamanca and Madrid – all of them run by relatives working closely with one another.

Some of the family worked in collaboration with printers. Others, without ceasing to use outside printers, owned their own printing shops. Often substantial publishers made efforts to set up their own print shops in which there was a division of labour and the journeymen had sharply defined responsibilities. The big publishers had two aims: to produce books at competitive prices by rationalising the organisation of work, and to ensure a better quality of product. In fact, the finest publications of the 16th century could not have been achieved without such production lines. It was in this way that Andrea Torresano, a rich citizen of

Asola, established himself in Venice as a bookseller where he employed printers and appointed a poor scholar, Aldus Manutius, as his shop manager. Aldus thereupon married his patron's daughter Maria, aged 20, when he was 50, thus neatly benefiting from her large inheritance. With such powerful patronage Aldus was able to carry out his ambitious and celebrated programme of printing classical texts (especially Greek) assisted by the scholars employed by Torresano.

Anton Koberger of Nuremberg[184] perhaps the most powerful publisher of his day, who brought out between 1473 and 1513 at least 236 books, most of them of the first importance, in the best possible format, used very similar business practice. Born in 1440 into a family which numbered a burgomaster among its members, he probably began his career as a goldsmith, and became a printer sometime between 1470 and 1472. In 1473 he published his first book, Boethius's *De consolatione philosophiae* with Aquinas' commentaries. Right from the start Koberger specialised in works of theology and scholastic philosophy and he published works of Vincent de Beauvais, Guillaume Durand, Duns Scotus, St. Thomas Aquinas, St. Jerome, St. Ambrose and St. Augustine. In addition numerous Bibles including the first one in German came from his presses, together with the *Decretals* and many books of canon law – in a word, all the conventional, traditional material needed by students of the Faculties of Theology and Law.

Koberger catered above all for university requirements. He therefore published very few classical texts. But he took great pains over the accuracy of the texts he edited and was a close collaborator with humanists of the calibre of Conrad Celtes and Pirckheimer. He enlisted men like Amerbach, Frissner, Pirckheimer, von Wyle, Wimpfeling, Berckenhaut and Busch among his publisher's readers and while publishing the Bible of Hugues de St. Cher in 8 volumes, he commissioned Busch to find the best manuscripts during his stay in Italy. But let there be no mistake. Koberger was first and foremost a businessman and manufacturer, anxious to increase the profits from his investments. By 1509 he employed no fewer than 24 presses and about 100 pressmen, correctors, engravers and binders. His bindery, where his solid and standardised bindings were created, was a main feature of his organisation, and on the design side for some of his editions he had the benefit of his friend and compatriot, Dürer, to advise on illustration and general format.

But his own workshop was not enough to cope with the expanding business. Koberger and his successors after him often recruited other printers to help in production: Jean Grüninger of Strasbourg, for example, and Amerbach, who had worked with Koberger before settling at Basel, and who maintained close relations with his old patron. To market all his products he needed a large commercial network and we find his agents not only in the biggest German cities – Frankfurt, Leipzig, Vienna, Cologne, Basel and Strasbourg – but in all the most important cities of Europe – Budapest, Warsaw, Venice, Florence, Antwerp, Bruges and Leyden, and of course, Paris. He became the indispensable entrepreneur, a broker between the lesser booksellers whose business was less extensive.

The most famous printing establishment of all, from the point of view of capital investment, was that of Plantin of Antwerp.[185] The case of the Plantin firm shows very clearly how availability of capital in a great commercial city like Antwerp, with connections throughout Europe, favoured the development of the printing industry.

Plantin had no private fortune. He was born in Touraine in 1514, began his career working in various printing offices in Rouen and Paris, and set himself up in Antwerp in 1549. He gives us the reasons for his decision in a letter written long afterwards to Pope Gregory XIII: 'From my point of view I could have easily assured myself of the greater advantages offered me by other countries and cities, but I preferred Belgium and, above all other towns, Antwerp. What chiefly dictated my choice was that in my judgement no other city in the world could offer more facilities for practising the trade than this one. Access to the city is good – the many different nations to be seen in the market square there testifies to that. And in Antwerp all the materials so necessary to the art of printing may be found. Manpower enough to train in any of the crafts can be found without any difficulty . . . and finally there flourishes the University of Louvain, outstanding for the learning of its professors in all subjects and whose learning I reckoned to turn to profit for the general well-being of the public in manuals, textbooks and critical works.'

To make his living at the outset Plantin had to work at binding and leather-working, after which he became a printer. His beginnings were modest, and he only produced one really important publication before 1562, the magnificent and sumptuous *Account of the Funeral Ceremonies of Charles V*, printed at the expense of the state. He had to leave town in 1562 for a few months, accused of printing heretical books, and the inventory of his goods which were seized after his departure showed them to be not yet of great value.

The members of the sect, called 'The Family of Charity', to which he belonged began to show interest in Plantin, and after his return to Antwerp in 1563 he formed a syndicate of publishers with some of the rich bourgeoisie of the city, including Cornelius and Charles Van Bomberghe, Jacob Scotti, a banker, and Goropius Buhnno, a doctor. During the five years of the syndicate's existence, 260 works were published; editions of classical authors, Hebrew Bibles and liturgical books. Once 'launched', Plantin could call on powerful patrons like Cardinal Granvelle and Gabriel de Cayas, Secretary to Philip II. Through this connection, he obtained financial and legal support from the Spanish king who bore the costs of his Polyglot Bible, the work which made Plantin famous, and gave him the monopoly of sales in Spain and her colonies. The king also ordered the publishing of the reformed liturgical books authorised by the Council of Trent. By early 1572 tens of thousands of breviaries, missals, psalters and antiphonies were sent from Antwerp to Philip II who ordered the monks of the Escorial to see to the distribution and sale of the books in his territories. Plantin at that time had up to 24 presses in active production and had assembled for the purpose a unique collection of punches and moulds. More than one hundred workers were employed in his shops and he had depots and other trade outlets in every European city from Frankfurt to Paris, from Danzig to Bergen, from Lyons to Nuremberg, from Venice to Madrid, from Rouen to Lisbon and London. A share in Antwerp's available capital and the support of the Spanish State were the mainsprings of Plantin's business and the reason why he could create the most powerful book manufactury to exist before the 19th century.

Plantin's is an extreme case of the workshop run on industrial lines. In fact, if we except a few large printing concerns like Koberger's and later the Elzeviers' and the Blaeus' in Holland, or the official publishing houses like the Imprimerie Royale in Paris, the Royal Publishing Office in Naples, or the Vatican, then quite clearly the craftsman's workshop was the rule. In 17th-century Paris, workshops with more than four presses and ten workmen were unusual. The wealthy booksellers who financed publishing preferred the putting-out system, which spared them work and allowed them to operate flexibly since they were not forced to keep a fixed number of presses continually replenished with material. On the other hand, if the financing of publications demanded a large amount of capital and so the intervention of large-scale investors, one must beware of unduly simplifying the actual organisation of the printing trade. A great number of other and lesser booksellers revolved around the major firms, living off the sale of books as well as from publishing, which was often done in association with the big names in various groups and syndicates, and using the trading network set up by the latter to provide them with their book stocks. This was how Sebastien Cramoisy who, either on his own or in association with others, brought out one tenth of all the books published in Paris between 1625 and 1660, came to be in charge of two companies which included almost all the booksellers of any reputation. One of the companies specialised in the works of the Church Fathers, the other in editions of liturgical works. He was also appointed trustee on behalf of many provincial booksellers, and even foreign ones, and the commercial network which he maintained covered the whole of Europe.[186]

In general the wealthy publishers acted as bankers for their less fortunate colleagues. This state of affairs was favoured by the method in regular use for the payment of accounts, which was by a triangular system of bills of exchange. Often, too, when a bookseller needed ready cash to back a new publication he arranged with a richer colleague for a loan under the form of a lease agreement. Denis Thierry made a speciality of this kind of deal in the 17th century.

Finally we must not forget the role of public authorities as backers in our consideration of the way the book trade was financed. Often bishops and chapters financed the publication of liturgical books. States and municipalities would often put up money for works they wanted printing, usually administrative records. A large number of printers, particularly in the small towns, lived on these commissions. Finally, the system of privilege and monopolies granted by the state to certain publishers for certain editions often prompted booksellers to combine to form groups and local or national syndicates. The state often intervened in this way in the financing of editions. It systematically encouraged large enterprises and attempted in that way to reconcile printers to becoming docile instruments of policy, eager to denounce dangerous books. By this means the power of the great publishing houses was greatly reinforced in the book market.[187]

The Little World of the Book   5

Having come into being more or less haphazardly, the book trade quickly acquired a modern character. From early on, to use Hauser's phrase, the printing shops looked more like modern workshops than the monastic workrooms of the Middle Ages.[188] In 1455, Fust and Schoeffer were already running a business geared to standardised production, and twenty years later large printing concerns were operating everywhere in all Europe. Already techniques were being perfected which increased both the speed and productive capacity of the press. The compositor was soon to work standing up, not seated, in order to work more productively. The need to produce ever more books at the cheapest price made printers rationalise their production methods. Although very free at first and respected because of their 'mystery', journeymen printers soon became like other workers, bound to finish a task in a certain fixed time for a wage; and from that moment the printing trade gave rise to a new kind of man, the typographer. Although working with their hands like any other worker they were also 'intellectuals', since they could read and often knew a little Latin. They lived among books, were acquainted with authors, and above all, in touch with new ideas; they liked to reason, and frequently rebelled against their conditions. Even in the 16th century they organised strikes which sound quite modern and, in support of their claims, wrote manifestos which the Syndicalists of 300 years later would not have disavowed, as Hauser has pointed out. In the 19th century, numerous printers were to be found in the ranks of the first Socialists.

Our objective in this chapter is to study the working conditions of apprentices and masters in order to find out how a trade which was both manual and intellectual caused its workers to look at things in a special way. We must therefore consider the relationship between masters and men, and the material and moral conditions which shaped their respective outlooks.

I
The Journeymen

First of all the journeyman printer. The future printer had to complete an apprenticeship and his age at entry varied from 12 years to over 21, the average being somewhere between 15 and 20. Apprentices came from all kinds of backgrounds, the sons of ordinary citizens, apothecaries, bailiffs, sergeants-at-arms at the Châtelet, wine merchants, locksmiths, cobblers, carpenters, weavers, and often of course the sons of printers. Many came up to Paris from the provinces. They had to be able to read and write, and usually the statutes of apprenticeship prescribed a knowledge of Latin; sometimes they insisted that they should be able to read Greek. Though necessary for a compositor, such knowledge was not indispensable for a pressman, and often masters would accept illiterate apprentices since they were more malleable as workers.

Conditions were normally specified in an indenture, agreed in the presence of a notary, between the parents and the master and countersigned by the apprentice. The period of apprenticeship varied between two and five years. The master was under an obligation to teach the apprentice his craft, to board and lodge him, keep him in clothes and allow him pocket money. For his part the apprentice swore to obey his master, to serve him faithfully and not leave the house.

During his apprenticeship the young printer underwent a severe regime. Occupying a little corner of the workshop, he was the errand boy for the journeymen, not the easiest of people to get along with. He rose before they arrived for work to get the workshop ready, light the fire in winter and set the table. He had to do the meanest, most disheartening tasks. It was he who prepared the ink and damped the sheets before printing. He was usually on the press, a less skilled but more exhausting job, and if he wanted to become a compositor he finished his time setting type under a journeyman's supervision. His happiest moments were when he was sent out for something, to fetch a set of proofs, for example. At the end of the day, after his workmates had gone home, he had to leave everything in order before going to bed. In addition to this he was often held in low esteem by his mates because masters, always anxious to get labour as near free as they could have it, often tended to multiply the number of apprentices in order to diminish the number of journeymen.

On the termination of his time the apprentice received his diploma and became a journeyman. Still young, free at last, and a bachelor – it was forbidden to marry during his time – he would start out on his journeys, often lasting years. While Germans and Flemings toured their countries and did not hesitate to go abroad, especially to Paris, French youths did the 'Tour of France'. They moved from town to town offering their services to printers in each locality, staying here a month, there a year or two, depending on whether or not there was work, and on the friendships they forged. On such trips they improved their skill and experience, learned the ways of different shops and made the contacts that would stand them in good stead if they became masters of their own businesses. Sometimes they married (preferably the daughter of a master printer) and settled down when they chanced upon a town where conditions were right for them to open their own workshop.[190]

But, most often, the journeyman returned to his native town once his travels were over, and hired himself to local master printers, taking his place in the order of seniority within the *atelier*. If capable, he could entertain hopes of becoming a head compositor, supervising the other workers. It was the head compositor's duty to assign work to the compositors and pressmen, and to oversee them. He corrected the first proofs, hence his need to know Latin, and to read varieties of handwriting. Finally he paid the workers their wages and was responsible for the conditions of the workshop.

Ranking below the head compositor were the trained workmen (*compagnons en conscience*), who were paid by the month rather than by the day. They were the core of the workshop who did the skilled work. After these came the piece-work journeymen (*compagnons à la tâche*) divided into two classes: the compositors who set the type, got ready the formes and laid out the pages; and the pressmen who pulled the sheets, i.e. did the actual printing. Compositors had to be reasonably well educated, but the pressmen need only have a taste for the work, a capacity for taking pains and strength: for working the press bar was hard work. The men were usually organised in teams, each team operating one press. Four or five workers was the normal complement from the 16th to the 18th centuries, comprising two compositors, two pressmen and an apprentice for running errands. To complete the picture we need to include the corrector. He was not usually a journeyman but a student or an educated man, possibly even a writer like Melanchthon or Beatus Rhenanus in the 16th century or Trichet du Fresne in the 17th century. But as a rule, proof correction, except in the largest establishments, was undertaken by the masters themselves, or a member of the family. It was one of the chief duties of men like Aldus, Joost Bade, Simon de Colines, Robert Estienne or Vitré.

How far was this division of labour actually observed in the majority of printing houses? In the largest ones, like those of Koberger, Froben, Plantin, Blaeu or the Imprimerie Royale at Paris, where there might be as many as 50 men on ten presses, each worker had his task strictly determined. The same was true in the houses which were particularly active and painstaking, like the Estiennes', or Vitré's, each of whom employed four presses. But printing was a craft skill and not always on such massive lines. In Geneva in 1570, out of twenty shops, three had four presses, five had two and the remaining twelve only one each. In 17th-century France the majority had only one or two presses, and the same was true of London.[191] Masters had no means of maintaining a large work force, especially when regular work was lacking; in fact it was usual for the master to work alongside his one or two workmen, helped when work was pressing by his wife or children. In such conditions the compositors must often have had to pull the press themselves.

In the big shops the workmen lived a hard life; the working day was longer than in many other trades. In Geneva it was fixed at the end of the 16th century at 12 hours, from 5 in the morning until 7 at night, with two hours off for meals.[192] In the Plantin-Moretus firm at Antwerp the men arrived at between 5 and 6 in the morning; they were allowed to return home between noon and one o'clock for lunch and went on working until 8 p.m.[193] At Lyons in the 16th century the men worked from 5 a.m. until 8 p.m. with only an hour for dinner; very often to get through work assigned to them they had to start at 2.30 a.m. and leave at 9 p.m.[194] At Paris in 1650, the working day began at 5 a.m. and ended at 8 p.m.[195] It was a long day, working by candlelight in their workshops at street level in the narrow streets where the sun scarcely shone at all, even at mid-day.

During the whole of this period high output was required of the men. While there is little hard evidence as to the work demanded from compositors, which naturally varied according to the difficulties of the text (the master printers of Frankfurt in 1563 proposed that the compositors complete each day from one to three formes according to the types used and the kind of work done), we have on the other hand plenty of information about the pressmen. At the close of the 16th century in Lyons they had to take off 3,350 sheets per day, and 2,650 in Paris. During the same period the master printers of Frankfurt required press pulls of 3,050 to 3,373 per day, depending on the difficulty of the work.

According to Monchrestien, the Dutch figure was 4,000 sheets in the early 17th century, the Paris figure 2,500: in the middle of the 17th century the number was fixed in Paris first at 2,500 and then 2,700 for impressions in black and red. These are high figures. Even if we take 2,500 as typical and remember that the working day was 14 hours, the rate per hour must have been 178 or one sheet every 20 seconds![196]

With such a workload printers do not seem to have been paid better than other tradesmen. By a royal decree of September 1572, it is true, the Paris compositors received 12 livres a month or 12 sols a day, while building workers received 10 livres a month. But in Lyons in 1539 the position was worse – the master printers offered their compositors 6 sols 6 deniers a day, a wage scarcely above other, less skilled, workers, and this at a time when the French printers were still the best paid in Europe. In Antwerp, Plantin's compositors earned a wage less than that of a roof mender. In Geneva, Pierre Bozon, a type founder, earned 8 to 10 sols a day in 1570, while an ordinary bricklayer earned 6.[197] Another curious fact is that sometimes compositors earned less than pressmen. In Paris in 1654, 24 to 27 livres a month was offered to ordinary compositors, and 33 livres to pressmen: a compositor might earn 33 livres if he could also set Greek. To these wages some extras could be added: journeymen used every occasion to demand a gratification from masters; they shared out tips given to them by authors, and the master often had to provide food and drink. It is no less true however that the wages of printers do not seem to have been much higher than those of other less skilled and less educated workers.

Like all workers of that age, printers were never sure of tomorrow. While a good compositor could always hope for stable employment in a large printing house, in times of crisis or even while there was a shortage of work the men could be dismissed virtually without notice; they were then unemployed and soon reduced to beggary. For printers who specialised in Statutes or Proclamations employment was seasonal when the Courts were in session. It is not surprising that printers were usually very poor. They generally lived in one room with their family, and their possessions amounted to no more than some working clothes and a few sticks of furniture. It is also not surprising that they were forced to many expedients to make a living when they were unemployed; we hear of some taking extra copies of sheets they had printed on the sly until they had made up a book which they would sell; others got involved (often using their wives as intermediaries) in the traffic in banned books or ephemeral pamphlets.

Yet journeymen printers were proud of their trade and their knowledge; they formed a distinct caste. To make it clear they were not mere mechanics they carried a sword. Quarrelsome and hasty, they insulted each other frequently and sometimes fought. Fines were imposed against anyone who slandered a fellow worker: at Plantin-Moretus they even recorded the scale of charges for each insult in the rules of the workshop.[199] In Paris agreements survive in the public archives in which the wronged party surrenders his right to complain on receipt of a sum fixed by common consent.

An awkward group cherishing their freedom, the men chafed under the discipline of the shop which was so much more exacting because presswork was teamwork and one man's absence threatened the work of the rest. They ceaselessly protested against the ban on taking their meals outside the printing shop or during hours convenient to them. Notorious for their appetite for food and even more for drink, they constantly sent out the apprentices for comestibles, and it was not easy to maintain much discipline in such conditions. Above all, they seem to have claimed the right to work when they felt like it and take time off when they wished. On the eve of Feast Days they were likely to leave early and return the next day to finish the job, and if the master enquired as to the reason for their absence he would get a rude answer.

Long hours spent together in the shop, the habit of team work, difficulties shared, the common meals – all these factors made for strong unity within the trade. They formed *Confréries* (Brotherhoods or Chapels) either works-based, as in big establishments like Plantin, or, more often, Brotherhoods of printers in a single town. Everywhere, they elected committees to look after their own welfare, with officers, funds, a scale of dues and a system of fines for ill behaviour or botched work. With the money accruing they would celebrate a Mass, arrange a banquet, look after sick workmates or a widow in want. Associations of this kind were not viewed kindly by the masters since they fomented grievances about conditions and bred strikes. Plantin-Moretus accepted the formation of a union in their business, and even threw in their mite for the funds and recognised a Father of the Chapel as the workers' representative, but the great majority of the master printers opposed such organised labour, which often united workers from several shops, and they tried to have such associations banned. Bans were repeatedly placed on unions, but as often as associations were officially dissolved they immediately reformed to continue the struggle, more or less clandestinely.

Thanks to the work of Hauser[200] we know what happened when the workmen at Lyons and later at Paris rose between 1539 and 1542, and brought almost all the presses to a standstill. Their masters, trying to reduce production costs and extort higher output, made strict economies in their food and brought in cheaper labour in the form of apprentices. Incensed by the fall in the real value of their wages against the increased cost of living, they went on strike. The municipality of Lyons, the Parlement of Paris, and finally the King had to intervene to re-establish order. In 1571–2 the confrontation broke out again and the masters were obliged to offer a number of concessions; in particular they were forced to abandon the right to take on more than two apprentices. A royal declaration to this effect, made on September 10th, 1572, was registered on April 17th, 1573.

Lyons and Paris were the likeliest places for such a confrontation because they were the largest book producers in 16th-century France, where more than 1,000 men worked in close proximity to each other. But the social movements we have just mentioned were not isolated cases. Everywhere in Europe the rise in prices and the economic crisis of the second half of the 16th century provoked conflict between masters and men. Three times between 1569 and 1573 the men at Plantin's went on strike.[201] In 1597 Johann Lauer, one of the great Frankfurt publishers, ordered his men to go and fetch their water from the well – and had a strike on his hands: it was not their function. That led to a lawsuit. The tribunal rejected the claims of both parties, refusing Lauer the compensation of 80 gulden he asked in damages for lost work, and the workmen the wages due to them for the time lost on strike.[202] Nearly everywhere the state was obliged to intervene in disputes between masters and men with a view to securing better regulation of their mutual interests. At Geneva the masters, often Huguenot refugees, had no wish for social conflicts to hinder the growth of an industry which was profiting from the decline of its competitors at Lyons, and regulations were passed by the City Council at Geneva in 1560 in a spirit of equity which contrasts strongly with the rigour of royal dictates in France of the same period. Genevan masters were forbidden to possess more than one apprentice to each press. Masters and men could not sever connection without very good reason and without notice. Each party's responsibility in a case of a job bungled or lost is carefully specified. The text of these agreements has the stamp of moderation and humanity about it and, while preserving the rights of the masters, clearly protects the men and apprentices. Yet even in these instances the authorities could not always prevent conflict. As in France, printers were fond of taking time off in addition to Sundays and Feast Days. In 1561 a dispute arose when leave was granted in some workshops to workmen on Wednesdays, while workers in other shops had to work. Eventually, every other Wednesday was made a holiday, but only after the issue had been brought to arbitration, in the course of which some journeymen did not miss the chance to attack their bosses.[203] On 22nd April, 1563, the master printers of Frankfurt presented a petition to the Town Council asking for a fixed daily quota of work for compositors and pressmen and an official list of holidays to be established. One day's holiday was to be granted at Christmas, one at New Year, one on Shrove Tuesday, another on Ascension Day, and, as at Geneva, one week-day in every fortnight was to be free. After this petition the first regulations for the trade were drawn up in 1573 and were regularly revised and amended.

Journeymen's agitation was not confined to the 16th century. In the 17th and 18th centuries as well, despite corporate regulations and the open support given by the state to the masters, French journeymen printers continued to press their claims and united in their attempts to secure their objectives, which remained always more or less the same. When the cost of living rose they demanded increases in wages. They also pressed for a reduction in the length of the working day, and for production norms to be reduced. During the 17th century, a period when the presses were often short of work, and even in the 18th, they were at pains to keep out workers from other towns who arrived in the course of their voyages looking for work and willing to take lower wages. The Parisian printers in 1702 demanded that their Flemish and German colleagues be allowed to stay only three months – time enough to see the sights, they felt. Anxious to protect their jobs, they fought against the efforts of some of the owners of large presses to multiply the number of apprentices they employed. They demanded that they know Latin and at least be able to read Greek, and that they be strictly limited in number by the regulations.[204] Masters increasingly looked for economies by using unskilled labour for the presswork. They hoped, in this way, to undermine the position of the journeymen, and so a new category of labourer, the hireling (*alloué*), made its appearance little by little, despite the complaints and demands of the journeymen. The *alloué* was officially recognised in regulations of the 18th century. The men did achieve some successes, however, in their fight with the masters. In the 18th century it was conceded that they could not be dismissed without one month's notice of termination of employment. The situation of printing workers continued nevertheless to be unbearable by our standards, although it was better than that of workers in other trades. Moreover it had worsened since 1666 when Colbert had limited the number of presses in each town in France, so that it became practically impossible for them to look forward to becoming masters unless they resigned themselves to marrying the widow of a deceased master.

2
The Masters

After the journeymen, we come to the masters, both publishers and booksellers, and whom we will study together, for the great majority of them carried out both jobs at the same time. Of course many book-shops, especially the small ones which published titles only very occasionally, did not own a printing press. But most printers kept a shop as well and invested the profits they made out of printing books for other people into publishing, either on their account or in collaboration with others. Joost Bade worked in this way. And if some of the biggest capitalist publishers who dominated the book trade like Cramoisy or some of the Giuntas owned no printing shops, others like Koberger or Plantin kept shops, as we have seen, in which they printed some at least of the books they financed as publishers.

Let us start by examining the professional activities of these men, and first of all of the master printer in his workshop. Let us take a typical case, a small printer with only one or two presses. There were very many of this sort throughout Europe from the 15th to the 18th centuries. Mostly this type of tradesman lived off odd jobs: bulletins, posters, prospectuses of all sorts required by people in the town, and ABCs and class lists for the nearest college. Sometimes booksellers would order the printing of little books that were easy to produce and intended for an undemanding public.

In the 16th and 17th centuries, such small establishments were often run by ex-journeymen who had managed to set themselves up in business and did their own work, helped only by their son, or even their wife or daughter. They called on transient workers if the job was urgent and sometimes they kept on permanently a worker on whom they relied and who shared the life of their family.

If a printer was of sufficient skill and had a good fount of characters he might attract a publisher's attention and he would then be offered regular commissions. Then he might come to need a more considerable work force in his shop. As we have seen, five people were needed to keep one press in full production. A master operating a business on this scale would be reckoned quite important by the standards of the time. Most 17th and 18th-century books came from printing establishments of this kind, containing two or three presses employing ten or so journeymen and apprentices.

The head of such a business had to be hard working and show initiative and also had to know the trade thoroughly. If the publisher was dissatisfied with the finished product, the printer risked losing orders from that source and so being short of work. He was paid generally by the sheet and sought to lower his printing costs by obtaining increased production from his workers. He had to set the example: rise early, perhaps be at the shop even before the journeymen, supervise their work, help and direct them with difficult tasks and, above all, ensure the accuracy of the text. He would normally be his own proof corrector and allow only members of his family to help him. As well as being a first-class printer he needed a sound knowledge of Latin. He would generally be the son of a master and have pursued his studies until his 15th or 16th birthday before starting work in his father's shop, or in a friend's, in order to acquire knowledge of the many varied tasks connected with presswork and composing.

Carrying on business with those who supplied him with orders, and always on the lookout for work to avoid idle presses, he had to spread the workload evenly, closely supervising the workmen's output, forever needing to be scrupulous over the painstaking business of proof correction which had to be completed to a strict timetable so that printing could continue. The master printer never lacked work to do, especially since he normally owned a bookshop near his workshop. If he made sufficient profits and could collect together some capital he published a book (sometimes associating himself, in order to cover the costs of publication, with another bookseller, with whom he could share the risks and the profits of publishing and who would undertake to distribute part of the edition). In this way a master printer might sometimes manage to become an important publisher.

The bookseller's business was as complicated as the printer's. He was usually a publisher to a greater or lesser extent and invested his capital in printing books. He would choose texts to edit, enter into negotiations with authors (if he published new works), secure his supply of paper (this was his duty, not the printer's), select a suitable printer and superintend the work. He had, above all, to arrange the distribution of the books he published and see to it that his shop was stocked with what his clients wanted. To ensure this, he needed a network of contacts, near and far, a complicated accounting system, and a knowledge of the market for the books offered to him, relating them to the known tastes of his customers. He needed to be an indefatigable letter writer. He would have to write dozens of letters a day and even in the largest publishing concerns he would have the assistance of no more than two or three clerks. They were employed to look after the consignment of books for despatch, and to check the contents of incoming bales – tricky work in an age when books were sent out as unbound sheets.

Often a letter was not enough to clinch complicated negotiations and the bookseller had to take to the road. In the bigger firms the owner would delegate this to an associate, a relative, or failing that, an agent. At a time when most businesses were family concerns the proprietor, who would have done enough travelling in his youth, would entrust this to his eventual heir, probably his son or a younger brother or nephew, and it would be his job to take the place of the older man at the great fairs where booksellers assembled, or on visits to correspondents. Consequently he would always be travelling to and fro about Europe.

Here for example is a letter which Laurent Anisson, a leading 17th century publisher at Lyons, sent to one of his sons in 1670, giving him instructions and reminding him of his obligations to the business during the course of just such a journey through Germany and Flanders.[205] I shall quote it in full:

Lyons 28 November 1670

'My dear son,
   If I hadn't received a letter of yours from Amsterdam I would have thought that you had not stopped between Frankfurt and Antwerp. You passed through Cologne without seeing anybody, yet it's a town better supplied with books for exchange or purchase than any other on your route. In the aforesaid letter from Amsterdam you say lightly that you took on a task which couldn't be finished for 15 days without telling me what the task was and what happened at Vasberg's and the other booksellers at Amsterdam and other towns you have visited since. You wrote me a letter from Antwerp on the 17th, and it was a real mish-mash, more like something written after a drinking session than after church. There is nothing about business in it except your writing to complain to Mr. König of Basel alleging that he

didn't honour the barter agreement you made with his son. It ought to have been drawn up by both sides so that he couldn't withdraw from it. There's a great difference between threatening Mr. Chinon with the law and trying to get something from him in a friendly way.

As for Mr. Meursius, you say he has no more copies of Cornelius and that you will make him find some, and that you can only exchange the copies of Bonacina with him if you grant him part of the rights on the Cornelius, which you intend to do. I have no idea what you're referring to. Don't undertake the Palavicini *Historia Concilii* (4°): it is not suitable for our business. We have known for a long time that prices charged by Flemish and Dutch printers were disadvantageous to us because they hold to our old prices and one must hold to the new ones or beware the consequences. Who gave you advice to act as you claim you did against Cornelius Hackius seeing that you are no longer on the spot? You ought to have made enquiries and found out to whom he entrusted the consignment he alleged he had sent to me, and to whom he addressed it in France. The batch sent him should have included three of Calepinus at a price of 22.10 each and one by Gassendi at 50, and which we charge more for now because of its rarity – unless you let a copy go in an exchange for some good book you should do the same. And there was no copy of Castillo in the parcel I sent him, I mean to the said Hackius.

What you say about Mr. Patin is of small account, and as for the question of the Spolmannus I will make enquiries. You can tell Mr. Papenburg what you know about the Calepin, which is that many more additions of greater importance have been discovered and that I am having them transcribed and sent to me. And what am I to make of the beginning, middle and end of your letter?

I received all the items you sent from Frankfurt in good condition, except for one parcel. We lack many ordinary books which are easily obtainable and these are the most suitable for our business. You sent 50 *Antidotum Melancoliae* vol. 2 (12mo) when 12 would have done, and 12 of Menzius on the Psalms (4°) when you should have sent three or four. Finally you really must understand that the cost of a trip like yours is high, and you must make the most of it and not be in too great a hurry as you seem to be, if you allow for the fact that there are so many book dealers in the towns you're in. So take care and mend your ways.

Believe me, ever your loving father,
Anisson.'

This is a typical letter and shows us clearly the kind of business the bookseller had to conduct in the course of his travels, and how booksellers were forced to move about Europe to settle their affairs. For the large firms travel like this was essential. Laurent Anisson's son whom we see in this letter vising Basel, Cologne, Frankfurt and Antwerp also made his way into Spain and Italy.[206]

Naturally enough booksellers and printers in the same town kept in close contact with each other. They met to discuss trade matters and exchange news, to help less fortunate colleagues, and above all to pray and celebrate the Feast Days, especially that of their own patron saint, St. John the Evangelist. Much the same reasons that made illuminators, binders and booksellers before the advent of printing form their own Guilds, led the later printers, booksellers and publishers to join them. The Guild of St. John the Evangelist, founded in 1401, was particularly active in Paris until the end of the 18th century. Twice a year, on the 6th May (Feast of St. John Porte-Latine) and on 27th December (Feast of St. John the Evangelist), printers and booksellers met to celebrate Mass and other solemn rites, often followed by banquets, and each Sunday the Guild met to hear Mass. The membership fee and the collections taken covered expenses and provided, above all, for a benevolent fund.[207]

In principle, the Guilds united all men in the same trade: masters, journeymen and apprentices. But in practice only the masters would join the Guild, the journeymen preferring to organise themselves in their own brotherhoods which, as we have seen, developed into centres of resistance against the bosses. It was largely to prosecute the struggle against journeymen that associations of booksellers and printers were set up all over the place in the second half of the 16th and in the 17th century. Until then the crafts connected with the book trade had been free. For a long time they were subject only to University regulation, a heritage which came down from the age of manuscripts, but this naturally only applied in those towns which had universities. Up to about the middle of the 16th century, while general affluence prevailed, the free regime continued. But as soon as economic crises provoked strikes and social struggles among journeymen – and we have emphasised their extent – and when legal cases multiplied, leading to state intervention and the elaboration of complex trade regulations, the masters were driven to form themselves into a body, and to empower certain of their members to represent them at law. Soon, lack of work forced them to unite to ban new recruits to the profession . ·I unemployment led to more and more pirated editions being printed and so caused them to meet regularly to settle the problems facing their profession. The state, of course, was favourably disposed to this development, which led to the establishment of corporations which were easier to manage politically, allowed greater surveillance and control of the trade and could be used to prevent the publication of the increasing numbers of 'seditious' books.

So, from 1548 in Venice, 1557 in London and about 1570 in Paris, and soon in all the great cities of Europe except perhaps in Holland, Companies of Stationers were granted charters of incorporation which gave them Masters and Wardens and power to impose ever stricter regulations. Meeting regularly, master printers, booksellers and on occasion binders discussed agreements to regulate trade practices. If a haberdasher tried to retail books, the Company acted swiftly. Had a banned book been on sale? The state at once demanded action from the Master to expose the defaulter. Had a bookseller from one town seen his copies pirated by a bookseller from elsewhere? The Company took action. Had an excessive privilege been granted to a particular bookseller? Those with grounds for complaint would bring them to the Company meeting. There too, booksellers of the same town would agree not to launch two separate editions of the same work and would get together to contend against booksellers from a rival town who had done them an injury.

In the little world of the book, rivalries were no doubt intense and in the big cities cliques were formed. Even if printers were a part of the same organization as booksellers they would band together on occasion against them. Or small printers and booksellers would unite against the great publishers always ambitious to dominate the Company. Booksellers would form factions within the organisation to fight a particular issue, usually against what they thought was an exorbitant privilege enjoyed by another member. Elections to the Court of the Company often led to rivalries and, in France at least, the state often interfered on behalf of the wealthy tradesmen, who in its eyes represented law and order. The function of the Masters of the Company of Stationers – and this called for diplomacy – was to arbitrate in the many quarrels which split the membership, and to act as intermediaries between the state and their fellow members, often a matter of personal relations with ministers. When this concerned the delicate question of censorship it was a role of vital importance.

Thus the social status of booksellers and printers varied considerably.

The nature of their profession undoubtedly gave them a certain prestige, especially in the sixteenth century. Their rank in university towns as necessary 'adjuncts' of the university entitled them to a high place in the processions and ceremonies, after the professors and students. But these honours did not prevent them from being, in fact, scarcely distinguishable from the other bourgeois of the town. Their children would be married to the children of businessmen of equivalent wealth. The richest booksellers were often linked by marriage to goldsmiths and at slightly lower levels they would marry into the families of haberdashers, candlemakers and wine merchants. In Paris the bookseller of the Palais, who published classics, often bound their children in marriage to neighbouring tradesmen, grocers, and linen drapers. It was a matter of hard bargaining: the size of the dowry and the principle that both parties to the marriage should be of equal wealth was the governing factor.

Sometimes the biggest booksellers were wealthy enough to be in the first rank of the town's citizens. In Paris and Lyons many of them became consuls and magistrates. As one would expect, once they had made their fortune booksellers looked to the day when they would obtain a post which would enable their children to ascend a rung in the ladder of the social hierarchy, and this meant abandoning their father's trade, in France at least. Elsewhere this did not always follow. The Moretus family, for example, retained their printing business even when they had secured noble status. In Italy as in the Low Countries some went into banking, like the Huguétans from Lyons who took refuge in Holland and became Counts Palatine and bankers.[208] Such cases were exceptional; it was far more usual everywhere in Europe to marry into the trade and hand it on for generations. The de Tournes were in the trade at Lyons, later at Geneva, and then at Lyons again, from the 16th to the 18th century.[209] The Barbou family likewise handed on the trade from father to son, working at Lyons, Limoges and Paris from the 16th to the 19th century.[210] Similarly the Desbordes carried on their business through the 17th and 18th centuries, first at Saumur and then in Holland. Over the centuries such dynasties helped to form a small closed world of men in the book trade with an outlook of their own.

3
From the Humanist Printer to the Bookseller of the Enlightenment

Living off and among books, in daily contact with men of letters, intellectuals and theologians, and also with students and the cultured public – in a word, with all who wrote and read – printers and booksellers naturally interested themselves in things of the mind as well as in commerce, if only to conduct their business more profitably.

From time to time writers turned printer – to print their own works, see them through the press ensuring their accuracy and good appearance, supervise their distribution and so have a direct influence on the reading public. This was and always will be an ambition common to many intellectuals. At times of intellectual crisis and of conflicts over questions of conscience, when polemical literature flourishes, this will be particularly the case. This kind of action on the part of intellectuals was never more influential than in the early 16th century when the vital mission of printing was the diffusion of ancient texts in their pristine purity, an age when philology was queen. Many scholars and writers were engaged as publishers' proof readers, and many turned to a career as printers and booksellers. Men of action as well as being humanists, living in an age of comparative economic prosperity, supported by publishers or investors able to recognise their qualities, they achieved many publishing successes in the service of the new humanism, and helped the victory of the cause. Let us look then at the humanist printer.

One of the earliest was Jean Amerbach.[212] Born at Reutlingen around 1434 when Gutenberg was beginning his experiments at Strasbourg, he began his studies in Paris under a fellow German, Johann Heynlin von Stein, who was later to be instrumental in starting the first printing press in France at the Sorbonne. Under Heynlin, Amerbach was taught the philosophy of Duns Scotus. Next we find him a Master of Arts and working for Koberger, the great Nuremberg publisher, where as an intellectual he saw the possibilities for the promotion through the press of an accurate knowledge of important texts. Around 1475 he opened an office in Basel, possibly with Koberger's help, and he concentrated on publishing the best available texts of the Church Fathers, continuing to work on this his chosen task all his life. In 1492 he published Ambrose, in 1506 Augustine, then in collaboration with Erasmus he concentrated on Jerome. The greatest minds of Germany agreed to collate manuscripts for him: Beatus Rhenanus, an outstanding scholar, gave up a journey to Italy to be his proof reader, while Reuchlin went to live at his house in 1510 in order to work with him. To understand Amerbach's stature in the contemporary world of printers and humanists we need only consider the letters he received from all over Europe, from Cologne and Paris, from Dijon and Strasbourg, from Dôle and Nuremberg, from Speyer and London and from Frankfurt, Freiburg, Berne, Sélestat, Tübingen, Heidelberg, letters from printers naturally, some of them established, some occasional. Men like Koberger, Adolf Rusch of Strasburg, Pierre Metlinger, the wandering printer from Besançon, Dôle and Dijon (1488–1492), Paul Hurus of Constance who was working in Barcelona in 1475 and Saragossa in 1480, Johann Heynlin, Johann Petri the uncle of Adam, Jean Schott of Strasbourg, grandson of Mentelin, all wrote to him; and there were letters from theologians and humanists, known and unknown, illustrious like Lefèvre d'Etaples, Reuchlin, Albrecht Dürer, notorious like Wimpheling, Sebastian Brandt, Ulrich Zasius the jurist, Trithème the geographer, and many more.

Amerbach, a tough worker, an untiring publisher, was also head of a family in the full sense of the phrase. He sent his sons, Bruno and Basil, to Lisieux College in Paris and wrote to them regularly, showering them with good advice. His correspondence brings to life the quarrels of the Schoolmen and the doings of the citizens of Basel living in Paris. Father is continually warning his sons about the dangers of Paris life. He urges them to follow the teachings of Scotus, not Ockham, for, faithful to his own education, he always supports the Ancients in their battle with the Moderns. Head of a business, devoted to his work, he is also concerned with other more immediate questions. He urges the boys to eschew bad company, keep a daily record of their expenses and avoid extravagance: 'Eat and drink to live, don't live to eat and drink' is the gist of his advice. But all the same, Amerbach does not forget his business or the Fathers, and when they return home he puts them to work on the great edition of Jerome, while employing John Kuhn, the famous Dominican from Nuremberg, as their household teacher. Amerbach's youngest son Boniface was the most brilliant and he too had to help his father. He later became a reader for Froben, Amerbach's successor, and acted as publisher for Erasmus, whose executor he was to be.

Amerbach's goal was to provide accurate editions of the Fathers. Another humanist, the Italian Aldus, set out to provide new and accurate editions of the Latin and Greek classics and to win a wider audience for them. Aldus,[213] like Amerbach, had been a student and even a professor, and his motives for turning printer are significant. He was born at Sermonetta near Velletri in the Papal States between 1449 and 1454. He underwent an education at the hands of traditionalist teachers. This meant learning by heart the eternal versified grammar of Alexandre de Villedieu – an experience which later encouraged him to write and publish a methodical grammar. He then went to Rome, completing his studies in Latin under Jasper of Verona and Domizio Calderino, two famous teachers, and later went on to Ferrara to study Greek under Guarini, a leading hellenist. He began to teach the better Greek and Latin authors himself and must have regretted the lack of good printed editions useful to his students, among whom were Strozzi the Florentine banker, and Pico della Mirandola. War broke out between Venice and the Duke of Ferrara, Ercole d'Este, and Aldus took refuge in the home of his pupil Pico who was at that time beginning his famous work. At Mirandola Aldus enjoyed generous hospitality for two years. There he formed the friendship of Adramyttenos, a Cretan scholar, corresponded with Politian, and was private tutor to the two nephews of Pico, Leonardo and Alberto Pio. He grounded his teaching as much on Greek as on Latin. The fall of Constantinople had driven many Greek scholars into Italy. Aldus then conceived the idea of establishing a printing house to specialise in Greek which Pico would finance. Since most of the refugees had settled in Venice where printers and booksellers were numerous and communications good, Aldus chose that city to open his business. He probably chose Cretan refugees, who had formerly been scribes, as his correctors and possibly his compositors. He had soon published the poems of Musaeus with a Latin translation, a Psalter, and the *Gallomyomachia*, inserting in the preface an ambitious programme of publication. In 1494 he brought out Lascaris' Greek grammar with Latin translation, and in 1495–6 Aristotle's *Organon*, Theodore Gaza's Greek grammar with commentaries by Greek grammarians and the works of Theocritus. Only then did he publish his first Latin work, the *De Aetna* of Bembo, and after that not a year passed without magnificent editions of Latin and Greek authors, especially Greek. In particular he published successive volumes of a monumental edition of the works of Aristotle. In order to complete this task for which he had had the most beautiful Greek characters cut, he associated himself with the best scholars, and above all hellenists, in Italy and even in all Europe. This was the foundation of the Aldine Academy, a product of the little academy of the Princes of Carpi. Scholars met in his home at a fixed time each day to decide which texts were to be printed and which manuscripts to adopt. Among them were Venetian Senators, future prelates, professors, doctors and Greek scholars. Among the many, let us note such names as Bembo, the poet, Alberto Pio, Prince of Carpi, Urbano Bolzani, Baltrita Egnazio, the famous professor, Sabellico, Girolamo Aleandro, later a cardinal, Gregoropoulos, Mark Musuros of Candia, who was to be Archbishop of Monembasia, and Erasmus. Soon Aldus expanded his list. He had an entirely new letter, the italic, cut by Francesco Griffo in 1501 and in this alphabet he printed his most famous books, the pocket classics in an octavo format intended to popularise the Latin classics and the Italian poets: Virgil, Horace, Petrarch, Dante, Ovid, Juvenal, Persius and Statius, and also Bembo, the *Adages* of Erasmus, and Boccaccio's *Decameron*. Till his death in 1515 the roll of authors he published in first editions is lengthy: among them are Aristotle, Aristophanes, Thucydides, Sophocles, Herodotus, Xenophon, Demosthenes, Aeschines, Plato, to mention only the Greeks.

Another significant figure in the gallery of humanist printers is Joost Bade.[214] Flemish by birth, he studied at a convent of the Brothers of the Common Life in Ghent and then went on to Louvain to finish his training. He was attracted to Italy to study Greek under the best masters and at Ferrara took lessons from Guarini. After this he received further instruction, at either Mantua or Ferrara, from Beroaldus the Elder, the greatest living master of classics, whose printed works were to be immensely popular throughout Europe. Bade was already making himself a reputation as a scholar and when his period in Italy ended he took teaching posts first at Valencia and then at Lyons. To help his pupils gain a knowledge of the ancients such as he had received from Beroaldus he prepared a new edition of that author's *Orationes*. It was published in 1492 in Lyons and was based on the one which had appeared the year before at Bologna. Then came the *Silvae Morales*, a collection of the choicest extracts from ancient and modern writers with a commentary, and an edition of Terence also with a commentary. Already Joost Bade recognised the power of the printing press. All the works produced by Bade were published by Trechsel, the great publisher of Lyons, and the regular contacts between the two men brought them to close mutual understanding. Trechsel gave Bade an important position in his business. It was Bade's job to revise the manuscripts and to correct the proofs, and often to compose the dedicatory epistles as well – a considerable burden for him while he continued to give his lessons, and one which prevented him from carrying on with his personal work. But it was absorbing labour for a dedicated humanist, who now gave the most important of the Lyons publishing houses a direction in harmony with his own ideas. Joost Bade found himself at the very centre of the humanist group in Lyons and his dedicatory epistles established his literary reputation. Indeed Trithème quotes him as being among the most celebrated authors on church affairs, young as he was. While on a trip to Paris in 1497 to copy a manuscript of Avicenna he made the acquaintance of Parisian scholars and printers sympathetic to the new trends, like Marnef. Trechsel died at this point and Bade married one of his daughters, but he seems to have fallen out with Trechsel's successors and he lost his job. He worked for several other Lyons printers, afterwards going to Paris, possibly at the invitation of Robert Gaguin, where he met the influential publisher, Jean Petit, who took him into his service. At the same time he resumed his publishing programme. We have seen how Jean Petit, a sharp-witted investor if ever there was one, helped Joost Bade to set up a printing shop.[215] As a printer Bade produced many books for Petit and also published in partnership with him and on his own account. Soon his house was a meeting place for the humanists of Paris and scholars in transit. Among his friends, whom he called the 'Ascensiani' or his 'assistants' were Lefèvre d'Étaples, Guillaume Budé, Pierre Danès, Jacques Toussaint, Jean Vatable, Louis de Berquin, Nicolas Dupuis known as 'Bonaspes', Beatus Rhenanus and François Du Bois – not to mention Erasmus with whom, like Aldus, he eventually quarrelled. This galaxy of famous scholars eased his task greatly, for they could notify him of the best manuscripts and would sometimes make copies for him when on their travels. In this learned atmosphere Bade was able to carry on his own work. He concentrated on giving his press a literary reputation and produced Latin and Greek authors in the main, being responsible for numerous annotated editions, each an advance on the one before. At the time of his death in 1535, he was the head of a prosperous enterprise which his son-in-law Robert Estienne carried on after him.

In this way the early dynasties of humanist printers were established. The most famous were those of the Aldi at Venice, the Morels and the Vascosans at Paris and that formed by the Estiennes, Simon De Colines and Joost Bade, all of whom were related by marriage to or descended from Guyonne Viart. She was married three times, first to Damien Higman, then to Henri Estienne I, and finally to Simon de Colines. One of her daughters by Damien Higman married a famous publisher

Régnauld Chaudière, and their descendants were still in business as booksellers in the 17th century. She also had a daughter and three sons by Henri Estienne. All three sons were printers, one of them being Charles Estienne the famous doctor-painter and author of the *Guide des chemins de France* and *Agriculture et maisons rustiques* and of a well-known treatise on anatomy. Robert Estienne I was another celebrated printer who produced many editions and translations of the Bible. He learned his trade in the business of his father-in-law, Simon de Colines, and then married Perrette Bade, the daughter of Joost, herself a fine Latinist who assisted in proof correction. Foreign scholars often stayed at Robert Estienne's, and Latin was spoken in the house, even by the children and servants. Several of the children were scholar-printers of the next generation: Henri II, a distinguished Greek scholar who worked at Paris and Geneva, François II and Robert II whose widow, the daughter of Jean Barbé the bookseller, married a second time to the Greek scholar Mamert Patisson, a proof reader in her first husband's printing shop.[216]

These humanist publishers were not only pure scholars concerned with the production of accurate texts and of their own scholarly publications. They were also, and possibly first of all, thoroughly professional printers just as concerned over the appearance and physical format of their books. We have seen how Aldus had more readable and elegant Greek characters cut than any previously used, and introduced italic. The humanist publishers of this period revolutionised the appearance of the printed book, making it much plainer. The Estiennes knew how to give the title page a sober, well-proportioned look, and some humanist printers were so in love with their art that they were more concerned about the appearance of a text than about its meaning. Geoffroy Tory[217] was one such. He had been a teacher at three Colleges, du Plessis, Coqueret and Bourgogne, and was a great admirer of Italy, a country he had visited several times. He set up on his own account after working for Gilles de Gourmont and Henri Estienne, whose widow he married, and he published a whole book on the proportions of letters, the famous *Champfleury*. He created a new model for the appearance of the French book, taking his inspiration from the Italian Renaissance. Such was the zeal of this veteran teacher that he is thought to have engraved his own plates, made his own binding tools and to have helped with the cutting and casting of his type.

Looking after a printing house business, correcting proofs ceaselessly, while at the same time carrying out the duties of a publisher; corresponding with foreign booksellers and with men of letters, while writing their own scholarly works – all this (we could be forgiven for thinking) would have exhausted lesser men than an Aldus, Joost Bade or Robert Estienne. It was a task that only the tireless enthusiast, the real Renaissance man, could sustain. Henri Estienne indeed explains, in the preface to his Thucydides, that he rose during the night to work on his scholarly editions as a relaxation from proof correction and the many routine cares he had as head of the firm! In fact many of the printers and booksellers of the 16th century whom we justly call humanists had neither the time nor perhaps the inclination to produce personal work. Men of culture and refinement, they were enlightened publishers and ensured that they were surrounded with writers and intellectuals for the greater good of their business. At the same time they encouraged them in their work and secured their services as partners and sometimes as close friends.

Take for example Sébastien Gryphe,[218] prince of the Lyons booksellers, populariser of the Aldine editions, tireless propagandist of Erasmus' writings, and above all of course a business man. Born at Reutlingen in Swabia in 1491, the son of a printer, he learned his trade in Germany and Venice after which he returned to Lyons, probably as an agent for the Corporation of Venetian booksellers, and set up as printer. He worked at first for this Corporation, printing law books in gothic type, then purchased roman and italic founts and specialised in the printing of Latin authors in a pocket sized format in imitation of the Aldine editions. He printed Latin translations of Greek authors and put out reprints of the translations of the best humanists of the time, men like Budé, Erasmus, and Politian. It was Gryphe who was granted the rights in the works of Sadolet, the liberal Bishop of Carpentras, and in Paleario's treatise on the immortality of the soul. Likewise he was commissioned to publish Scaliger's first work, the *De causis linguae latinae*, the *Thesaurus hebraicus* of Sanctes Pagninus, and Étienne Dolet's *Commentarii linguae latinae*, not to mention the scientific work of Rabelais. He also published some less serious works along with these, the *Arresta amorum* of Benoît Court, for example. Gryphe provided the text books for half Europe and was the quickening spirit behind the humanist movement in Lyons. The greatest writers and scholars praised him in their dedications, frequented his house, and sometimes worked with him as proof readers. So this printer, himself very highly cultivated, surrounded himself with men such as Rabelais, Alciat, Sadolet, Hubert Sussaneau, Claude Baduel, François Hotman, François Baudoin,

Antoine de Gouvera, Claude Guilland, Emile Ferret, Clément Marot, Visagier, Nicolas Bourbon, Maurice and Guillaume Scève, Salmon Macrin and Barthélemy Aneau. These men and many others were guests in his house. Thus Gryphe already provides a model for the editor who is the personal friend of men of letters; not himself a writer, yet no less cultivated than they.

Printers and booksellers, as friends, confidantes and protectors of literary men, were often led, if only for business reasons, to publish daring books that would sell better because scandalous, and they frequently sheltered writers suspected of heresy. Gryphe readily welcomed Dolet the heretic bookseller into his house after Dolet's release from prison in Toulouse. Being the first to read new manuscripts, they were naturally abreast of new ideas, and frequently among the first converts to them and among the first to fight on their behalf. Such were Thomas Anshelm,[219] a printer of Tübingen and Haguenau and a friend of Reuchlin, and his successor and brother-in-law Setzer, the friend of Melanchthon, who gathered a small circle of Lutheran reformers around himself. Both men made their presses available almost exclusively to Luther, Melanchthon and their friends, and even took on the opposition, printing in secret the pamphlets of a young Spanish doctor named Servetius. Serving the same cause was Simon Dubois, a printer at Paris and then at Alençon, and an indefatigable propagandist for the ideas and writings of Luther.

In the first ranks of the fight to spread new ideas, printers and booksellers were always the most vulnerable to victimisation, at the mercy of inquiries which might commit them to prison and often the stake. The Inquisitors of the 16th century were implacable in their dealings with printers. What better way to root out heresy than to punish severely those who initiated the publication of suspected books? The most celebrated humanist printers in Paris and Lyons were nearly all Protestant in the latter half of the 16th century and had to flee France to avoid the retinue of spies and informers employed by the censors and the Parlement. Robert Estienne and de Tournes both returned to Geneva and a great many others went with them. In Antwerp, which was first controlled by William of Orange and the Duke of Alençon in rebellion against the Spaniards, and won over to heresy, and was then recaptured by the troops of the Duke of Alba, Plantin, in order to continue practising his craft had himself to undergo an unknown number of conversions, sincere or not, before he felt it finally necessary to quit the city. Other printers and booksellers, less lucky, less cunning, or more sincere than he, paid with their lives for the unorthodoxy of their publications. Such a one, for example, was Augereau, a skilled type cutter and the publisher of Marguerite of Navarre's works, who died at the stake.

Among the printers and booksellers burnt at the stake along with their books, among the 'martyrs of the Book', the most dominant personality was that of Étienne Dolet. His was a complex and difficult psychology for the twentieth-century mind to grasp; and his case is one which we would not examine here if it did not concern a writer who turned bookseller and printer and ended up at the stake as a result of his activities as a bookseller, and if the psychological problems involved were not common in the interpretation of the life history of other printer-publishers and did not arise from their professional concerns.[220]

Dolet was brutal, violent, unbalanced. One day he killed a man in a brawl in mysterious circumstances. He was a passionate admirer of Cicero and a former pupil at the University of Padua. He preferred to stay outside the parties in the contemporary religious conflict but he eventually found himself in a claustrophobic environment, suffocating among the narrow-minded bigots he met in Toulouse on his return from Italy. He could not repress his contempt of persecution and his love of liberty when Jean de Caturce, one of Luther's disciples, was burned in 1532. Now a rebel, he was cast into gaol after abusing certain members of Parlement, and later freed after his friends had taken up his cause. He went on to earn his living as a proof corrector with Sébastien Gryphe at Lyons, who warmly welcomed him on the recommendation of one of his loyal friends, Jean de Boyssonne. While employed there he wrote original works, translating his beloved Latin authors and assembling materials for a masterwork designed to demonstrate the superiority of Cicero's style; he even engaged in a famous polemic with Erasmus with a view to defending his favourite author. Meanwhile he prepared about 50 books for publication by Gryphe and thus began his career in the printing business, which was only interrupted when he killed Nicolas Compaing, for which he was soon pardoned by the King.

Now we come to the year 1538. Dolet married and was soon to have a son. Was it a desire to ensure his family's future that made Dolet turn printer? Certainly he set up a printing shop with the help of a money-lender whose identity, despite the efforts of historians, is still a mystery. On 6th March, 1538 Dolet obtained a privilege from Francis I for his printing enterprise and soon his first book appeared. The surprise was that this lover of fine language, a fervent devotee of Cicero who prided himself in being above sectarian strife, should have chosen to offer to the public, not an edition of the classics, not a selection of Latin poetry or a work of philosophy, but a little book of piety, the *Cato christianus* which earned the praises of Guillaume Durand, the Principal of the College of Lyons, though later it was condemned by the Parlement of Paris. Was this a concession to public taste? A wish to give proof of his orthodoxy? The vanity of an author who wants to show he is as capable as anyone else of grappling with religious subjects? It is impossible to say. Perhaps it was a little of each. In any event this gesture had, from 1538 to 1541, no sequel. Dolet forsook religious topics to print books by his friends Cottereau and Claude Fontaine, the works of Marot, some medical books and again more Latin writers, Terence, Virgil, Suetonius, and his beloved Cicero. In 1541 he published a New Testament in Latin and a small work of Savonarola's. And then came 1542, the fatal year. His business was expanding and he set up in the Rue Mercier among the big booksellers and published 32 titles. Only five of them were classics. Of the rest, seven were medical works, six were works of literature and poetry, all of which were in French and were well chosen, among them a Rabelais and a Marot; and there were fourteen religious works. All these latter were suspect, among them the *Enchiridion* of Erasmus, works of Lefèvre d'Etaples, Sadolet and Berquin. Marot's rendering of the Psalms and a New Testament in French. These works were not exactly iconoclastic, but were books which taught a love of the Gospel. At the same time Dolet prepared a translation of the Bible, following that of Olivétan. All this was sufficient to draw the attention of the authorities to him. Soon his premises were searched and a copy of Calvin's *Institutions* came to light along with Olivétan's French Bible and some of Melanchthon's works. Martyrdom at the stake followed on 3rd August, 1544, in the Place Maubert where Dolet was burned along with his books.

Such are the facts, and they present us with a problem in psychology. How and why did Dolet, this man of letters and lover of style, a libertarian who for so long disdained to join either side, suddenly enter the arena and take sides? Was it to make money? Did he begin to publish books that represented the new trends because that was what paid off? Or did the great religious issues grip him as he grew older, after the birth of his son? Such answers are too simple. There is no opportunity to solve the Dolet mystery here. But it is worth referring to, because it demonstrates the problems that are encountered whenever one has to do with the case of the printer or bookseller who is willing to take risks in support of a cause.

From the end of the 16th century the attitudes of printers and booksellers changed, as did relations between authors and publishers. The great generations of humanist printers disappeared in the upheavals at the close of the century. After a hundred years of exceptional prosperity printing was in crisis. The innumerable editions of books had glutted the market, capital to finance publishers was not forthcoming because of the general economic crisis, and unrest and strikes broke out among the workers. The first concern of publishers was simply survival, especially in France. Then, while Germany, which had been least affected by the crisis, was being devastated by the Thirty Years War, the trade slowly pulled round in the rest of Europe at the beginning of the 17th century. The world of the book emerged impoverished and diminished from economic turmoil. In general, booksellers and printers had by now formed into guilds and corporations; the scholar who starts a new firm is no longer on the scene. The masters found themselves in an overcrowded trade, had difficulties in making ends meet, and often lived in pitiable conditions with the social status of petty artisans. Publisher-booksellers were no longer concerned to patronise the world of letters, but only to publish books with a guaranteed sale. The richest made their money on books with an assured market, reprints of old best sellers, standard religious works and, above all, the Church Fathers. The leading firms were those on the side of the Counter-Reformation – important merchants but humble servants of Jesuit policy, supporters of the ultramontane faction.

Publishing was in total subjection to authority. Originality was shunned, and new works, which by now were usually in the vernacular, were not favoured. The publishers of the great French classics cut a modest figure, and writers were not interested in mixing with small shopkeepers and tradesmen who were in any case poorly educated and from an inferior class. Writers and scholars no longer gathered in printers' houses or workshops but in the literary salons of high society, or in the libraries of the aristocracy, at the invitation of learned librarians and under the patronage of powerful individuals, or even in monasteries. Of course leading publishers like Cramoisy or later on like Léonard were on good terms with men like Chancellor Séguier, the Minister in charge of Censorship.[221] Admittedly too, leading booksellers like Camusat, bookseller to the Académie Française, and Desprez, bookseller to the Jansenists, continued to serve literary men in many ways. But they were now like servants in relation to their customers, not their equals or even their protectors as they had been in the 16th century.

Gabriel Naudé, librarian to Cardinal Mazarin, gave Camusat a brace of pistols as a New Year gift. Later on still, Balzac, in his letters, consigned Rocollet to public obloquy, and Chapelain, more benevolent by nature, refers condescendingly to great booksellers like Rocollet and Léonard as 'my good man' and 'my dear fellow'.[222]

Times had certainly changed since the age of Aldus and the Estiennes and the trade looked back sadly on the early days. Historical scholars were the only literary men to have conserved friendly relations with the printers and publishers on whom they relied for the printing of complicated works. Du Cange and Mabillon were in regular correspondence with the Anissons of Lyons, and the two sons of Laurent Anisson gave directions to Mabillon when he set out on his search for manuscripts in the monasteries of Italy.[223] In the same way the professors at the University of Leyden had great respect for the knowledge and skill of the Elzeviers whose friend and protector was the learned statesman Heinsius. To some extent the Elzeviers were carrying on the traditions of the humanist printer of the previous century. On their unending journeys they received warm welcomes from Chapelain and from Pairesc.

At this time few booksellers or printers escaped that dingy region where the tradesmen and artisans who made up the majority of the trade intermingled. Still, some kept up the highest traditions of their profession, albeit more modestly than their humanist predecessors. Antoine Vitré of Paris, for example, knew no Latin yet devoted one whole period of his life to the production of a polyglot Bible in five languages and seven volumes which eclipsed Plantin's. There was Edme Martin, a first rate hellenist much respected by the learned men of his day and the only printer in Paris capable of printing correctly in Greek, and Palliot of Dijon, a scholar and respected genealogist who printed his own books.[224] Most distinguished of all, perhaps, was Blaeu, the pupil of Tycho Brahe,[225] a former instrument maker turned printer, who founded an important publishing house in Amsterdam and made improvements to the press. He made tremendous progress in the production of atlases. But such men were uncommon at this period except perhaps in Holland.

At the same time the trade was subjected to increased regimentation. Both printers and booksellers were under surveillance by the Church, or rather by both the Catholic and the new Protestant Churches, and also by numerous secular authorities who often came to contradictory decisions, making it difficult for even the most orthodox printer, however obedient, to avoid the rigours of censorship. Cramoisy himself, having received copies of Santarelli's famous *Tractatus contra tyrannos* from Rome, was ordered by the Parlement to pay a fine.[226] Printers and booksellers who were not brought to trial at least once in their lives were rare, although normally the sentence was light. And if booksellers willing to break the law were numerous, and their profession required as much, they did not have the stature of their predecessors in the 16th century. The authorities sensed as much, and often showed an extraordinary leniency towards them at the same moment as they meted our harsh punishment to authors. So Sommaville, Estoc and Rocollet, who published the *Parnasse satyrique*, were not brought to trial, whereas the author Théophile de Viau was condemned, *in absentia*, to death by burning. This leniency made some think that they were actually the agents of Father Garasse, Théophile's mortal enemy! But the government knew well enough that there was no point in attacking the printers and booksellers who, though they might print and sell forbidden books, did so nearly always out of cupidity, not conviction: they had to supply their clients. Sometimes, though, they may have acted out of loyalty to an author or the parties who protected him. Such seems to be the case with the publishers of Port-Royal, such as Desprez and Le Petit who printed the *Provinciales*. They ran risks they knew to be grave, despite the friendship and sympathy their patrons enjoyed even in the Chancellery itself.[228] Through their representatives they would keep in touch with the reactions of the Chancellery and the members of the government, and they would try to halt publication before any serious investigation had started.

The printers who worked on their own without powerful friends were in a more exposed position. These were poor men who, with nothing to publish, occasionally had to resign themselves to the risk of printing some pamphlet or other. From the time of Colbert they were hunted without pity and many were imprisoned in the Bastille. The same fate was prepared for those who operated not in banned books but in piracies. One Ribou was gaoled several times for libels on the King, and he escaped the galleys only through ill health.[229]

The situation changed again at the end of the 17th century, when the struggle against royal absolutism began to develop after the Revocation of the Edict of Nantes, and took a new form during the 18th century at the time of the Enlightenment and the *Encyclopédie*. Religious passions and persecutions flared up and many printers were forced to flee abroad where they printed vitriolic pamphlets intended to do as much damage as possible to the King who had driven them into exile. From this a polemical literature developed, and at the same time the printer-journalist and the daily newspaper appeared on the scene. In these struggles printers and booksellers were of central importance. The *philosophes*, who were in continual conflict with authority over censorship and wanted the widest possible diffusion for their own works, needed to value their publishers afresh. Men of letters had often to be their own publishers and printers in order to propagate the new ideas, just as they had had to be in the 16th century. Beaumarchais, for example, opened a printing shop in Kehl to bring out a complete edition of Voltaire out of the reach of the French censors. In frontier towns, just outside France, writers of secondary importance, above all journalists, issued books and news sheets from small printing shops, helping to spread the radical ideas and writings of the philosophers. Pierre Rousseau was one of these.[230] Born in 1716 at Toulouse, he was taught there by the Jesuits, and then enrolled in the Faculty of Medicine in Montpellier. Having given up his studies, he came to Paris at the age of 24. A polemicist who had literary ambitions, he frequented the cafés near the Tuileries and the Palais-Royal – all the public places where politics and the arts were eagerly discussed – and made friends with men such as D'Alembert. Rousseau wrote plays and in 1750 founded a paper, *Les Affiches*. At that time the *Encyclopédie* was beginning to appear and Rousseau was carried away with enthusiasm for the views it expressed. His aim thereafter was to start a *Journal Encyclopédique* and to promote the works of the encyclopaedists by means of a special publishing company.

But the first two volumes of the *Encyclopédie* were suspended. D'Alembert and Diderot had many problems to contend with and obviously Rousseau would get no privilege for any *Journal Encyclopédique*. Then he thought of Liège, a town where he could easily be in touch with all the countries of Europe while remaining close to France. Thanks to the brothers Paris, leading bankers who were prepared to protect the philosophers, he managed to get a recommendation to some agents of the prince-bishop of Liège, and obtained authorisation to start a fortnightly newspaper in the town. He had to flee the place after four years, in 1759, after protests from the clergy, and went first to Brussels and finally to Bouillon. From then on he prospered, busying himself with editing his journal. He drew literary men round him to write for it, and his brother-in-law, Maurice Weissenbruch, managed the printing side. Every other week a thick issue came out, almost a book in itself.

Later Rousseau and his brother-in-law engineered even more efficient propaganda on behalf of the *philosophes* through their large and enterprising publishing concern called the *Société Typographique*, established in 1769 with a new printing house of six presses which poured out books across Europe for 25 years, among them the novels and stories of Voltaire, the *Fables* and *Contes* of La Fontaine, the *Histoire générale des dogmes et opinions philosophiques*, the *Essai sur les règnes de Claude et de Néron* as well as a complete set of Diderot's works, the complete works of Helvétius, the *Mémoires sur la Banque de Madrid* by Mirabeau, and other works by Voltaire, Jean-Jacques Rousseau, and their friends.

Numerous other writers and propagandists for the Enlightenment were now at work, all issuing books and newspapers from the printing shops they had set up. But a small number of great publishers had a still greater impact. The new philosopher-bookseller was the equivalent of what Gryphe had been in the age of Rabelais: a combination of businessman and man of taste, supporting the new ideas for reasons both of conviction and self-interest. In the course of their struggles against censorship such men became the friends and confidants of Diderot, Voltaire or Rousseau. Le Breton for a time held such a position. He may well have been the first to conceive the idea of the *Encyclopédie* and played a key role in its development and publication. Others were foreigners who helped in the struggle against the French police from behind the shelter of their national frontiers, like the important Dutch publisher Marc-Michel Rey, friend of Jean-Jacques Rousseau, whose neurotic distrust he managed to overcome. He asked Rousseau to be godfather to his daughter, and published the majority of his works.[231] Gabriel and Philibert Cramer from Geneva were of the same characteristic type. They were the official publishers of Voltaire, men of the world and suave diplomats, people of high culture and shrewd businessmen. Coming from a family of booksellers and connected on their mother's side with the de Tournes, they were direct descendants of the famous humanist publisher of 16th-century Lyons. They were European in range, operating from Stockholm to Naples, from Venice to Cadiz, Linz, Alicante, Lisbon and of course Paris. Having great wealth, they played an active part in Genevan politics. Philibert, indeed, slowly withdrew from publishing in order to concentrate on his public appointments which brought him into personal contact with Choiseul and Necker. He moved in the highest society. He was invited to La Rochefoucauld's house, and Voltaire described him as a man of *esprit* and good taste. His brother Gilbert was perhaps less outstanding. He remained a publisher, and was a musician and a great lover of women. At one time he was a member of the Genevan Council of Two Hundred, and later he was an auditor. A friend of Voltaire and an actor as well, he appeared in almost all the plays of Ferney and the Délices, as did his wife. She was ebullient, sensitive, and lively, and was in regular correspondence with Rousseau. The Cramer brothers were fashionable and cultivated publishers but on the fringe of the aristocracy, and so appealed to Voltaire, almost all of whose works they published between 1756 and 1775, even the most outrageous, like the *Dictionnaire philosophique*. Through his recommendation they also published the works of D'Alembert and the Abbé Morellot, distributing them throughout Europe and smuggling them into France.

Largely because circumstances in the 18th century favoured the development of publishing (as they did in the 16th century) small publishers, like Pierre Rousseau and Beaumarchais, and great ones, like Rey and Cramer, were able to expand their enterprises. This was a time of great material affluence and fevered intellectual life: everyone was interested in intellectual matters, and cultured and enterprising booksellers could confidently launch grand schemes. Coustelier gave his name to a collection of early French poetry which is still famous. Barbou published a series of Latin classics in an attractive format. Panckouke assumed publication of an enormous systematic encyclopaedia in 166 volumes. Meanwhile Zedler at Leipzig brought out a universal lexicon in 64 huge volumes. This gives some indication of the role played by the big publishers in the world of letters.

The rapid expansion of trade, a result of the new demand for fine editions, of a general increase in the number of titles published, and of the growth of the newspaper, prompted the search for new ways to improve the appearance of publications and above all for technical improvements to increase production. Throughout Europe in the 18th century we find a new race of printers, worthy successors of Aldus and Tory. Often former letter founders and designers, they introduced new founts, and their researches into presswork and papermaking paved the way for the technical revolution which transformed the trade at the beginning of the 19th century.

Baskerville (1706–1775), an English writing master and monumental engraver, became interested in typography in 1750 and spent two years designing a new fount, cutting his own punches, while perfecting a new process which gave a satin finish to his unlaid paper, known as wove. He published his first book, an edition of Virgil of outstanding quality, in 1757 and died a ruined man. His materials, bought from his widow by Beaumarchais, were used in the Kehl edition of Voltaire.[233] The Italian Bodoni, engaged as a very young compositor in the Tipografia della Propaganda in Rome, also cut a new fount on different principles. Requested to set up an official press at Parma by the Infante Ferdinand in 1768, he continued to cut types or have them cut and published books of remarkable quality.[234]

Baskerville, Bodoni, or to take another example, Caslon were all printers who gave their names to founts which have been a source of inspiration down to the present. The most outstanding and in some ways most characteristic of these artist-technicians who were in love with their art and felt passionately about fine printing were the Didot family.[235] This typographic dynasty began with François Didot who published the Abbé Prévost and the *Histoire générale des voyages*. One of his eleven children, François-Ambroise Didot improved printing equipment which had remained unchanged since the 16th century, his greatest achievement being the perfecting of a single-action press. He engraved new letters, introduced wove paper into France, brought much needed order into the confused measurement of type by inventing the points system, and published many fine works illustrated in the style of the painter David. Under the Empire his sons Pierre and Firmin continued his work while another Didot, Pierre-François, bought, in 1789, the paper mill at Essonnes where the first continuous papermaking machinery was constructed seven years later.

4
Authors and their Rights

The last profession associated with printing, one that was bound to the press and was born because of it, is the profession of author.

Today the author benefits from the sale of copies of his work by means of the royalty system, which is now taken for granted, but was a long time in conception. Before the advent of printing it was inconceivable. True, manuscripts were mass produced by copyists, but how could anyone imagine remuneration of the author for a text in which he had no monopoly and which anyone could copy? In such conditions an author could not be assured of an income, and if he did not write for the sake of prestige alone, he turned for protection to some great personage, a Maecenas, and sold copies made under the patron's supervision. After the introduction of printing there were few immediate changes. Printers, like the copyists before them, had no monopoly in the texts published and for the most part they printed ancient texts, for which they required only secondary aid by scholars and linguists in choosing a manuscript to edit and in proof correcting. It was as a proof corrector rather than author that the literary man made his entrance into publishing. Humanist scholars with an interest in letters became readers for the press, as we have already described.

Soon the supply of unpublished texts dried up. Piracies began and multiplied; and to protect themselves printers sought privileges granting them a monopoly for a number of years on the publication and sale of works they had printed. In addition they sought out new work to publish. Authors, sensing the influence they could bring to bear through the press, submitted their work to booksellers. For many committed humanists the problem of making a living was of pressing immediacy. Not all were lucky enough or reliable enough to find regular employment as proof readers. To ask money from the bookseller to whom they had entrusted their manuscript and who would profit from its publication – to sell the fruits of their intellect – was not yet common practice before the late 16th century. Even thereafter many authors still refused to accept the new convention and many continued to have recourse to the traditional system of patronage. When a work of theirs was issued the contemporaries of Erasmus asked for a number of copies, and they would send them to some great nobleman and patron of letters with a flattering dedication, for which present they anticipated reward in the form of a gift of money. In the 16th century this, and the custom which was quickly adopted of printing, at the beginning or end of the book, letters or laudatory verses to a powerful patron, seemed quite the honourable thing to do, and was usually recompensed. Authors were then free to let it be known how mean the patron in question was if the sum they received was insufficient. The humanist Petrus de Ponte, the 'blind man of Brussels', disappointed by his patrons, dedicated a work to his pupils, denouncing the lack of generosity shown by those in whom he had placed his hopes of financial reward.

This system, which seems distasteful to us, seemed natural at the time and more creditable than selling your copy to a publisher. When one of

Erasmus' enemies reproached him for taking money from his publishers, he replied indignantly that he received nothing beyond what the friends to whom he gave his copies never failed to offer him. We need not be under any illusions: Erasmus lived well on the rewards of his writing. He enormously increased the numbers of dedicatees; his reputation allowed him to demand more complimentary copies from his publishers; and he organised a network of agents across the length and breadth of Europe who were active in the distribution of his works and in the collecting of his rewards.[237]

Authors who received a large number of complimentary copies, as Erasmus did, seem to have been few in number throughout the 16th century, as the Plantin-Moretus archives show. In some cases even, when a limited edition was announced, Plantin required of his authors that they undertake to buy a proportion of the copies printed. Nicholas Mammeranus had to promise to buy 400 to 500 copies of his *Epithalamia Alexandri Farnesii* in 1586, and again in 1572 Serianus bought 186 copies of his *Commentarii in Levitici Librum* for 200 florins, out of an edition of 300 copies. Such cases were common, especially with editions of works of music. Authors are still requested to subsidise editions of books with slight appeal, but it is none the less surprising that in Plantin's time few authors received any honorarium at all. Sometimes he made his authors a present of some books, as he did to Georges Buchanan. Thus Jean Isaac, who received 100 copies of his *Grammatica Hebraea* (1564), and Augustin Hunnaeus, to whom Plantin gave 200 copies of his *Dialectica*, must have reckoned themselves lucky. At other times Plantin gave trifling presents to his authors: in 1567 Adrian Funius received 6 lengths of fine velvet for his *Nomenclator* and was given lodgings for three days. Occasionally Plantin did give his authors sums of money in addition to copies of their books, but that was unusual. Pierre de Savone had 100 copies and 45 florins for his *Instruction et manière de tenir livres de compte* in 1567 and in 1581 Guicciardini received 50 copies and 81 florins for revising his *Descrittione di tutti i Paesi Bassi*.

Soon, however, it becomes usual for authors to sell their manuscript outright to a bookseller for a sum. Many, especially the gentlemen of quality, refused to accept money, but most writers – particularly dramatists and novelists – were not so proud. Boileau and La Bruyère did not sell their manuscripts (for which fact they did not fail to claim credit), whereas Benserade, Corneille, Rotrou, La Fontaine and Molière sold their comedies and tragedies. In 1614 Honoré d'Urfé, too great an aristocrat to accept money from his bookseller, gave his valet the third part of *Astrée* and so the valet received from the bookseller 1,000 livres as an honorarium plus 60 copies of the edition. After 1660 the figures have often survived, and some quite considerable amounts are involved: Scarron had 1,000 francs for his *Roman comique*, 11,000 for *Virgile travesti*; Varillas obtained 30,000 francs from Barbin for his poem *Hérésie* and the heirs of M. de Saci received 33,000 francs from the bookseller Desprez in exchange for his manuscript.[239] One can understand the well-known lines of Boileau:

> 'Je sçai qu'un noble esprit peut sans honte et sans crime
> Tirer de son esprit un tribut légitime
> Mais je ne puis souffrir ces auteurs renommés
> Qui, dégoûtés de gloire et d'argent affamés,
> Mettent leur Apollon aux gages d'un libraire
> Faisant d'un art divin un métier mercenaire.'

But authors who could command large sums from their publishers were very few. In fact, except for a few isolated cases mainly from the end of the century, the money an author received was still meagre. To subsist it was necessary to have recourse to other means and to continue to sell prefaces and dedications. Corneille dedicated his *Cinna* to a financier, M. de Montauron, who gave him 200 écus,[240] and this is only one example among many. The nobility, more out of concern for their own prestige than love of literature, continued to support writers in their households. And what self-abasement the competition for Louis XIV's pensions drew from authors! The simple fact was that the man of letters had not yet lost his dependence on the high and the mighty, at least in France.

This was the situation because at that time authors' rights were not protected. Once his manuscript was bought outright, the author had no further rights over the publication of his work. Further, since the principle of literary property did not exist, any bookseller had the right to publish any manuscript which he had managed to procure without consulting the author. For example, we know that the bookseller Ribou, after successfully getting hold of the text of *Précieuses ridicules*, forthwith published it without Molière's authorisation and even went so far as to secure a privilege in the play which legally forbade the author to publish it himself. Molière succeeded in quashing this privilege[241], but not all writers were so lucky or well established. In any case the author's remuneration was likely to raise all kinds of dispute and provoke bitterness. The amount an author was given was worked out and paid before publication, but the difficulty was to estimate the likely success of the book – if reprints were produced the author would get no more. It is understandable in such circumstances that booksellers often had occasion to complain of the pretensions of authors, whom they saw as inclined to overestimate their work and so demand excessive sums for their manuscripts. It is equally understandable that many writers had the impression that they had been cheated, especially since in the 18th century booksellers were commonly able to prolong their privileged rights in a book and in practice enjoyed a permanent monopoly over the right to publish a book once they had bought the manuscript, thus, occasionally, building great fortunes while the creators of those fortunes or their descendants were left in penury.

From the end of the 16th century many authors also tried their luck as publishers on their own account, with the intention of obtaining the profit of their work for themselves and of supervising the circulation of their books. Cyrano de Bergerac and Saint-Amant[242] did so, along with many others in France, Germany and England. Such initiative was usually frowned on by booksellers and printers, who tried to hinder by various means the sale of books 'privately published by the author'. Their corporations even got together to try and ban the practice, sometimes successfully. In 1773, largely through pressure of public opinion, this type of enterprise by writers, which more or less required that they should turn themselves into businessmen, narrowly failed to become the general rule in France. Meanwhile in Germany writers like Lessing published their own works and writers' co-operative publishing houses were started, of which the most important was the *Gelehrtenrepublik* of Klopstock, set up in 1774.[243]

The current solution to the problem of author's rights was eventually worked out in the legal recognition of copyright, which is vested in the author for a fixed period of time during which it is exclusively his, and after which it reverts to the public domain. With copyright came the system by which the author shares, whenever practicable, in the profits arising from the sale of his work through various types of contractual arrangement.

England led the way here. From the 17th century, it seems, publishers sometimes undertook not to put out a second impression without the author's consent, which was naturally not obtained without a further payment. When Milton sold the manuscript of *Paradise Lost* on 27th April, 1667 for £5 to Samuel Simmons, he was promised another £5 by Simmons if the first edition of 1,300 copies sold out, and the same sum was to be given to him when the second and third editions, should they be printed, sold out. An Act of Queen Anne in 1710 tried to regularise this procedure, the author and not the bookseller being legally recognised for the first time as the proper holder of copyright. Henceforth it was the author who was required to register his work in the Stationers' Register to secure his rights and so retain control over the publication and sale of his work for 14 years, and for a further 14 years if he was still alive at the expiry of the first period. English authors from that date began to receive, on occasion, sizeable sums from their publishers.[244]

On the continent the recognition of authors' rights was delayed longer. Booksellers continued to buy manuscripts outright and thereby claim copyright. However, manuscript prices seem to have risen during the 18th century. In the second half of the century the publishers of Leipzig, in Germany, sometimes paid large sums for a manuscript. French authors were not well paid by their publishers until after 1750. The publisher Prault gave Voltaire 1,000 francs for his *Enfant prodigue*, and that was more than Crébillon or Destouches received, neither of whom was an unknown author. According to J. J. Rousseau, Condillac was hard put to it to sell his *Essai sur l'origine des connaissances humaines* for 300 francs to Durand in 1747; Rousseau had 500 francs for his *Discours sur l'inégalité*, 600 for his *Lettre à d'Alembert*, and 6,000 for the *Emile*. Buffon made more than 15,000 francs for each volume of his *Histoire naturelle*, although he incurred heavy costs for the plate making which was done at his expense. In general however from 1770 even the second rank of authors were earning higher rewards.[245]

The bookseller, although paying more for the manuscript, was not normally willing to include the author in his profits. It is true that, from the beginning of the century, Thomas Corneille seems to have had an interest in the sale of his Dictionary, but this was most unusual. Sometimes, in such exceptional cases, publishers agreed to pay part of the profits to the authors once all their expenses had been covered. Rousseau concluded such an agreement in 1742 for his *Dissertation sur la musique moderne*, but no profits ever came his way. D'Alembert did the same in 1753 for his *Mélanges de littérature, d'histoire et de philosophie*. However a system which, in Diderot's words, required 'too much trust on one side, too much integrity on the other' was the exception.

Increasingly, throughout the century, authors wrote pamphlets and went to law to establish their rights, until eventually certain procedures were agreed by the trade. It was particularly galling for authors to see the copyright on their work sold when a publisher went out of business, without them gaining anything from it. In 1736, when a booksellers' syndicate bought up the stock belonging to the firm of Ribou, including five plays by Crébillon, the latter opposed this at law. They then made him an offer of 500 francs outright if he would revise the works and, being short of money, he accepted. Fifteen years later in 1752 he obtained a royal privilege for a collected edition of his works printed at the Imprimerie Royale. The booksellers who had bought Crébillon's manuscript opposed the registration of the privilege which was to begin in 1755 after the expiration of the one which they had obtained in 1746 (but for which they would normally have expected to obtain an extension).

The outcome of this affair is unknown. But publishers in general soon received an important set-back. In 1761 La Fontaine's grand-daughters secured copyright in his *Fables* and *Contes*. The publishers tried to resist with the argument that these works were their property by virtue of an agreement of 1686 signed by Barbin, La Fontaine's publisher, and subsequent extensions of that agreement up to the present date. A decree of the Council of State dated 14th December, 1761 declared their case invalid in the light of the arguments of Malesherbes. Authors' rights were again confirmed by a judgment which rendered invalid a distraint obtained by the publishers upon an author called Luneau de Boisgermain, who was publishing his books at his own expense and retailing them.

Thereafter, memoir after memoir dealt with the rights of authors and publishers. The publishers instructed Diderot to defend their position, while Malesherbes and then Sartines, by virtue of their position of supervisors of the book trade, were set to examine the whole question. Both found favour of authors. Finally in August, 1777, five decrees were passed in an attempt to settle the matter and to them was soon added a further decree of 30th July, 1778. Henceforth writers would enjoy perpetual copyright, while booksellers would hold a temporary copyright, for a period of 10 years at least, which could be renewed only for a further one quarter of that period. Authors obtaining copyright in an edition had the right to sell their work in their own homes, and could have a printer reprint it as often as they wished at their own expense, and have a bookseller sell the copies, without such arrangements being considered a transfer of copyright.

Sixteen years later, the Convention passed a law regularising the rights of authors which is the basis of modern legislation: the author had the right to sell and distribute his work and to assign his rights in whole or part, and rights in the literary property of an author were extended to his heirs for ten years after his death, a period increased today to 50 years. And so, slowly, laws analogous to these, passed mainly at the end of the 18th and the beginning of the 20th century, have established authors' rights throughout Europe. From this point on, authors were in a position to defend their interests. In the 19th century most of them concluded contracts with their publishers for the printing of a specific number of copies of their work, and reserved their rights if a new edition was required. The craft of authorship did not automatically guarantee a large income. Balzac, who it is true was hopeless at keeping accounts, lived in crippling debt despite prolific output. But at least writers could look for remuneration which was commensurate with the success of their work.[246]

So little by little the profession of author was created. Slowly the author came to recognise and to obtain recognition for his right to profit from his work and to have rights over his product. At the same time he freed himself from ties which had long bound him to a private patron or to a state pension. But some constraints remained. Now that he had a share in the profits he had to try and produce a best seller; and so he had to aim at the widest possible readership. In the end this perhaps served to encourage hack writing rather than work of the highest quality.

The Geography of the Book

I

The Journeys of Printers

Gutenberg, Fust and Schoeffer, once they had perfected printing in their workshops in Mainz, must have wondered whether they would retain their monopoly or would have to face competition. Schoeffer appears to have tried to stop any leakage of technical information, and there is a tradition that he required his workmen to swear an oath that they would not reveal the secrets he had taught them. But too many inventors had for some years been seeking to resolve the problem of printing, and the new invention was of too great importance from both an intellectual and a commercial point of view for the secret to be kept. There is a story that the King of France sent a spy to Mainz in 1458.[247] The inventors perhaps had the monopoly for ten years, no longer – for Menthelin printed a Bible at Strasbourg in 1459. Several new printing shops opened in Mainz. Soon there were printing shops in the Rhineland towns and by 1475 there were many printers in the Po Valley. Paris, Lyons and Seville and many other towns had workshops by that date.[248]

For a long time the printer's art, like that of the gunsmith, was almost exclusively German – the master printers in the first ateliers were either apprentices of Gutenberg and Schoeffer or workmen who had learned from these apprentices. The history of this small group of men is remarkable. Their enterprise and spirit of adventure amazes us. They were willing to leave their master's shop and travel the length and breadth of Europe, like many other journeymen of the period, carrying their equipment with them and practising and instructing in the new art. They must have led nomadic lives, their chief asset experience, their equipment of the most elementary sort; they would stop in a town, hope for orders locally, probably suffering poverty very often. What they sought was someone to provide capital so that they could establish themselves permanently, and a town which met the conditions for the establishment of a successful printing shop. Nothing stopped them: did not Jerome Münzer, a doctor of Nuremberg, meet three German printers already established in Granada in 1494, only two years after that city's liberation from the Arabs? Two others, from Strasbourg and Nordlingen, settled in far away São Tomé, an unhealthy island off the African coast in the Gulf of Guinea.

Johann Neumeister,[250] for example, was a cleric who quite probably worked with Gutenberg (he is thought to have been his associate in 1459–60). He left the Rhineland a few years later and, like many others among the first printers, succumbed to the lure of Italy, where he hoped for big profits since it was a country which respected learning and literature. Was he perhaps numbered among the group of German workmen whom Sweynheym and Pannartz took with them to Subiaco and to Rome in 1464, or was he summoned to Rome with Ulrich Hahn by Cardinal Torquemada? We know he had settled at Foligno, a small Umbrian cathedral town, by 1470, and had found backers and partners in Emiliano Orfini, a goldsmith, and his brother Marietto, who were followed by Evangelista Angelini. There he published Bruni's *Historia belli adversus Gothos*, the *Epistolae ad familiares* of Cicero and the first printed editions of Dante.

But his partners gave up, presumably finding that there was little profit to be made in printing. Business was tough for German printers in Italy. The book market was still ill-organised and could not support many printers; in Rome itself Sweynheym and Pannartz were near bankruptcy with a warehouse full of unsold works. They had to apply to Pope Sixtus IV for aid. Neumeister was forced to return home after a spell in gaol for debt and the craftsmen he had gathered together dispersed. Some went to Perugia where Bracio Baglione, a rich patrician, set up a new printing business. Neumeister did not follow them. He almost certainly returned to Mainz. It was probably there that he printed an edition of the *Meditationes* of Torquemada in 1479, illustrating them with engravings on metal which betray a Rhenish origin. But he did not stay in that town, for competition was too strong and capital was probably in short supply. We surmise he moved on by way of Basel, where he would have met with many fellow-workers, to Lyons, a town into which there poured a flood of German printers; then he set out on the route to Toulouse, a road made busy by the merchants of Lyons, some of whom already carried books with them as part of their stock. In 1480 he was at Albi, a rich and important cathedral town, where a printer could hope to start a good business. He may have been invited there by the bishop, an Italian called Lerico. There he printed a little moral treatise of Aeneas Silvius called *De amoris remedio*, a *Historia septem sapientium*, another edition of the *Meditationes* of Torquemada with the same plates, and a large folio missal – a work with a guaranteed sale because it was ordered by the Chapter at Lyons (in fact sales were so certain that a pirate edition was issued almost immediately by a Lyons printer Matthew Husz). Neumeister left Albi for Lyons, perhaps at the request of the Bishop of Lyons, Charles de Bourbon. There in 1485 he produced a new missal of particularly high quality. He also found a new patron, the Count Archbishop of Vienne in Dauphiné, Angelo Catone, friend of Philip de Comines who wrote his *Mémoires* at the Archbishop's request. In 1489 Neumeister printed for the diocese a breviary corrected according to the instructions of Archbishop Catone. In 1495 he published the missal of the diocese of Uzès in partnership with Topié. Despite what seems to have been a busy life, and despite all his travels, printing brought no lasting prosperity to this veteran colleague of Gutenberg. In 1498 he was classed as a pauper and exempted from taxation, and in the same year was forced to seek employment as a journeyman in the business of his old partner Topié. Eventually he died in obscure circumstances in 1507 or 1508.

Not all of Neumeister's contemporaries suffered the same fate; many did well and established themselves more quickly. But his example is instructive, for it shows us how the first printers – the colleagues of Gutenberg and of Schoeffer, and later on their pupils – taught the craft of printing to all Europe. It also shows why nomadism was a common characteristic of a printer's life. Over a long period we encounter these travelling printers. During the 16th and even the 17th centuries the south-west of France is particularly crowded with travelling printers who stop in one little town or another for a few months, or even for a few years, before setting out again. Nor would their life have seemed peculiar. We have only to compare them to the Belgian stone masons who specialised in making altars and who led the same itinerant life at the same date. In the 17th century, many journeymen, in the course of their travels around France, found the opportunity to stop in a town and settle down, having found at one and the same time a wife and sufficient capital to set themselves up in business. Or they returned after an interval of several years to a town which had seemed to them to be particularly promising as a place to set up in business, whether as a printer or as a bookseller.

2
Places to Set Up Business

What were the attractions which drew the first printers, who had set out from Mainz and the Rhineland, and their pupils and rivals after them, to certain towns? Who supplied these penniless men with capital? How did printing, over a period of 300 years, spread slowly across the whole of Western Europe?

The prime factor in the spread of the press, especially in the earliest days, was the interest certain influential men and institutions had in making texts accessible. Let us look first at the individual patrons. Men like Jean de Rohan, Lord of Bréhan-Loudéac, not quite so rich and powerful as his name might suggest (for he was descended from the younger son of a Rohan), but a man of letters who owned a magnificent château still to be seen close to St. Étienne du Gué de l'Isle. Nearby he installed two printers, Jean Crès and Robin Fouquet, in 1484, and in the space of nine years they produced ten books which together provided an ideal course of study for any cultivated aristocrat of the time: *Le Trépassement de Notre-Dame*; *Les Loys des Trépassés avec Le Pèlerinage Maistre Jean de Mung en vision*; *La Patience de Grisélidis*; *Le Bréviaire des Nobles*, a poem in 445 stanzas; *L'Oraison de Pierre de Nesson*; *Le Songe de la Pucelle*; *Le Miroer d'Or de l'Ame Pécheresse*; *Les Coustumes et Constitutions de Bretaigne*, and of course a *Vie de Jésus-Christ*, with the inevitable *Secret des Secrets d'Aristote*.[252]

Examples like this are not rare. Sometimes even uninfluential people invited printers to their houses, so great was the interest aroused by the printing press. But on the whole the men most favourably disposed to the new art were the ecclesiastics. In the beginning the Church was strongly in favour of the new process. The value of the press was evident in the 15th and early 16th century because of the destruction, during the wars, of many churches and of the liturgical books in them. The canons of Dôle, for instance, complained in 1508 of the loss of 'their music books and other things needful for the singing of matins' in the sack of their town by the French. Canons after all have to be able to sing matins. Printers worked hard to provide church books, for there was a large demand; the Besançon missal is proof of that – after its printing at Salins in 1484, it was printed in Paris by Nicolas Du Pré in 1497 and pirated in Lyons by Maillet in the same year under a false Venetian imprint. Multiple reprints like this indicate the number of copies of such works that were sought. In many places bishops had printers come and set up shop in order to print the books they needed, as was the case with Neumeister. In many cases mere canons decided to defray the cost of setting up a press to turn out missals and breviaries. Charles Du Pré, the finest printer of his day in Paris, was invited to Chartres by a canon of the cathedral and set up in the canons' house to produce a breviary and missal for diocesan use in 1482–3.[253]

Liturgical works were not the only commissions given to printers by ecclesiastics, although the demand for them was the greatest. The scriptures and theological works were commonly published in order to assist theologians in their labours; works of classical antiquity and texts for students' use were often published for general educational purposes; above all, works of popular piety in tract forms were common. The press thus seemed best fitted to serve the needs of scholarship, education and popular devotion. The first important book printed in Mainz was the Bible and we hear the Archbishop of Mainz, Bertold of Henneberg, describe printing as 'a divine art'. German bishops often issued indulgences to men who printed and sold books. The clergy's enthusiasm for printing appears to have been general and the author of the Chronicle of Koelhoff could write, on seeing the work of the first printers: 'What an ascent towards God! What ecstatic devotion must we feel on reading the many books which printing has given us!' And we read in an edition of the *Fasciculus Temporum* the following lines: 'Printing, lately invented in Mainz, is the art of arts, the science of sciences. Thanks to its rapid spread the world is endowed with a treasure house of wisdom and knowledge, till now hidden from view. An infinite number of works which very few students could have consulted in Paris or Athens or in the libraries of other great university towns, are now translated into all languages and scattered abroad among all the nations of the earth.'[254]

Churchmen, particularly those who were interested in classical literature, took the lead in supporting the press. In 1466, Cardinal Torquemada appears to have contributed to the cost of inviting Ulrich

Hahn of Ingolstadt to Rome and entrusted the printing of his *Meditationes* to him, while Cardinal Caraffa in his turn invited George Lauer of Würzburg to Rome in 1469. He printed at least 33 works there between 1470 and 1484, including the *Canzoniere* of Petrarch. In Paris and elsewhere there were many similar cases.

Numerous monasteries also welcomed printers into their midst and monks even did some printing. Wenssler, an early printer, was invited to Cluny;[255] while John Metlinger of Augsburg went to the Abbey of Citeaux at Dijon at the invitation of Jean de Cirey, the abbot, moving there from Dôle in 1490.[256] In Germany, the Brothers of the Common Life founded a press at Rostock and in one of the first books printed by them termed printing 'the universal mother of all knowledge' and 'handmaid of the Church'. Of themselves they said they were 'God's priests, teaching not by the spoken word but by the written word'.[257]

Among the canons regular of Beromünster in Aargau a press was in use by 1470 and the Benedictines of Saints Ulrich and Afra had one in 1472 at Augsburg, in 1474 at Bamberg and in 1475 at Blauberen; the Premonstrants of Schussenried had one in 1478, while the Augustinian hermits of Nuremberg and the Benedictines of St. Peter at Erfurt obtained theirs in 1479.[258] In Italy there was a similar development. Leaving aside the disputed example at Subiaco, there was a press in use in the monastery of St. James of Ripoli in Florence for more than twenty years, and there Marsilio Ficino's works were among those printed.[259]

These are a few examples among many. But despite all this activity, the Church could not assume in the age of printing the same rôle as in the age of manuscripts, when she had been able to control the distribution of texts. To get hold of a printer, to provide him with the necessary capital and to give him some commissions, or to install a press in a monastery and teach the monks to print, was not enough when printing was really an industry. If a printing press was not, after a certain period of time, firmly based on a business footing and capable of realising profits or at least breaking even, then it was doomed to failure. Consequently, among all the presses founded by rich patrons or churchmen, or set up as a result of their encouragement, only those which existed amid conditions suitable for commercial success lasted any length of time.

The crucial problem was that of finding a market. It was vital to discover, preferably on the spot, a regular and fairly extensive clientele. For this reason, as we have mentioned, presses multiplied and prospered in the great university towns. The history of the first printers in Paris is particularly enlightening in this respect. There is no better example of the frame of mind in which, and the motives for which, a small group of clerics could be led to invite some printers into a town; nor of the favourable conditions, and the freedom to alter their business strategy, which allowed these early printers to succeed in establishing themselves and prosper.

The English military occupation and the wars of the first half of the 15th century had damaged the educational institutions of Paris both financially and culturally. By the time printing was discovered, however, Paris had become once more a great university town with a large academic population drawn from all over France and other European countries. Its strength lay in Law, Medicine, the Liberal Arts and, above all, in Theology. Twenty-four stationers, supervised by four leading booksellers, were strictly organised on traditional lines and employed by the University to copy the indispensable texts: Hippocrates, Galen and their commentators for the Faculty of Medicine; the codes and their commentaries for the Faculty of Law; Aristotle and the commentaries of Aquinas, William of Ockham, Duns Scotus, and Buridanus, and the treatises of Alexander de Villedieu on doctrine, of Boethius on arithmetic, of John of Hollywood and Pierre d'Ailly on astronomy, for the Faculty of Arts. For the numerous students in the Faculty of Theology they supplied the Bible and the *Sententiae* of Peter Lombard. These same bookshops furnished certain other texts for clergy associated with the university who wished to build up a library of religious books: St. Augustine, St. Bernard, St. Bonaventure, Nicholas of Lyra, Vincent de Beauvais, which the richer clergy would be proud to possess, and, above all, Ludolphus of Saxony's *Life of Christ*, the sermons of Jacques de Voragine and other such works of devotional piety and practical morality. Another category was manuals for the guidance of confessors, which were in greater demand because they were of simple format, of more general use, and less costly and heavy than the massive folios which enshrined the Schoolmen and the Church Fathers.

However, the works of the Italian humanists began to make their way into France. The great Parisian university teachers of the end of the 14th and the beginning of the 15th centuries were no more ignorant than their 13th-century predecessors of classical studies and no more incapable of an elegant Latin prose style, for knowledge in these fields never entirely died out. In addition, contacts with Italy were close in the second half of the 15th century. Around 1470, Guillaume Fichet, who made numerous journeys to Italy, and who was to die in Rome, was the central figure of a group which professed, along with reverence for the doctrines of St. Thomas and of Scotus, a love of ancient Rome and of the Latin classics. This group felt the lack of accurate texts of the classics keenly. Although manuscript copies of the authors on the syllabus were relatively numerous, the copies of the works of Cicero, Virgil and Sallust were both rare and faulty. It would have been impossible to reproduce these texts exactly and in great number, if there had been no knowledge of the new technique of printing. Printed books had been known and used in Paris for several years. Fust and Schoeffer sold some of their stock there and Fust, who had in his youth been part of the German contingent at the university, had already made numerous business trips to Paris. He even had a permanent agent there, Hermann of Statboen. It was quite natural, then, that another German, Johann Heynlin von Stein, who was prior of the Sorbonne, should, in 1470, have had the idea of getting printers to come from Germany and of installing them in the buildings of the Sorbonne. This was how the first Paris press started. It was run by Ulrich Gering of Constance, Michael Friburger of Colmar (an arts graduate of the university of Basel who must have known Heynlin as a student) and their assistant, Martin Krantz, a journeyman printer from Heynlin's home town. The Sorbonne printed, in the course of three years, editions of the *Letters* and the treatise *On Orthography* of Gasparino of Bergamo, the works of Sallust and of Valerius Maximus, Cicero's *De Officiis*, Valla's *Elegantiae* and Fichet's *Rhetoric*, in which the author, who had encouraged the efforts of Heynlin and Gering, summarises the principles of a correct Latin prose style.

The circle of humanists at Paris was still small and men of letters few in number; the market was soon saturated. Moreover ancient texts to edit were hard to come by and when Fichet departed for Italy the inspiration of the group was gone. Gering and his two associates had to alter their objectives, consequently, and aim their editions no longer at the small number of humanists who had brought them to Paris, but at the university in general. Thanks to profits from the work done at the Sorbonne they were able to leave their old workshop, renew their equipment and pay for a new installation, probably larger than the old one, setting up an independent business which proved successful. This involved no break with their old patrons; after all Heynlin had once printed at the Sorbonne, on the same presses which had produced editions of the *Letters* of Plato, the *Tusculan Disputations* of Cicero and Scotus' *Commentaries* on the Fourth Book of Peter Lombard's *Sententiae*. The university of Paris was loyal to the doctrine of St. Thomas, and its leading spirits belonged to the old school, disciples of Scotus and St. Thomas at the same time as lovers of the classics.

The new press was opened at the Golden Sun (*Le Soleil d'Or*) in the Rue St. Jacques, and from it came the occasional classical text, notably of Virgil, and, to reach a wider public, the texts of the medieval philosophers, theologians and canon lawyers in black letter, not roman, type. Some works of Aristotle, the *Postillae* of Nicholas of Lyra, a new edition of the *Commentaries* of Scotus on the 4th book of the *Sentences*, which they had already published at the Sorbonne, were thus produced. But above all they concentrated on devotional works, treatises on everyday morality and manuals for confessors: all were sure sales. In this category there were the *Manipulus curatorum* of Guy de Montrocher, the devotional works of Johannes Nider, the *Sermons* of Utino and, inevitably, the *Golden Legend* of Jacques de Voragine.

The first Parisian printers were led to publish works for which there was most demand by the need to obtain high sales, in order to put their business on a firm footing and make profits. This proved to be the classic situation in the book trade: in every age thereafter the biggest firms have been obliged sooner or later to produce books not just for a restricted academic market, but also for a popular market. In addition to producing books intended for libraries and scientific publications, they have produced little books at cheaper prices and with a market large enough to guarantee frequent reprints.

By the time Gering started his new series he was not the only printer established near the university. Next door but one to the Golden Sun another press opened at the *Chevalier au Cygne* (the Knight and the Swan), opposite the Rue Fromentalle and almost opposite the *Collège de Cambrai*. It was run by two Germans, Peter Caesar, a master of arts, and his associate Johann Stoll. Caesar started in 1474 with the evergreen *Manipulus curatorum*; then, with Stoll, he edited the *Speculum vitae humanae* by Rodriguez, Bishop of Zamora, the *Casus longi* of the lawyer Bernard of Parma (1475), some treatises of Aeneas Sylvius, Panormitano's *Apparatus in Clementinas*. Like Gering they spent part of their time on works favoured by the humanists, like Perotto's *Rudimenta Grammaticae*, Eyb's *Margarita Poetica*, the works of Cicero, Sallust, Terence and Seneca. Often they had already been edited by Gering, and they were of course intended for the same limited market among the teachers and students of the university of Paris.

Such is the story of the birth of printing at Paris; it shows how the press began, and how it was possible for it to develop, thanks to the bookish tastes of the clerics associated with the university. The same developments could be shown to have taken place in all the great university towns of Europe, Cologne providing a most striking example. Later on, at the end of the 16th century, when Leyden got its university, which quickly became important, a flourishing publishing business of the foremost importance developed almost at once. Plantin was there for a time and his son-in-law set up a durable local business. Then the Elzeviers were appointed booksellers to the university and began in Leyden the astonishing career which was to make them perhaps the greatest publishers of their day.[261] Jean Maire, famous as the publisher of Descartes' *Discours de la Méthode*, worked near the Elzeviers. Similarly, when the French Protestants at Saumur founded a university, which was very popular at the beginning of the 17th century, the same developments are evident; large publishing firms like the Desbordes were very active there.[262]

But the university clientele was not the only market to attract printers and booksellers. The rich clergy to be found in archiepiscopal towns and in the larger cathedral cities were good buyers, while the presence in a town of Courts of Justice with all the lawyers attendant thereon provided still better prospects. Lawyers were as good clients for booksellers as ecclesiastics – perhaps even better ones. They bought not only religious works but books of Common Law and Statutes and, above all, books of secular literature. Often, to satisfy their tastes, French booksellers and printers set themselves up in the neighbourhood of the Parlements. Most of the bookshops in Paris and almost all the presses were on the Mont Ste. Geneviève and along the Rue St. Jacques, in the university quarter. But a very successful group of booksellers set themselves up inside the buildings of the Law Courts and in the neighbouring streets. There Vérard's main shop was to be found in the 15th century, Corrozet's in the 16th century, and in the 17th century those of Barbin and of Thierry, who published the major works of classical literature. The shop fronts and stalls of these booksellers stood next to those of haberdashers and drapers. Their clients were members of the Parlement, public prosecutors and defence counsel, the hordes of litigants, and also the fashionable gentlemen and the merchants who came to the Law Courts as a suitable place to take a stroll. They sold not so much text books on law as books about current affairs and works of literature, usually in French translation. Similar shops were to be found clustered around law courts in the French provinces and in other countries. In Rouen and in Poitiers many booksellers has stalls set up within the law courts. Later, in the 17th century, booksellers at the Hague established themselves within the Parliament building.[263]

A university, a High Court or a French Parlement guaranteed a market. This was their attraction for the printers and booksellers of the 15th and 16th centuries and the reason why many of them were important centres of printing and bookselling. At the end of the 16th century, all the towns of Europe where institutions of this type were to be found contained a considerable number of printers' workshops and of bookshops. At this time new universities were still being founded – especially in Protestant lands, as we have seen in the cases of Leyden and Saumur. These new universities provided a market for new printing and bookselling businesses. But in the greater part of Europe, and in Catholic Europe especially, the picture was very different: in these years of financial crisis the bookshops in business in the neighbourhood of the law courts had a hard time making ends meet, and were engaged in savage competition with each other. Meanwhile the universities were declining in importance and this often brought about the bankruptcy of those businesses in the book-trade which had opened up near them. Henceforward the booksellers and the printers who planned to set up in business were attracted elsewhere, often to the less important towns. In their search for a stable clientele, they established themselves not by a High Court but by a petty sessions. They lived off jobbing work on posters, official announcements, pamphlets; the growth of bureaucracy in the 17th century offered a new type of work. The Jesuits and Oratorians were active in the educational field, opening their Colleges in many towns, and these too provided work and attracted printers. The Jesuit colleges were particularly promising since they needed textbooks and other material for their educational programmes, as well as the devotional works and the polemical tracts which were an essential part of their ministry. In a small town called La Flèche where there had hitherto been no established printing business, the Jesuits in 1603 opened a college and brought in a printer, Jacques Rezé, who printed numerous books for the college and for the Order, whose colophon he adopted.

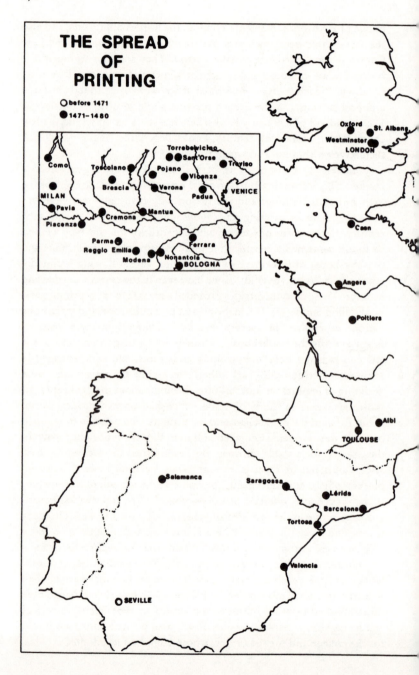

THE SPREAD OF PRINTING

○ before 1471
● 1471–1480

Como, Toscolano, Torrebelvicino, Sant'Orso, Treviso, Brescia, Pojano, Vicenza, Verona, Padua, MILAN, VENICE, Pavia, Cremona, Mantua, Piacenza, Parma, Reggio Emilia, Modena, Nonantola, Ferrara, BOLOGNA

Oxford, St. Albans, Westminster, LONDON, Caen, Angers, Poitiers, Albi, TOULOUSE, Salamanca, Saragossa, Lérida, Barcelona, Tortosa, Valencia, ○ SEVILLE

He was followed by three other printers and a large number of book-sellers who all established themselves in the neighbourhood of the college.

However, it was not only the printers who set up business in towns like La Flèche who did well. Clergymen and lawyers were not the only people who bought books. The idea of building up a personal library was popular among wealthy merchants, among the comfortable bourgeoisie, and even among the successful artisans in the commercial cities, especially in the 16th century. In such cities, moreover, enterprising businessmen were financing presses to publish books for export. Barthélemy Buyer who, as we have seen, founded the first publishing house in Lyons, was a merchant.[265] The skinners and furriers of Leipzig financed the book-sellers in that town in the 16th century, and when Plantin started he had little difficulty in finding backers in Antwerp.[266] Such towns, which maintained trading relations throughout Europe, provided increasingly efficient facilities for the settling of accounts and the transport of both paper and books.

Since transport by water was less costly, publishers opened businesses near ports – such as Rouen, whence books were shipped to Flanders, the Low Countries, Spain and, above all, to England. At the same time they could easily be transported to Paris, by boat up the Seine. In Spain, the Crombergers exported books from Seville to America. In the 18th century Rainier Leers transferred from The Hague to Rotterdam, thus facilitating the export of the writings of Bayle and Le Clerc to France, England and Northern Germany. Lübeck in the 15th century, Antwerp in the 16th and Amsterdam in the 17th were all further examples of ports in which great publishing houses established themselves.

3
Geography and Publishing

We will now try to establish the dates when printing spread out from its birthplace in Mainz to the various European countries, and to locate and describe the major publishing centres in the three and a half centuries between 1450 and 1800.

It may appear to the 20th-century reader, accustomed to technical revolutions, that printing spread very slowly. Yet when we think of the innumerable problems posed for the people of the 15th century by slow communications and a rudimentary technology; when we consider that in the years between 1450 and 1460 only a handful of men based in a few workshops in Mainz were acquainted with the secrets of printing, itself a craft of considerable technical sophistication by contemporary standards; when we remember the multiple difficulties that those who established new workshops had to overcome if they were to gather together the necessary raw materials (to take but one example – steel for the punch, copper for the moulds, a mixture of lead and of tin for the type); when we take into account the shortage of technicians, of engravers for the punch, of type-founders and of compositors – then it becomes evident that the spread of printing was far from slow. If we consider all the difficulties involved in setting up a new industry formed out of a number of different skills and processes, and in building up the commercial contacts to provide outlets for mass-produced books, then we must admit that printing in fact spread surprisingly rapidly, and that the men of the 15th century were particularly keen to innovate, as a few dates and a glance at a map will show.

From 1455–1460[267] there were several workshops in Mainz about which we know little, although it is plain that the most important was the one run by Fust and Schoeffer. At this early period printers were already planning trade outlets in university towns; Fust and Schoeffer were supplying books for sale in Frankfurt, Lübeck and Angers, and were about to open a bookshop in Paris.[268] Avignon also boasted bookshops selling printed books at this early period.[269] From 1460–1470 printing expanded markedly and the trade improved its organisation in its home country, Germany – a land of mines, possessing prosperous commercial cities with skilled metal workers and a rich merchant class to finance the new trade. By 1460 Mentelin, a former illuminator and episcopal notary, had opened his printing shop in Strasbourg. But he soon had to face competition from Heinrich Eggestein, keeper of the episcopal seal, and from Adolf Rusch, the mysterious printer of the 'crazy R', and from many others after them. Around the same date, Pfister, who may have been a pupil of Gutenberg's, set up a printing press at Bamberg, and soon began to publish illustrated books. From 1465 former journeymen who had worked under Gutenberg and Schoeffer were opening businesses in a number of towns: Ulrich Zell of Hanau, clerk to the diocese of Mainz, established himself in Cologne (1466), Berthold Ruppel set up shop in Basel (1468), Heinrich Kepfer and Johann Sensenschmidt in Nuremberg (1470), and at about the same date and in the same town Anton Koberger started his career as a printer and publisher. In 1468 the first book printed in Augsburg was published by Günther Zainer, while in 1464 or 1465 Conrad Sweynheym and Arnold Pannartz had left Germany for Italy to produce in the monastery of Subiaco (or perhaps in Rome) the first book printed in that country. In 1469, John of Speyer, also an immigrant from Germany, printed Cicero's *Epistolae ad familiares* in Venice. And in 1470 Neumeister, whose career we have already followed, started work in Foligno.[270]

Between 1470 and 1480 the industry's rate of growth increased still further. There were printers in Speyer in 1471, Ulm (1473), Lübeck (1475), Breslau (1475) and many other German towns. In Italy a great number of printers, mostly German, worked at Venice between 1470 and 1480; workshops opened at Trevi (1470), Ferrara, Milan, Bologna, Naples, Pavia, Savigliano, Treviso, Florence, Iesi, Parma, Mondovi, Brescia, Fivizzano and Mantua between 1471 and 1472; and many more followed soon after this in other cities. In France the first book printed in Paris was published by Gering and his assistants at the Sorbonne in 1470, and in 1473 Guillaume Le Roy arrived in Lyons and printed the *Compendium Breve* of Cardinal Lothaire, financed by Barthélemy Buyer. From then on presses multiplied in Paris and Lyons where German printers arrived to set up in business. In 1476 presses began work in Angers and Toulouse, and at Poitiers in 1479. Already there was a press in Poland at Cracow (1474), while in the Low Countries Thierry, Martens and John of Westphalia were working at Louvain in 1473 and Gerard Leeu at Gouda in 1477, producing a stream of illustrated books. Finally in 1476 William Caxton, an English merchant who had learned his printing in Cologne and who operated a press in Bruges, went back to England and set up a press at Westminster. In Spain, German printers were active in several towns.

By 1480 printing presses were in operation in more than 110 towns throughout Western Europe, of which around fifty were in Italy, around thirty in Germany, five in Switzerland, two in Bohemia, nine in France, eight in Holland, five in Belgium, eight in Spain, one in Poland and four in England. From that date it may be said of Europe that the printed book was in universal use. In Germany and Italy large firms had been established with good connections everywhere. In Italy, thanks to German immigrant printers, there was not a single town of any importance which did not have at least one well equipped press, and some of the Italian towns were as important publishing centres as the great German cities. An examination of catalogues of incunabula printed between 1480 and 1482 makes it obvious that Venice had become the capital of printing – because of its geographical position, its riches and its intellectual liveliness. 156 editions are known to Burger and positively identified as Venetian publications of the years 1480–1482,[271] without counting lost and unidentified works. Among the big firms were those of Jenson, Herbort, Manzolies, Maufert, John of Cologne, Blavis, Scoto, Torti, Girardengo, Ratdolt and others. Second came Milan where the Pachels, the Zarotti and the Valdafers produced numerous editions of Latin classics (82 known editions). Augsburg is next with 67 editions, an important centre of map production and wood engraving, where Sorg, Schönsperger and Baemler turned out illustrated books. Next comes Nuremberg with 53 editions. Here there was probably the most highly organised and productive printing house of the period, the Kobergers. In Florence, a city noted for its culture, printers worked mainly for the local market – 48 editions were published in the same period; while in Cologne, the centre of ecclesiastical and university life on the Rhine, where the Quentells and the Koelhoffs worked and where mainly religious and scholastic books were published, 44 editions are recorded. Then come Paris (35), Rome (34), Strasbourg (28), Basel (24), and Gouda, Bologna, Treviso, Lyons, Padua, Delft and Louvain (from 25 down to 15 editions).

Mainz by this time had lost some of its initial importance. Major centres of the printing industry were numerous in Central and Southern Germany, but there were already more, and more productive, printers in Italy than in Germany. In Italy the first editions of classical authors and of the great works of Italian literature appeared in Roman type on the good paper which was at that time available locally, along with law books and religious texts in gothic and bastarda type. Printers were still scarce not only in England and Spain but also in France, even though by 1480 they were numerous in Italy and Germany. While only Gering's, admittedly large, publishing house was operating in Paris, books had to be procured from Germany for the lecturers and students. Although the publishing industry had existed in Lyons for several years, it was still on a very small scale.

This evidence allows the progress of printing in the following decades to be better understood. Spain and England, despite the establishment of several new presses, remained dependent on imported books. France, however, caught up on her late start during the last twenty years of the 15th century. In 1480, only nine French towns had had a printing press; by 1500, presses were functioning in forty towns. But above all the

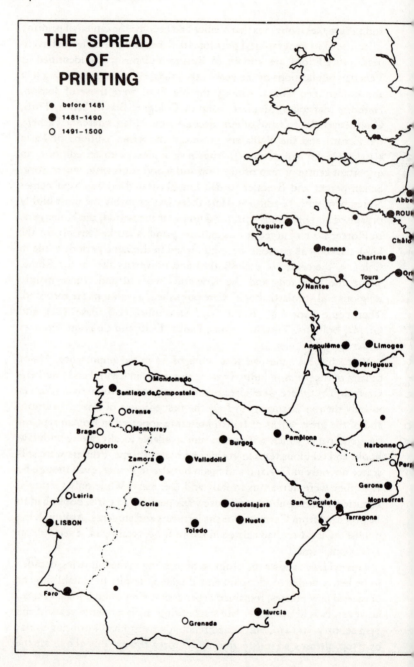

THE SPREAD OF PRINTING

- ● before 1481
- ⬤ 1481–1490
- ○ 1491–1500

Abbe
● ROU
Treguier ●
Châlo
● Rennes
Chartres ●
Tours ● Orl
○ Nantes
Angoulême ● ● Limoges
● Périgueux

○ Mondoñedo
● Santiago de Compostela
○ Orense
○ Monterrey
Braga ○ ● Burgos ● Pamplona
● Oporto
Narbonne ○
Zamora ● ● Valladolid
Perp
Gerona ●
○ Leiria ● Coria ● Guadalajara San Cuculate Montserrat
● LISBON ● Huete Tarragona
Toledo

Faro ●
● Murcia
○ Grenada

printing industry had developed in Paris, thanks to the labours of Marchant, Vérard and many others; while a little later on, it had also developed in Lyons, where the German Trechsel had been very productive. A similar, though less marked, evolution had taken place in Northern Germany. Lübeck had become an important centre for publishing and a staging-post from which the industry spread to Scandinavia. In the Centre and the South of Germany, on the other hand, the great centres of the previous period subsisted, but without developing greatly. The single exception was Leipzig, which began to become, with the firms of Kachelofen, Stöckel, Lotther and Landsberg, an important centre for the new industry. In Italy at the same time, while the printing press continued to spread to the smaller towns, large-scale production seems to have increasingly been concentrated in Venice, while Milan appears to have already begun to decline.

A scrutiny of books printed between 1495 and 1497 helps to measure the evolution of the industry. Of the 1821 editions that we have been able to identify, 447 or almost a quarter, were from Venice where large printing firms were numerous. This was undoubtedly the age of the great Venetian publishers: the Locatelli, the Bevilacqua, the Tacuini, the Torresani, the Aldus family, and the firms of Pincio and De Gregori. If Venice remained by far the most important centre of the industry, Paris and Lyons followed immediately behind.

181 editions are known to have been produced in Paris, where there were not perhaps many large firms, but where there was an immense number of printers and booksellers. From Lyons we know of 95 editions, and of the Lyons publishers Trechsel was the most important. Behind those come Florence; Leipzig, a newcomer to the list of leaders; Deventer, another newcomer, largely as a result of the work of Jacques de Breda and of the Paffroet firm; Milan, where Pachel and Scinzenzeler were the important firms; Strasbourg, where Grüninger and Flach were established; and finally Cologne, Augsburg, Nuremberg and Basel.

Thus by the close of the 15th century, about 50 years after printing began, at least 35,000 editions had been produced, amounting, at the lowest estimate, to 15 or 20 million copies, and the press was established in all parts of Europe.[272] First in Germany, then in Italy and finally in France, the industry had developed centres of large-scale production. No fewer than 236 towns had seen printing presses installed during this fifty years.

This growth continued into the 16th century, when presses regularly opened up in new cities. For the first fifty years of the 16th century saw an unprecedented prosperity, an age of exceptional economic boom, and of literate humanism. The book trade was now more than at any other time a great industry under the control of wealthy capitalists; in the golden age of printing, publishing was big international business. It was the age of Froben, the Kobergers, Birckmann, Aldus, Jean Petit and other influential publishers, all more or less humanists, whose many business contacts throughout Europe provided the basis for the intellectual relations of the intelligentsia. Spurred on by capitalist investors – although small businesses continued to open up in many towns – the book trade looked for its most lucrative markets and found them in the university cities and the great commercial centres, especially in the Low Countries. Even before Plantin, Antwerp, a great commercial city undergoing rapid expansion, was second after Deventer at the end of the 15th century in the league of great printing centres, and quickly reached first place. Antwerp publishers sought to satisfy their merchant customers and the wealthy bourgeoisie, who were numerous in such a great commercial centre, producing for their delectation illustrated romances of chivalry and devotional works, in Flemish and French. But very soon they began to produce for export, printing books, for example, in English. Thus Antwerp soon enjoyed a predominant position in the trade in the Low Countries. Of the 133 printers in the Low Countries between 1500 and 1540, 66 or nearly one half, were in business in Antwerp, and of the 4,000 (more or less) books published in the Low Countries, 2,254 – more than half – were from Antwerp.[273]

In the wealthy German towns between the Rhine and the Elbe, where there was a rich and cultivated bourgeoisie, the book trade continued to expand at the end of the 15th century and in the first quarter of the 16th. Strasbourg, in particular, very rapidly became a centre of foremost importance. From the early days of the trade, a son-in-law of Mentelin, Adolf Rusch, financed numerous editions and expanded into the paper trade (1466–1489), while his brother-in-law Martin Schott (1481–1499) was also important though not perhaps as active as Jean Prüss (1480–1510) or Henri Knoblochtzer (1476–1484). The art of illustration had meanwhile developed in that city, reaching its apogee in the work of Jean Grüninger (1482–1531). The presses of Strasbourg were famous for their high quality editions; they received orders from everywhere. Grüninger sold a complete edition of 1,000 copies to Schönsperger, the famous publishers of Augsburg, while Jean Schott was printing for booksellers as far away as Leipzig, Vienna and Milan.[274]

But Basel was still more important. There the humanist Amerbach was engaged in vigorous trading activity, while as we shall see, nearby Johann Petri was bringing out weighty treatises in theology and canon law, and publishing the works of Augustine in 11 volumes. After their deaths in 1511 and 1513, Froben extended his business with the assistance of his son-in-law Wolfgang Lachner. He made much use of roman type, devised his own italic based on that of Aldus, and his own Greek type, whose founts he sold to Joost Bade, and whose matrices he sold to Melchior Lotther. In 1536 he bought the type foundry which had belonged to Schoeffer. He engaged artists of the first rank to engrave his illustrations, title pages, head bands and initials: first he hired Urs Graf and then after 1516 the Holbeins, Hans and Ambrosius. His proof-readers were his brother-in-law, Boniface Amerbach, and Beatus Rhenanus. He was Erasmus' editor – the great humanist extended a visit to him which had been intended to last several days over three years (1514–1517).

In most of the great cities of Germany the presses were constantly busy. At Mainz, the old firm of Schoeffer was active over a long period. Peter Schoeffer, son of the founder, and a friend of Ulrich von Hutten, printed the latter's writings in Mainz. He possessed an immense stock of equipment, which was later sold to Froben, and he constantly added to it. Erhard Ratdolt was at Augsburg and until about 1520 produced numerous liturgies, including some fine illustrated works like the Constance Missal (1516). Johann Schönsperger the Elder worked for the Emperor Maximilian in the same town and printed among other books the famous *Teuerdank*, an allegorical description of the Emperor's marriage, for which he used types whose design was based on the Imperial Chancellery script, and which provided the prototype of *Fraktur*. There Hans Otmar published the sermons of Geiber and of Kayserberg, and after him his son, Sylvan, multiplied their editions of Lutheran books. Meanwhile, Johann Miller published editions of the works of Konrad Peutinger and Ulrich von Hutten. At Nuremberg, where the Kobergers were still doing tremendous business, there were other important printers too: Hieronymus Höltzel was extraordinarily productive until 1532, and new printing concerns of considerable importance opened up: those, for example, of Friedrich Peypus (1510–1535), of Jobst Guntknecht (1514–1540), of Johann Petrejus (1519–1550). In a more modest workshop Hieronymus Andreae was using a new and beautiful kind of *Fraktur* type which he had specially cut, and was printing the *Triumphwagen* and theoretical works by Dürer.

At the start of the Lutheran Reformation the great printing towns of Germany were numerous. Others, many of notable importance, deserve to be mentioned – Leipzig, for example. We will see that many new centres of book production developed during the life of Luther and in the second half of the century. But for the present we will only emphasise the importance of the Catholic city of Cologne, which after a decline in the early 16th century (Heinrich Quentell worked there alone, publishing numerous theological treatises) later responded fully to the demands of the thousands of students coming to the university. The publisher Hittorp had many of the town's presses working for him and gave orders for works to be printed in Paris, Basel and Tübingen. His business contacts extended across all Europe. With his associate Horunken he owned branches in Paris and Leipzig, Wittenberg and Prague. Again in Cologne Eucharius Cervicornus was publishing Latin authors edited by the humanists Hermann von dem Busche and Murmellius. Birckmann, the bookseller, who acquired a printing shop in 1526 and employed printers from Antwerp, had a branch in London. Many other such businesses made Cologne one of the largest centres of German printing – indeed (if we may judge from the catalogues issued at the Frankfurt Book Fair) perhaps the biggest in some periods, though third in rank by the end of the century, following Frankfurt and Leipzig.[275]

There were 140 towns in Germany during the 16th century where the printing press operated, at least for a time, and where it had never operated before. In France too the printing industry expanded rapidly, particularly in the first half of the century. Printing shops were set up in town after town. Lepreux has listed 39 presses established between 1501 and 1550, and 40 in the second half of the century.[276] Paris and Lyons, with Venice, were the most productive cities in Europe and it would be tedious to try to enumerate even the largest firms in a period so fertile. A total of 25,000 books were printed in Paris from 1500 to 1599, and 15,000 in Lyons. Rouen, Toulouse, Poitiers, Troyes, Angers, Grenoble and Bordeaux came far behind. For the year 1530 Philippe Renouard has listed 297 volumes printed in Paris, 110 in Lyons, 5 in Caen, 5 in Rouen, 4 in Poitiers, 3 in Bordeaux, Grenoble and Toulouse. Thirty-two, however, came from Strasbourg presses, and 19 from Haguenau.[277] France became typographically two zones. In the North books produced in Paris dominated the market, with Troyes and even more so Rouen complementing the capital, their printers often working for its booksellers. The latter were in close contact with Cologne and Basel printers, who sometimes came and set up presses in Paris. On many occasions, Parisian and Norman printers went over to England or produced books for the English market. The other zone, in the South, was ruled by Lyons. Its booksellers also did business with Basel and the Rhineland; while its great book fairs helped develop the export trade which formed the most important part of their business. The booksellers of Lyons had excellent contacts with their opposite numbers abroad, especially in Italy. It was at this period that the Giuntas owned branches in Venice, Florence and Lyons, as well as in Spain; while many Lyons publishers had Italian editions copied and were strong competitors of the Venetian trade. Often they had branches in Toulouse and there were many of their agents in Madrid, Salamanca, Burgos and Barcelona.

The Italian book-trade was not so vigorous at the turn of the 16th century as that of France and Germany, conditions in Italy being less favourable to rapid expansion. Venice continued to dominate the trade. At the beginning of the 17th century its products were more in evidence in Germany than even Antwerp's. The House of Aldus went on producing its famous editions, and the Giuntas, the Nicolini of Sabio, the Marcolini, and the Pagnanini were all producing in quantity. But the old quality seems to have been lacking; there was an emphasis on volume rather than on innovation. After about 1530, there seems to have been a definite decline. While the Blado family did good work and the Vatican Press kept up high standards in Rome, where the popes of the Counter-Reformation helped with their policy of maintaining the book-trade and the printing industry, at Milan there was a steady decline, in spite of the work of the Pachels, Bonacorse, Legnani and Le Signere. At Bologna the position was similar, despite the activities of the Faelli and Bonacci. Florence, too, declined, the Giuntas and their competitors the Doni now producing more and more only for a local market.

Spanish printing made hardly any progress at all during this period. It was deeply conservative in its use of black letter type and until the middle of the century wood-cuts of archaic form and foreign style were still used. Although Cardinal Ximenez, assisted by the humanist Antonio de Nebrija, produced his famous polyglot Bible at Alcalá between 1514 and 1517, printed for him by Arnao Guillon de Brocas (who may have come from a township of that name in the South of France), only three places gave proof of any real life; Salamanca, Barcelona and Seville, where the

Crombergers were turning out chivalric romances. There was some increase in activity in the second half of the 16th century at Madrid, where the printing industry developed considerably in the next century. However, even then Spain largely continued to be a market for foreign books, chiefly from Lyons and Antwerp.[278]

In England on the other hand printers and booksellers were successful in creating an independent trade.[279] The Reformation in England cut off contact with European Catholic states and so favoured home production, while the Tudors enforced rigorous protectionist policies to assist the native industry. The history of English printing at this period is singular. In the 15th century there had been attempts to try and attract foreign publishers and printers to England. By an Act of 1484 restrictions on foreign workers were relaxed on any who were occupied in the book business. By the first decade of the 16th century the chief printers in England were from the continent. Wynkyn de Worde, Caxton's successor, who printed 700 works up to 1535, came from Worth in Alsace. Guillaume Faques (anglicised as Fawkes) and Pynson, whose presses produced some 400 titles between 1490 and 1530, both King's Printers, were Norman, and Julian Notary was probably French, as were others. From 1476 to 1536, two-thirds of the printers, booksellers and bookbinders in England were foreigners. The equipment was often French, and the same was true of Scotland where Andrew Myllan used types like those of Marnef. From Paris, Rouen and soon from Antwerp, books intended for the English market were exported; while several Paris booksellers like Vérard and, later, Regnault had branches in London.

When British born printers began to increase in number, the English were forced to react against the foreign domination of the trade. In 1523, for example, foreigners were forbidden to take on apprentices who were not English or to employ more than two foreign journeymen. Eventually an Act of 1534 annulled the Act of 1484, and in 1543 the King, satisfied that English printers were capable of production of high quality, granted an exclusive privilege in Church prayer books to Richard Grafton and Edward Whitechurch. Finally in 1557 Queen Mary granted a charter to printers and booksellers to found the Stationers' Company.

English production grew all the time. From 1520 to 1529, 550 books were printed; from 1530 to 1539, 739; from 1540 to 1549, 928. Such figures seem meagre when compared with Paris, which alone produced 300 titles a year, but they do indicate progress. In the second half of the century many more books appeared and more and more printing houses were established. The desire to control the output of the press and to ensure that its expansion did not lead to a multiplied production of seditious pamphlets, led the state to concentrate the industry in London by a Decree of 1586, and to limit the number of presses. In 1615 the number of printers in London was fixed at 22, and the only authorised persons allowed to print outside London were the university printers of Oxford and Cambridge. In 1662 York was likewise allowed a press. It was not until 1695 that this draconian legislation was abolished, after which the trade expanded; by 1725 there were presses in Manchester, Birmingham, Liverpool, Bristol, Cirencester, Exeter, Worcester, Norwich, Canterbury, Tunbridge Wells, York, Newcastle and Nottingham.

The Reformation which led the kings of England to intervene to stop the trade in books between England and the continent, revolutionised the geographical distribution of German printing presses. From 1520 the Lutheran Reformation began to have effects in Germany. Leipzig, which had been a busy centre at the beginning of the century, with the success-ful firms of Martin Landsperg, Wolfgang Stöckel, Jakob Thanner and, greatest of all, of Melchior Lotther, suffered an eclipse when George, the ardently Catholic Elector of Saxony (1471–1539), began to persecute publishers of Reformation literature. Stöckel, for example, went to Eilenburg to escape censorship. Yet on the other hand Luther's move-ment created the right circumstances for the vigorous growth of publish-ing at Wittenberg. The founding of a university there in 1502 attracted the printer Johann Rhau-Grünenberg in 1508; in 1516 he published Luther's earliest works and almost certainly the famous theses on Indulgences of 1517. From that year the printing trade developed steadily at Wittenberg. Melchior Lotther of Leipzig opened a branch there in 1519, which his son Melchior Junior was put in charge of in 1520. This press was entirely at Luther's service, printing and reprinting his translations of the Scriptures. Christian Döring owned a press which also worked on the Lutheran Bible in German and soon there were many others, all devoted to the Reformation – Nickel Schirlentz, Joseph Klug, Hans Weiss and Hans Lufft. Large numbers of printing firms published Luther in hundreds of thousands of copies: his translations, sermons, polemics were pirated and reprinted in the towns supporting the Reformation. German presses from this time on concentrated on producing cheap pamphlets and propagandist tracts in the vernacular, a literature of revolt spread far and wide by pedlars.

Later we will take stock of the consequences of this.[281] For the moment let us consider those factors which affected German book production. While printing shops had previously been concentrated largely in the South of Germany, where they were numerous, the presses in the North, which had done little business until around 1520, produced an enormous quantity of books between 1520 and 1540. They declined somewhat between 1540 and 1575, but revived at the end of the century. Consequently, the superiority of Southern over Northern Germany as regards the book-trade became less marked during the course of this period, owing to the impact of Luther and of the Reformation.

But religious dissension was not confined to Germany; while at the same time the economic crisis which characterised the second half of the 16th century brought about the decline and even the ruin of some publishing centres. These two factors were the cause of many important changes. In France the spread of Calvinism gave rise to the establishment of often short-lived printing presses in many towns of the South, all of them in support of the Protestant cause. From around the year 1550 we note a decline in Lyons, which grew steadily more pronounced up to about 1630. Often well disposed to the new ideas, or even converts to Calvinism, and, yet more important, hampered by their workers' strikes and demands, master printers and booksellers quit Lyons en masse to avoid persecution and to work more peacefully elsewhere. Calvin, like Luther at Wittenberg, created an important publishing centre in Geneva. Geneva was not far from Lyons, the labour force there was disciplined and comparatively docile, and soon there were many papermills in the neighbourhood. The large firms took refuge there, and soon the journeymen of Lyons, short of work, had also to take the road to Geneva.[282]

A third city – Frankfurt – was to profit, thanks to its fairs, from the competition between Lyons and Geneva. Printing did not arrive there until relatively late, in 1511. But by 1530 Egenolff, who was to become a major publisher, was in business and soon the Frankfurt Fairs became, as we shall see, the meeting place for the publishing trade of all Europe, which congregated there to display its latest wares. Until 1625 this town remained the headquarters of the European book-trade.[283]

The Catholic Revival or Counter-Reformation began to take effect after about 1570. It, too, brought about another revision of the existing map of the book trade. The decision taken at the Council of Trent to authorise an official text of the liturgy and to revise the old texts to make them conform with Roman usage encouraged a rebirth of the Catholic press. A number of wealthy publishers, supported by the Church or Catholic princes, secured monopolies in the publication of the liturgy and so were able to extend their businesses considerably – this, as we have seen, is how Plantin first made his fortune. The Jesuits, at the same time, were founding colleges throughout Europe and encouraging the establishment of printing presses alongside them. In addition, numerous new monasteries and convents were being founded throughout Catholic Europe, each of which sought to build up its library. This, combined with the renewal of popular piety, along with which went a new religious literature, led to the expansion of the Catholic press.

In Catholic Europe, the great publishing centres were thus the great centres of the religious Renaissance. In Germany, printing once more flourished in the South and in Cologne. In the Spanish Netherlands, at Antwerp, which since the Spanish reconquest had become a stronghold of the Counter-Reformation, the Moretus firm long produced vast numbers of service-books revised according to the Council of Trent – which they sold throughout Europe and in the Americas. Along with the Verdussens, another of the great Antwerp firms, they printed a large quantity of learned works composed by Jesuits. In France, Cramoisy and his relatives and associates dominated the Parisian trade, enjoying the protection of the Church and the Jesuits. Printing in Lyons revived to some extent, especially after 1620, because of the same Jesuits. Venice too saw some growth in the trade. At Rome, Paulus Manutius established himself in the Holy See and placed his presses at the disposal of ortho-doxy.

A network of Protestant presses faced the Catholic ones. In France, Protestant book production flourished at La Rochelle before the siege, and above all at Saumur, to those Protestant university English students came as well as those of the Low Countries and Germany. Their presence encouraged the development in this small town of several quite important firms. At Sedan, in the principality of Souillon, the university similarly made possible the establishment of printing presses. In Switzerland, Basel was in decline, and in Geneva printers were obliged to print books for Catholic countries under a series of false imprints. By contrast, Holland, freed from the Spanish yoke, became the metropolis of Protestant printing and saw a multiplication of printing firms. At Leyden, whose university was founded by William of Orange in 1576, new workshops were particularly numerous – here the great Elzevier firm began. As much as theology, the study of philology was paramount here and the Elzeviers printed countless editions of classical authors, which were in demand among specialists all over Europe, Blaeu, the famous map and atlas printer, founded his important business in Amsterdam,[284] and the Elzeviers set up, in addition to their Leyden workshop, a press in Amsterdam and began to pirate the works of the greatest French and English writers, selling these books throughout Europe, under false imprints, by means of an excellently organised trade network.

New tendencies were once more apparent from the middle of the 17th century. The era of the Counter-Reformation was ended and with it the prosperity of the great publishers who had specialised in religious books. Massive tomes, like the editions of the Church Fathers, were now more difficult to sell. Fewer new monasteries and convents were being created. The libraries of those establishments that had recently been founded, and those too which had been replenished in monasteries that had been pillaged during the wars of religion, were now complete. At the same time there began in France, Spain, England and, shortly after, in Holland, a vogue for vernacular, secular literature intended for a public ignorant of Latin. The scarcity of money which restricted the expansion of business in the second half of the 17th century made publishers seek small profits and quick returns with less ambitious books. They concentrated on vernacular literature which sold easily and this central change of direction once more changed the geography of the trade.

Between 1640 and 1660 the prevalence of pirated editions created a situation of cut-throat competition which brought about the ruin of many small printers. In Antwerp, the publishers who relied on monumental religious works saw their profits diminishing every year. Moretus played safe by restricting himself to the publication of prayer-books, which retained a ready market. At Lyons, there was a process of rationalisation; soon the only large firm left was Anisson, who became engaged in deadly competition with Paris. Cologne and Venice were in decline.

With the growth in vernacular printing, the major part of the book trade ceased to be an international European affair. English printers in particular seemed to have no wish to maintain business relations with their opposite numbers on the continent. In Germany, Frankfurt ceased to be the great book centre after the crisis of the Thirty Years'

War. Though the Leipzig fairs replaced it as the main market, they were significantly attended only by Germans, unlike the Frankfurt fairs which had drawn publishers from every country. French scholars complained of the difficulties they experienced in ordering books from across the Rhine. In France, only Paris remained a major printing centre; for intellectual life was increasingly focussed there, while the printers of Rouen, Lyons, Troyes and Toulouse, unable to obtain new works to publish, had to resign themselves to living off pirate editions.

At such a time of latent – and soon overt – crisis, French publishing faced enormous problems. These were all the greater because over the previous 200 years, until the 1650's, the number of presses had steadily multiplied, to reach finally an astronomical figure. Every township had its master printer turning out ABCs, local Acts, primers and pamphlets and doing jobbing work. Many journeymen on their travels were unable to resist buying a cheap second-hand press and setting up their own workshops, where each could be his own master. There were 75 establishments with 181 presses in Paris in 1644, 16 of them having only one press and 34 only two. As a consequence, about half these presses lacked regular work. To remedy this and deter would-be pirates, and above all to prevent printers who were short of work from printing seditious or pornographic books and pamphlets, Colbert instituted harsh legislation. He issued strict regulations about copyright privileges and in 1666 shut down some presses. He forbade the appointment of new masters and the setting up of new shops, a measure enforced without pity until 1686.[285] Right up to the time of the French Revolution the number of printing shops was severely restricted,[286] a draconian policy rather like the one enforced in England a century earlier. Its consequences were unfortunate and it failed in its principal objective. Far from suppressing the publication and sale of contraband books, it merely resulted in an ever greater proportion of French books, among them some of the most important, being printed abroad. By the close of the 17th century supremacy in publishing was passing to Holland, while French publishing underwent the most terrible depression.

The history of the book trade in Holland is astonishing.[287] Its development began, as we have seen, in the early years of the 17th century, at a time when Holland was freeing itself from Spanish tyranny and was herself launched on a programme of imperialist expansion. The 17th century – Holland's golden age – was a period of great prosperity. The book trade was peculiarly suited to the temperament of the Dutch merchants, who were keen for liberty and connoisseurs of the arts. At this time Vermeer, Rembrandt and Franz Hals gave the Dutch School of painting its renown. Men of learning thronged the cities and engaged in correspondence with their equals in foreign countries. Men like Huygens, who was in touch with the intellectuals of three different countries – France, Germany and England – themselves more or less unknown to each other, acted as the unifying agents in the world of letters. They produced the innumerable Dutch gazettes of news, the original newspapers. Many French intellectuals stayed in Holland – for example, Balzac, Théophile de Viau and, of course, Descartes. French was spoken at the Court of Prince Maurice of Nassau and French books were to be found in plenty in the bookshops of The Hague. After each outburst of persecution, French Protestants took refuge in this predominantly Calvinist country. During the reign of Louis XIV they were especially numerous, this being the time of the *dragonnades* and of the Revocation of the Edict of Nantes. Wealthy publishers like Desbordes and Huguétan arrived from France and met other refugees from Walloon country like the Mortiers. There too they met French writers, among them some of the most important. So, by the close of the 17th century, Amsterdam was, after Paris, the next largest centre of French book production. The great Dutch booksellers like the Leers of Rotterdam were able, through their extensive business contacts and the favoured geographical position of their country, to promote throughout Europe, from London to Berlin, the works of Bayle and pirated versions of Paris editions of the best French writers. They were soon in bitter competition with French publishers, since their publications reached Paris without any difficulty – except when it was a matter of banned titles or forged works. Even then it was usually merely a question of taking some prudent precautions. The traffic in banned works grew during the 18th century as French became the international *lingua franca*. Soon Dutch publishers, along with a few Belgians and Swiss, were to be the strongest supporters of the *philosophes* – the name of Marc-Michel Rey is sufficient evidence.[288] In that one century, from 1690 to 1790, the works of the most famous French writers were read throughout Europe in editions published outside France.

4
Printing Conquers the World

With the rapid expansion of printing in Western Europe, there was scarcely an important town in Germany, Italy, France or the Low Countries which had not had its own press since the 15th century. From a slightly later period, the same was true of Portugal, Spain and Poland too. In England the trade was artificially confined, more or less, to London by government restrictions. How, and when, was printing introduced in the countries of Northern Europe, with their less dense populations and their greater distance from the original centres of the trade? How did it adapt itself to the Slav countries, especially to those where a different alphabet was used? How did it adjust to the entirely new conditions encountered by Europeans in their conquest of the New World, where it was necessary to master vast expanses of territory which long remained almost uninhabited? How, finally, did the technique of reproducing texts which had been perfected in the West manage to establish itself within the ancient civilisations of Asia, many of which already employed techniques of reproduction which, if more rudimentary, might still have seemed better adapted to local needs? These are some of the many questions to be faced if we are to gauge correctly the whole range of impact of the printed book.

A. The Slav Countries *

Bohemia and Moravia

Bohemia, in what is now called Czechoslovakia, was the first Slav country to make use of Gutenberg's invention. Two cities were predominant in this highly cultured land: Prague the capital, which had had its own university since 1348, and Pilsen. As elsewhere in Europe, a merchant class had grown up alongside the old nobility and was able to exercise considerable influence through its economic importance. The tragic death of John Huss in 1415 led to religious and political disturbances which lasted for many years, overlapping with the beginnings of the Renaissance; but this may possibly have been a blessing in disguise as

* This section has been written by Mme. A. Basanoff, librarian in the *Bibliothèque Nationale*.

far as the spread of printing was concerned, for the notion of influencing people by the written word took root in Bohemia more than in any other Slav country. While Prague, under the benevolent government of the King Jurii Podiebrad, resounded with Hussite propaganda, Pilsen, a wealthy commercial centre – situated at the crossing of a number of important roads and at the confluence of several rivers – and a town renowned for its Catholic sentiments (it was known as *Pilsna christianissima semperque fidelis*), was operating its first press in 1468. Printing in Bohemia began with the work of an anonymous printer who produced a translation from the Italian of Guido di Colonna, called *Kronika Trojanska* (History of Troy). This was the first book to be published in Czech. The fact that a secular and not liturgical text was chosen by this printer to be the first book produced in Bohemia is significant (the work had already had a great vogue as a manuscript which was widely read in Western Europe and it attained permanent popularity after it was printed). In the other Slav countries the first printed books were invariably religious. The *Kronika Trojanska* was set in a bastarda type of great beauty. The face that was utilised (which includes a large number of ligatures between letters) was related to that of Ulrich Zell of Cologne, but it had been developed by the introduction of new diacritical signs peculiar to the Czech language. The unknown printer, possibly German, must have had local help to set the work up and he has taken his inspiration from old Czech manuscripts. In 1476 the *Statuta Arnesti* appeared in Latin printed in textura type.

Mikuláš Bakalář (1489–1513) had set up a permanent press in Pilsen towards the end of the 15th century and produced at least 22 books which sold widely. The *Holy Pilgrimages* of Bernhard von Breydenbach, the *New World and Newly Discovered Countries* of Amerigo Vespucci and *Barlaam and Josaphat* were produced, as well as the first Czech Psalter (1499) and dictionary (1511). Bakalář's output included certain features which were common to all his books: Schwabacher type, a page of 20 lines, and a text in Czech. We also owe the first satirical book, *Podkoni a Žak* (*The Stable Boy and the Student*) published in 1498, originally composed in Latin in the last quarter of the 14th century, to Bakalář. He was a linguist of some ability, a publisher, a bookseller and perhaps also his own printer.

In Prague three separate presses were established. The oldest was that of Jonata de Vykohevo Myto (1487), who did a Psalter and a *History of Troy* printed in a specifically Czech type face which represented a cross between rotunda and bastarda. The press of Jan Kamp and Jan (?)

Severyn (1488–1520), who were associates, was the next to be set up. Severyn was the publisher and the owner of the business. He was the founder of a family of printers which after 1520 became, under Pavel Severyn, the most important in Prague. To these partners belongs the honour of printing the first complete Czech Bible in 1488, called the Prague Bible, one of the most beautiful of Bohemian incunabula. Severyn and Kamp were the first to receive a royal privilege, in 1499. They produced 20 titles richly ornamented with wood-cuts that suggest affinities with those of Nuremberg: in 1488 an edition of Aesop, one of the oldest illustrated Czech works in print, and a book on the Passion in 1495. The first illustrated title page appeared in their edition of a Czech translation of Petrarch's *De remediis utriusque fortunae* in 1501. Until 1513 the press used bastarda type and after that date textura.

Beneda was another Prague printer, producing for a larger public, and he acquired something of a reputation for his Calendars in Schwabacher type, with wood-cuts. He relied on members of the university to provide him with the annual almanacs. Other Czech towns also had printing before 1500, encouraged by the Bohemian Brothers (the disciples of Chelicky, a Tolstoyan of the day) and by economic and cultural factors too. At Kutno, in 1489, Martin de Tisnova put out two Bibles in the Nuremberg style; at Winterberg, Allakraw was working after 1484; at Brno, in 1486, Konrad Stahel started the first Moravian press; at Olomuk, printing began in 1499. In the same period it penetrated Bratislava in Slovakia.

Thirty-nine incunabula survive from Bohemia, five in Latin, the rest in Czech; the eleven from Moravia are in Latin with only one exception. Despite the work of these Czech presses, they failed to meet the rising demand, especially for liturgical works, which had to be satisfied from foreign sources, usually Strasbourg, Nuremberg and Venice.

Poland

If printing was promoted by the rich city merchants of Bohemia, this was not the case in Poland. At the beginning of the 15th century Poland was on the eve of great political and economic advance. The conquest of Danzig opened a way to the Baltic and control of the coast, and her victory over the Teutonic Knights in 1410 established Poland as a political and military power. Yet the only city to have printing presses in the 15th century was Cracow. The capital was an ancient university town and known far beyond the frontiers as a great cultural centre, yet scholars were obliged to have their books printed abroad because of the lack of local printers. Humanism had had a marked influence from an early date, through the young Polish intellectuals studying at French, Italian and German universities.

Hungarians, Czechs, Ukrainians, Bavarians, Silesians, Alsatians and Franconians gathered in Cracow. The first printers came from these foreign communities, but were freemen of the city despite their foreign nationality. The first book printed in Poland, probably the work of one of Gunther Zainer's journeymen, was the *Explanatio in Psaltetium* of Jean de Torquemada, produced about 1474. It was followed by Augustine's *Works* a little later. More presses were started in 1476–1477 by a Bavarian, Gaspard Hochfeder of Heilsbronn, by Jan Krieger or Krüger and by Jan Pepelaw. But the individual who dominates the history of printing in the Orthodox Slav lands is Swiatopolk Fiol from Franconia (1475). A gold embroiderer of the Goldsmith's guild in Cracow and inventor of a device for draining mines, Fiol produced an immense quantity of books. He enjoyed close contacts with the 'Slav Benedictines', who were working for the union of the Orthodox and Catholic Churches, and planned to sell the books he produced to Orthodox Slavs. He thus concentrated on their liturgical literature and was the first to use Cyrillic type. The wide distribution of his books is attested to in many places; copies are found, for example, as far afield as Leningrad and Moscow. Fiol had acquired printing equipment in 1483; eight years later in 1491 his workshop was busy with five books: *Osmoglasnick* (Plainchant); *Časolovec* (a breviary); *Psaltir* (Psalter); *Triod Postnaja* (a Lenten liturgy); *Triod Cvětnaja* (Pentecostal liturgy). After this date Fiol's presses closed down. Accused of Hussite heresy, imprisoned and then released, he left Poland for Hungary.

Jan Haller of Franconia was the founder of a permanent printing tradition in Cracow; a wine merchant and cattle dealer, he was a well-known capitalist and went into publishing at the end of the century. His activities in the world of books expanded considerably after 1505, when King Alexander granted him a monopoly in all the Polish territories. He then founded a printing business putting out books in Latin and Polish. It was for his masterpiece, the Cracow Missal, that he obtained his monopoly of both printing and sales. He opened a paper mill and a bindery with his own capital and was the first in Poland to combine the jobs of printer, bookseller and publisher as his great contemporaries in the West did. He inundated the market with his breviaries, missals, graduals and devotional manuals. The patent of monopoly which he held also stipulated that books printed abroad could not be imported into Poland if the title appeared in the catalogue of Haller's bookshop. This measure for a while assisted the sale of locally produced books within Poland, freeing them from the crushing competition of imported books, especially those brought in from Italy. Haller made a major contribution to Poland's cultural life; as a patron of poets and writers he was considered the '*fautor humanissimus vivorum doctorum*'.

Florjan Ungler, on the other hand, who came originally from Bavaria, was only a printer. His workshop produced the first Polish book to survive to our day, in or around 1514. It was the *Hortulus animae* of Biernat de Lublina (c. 1514), itself an adaptation of the famous treatise by Nicolas of Salicet, *Antidotarius animae*. The *Hortulus animae* was expanded with additional practical advice and was enhanced by a series of wood-cuts. Ungler was in correspondence with Rudolf Agricola, Pawel of Krozna and other scholars and was abreast of all current scientific advances. He was the first to adapt the language spoken by the great majority of Poles to the press. Zaborovsky's book on spelling, published at this time, was perhaps related to this development. The *Hortulus animae* in its expanded form marks the first step towards the eventual popularisation of the printed book.

Haller's 1505 monopoly delayed the development of the third great Polish press, that of Wietor, who came from Silesia. As soon as Haller's monopoly expired in 1517, Wietor, who had just established a press in Vienna, came to instal himself in Cracow. He issued Latin, Hungarian and Polish works from 1518 to 1546; their superiority to Haller's production is undeniable.

In the first half of the 16th century, Mark Scharfenberg makes his appearance. He is remembered for his struggle with and victory over the famous Haller. Until the beginning of the 17th century the Scharfenbergs were printers, son following on father. Nicholas, Mark's son, was appointed Printer to King Stephen Báthori, who ruled from 1576 to 1586. In the wars between Russia and Poland (Ivan the Terrible and Báthori) he printed proclamations and broadsides. It could be said that the Scharfenbergs were in Poland what the Kobergers were in Germany or the Plantins in the Low Countries.

Around the mid-16th century, the Reformation swept into Poland. Printing offices opened on all sides, not only in the towns but on their outskirts and on the great landed estates. In Czechoslovakia the 16th century was the golden age of printing.

The innovatory work of S. Fiol, the Cracow printer, was continued by Fracisk Skorina, who had started life in Polozk, a town in the North-west of Russia. Having studied philosophy at the university of Cracow and then medicine at the university of Padua, Skorina went to Venice, where he must have known the publisher-printer Božidar Vuković, who owned a set of Cyrillic type. He made Prague his home base and worked chiefly on Orthodox service-books. We owe the first Slavonic Bible to him (Prague, 1517–1519); this contained 23 books of the Bible, was printed in Cyrillic characters, and was illustrated with numerous woodblocks. Skorina's scientific knowledge, and his translations and publications, had a considerable influence on the culture of those Slavs who belonged to the Orthodox Church. In 1525, for reasons which are no longer apparent, he left Prague, taking his equipment with him. He set himself up at Vilna, Lithuania, in the home of the magistrate Jacob Babič. There he printed a further two books in 1525.

A pupil of Melanchthon, one Melantrich, was another of the out-standing printers in the Prague of the 16th century, as was his brother-in-law and successor, Adam Veleslavine. Both were in close touch with the University of Prague. Melantrich used Schwabacher and roman type and took great care over his texts, which were in four languages. His shop employed eleven compositors, whose weekly wages we know – they varied from 18 Czech groschen to a Rhenish gold piece.

Adam Veleslavine (1545–1599) was a professor at the University of Prague and carried the Czech book to its highest pitch of perfection. The Renaissance reached Bohemia through this scholar-printer, whose importance is comparable to that of Amerbach. The 16th century was the golden age of Czech and Polish printing. The art suffered a decline in the 17th through censorship, wars and the economic crisis and only began a slow rebirth in the 18th century.

The Southern Slavs

The influence of Germany, as we have seen, lay behind printing in the Western Slav territories. But in the lands now included in Yugoslavia it was Venice which was the predominant influence, for these regions were closely linked to that great trading city. This connection made possible the development of printing among the Southern Slavs and the production, in a number of cases, of masterpieces of the art.

The first press in Montenegro was in Cetinje, near the Adriatic coast, under the protection of the reigning Prince Durad Crnojevic, who was married to a Venetian. However, his father Ivan had already installed a press, it is thought, at Obod in 1490 and this was later transferred to Cetinje. A monk called Makarii was the printer in charge of this press. He had learnt his trade in Venice and had bought the type for the press there. He came second after Fiol of Cracow in his use of the Cyrillic alphabet. The first Montenegrin book was a Plainchant published in 1494, followed by the Cetinje Psalter next year, a very rare book whose workmanship reflects the influence of the Venetian Renaissance. Makarii was at Tergovisče, in the service of the vojvoda of Wallachia and Moldavia, in 1508. He introduced printing there and produced three liturgies (1508, 1510, 1512) printed in a typeface slightly different from those of Cetinje. At the start of the 16th century Božidar Vuković opened a workshop using Cyrillic type in Venice itself.

Printing came to Serbia in the 16th century, while it was still under Ottoman control, and established itself in the monasteries or under the patronage of princes. In either case the majority of printers were Orthodox monks and they produced nothing but liturgical books: in 1531 a prayer book was printed at Goražde; in 1537, at the monastery of Rujansk, a monk called Theodosius did an edition of the Gospels, using wooden letters to overcome the deficiencies in his type; in 1539 a Plainsong was produced at Gračanica and a Psalter was produced in 1544 by the monks Mardarii and Fedor at the monastery of Mileševa in Herzegovina. At Belgrade, Prince Radiša Dimitrović founded a press in 1552 which was continued after his death by Trojan Gundulić; it was here Mardarii printed his edition of the Gospels. At two more monasteries – Merkšin in 1562 and Skodar in 1563 – presses were set up by the monks.

All the Serbian presses had a floating existence lasting only about 50 years in all. The printer-monks were hampered by their growing poverty, so that after their type wore out they had, in the absence of skilled casters, to cut their own by hand in brass or iron. They had not the resources to print more than a handful of books, and were soon forced to go back to the ancient methods of reproducing manuscripts in their scriptoria. Illustrations in Slav books from these regions preserve features of Slavo-Byzantine manuscripts. They are arabesques of complicated patterns in black and white, but the ingenuity of the designs hardly conceals a certain clumsiness on the part of the engravers.

The situation in Croatia was very complex in the 15th century. The

North of the country and Zagreb had obvious affinities with Bohemia and Hungary, while the Adriatic was under strong Venetian influence. Printing began late in Croatia. Regular production at Zagreb began only in the 17th century, attempts in Nedelišće (1574) and Varaždin (1586) having been negligible. Latin works by Croatian writers of the 15th and 16th centuries were mainly printed in Italy.

From 1483, Croatian books were printed in Venice in Glagolitic print designed for the liturgies of Dalmatia, Istria and the Kvarner islands; but in Croatian territory itself Glagolitic presses were not very productive, though they operated at Senj (1491–1508) and Rijeka (1530–1531).

The Reformation came to Slovenia in the person of Primus Trubar (1508–1586), a professor and a canon of Ljubljana, whose sermons were popular but who left under pressure from the Catholic Church and took refuge in Germany. At Tübingen he edited a catechism and an ABC in Slovenian in 1550–1551. He associated with Baron Ungnad, a convert to the Reformation who founded a press at Urach specialising in the production of Croatian and Slovenian books for export.

At Ljubljana printing did not start until 1575–1578, and in Dalmatia not until 1783, when a press was established at Dubrovnik (Ragusa). But a great number of emigrés from these countries settled in Venice, Padua and elsewhere in Italy and helped to produce the fine Italian books of the 15th and 16th centuries. Among them were the Croatian Andrija Paltašić from Kotor (Andreas de Paltasichis Catterensis), the Croatian Dobruško Dobrić, who in Italy called himself Bonino Boninis, the Dalmatian Grgur Dalmatin and the Slovene Matheus Cerdonis de Windis. None of them, however, used Cyrillic or Glagolitic print.

Russia

We do not know by which route printing entered Russia. Was there a branch-off from the curve that led from Fiol to the monk Makarii at Cetinje, and from him to Božidar Vuković and on to Skorina? Books published by Western Slav printers and even more so those by Southern Slavs were certainly known in Moscow. The first dated book produced in Moscow is the *Apostol* of 1563–1564; this date is generally agreed as marking the beginning of printing in Moscow, although some undated anonymous works may go back as far as 1553. From the start printing was an enterprise monopolised by Church and state in Russia. It had its origin in the administrative measures instituted by Ivan the Terrible after the conquest of Kazan in the middle of the century, being intended as a response to the growth of the artisan and merchant classes and to the urgent need for government censorship of liturgical books. It was an instrument of the policy of centralisation and coercion.

The 'Anonymous' printing office, the first in Moscow, produced six books: the Gospels (1555–1557, 1559 and 1565–1566); a Psalter (1557? and 1566–1567); and a *Triodion* for Lent (1558–1559). Two printers, Marusha Nefediev and Vasjuk Nikiforov, are believed to have worked there. After 1567 the Cyrillic types used by this workshop disappeared completely, perhaps in a fire.

The first printing-shop worker known to have had his name in an imprint was Ivan Fedorov, a church deacon. He printed the *Apostol* (1564) and two editions of the *Casovnik* (1565), the first copiously illustrated with wood-cuts. In 1566 he and his partner Petr Mstislavec left Moscow, taking with them part of their type and almost all of their engraved wood-cuts. They went and settled in Zabludov, in Lithuania, and were employed in the service of Prince Khodkevich. Ivan the Terrible had given them permission to emigrate to Lithuania, possibly because he saw an opportunity to extend Russian influence there. After the unification of Lithuania with Poland, Fedorov left to settle in Lvov in Poland in 1572 and then in Ostrog in Volhynia; he printed a Bible there in 1581, using a fount different from the one he had previously employed.

In the history of Cyrillic books Fedorov's role is crucial and his New Testament was influential over nearly two hundred years; some of the wood-cuts in that book were still used in editions produced in Lvov as late as 1722.

Andronik Neveja succeeded Fedorov at Moscow and printed two Psalters, a Lent *Triodion* in 1589, a Pentecostal *Triodion* in 1591, and in 1597 an *Apostol* in an edition of 1,050 copies. His career lasted until the early 17th century, by which time books were being printed in Moscow, Kiev, Lvov, Novgorod, Chernigov and other great cities, in Belorussia, and in a number of monasteries.

Prayer books alone were the staple for nearly a century. Only in the mid-17th century did secular works appear. The first was an ABC written and printed by V. F. Burschev in 1634, with a further edition in 1639 of 6,000 copies, this time with secular engravings, an unprecedented feature. The second secular book was the translation from German of a military textbook in 1647. The title page of this work was engraved according to the design of Grigorij Blagushin. In spite of the activity of the presses (largely producing Church service-books), even as late as the

18th century the tradition of the manuscript book persisted. Lives of saints, accounts of travels, history books and even scientific works were all copied in the scriptoria.

Despite their diversity, there was a strong bond linking all the books of the period and that was the use of Cyrillic type imitating the Church hand. Although introduced late in the day, the printing industry in Russia was to undergo a remarkable expansion; in the 20th century, the statistics for books published there reached record figures.

B. The New World

Almost contemporary with the invention of the printing-press, that is during the last fifty years of the 15th century and even more during the very first years of the 16th century, other great 'discoveries' rapidly enlarged the horizons of the world known to Western man. These discoveries were geographical and with them a new epoch began in European history, as Europeans struggled to master the expanses of land and sea which opened up in front of them. They entered into relations with worlds previously unknown to them, or only glimpsed through more or less legendary accounts. The epoch which begins with these discoveries has yet to come to an end, and throughout it Western civilisation has acted to transform the rest of the world. In this process of transformation the printing-press has had its own role to play.

In America first of all. In the conquest of the Americas, printing from the beginning had an important influence. We wonder what motive lay behind the assaults by the Conquistadors; was it greed for gold, a taste for adventure? These had their part to play. But their vision of the Indies had been fed by countless stories of chivalry printed on Spanish presses during the late 15th and early 16th centuries; in these, far off lands were described populated by happy peoples blessed with fabulous riches. They were fired with a desire to enjoy adventures similar to those their heroes experienced. It was not by accident that, during the Conquest, the printer Cromberger at Seville was bringing out books like the *Sergias de Esplandian*, the second of Monteverde's novels, the sequel to his *Amadis de Gaulla*, which deals with Amazons living in California; the novel was frequently reprinted during Cortez's conquest of the vast kingdom of Mexico, and when Pizarro and later Almagro were exploring the Amazon Basin (with its symptomatic name) looking for Eldorado. This shows that the romances of chivalry popularised by the press helped to create a favourable climate for exploration of the New World. These tales, moreover, were constantly present in the minds of the Conquistadors and we know that Cromberger shipped large consignments of his novels to New Spain. Hardly a ship sailed at certain times without such books in its cargo.

The printed book quickly spread through the territories conquered by the Spanish. Soon a few presses appeared in the great conurbations which became the two capital cities, Mexico City and Lima. But these printing shops did not print chivalric romances. The all-powerful Church authorities would not stand for it. The very importation of works of fiction into the new continent was in theory forbidden – and in practice only grudgingly tolerated. For a long time, moreover, the religious books needed in South America were imported from Europe, to the profit of the firm of Plantin-Moretus. The New World thus long provided a market for the publishers of Spain or of Antwerp. Indeed, the printing shops of America, all of which were established by the ecclesiastical authorities, had in the beginning the strictly limited purpose of providing the volumes needed for missionary work among the Indians and keeping the developing colony supplied with essential text books and the indispensable works of religious piety. The history of the first Mexican press whose existence can be clearly dated, which was certainly the first press established on a permanent basis, is characteristic in this respect.

Only thirteen years after the Battle of Tolumba – the start of Cortez's conquest – Juan de Zumárraga, Bishop of Mexico to King Charles V of Spain, in a communication indicated a wish to set up a paper mill and printing office. His plan was realised in 1539, with the Spanish Viceroy's approval. Cromberger sent over a press from Seville with a printer named Juan Pablo – having first guaranteed himself against his future competition with a tightly drafted contract. Pablo began, it seems, by printing ABCs, elementary tracts to convert the Indians, devotional manuals and some law books – a modest start which however proved the existence of a local clientele. Little by little printing developed in Mexico City. In 1550 Antonio de Espinosa, a type founder of Seville, arrived in the town and began casting new roman and italic types for Pablo, to replace the gothic he had been using. De Espinosa founded a second press in 1559. Other presses were established before the end of the 16th century and, in greater numbers, during the 17th century. In the 16th century the number of titles published in Mexico City was 116, and in the 17th it was 1,228, a total much higher than in many European cities. This is even more remarkable when it is remembered that the paper had to come from Europe.

Mexico City was already so large that printing was bound to do well there. Its population just after 1600 was 25,000, of whom 12,000 were Europeans. At Lima, capital of Peru, presses also soon began to operate. An Italian printer, Antonio Ricardo, who had worked briefly in Mexico, set up a press there in 1584. He had been attracted to Lima by the Jesuits, who had a large college there and who had, since 1576, expressed a wish to have a printing press operating in the vicinity, so that they could have the books necessary in their missionary work among the Indians. Naturally his first major work was a catechism in three languages. From that small beginning printing developed in this city, which had in the 17th century 10,000 inhabitants (including the *mestizos*) and possessed five colleges (one of them for the natives) and a university with 80 teachers: by 1637, three printing offices were in simultaneous operation.

Thus, fairly early on, two major centres of the printing industry began to develop in the two largest towns of the Spanish American empire. But apart from the two cities there was, for a long time, little else. Four books are known bearing the imprint of Juli on the shores of Lake Titicaca, where there was a Jesuit seminary, but these books seem in fact to have been printed in Lima. In 1626–1627 a press was working in Cuenca, Ecuador, and another at Santiago in Guatemala from 1660 on. Very little thus appeared outside Mexico City and Lima before the 18th century, which indicates that the Spaniards had not yet subdued and developed the vast regions they had conquered. It was very different in North America where the press, in the wake of the pioneers, gradually and methodically occupied the new territory.

The first printing office in what is now the United States was opened in 1638 in the New England colony of Massachusetts Bay, which had been founded some twenty years before by the Pilgrim Fathers.[289] Educated men were numerous among the first immigrants and those who followed them. There were many lawyers and dissenting clergy (graduates of the university of Cambridge in many cases) who went to New England to seek religious liberty. Quite early on, the colony felt it needed a college. Among the bequests and gifts granted to the new foundation, the largest was that of John Harvard – £800 and 320 books. By 1636 plans were complete and the college was inaugurated in a village called New Town, later rechristened Cambridge in 1638. Glover, a nonconformist minister, who had only recently arrived in America, returned to England with a view to securing printing equipment and any printers willing to make the trip. He bought a press and made an agreement with a locksmith, Stephen Day and his two sons, one of whom, Matthew Day, 18, was a printer. All three accepted an engagement offered by the minister, and went to America. Glover died on the return voyage and his widow took over the business, setting up near the new college in Cambridge. The first titles published were: the *Freeman's Oath* (the formula for the oath of allegiance required by the Government of its citizens), an almanac and a translation of the Psalms. In 1643 came the *Capital Laws of Massachusett's Bay*. Under Matthew Day's control and then Samuel Green's (1649–1692), this press gave proof of vigorous activity. It published material related to the activities of the college, almanacs, catechisms and in 1663 an Indian language translation of the Bible.

A long time elapsed before other presses appeared. In 1674 John Foster set one up at Boston. In 1685 William Bradford began in Philadelphia; there, along with two associates, he started the first American paper mill in 1690, before moving to New York in 1693. Farther south the printer William Nuthead started business in Jamestown, Virginia, in 1682; evicted by the Governor, he went to Maryland, where he set up in St. Mary City in 1685. But clearly, print shops were few and far between in the North American colonies in the 17th century.

This was hardly surprising. In the early 18th century the future United States had a population of less than 400,000, scattered over vast areas. The books they read came from England. In such conditions, American printers largely made a living out of printing routine matter like Acts, local laws, almanacs, ABCs, collections of sermons by local ministers, commercial leaflets and prayer books. The publication of laws, bye-laws and official regulations, remained, for a long time, their principal source of revenue. As a result, in practice only those printers could survive who were appointed as official printer to one of the colonies. Even then their position was far from secure. Often colonial governors distrusted printers and hesitated to give them permission to establish themselves, keeping a very close watch on them after they had done so. Moreover the local representative assemblies, who paid the printers' wages, also claimed for themselves the right to censor their productions.

Printing did not really develop in America during the 18th century until the printers discovered a new source of income – the newspaper. Far from their homeland, in sparsely populated areas, the pioneers felt cut off from contact with the rest of the world; probably that is why the newspaper developed more quickly in America than elsewhere. The first American gazettes, from before Franklin's time, often copied their stories from European papers; but priceless information about local events can also be found in them. Print runs were often very modest and many papers disappeared after a short life; yet no fewer than 2,120 papers were published between 1691 and 1820, in thirty colonies and states, and 461 of these lasted more than ten years.

Therefore, printers starting a new press never omitted to include a newspaper in their production, to which they were usually the main and sometimes the sole contributor. The printer-journalist is an essentially American phenomenon. In those vast regions, the main problem was to reach their readers; this was only possible with the aid of a new functionary, the postmaster. Naturally, therefore, printers produced their newspapers in close collaboration with postmasters. Often postmasters became printers and printers postmasters. In fact the official postal system in America was the work of a printer. The printer's office was often a relay station in the postal system. It was often a bookshop too, but one which sold more than just books. It was, in short, a centre of news and communications – hence frequently of local public life as well. Thanks to the systematic organisation of the postal service, which was perfectly adapted to the needs of the country, the number of printing shops in America multiplied in the course of the 18th century. More often than not the establishment of a printing press was followed by the inauguration of a newspaper. During the century nearly every colony came to possess its own press. After Massachusetts came Virginia, Maryland, Pennsylvania and New York State, all of which had presses in the 17th century. In the 18th century Connecticut (New London 1709); New Jersey (Perth Amboy 1723); Rhode Island (Newport 1727); South Carolina (Charleston 1731); North Carolina (New Bern 1749); New Hampshire (Portsmouth 1756); Delaware (Wilmington 1761); Georgia (Savannah 1762); Louisiana (New Orleans 1764); Vermont (Dresden, now Hanover 1778); Florida (St. Augustine 1783); Maine (Falmouth, now Portland 1785); Kentucky (Lexington 1787); District of Columbia (Georgetown 1789); West Virginia (Shepherdstown 1790); Tennessee (Hawkins Court House, now Rogersville 1791); Ohio (Cincinnati 1793); Michigan (Detroit 1796) followed one on the other.

This list proves that the Anglo-Saxon settlers were able to develop the territories they had acquired, and that, though long limiting their endeavours to production of modest works of simple utility, they created fairly quickly a busy printing trade, soon backed up by a papermaking industry which made them independent of the Old World.

C. The Far East*

If we pass from Spanish America and North America to the lands which had been under Portuguese control since 1500, we can see once more the force of Cournot's observation that in every civilisation the discovery of writing was a critical moment in its history. Neither the Aztecs of Mexico nor the Incas of Peru had a knowledge of writing; nor *a fortiori*, did the various Indian tribes in New Spain or Portuguese Brazil. This goes far towards explaining the comparative delay in the development of the European book in South America.

But in their African and even more in their Asian territories, the Portuguese quickly grasped the importance of the medium for propaganda purposes. There is much to be learnt from the fact that while the first book printed in Russia was dated 1563, the first in Constantinople 1727 and the first in Greece 1821, one was actually imported into Abyssinia as early as 1515 and presses were operating in Goa by 1557, in Macao by 1588 and in Nagasaki by 1590. The first 'exotic' types to be cast in Europe were made in Lisbon in 1539 for the historian Juan de Barros and intended to be used in books for child readers in Ethiopia, Persia and India; they were for a grammar and a catechism. The Kings of Portugal from an early date made it a policy to send books in the cargoes of ships carrying explorers – for example, in 1490 when an expedition was sent to the Congo (two German printers were also sent to that country in 1494, although it is hard to know what they could have hoped to accomplish there). When St. Francis Xavier left Lisbon in 1541, King John III provided him with a library worth 100 cruzados.

In Portuguese India there was scarcely any contact with educated Hindus, until the efforts of Father de Nobili in the early 17th century. As a result, the pamphlets printed from 1557 at Goa (there were three printers there), Rachol (five printers), Cochin, Vaypicota, Punicale and Ambacalate, were rarely anything but catechisms and prayer books.

* This section is the work of the Reverend Father Henri Bernard-Maitre.

Sixteen are known up to the present in Portuguese and between twenty-four and twenty-seven bilingual texts or texts in various Asian languages (one in Malaysian, two in Abyssinian, one, produced in Lisbon, in Portuguese and Tamil, between four and six in Indian languages printed in Portugal, one translation from Indian into Portuguese, etc.).

When, on the other hand, the Portuguese arrived in China in 1513, and even more when they arrived in Japan in 1542, they found an indigenous printing process already highly developed: xylography, a form of writing in wood-cut. Missionaries, especially the Jesuits, lost no time in transplanting the latest Western printing techniques to the Far East. However, we must not forget that little religious books were being printed in Chinese at the end of the 16th century by xylography in Parian, a suburb of Manila, under the direction of the Dominicans.

St. Francis Xavier (from 1549) and his first successors (Father Ruggieri was in China from about 1584) only envisaged the use of local xylographic methods at first; but Father Alexander Valignano, who left Japan in 1584 with four little 'ambassadors', was soon planning to supply these lands with moveable types cast as in Europe. This idea came to fruition at Macao with the production of a school text book in 1589 and a work in Latin, the account of the journey undertaken by the ambassadors, in 1590. During the so-called 'Christian century' in Japan (1549–1644), no fewer than twenty works were produced, reflecting a variety of interests. Including major adaptations of 'Calepin', a European dictionary, they are sought out as keenly as Gutenbergs or first editions of Shakespeare. These Japanese 'incunabula' have the same importance in the history of literature as the earliest transcripts of the Buddhist works which translated the sacred Sanscrit texts into Chinese. Scholars examine these first printed books in minutest detail, not only to study the contemporary dialects, but also to observe the virtually indetectable modifications in Japanese grammar and vocabulary as it became influenced by European thought.

Analogous information can be obtained from the adaptations, which have generally survived only in manuscript form, of Western works into Chinese, Vietnamese, Korean and the languages of the East Indies. But in comparison to these half-hearted attempts to introduce Western ideas, the Western influence in China was of much greater importance. Besides the xylographic publications in European languages, of which there were about a dozen, the first Catholic missionaries, known as the Peking Fathers, created a veritable library of European texts in Chinese. The story is worth briefly summarising.

The first editor and translator of Christian texts in China was Father Ruggieri, from Naples. He was joined in 1583 by Father Matteo Ricci, an Italian of remarkable abilities who, after devoting many years to the study of Chinese as it was written and spoken by the mandarins, translated what little was available: some scientific works, particularly on navigation and astronomy, and humanist compilations, for example a collection of Adages in the manner of Erasmus and the Stoics. After his death on 11th May, 1610, the Jesuits in China sent one of their number, Nicholas Trigault of Douai, to Europe to assemble, among other things, as large a collection of books as possible for the Chinese mission. Trigault arrived in Rome in 1616. Almost at once he obtained as an assistant Johann Schreck, known as Terrentius, a former doctor who entered the newly created *Accademia dei Lincei* with Galileo. Thanks to some connections in high places, especially with Cardinal Borromeo, founder of the Biblioteca Ambrosiana in Milan, Terrentius and Trigault got together an impressive collection in a very short time – one worthy of any of the best libraries in Europe. They bought books, for example, at the Frankfurt fair. After many vicissitudes this unique collection (more than 200 volumes on medicine alone have survived from it) arrived in Pekin. It was preserved almost intact down the years (despite catastrophes like the burning of Pekin after the fall of the Ming dynasty in 1644 and the Boxer Rising of 1900) and was enlarged by many gifts, notably from the 'French' Mission sent by Louis XIV in 1688 and from other missions and missionaries down to the 18th century. Today more than four thousand books survive, including several incunabula, in the Petang Library in Peking. A meticulous catalogue was compiled by M. Verhaeren, a Lazarist priest, with help from the Rockefeller Foundation.

This early collection of European literature in the heart of China was intended to be used for translating the finest products of Western culture and literature into Chinese. The first man to tackle this daunting project was a German from Cologne, Adam Schall. With the assistance of a Chinese scholar, Paul Hsu Kuang-chi, he eventually published an encyclopaedia of mathematics and science in 100 volumes. When the Ming Dynasty fell in 1644 and the Ching Dynasty of the Manchus came to power, the enterprise was momentarily interrupted. But under the patronage of the first Manchu Emperor, Shun-chi, Schall was made President of the Society of Mathematicians and reprinted the encyclopaedia. He fell into disgrace in 1661 and was succeeded by a Fleming, Ferdinand Verbiest, who had been the first schoolmaster of the great Emperor Kang-hsi (1661–1722).

The arrival of the five mathematicians sent out by Louis XIV under the direction of the Frenchman de Fontaney in 1688 was intended to lead to the foundation of an Academy affiliated to the *Académie des Sciences* in Paris. One of their most noteworthy efforts was the mapping of the Manchu Empire, begun in 1706. Their works printed in Chinese won Leibnitz's admiration – he was a convinced advocate of a Eurasian policy. But the successor of Emperor Kang-hsi, his grandson Chien-lung (1735-1799), did no more than tolerate European missionaries in the Society of Mathematicians. However, he at least gave orders for the buildings known as the Peking Versailles to be erected, and the survey of the Empire came out in a second edition in his reign.

The production of Chinese works of this kind, which came to number several hundred titles, began gradually to fade out for various reasons, among which was the suppression of the Jesuits in 1762. It was compensated for in part by the publication in 18th-century Europe of works by missionaries, generally French, which were to provide the basis of scholarly Sinology. These included the *Lettres édifiantes et curieuses depuis 1702*, the *Description de la Chine* by Father du Halde, which was published in 1735, and the sixteen volumes of the *Mémoires concernant les Chinois*.

Developments in India were similar to those in China, but on a smaller scale. Astronomical observatories were built, the one at Agra being the most noteworthy, and several of the most important works of Indian literature, above all the Vedas, were translated. Some epic poems were even composed in Tamil by P. Beschi. But the French Revolution and the Napoleonic Wars interrupted contacts between the West and the East. Afterwards relations were slowly restored, mainly by Protestant missionaries acting in a totally changed context. The temporary eclipse of the Eastern civilisations by Western technology prevented any two-way exchange on equal terms. Particularly after the 1840 Opium War, Europe achieved almost total dominance in the East. The printed book played an important role in this domination, but only in order to serve the interests of the Western nations, until the day when first Japan, after the restoration of the Meiji Emperors in 1853, and then China, with its literary renaissance after 1919, took up on their own behalf the torch which first blazed in the 16th century.

The Book Trade 7

Between the 15th and the 18th centuries, as we have seen, the number of presses multiplied. The number of books produced increased continuously as well. But let there be no mistake, it was in no way comparable to the present quantity. Calendars, almanacs, ABCs, prayer books, religious tracts and, from the end of the 16th century onwards, the old chivalric romances were read by everybody and made up the bulk of the bales of books transported from town to town. In addition, the multiplication in the number of schools and colleges created, from the end of the 16th century onwards, a growing demand for text books. Apart from these works only the major bestsellers reached a wide audience. All the other books produced, that is to say the great majority, were of interest only to a very small number of readers. Consequently throughout this period publishers were faced with a basic problem, a problem which was more severe for them than for publishers nowadays, but one which they had in common with all those who run a business which produces a large number of identical objects – the problem of finding enough retail outlets. The task of organising a commercial network which would enable them to sell the books they produced as rapidly as possible was, for a long time, the constant and central preoccupation of publishers.

I
Some Basic Data: Sizes of Editions

Once set up in type, a text could be reproduced in an almost infinite number of copies; there were no technical difficulties about producing 'large' editions even with the earliest, or almost the earliest, presses. Financially, moreover, the cost of setting up type and the inescapable charges that had to be met before printing could be begun formed a fairly large proportion of the eventual cost of producing an edition. As a consequence printers and booksellers naturally had an interest in printing a relatively large number of copies of an edition in order to offset this expenditure and so reduce the cost of producing each copy. Yet once a certain figure was reached in a print run there was no great advantage in printing any more. For, on the one hand, the reduction in the cost price resulting from the offsetting of the initial investment diminished in proportion to the number of copies printed, until it reached a fairly insignificant sum; and on the other – and here the crucial problem of retail outlets came to the fore – there was absolutely no point in a publisher printing more copies of a particular book than the market could absorb within a reasonable period of time. To ignore this meant many unsold copies or, at the best, tying up a substantial capital sum in a commodity that sold all too slowly.

Some figures relative to this: firstly for books published in the earliest years of printing, up to 1480 or 1490, when the book market was still in a relatively unorganised state.[290] The figures seem modest to us. In 1469 John of Speyer printed in Venice only 100 copies of Cicero's *Epistolae ad familiares*, the same number as for St. Antoninus' *Confessionale* printed in 1477 and 1480 and for a Statius produced by the presses of the monastery of St. James of Ripoli in Florence. In the same period, according to hints he gives us in 1472, Johannes Philippus de Lignamine printed, in Rome, editions of 150 copies on average, yet already in the same city his competitors Sweynheym and Pannartz printed 300 copies of Donatus and commonly produced print runs of 275. However these quickly proved too many for the time and Sweynheym and Pannartz complain of poor sales of classical works, even in Rome; the market just could not absorb them. Johannes Neumeister printed in Foligno a Cicero in 200 copies in 1465 and Andrea Belfortis printed the same number of Justinian's *Institutes* in 1471 in Ferrara. Thereafter editions grow larger, notably at Venice, an important commercial and cultural centre from which it was easy to export bales of books in all directions. As early as 1471 Wendelin of Speyer printed 1,000 copies of Panormitano's commentaries on the Decretals in Venice, and in 1478 Leonard Wild printed for Nicholas of Frankfurt 930 copies of a Latin Bible. These are enormous figures for the period and may explain Wendelin's sudden financial difficulties.

By 1480 the market was beginning to be better organised. At this time the Kobergers, the first truly international booksellers, began to do business on a large scale. The price of books dropped to a fraction of what it had been and the average number of copies per edition grew.

Between 1480 and 1490, according to Haebler, printings of 400 or 500 would be average and higher figures were increasingly common. In 1490 Hans Rix printed more than 700 copies of the romance *Tirant lo Blancho* in Valencia and a few years later Alonzo di Alopa printed Plato's works in 1,025 copies in Florence. In 1491 Matteo Capcasa in Venice did a breviary in 1,500 copies and in 1489 Matthias Moravus reached 2,000 in his edition of Roberto Caraccioli's *Sermones de Laudibus Sanctorum* printed in Naples, while Battista Torti published Justinian's *Codex* at Venice in 1490 in an edition of 1,300. In 1491 and 1494 he produced two editions of the *Decretals* of Gregory IX, each of 2,300.

By the close of the 15th century therefore some of the biggest publishers reached 1,500 copies. This figure represents more or less the size Koberger planned for his great editions.[291] After that, editions settled at that figure for a long time. Joost Bade may have declared as late as 1526 that he published only 650 copies of Noël Beda's *Annotatione* against Lefèvre d'Étaples. But that was in reply to an enquiry by the Parlement which had just censored the work, and this fact may have inhibited Bade from claiming a large run. We know that two years later he published a Thucydides in 1,225 copies. Bonnemère published an edition of 650 copies of Augustine's *Commentary on the Psalms* which had been ordered by Wechel in the same year,[293] but he printed 1,500 of Pierre Doré's *Collège de Sapience* in 1539 for Le Bret and Brouilly.[294] At about the same time Lucian's *Palinurus*, a very short book, was printed in 1,500 copies at Avignon in 1497, and 750 copies of Raymond Lulle's *Ars Brevis* were produced in 1511.[295] Finally at Hagenau the printer Gran printed 1,500 copies of the *Sanctorale* by the Spanish preacher Petrus de Porta in 1515.[296] Such facts suggest an average edition of somewhere between 1,000 and 1,500 copies in the early 16th century, with occasional figures below that. It has sometimes been thought that works which we know to have been tremendously popular were published in much larger editions, a conclusion based on a letter of Erasmus written in 1527 in which he claimed that Simon de Colines had put out a pirated edition of his *Colloquies* in 24,000 copies. But Erasmus quotes the figure from hearsay and it is contested by the more reliable bibliographers.[297] This unique figure must have been put forward by Erasmus as a boast. In fact it is probable that even works which were guaranteed to be highly successful were not published in much greater numbers than normal. Erasmus' *In Praise of Folly* was printed by Froben in Basle in 1,800 copies in 1515,[298] and Luther's German Bible was first printed in 4,000 copies.[299] Not that works like those were not widely circulated, but their dissemination came from repeated printings often by different printers.

Thus in this period the size of editions remains fairly stable. Plantin, one of the greatest printers of the second half of the 16th century, and with a highly developed network of commercial contacts, worked as a rule only to 1,250 or 1,500 copies. Occasionally he produced smaller editions of around 800 for special works, such as Dodoens' *Frumentorum Historiae*. But sometimes he produced bigger runs of scholarly and liturgical works. Clénard's Greek grammar of 1564 and the *Corpus Juris Civilis* in 1566-1567 both reached 2,500. He even printed 2,600–3,000 copies of some books of his Hebrew Bible which he reckoned to sell in part to Jewish colonies in North Africa.[300] By the Decree of Star Chamber dated 1587, editions in England were limited to 1,200–1,250, with some few exceptions reaching 3,000.[301]

Similar figures are to be found in the 17th century. Three plays of Corneille, *Nicomède, Pertharite* and *Andromède* came out in editions of 1,200–1,250.[302] Boileau's publisher thought 1,200 a creditable number for his poem *Le Lutrin*.[303] Luynes, a major publisher in the field of classics, printed Primi's *History of the War in Holland* in 1,000 copies for the French edition and 500 copies for the Italian.[304] Each of the first eight editions of La Bruyère's *Characters* appears to have been put out in 2,000 copies or thereabouts.[305] In Holland, Elzevier did a reprint of Grotius' *Truth of the Christian Religion* (1675) for the English market in 2,000 copies,[306] and in 1637 the printer Jean Maire of Leyden printed, as we have seen, a first edition of 3,000 for the *Discours de la Méthode*.[307] While some important and famous works were published in editions of under 1,000, most editions of important reference books and of text books fluctuated between 1,000 and 2,000. The first edition of the *Dictionnaire de l'Académie Française* to be put on sale was printed by Coignard in an edition of 1,500.[308] Pithou's edition of the *Corps de Droit canon* published in 1687 ran to 1,500 copies; an edition of the less ambitious *Practicien Français* was printed in Lyons by Antoinette Carteron in 1,500 copies in 1704.[310] The Antwerp publisher Verdussen published a theological work in 1677, Ariaga's *Disputationes Theologicae*, in 1,530 copies, and Anisson's edition of the same work at Lyons was in 2,200.[311] Franz Halma of Amsterdam printed 1,500 copies of Pieter Marin's new Dutch-French Dictionary in 1701.[312]

The only works regularly to pass the 2,000 mark in this period were religious titles or text books. Some Bibles from Holland seem to have been printed in editions exceeding 3,000 or even 4,000 copies.[313] Towards the end of the 16th century pirate printers in Luxembourg and

Liège ran off 2,500–3,000 copies of Saci's French Bible, the copyright of Desprez of Paris.[314] At Narbonne the printer Besse printed an ABC in 3,000 copies[315] and André Molin in Lyons pirated a Latin-French dictionary called the *Petit Apparat Royal* in 6,500 copies.[316]

In the 18th century print runs were still generally less than 2,000, although some reached a higher figure if they were certain to be a major success. The folio volumes of Montfaucon's *Antiquité Expliquée* were published in a first edition of 1800 which sold out in two months, but a second edition of 2,000 did not sell so readily.[317] Moreri's *Dictionary* printed at Paris by the bookseller Coignard went into several reprints each of 2,000.[318] Bayle's *Dictionary* on the other hand was, it seems, the subject of a bigger print run (more than 2,500).[319] In 1770 Panckouke planned to print 2,150 copies of his *Encyclopédie*, and Diderot's *Encyclopédie* was finally printed in an initial edition of 4,250.[320] The Société Typographique of Liège put out three editions of Helvetius simultaneously, one in 4vo of 500 copies, the other two in 8vo, one of 1,000 and the other of 2,000 copies. The same group published a pirate edition of Sébastien Mercier's *Tableaux de Paris* in 1,500 copies which sold out quickly within the neighbourhood of Liège, as did an illustrated edition of *Daphnis and Chloë*, and they planned an edition of 1,500 of Rousseau's collected works in 1788.[321]

These figures show that even in the 18th century publishers hesitated to order really large editions. The only literary works which were an exception to this rule seem to have been the works of some of the *philosophes*, Voltaire in particular. Cramer published his *Essai sur les moeurs* in an edition of 7,000, and promised to send 2,000 copies of the *Histoire de l'Empire de Russie* to Paris as soon as the printing was completed – which suggests a large overall number. The *Siècle de Louis XIV* appeared in Berlin in an edition of 3,000.[322] If we exclude for the moment text books and chapbooks, it is clear that print runs remained comparatively modest in the 18th century. We also have the impression that no matter how successful a title might be guaranteed to be, publishers did not dare print many more than the conventional number. Let us see why.

Even when we look at publisher's accounts today, it is surprising how a remarkably small number of copies of a book will normally exhaust the potential readership in a city of middling size, with some exceptions: in France, titles which win the Prix Goncourt, for example. Hence we may guess the difficulties facing a bookseller in the 16th, 17th and even 18th centuries when the population of the towns was much smaller, the proportion of readers much lower, transport was much more difficult and there was a much greater risk of piracy.

Some figures will help us understand the logistics of book distribution: how normally books had to be sent out in very small consignments, with only a few copies of a particular title, sometimes only one copy, being included in each consignment. Here are Joost Bade's sales of his edition of Beda's *Annotationes* on Lefèvre d'Étaples and Erasmus in 1526: 32 to Melchior Koberger in Nuremberg, 50 to Bade's agent in Lyons for sale in Italy, 50 to another agent, 20 to Conrad Resch, a bookseller in Basel and in Paris, 62 to England, 40 to Rouen and 6 to Orléans.[323] In the 17th century bales of books would hold equally small numbers. Here is one list, among many, of titles ordered by Moretus from Sébastien Cramoisy, dated 17th February, 1639: 3 copies of the works of the legal expert Chopin, 10 of the *Preuves des Libertés de l'Église Gallicane* by Pierre Dupuy; 6 of the *Institutes de Practique en Matière Civile et Criminelle*; 3 of the *Dies Caniculares* of Simone Naioli; 3 of the works of Polybius; 3 of the works of Aristotle; 6 of the *Commentarii in Patrias Britonum Leges*; 3 of the works of Du Perron.[324] In the second half of the century the orders were of much the same size. In the course of an enquiry, Guillaume de Luynes declares that he has sent 24 copies of Primi's *Histoire de la Guerre de Hollande* to Anisson and Posuel at Lyons, 5 to Hugueville at Nantes, 8 to Garnier at Rheims, 6 to La Court of Bordeaux, 4 to a bookseller in Douai.[325] Admittedly this is only the beginning of his sales effort, but these figures nevertheless reveal how small were the quantities sent out in response to orders.

There is no point in giving further figures. Let us limit ourselves to one final example which is particularly striking – the way the Cramers distributed copies of the complete set of Voltaire's works during the year of its publication.[326] They sent, some separately, some in large consignments, 1,600 volumes to Robin and 600 to Lambert, both Paris booksellers; 142 to booksellers at Avignon; 80 to Basel; 36 to a retailer in Dijon; 50 to Marc-Michel Rey in Amsterdam; 75 to Pierre Machuel in Rouen; 25 to Bassompierre; 25 to Gaude at Nîmes; 25 to Gillebert, a canon of the cathedral at Besançon; 25 to Reycendes and Colomb in Milan; 20 to Jean de la Ville, 18 to Jeanne-Marie Bruyset, 12 to De La Roche and 15 to Camp, all booksellers of Lyons; 24 to Christian Herold in Hamburg; 16 to Boyer and the same number to Joseph Colomb, both in Marseilles; 12 to Claude Philibert in Copenhagen; 12 to Barbou in Limoges; 10 to Pierre Vasse in Brussels; 7 to Pierre Chouad also in

Brussels; 6 to Jean-Georges Lochner in Nuremberg; 6 to Elias Luzac in Leyden and smaller numbers of copies to Genoa, Cadiz, Turin, Milan, Parma, Berne and Venice, not including some volumes sent off separately to individual buyers.

2
Some Problems for the Trade

It was necessary to organise an efficient distribution system, and the difficulties were all the greater if books had to be sent across all Europe in such small consignments. Firstly transport. Books were precious merchandise, but heavy and cumbersome. Throughout this period transport costs were high and often had a severe effect on book prices. In order to reduce the weight and bulk of books it was the habit to despatch them 'white', i.e. without their binding. But this practice had obvious disadvantages. The man who got the consignments ready in the shop had to see that the right sheets were included in the correct order. Many mistakes were made and booksellers' correspondence of the period is full of demands for missing sheets needed to complete defective volumes.

But the book was also a fragile commodity. There were only two forms of transport available, boat and wagon, so that books risked being ruined by seawater at the bottom of a ship's hold or by rainwater in a carrier during bad weather. Normally they were placed in great wooden crates for protection, but even so they often arrived soaked or otherwise damaged, and when books were transferred from one vehicle to another several times during a journey the risk was even greater. We know how the Antwerp booksellers despatched their cargoes. Those destined for Paris either went all the way in carts driven by carters who more or less specialised in this form of merchandise, or else they were despatched by sea to Rouen and were then transferred to barges on the Seine. Those bound for Lyons went by carrier, sometimes direct, more often by way of Paris, where an agent of the Lyons bookseller would take them into his care and relay them to their destination partly by land, partly by water. The many books Plantin sent to Spain went by sea to Rouen or one of the ports in Brittany and thence on by sea to a Spanish port, and often from there to America. Moretus, who exported to Danzig, Bergen and England, was constantly concerned about sailing times, impatiently waiting news of ship arrivals and dreading bad weather or, in time of war, attacks by pirates like Jean Bart. When war came, the whole trade was at risk. In Richelieu's day, during the war between France and Spain, the Low Countries could not deal directly with France because of various royal prohibitions. So that trade could be carried on, a subterfuge which then amounted to common practice went into effect: books were sent first under a neutral flag to a bookshop in Dover which then arranged for them to be sent on to Paris. Even in peacetime the risks were great, particularly for the booksellers of Lyons, who exported much of their wares to Italy and Spain – to Italy across the Alps in carriers; to Spain by land as far as the Loire, then by river to Nantes and thence on the Atlantic to a Spanish port, then again by land to Medina del Campo for distribution.[327]

Most of the time transhipments meant that a bookseller needed to have an agent on the spot. There was always an additional risk of cargoes going astray during transhipment because so many people could not read. Usually, in addition to the written address, a monogram was inscribed on the crate indicating the destination of the merchandise, but this often only compounded the confusion. It is problems like these that explain why the trade developed in ports and those other growing commercial centres where communication was easier.

The crate arrives in good condition, to the relief of sender and recipient, and all that remains is to pay for the cargo. More and greater problems confronted the bookseller at this stage because the banking system then was still badly adapted to this kind of commerce. It was often impossible to pay in hard cash. How could a bookseller living abroad send the money each time he received his goods? The difficulties were usually too great. He had to use other methods even if they served to raise the price.

Until the late 17th century there were two other methods in common use: barter and bills of exchange. Quite often both were employed at once. It generally worked like this: on receipt of a consignment the bookseller made a note in his account book of what he owed and similarly when he sent out a consignment he made a note of what his client owed him. After what were often quite long intervals they balanced up the accounts and the debtor settled up by using the traditional method of the bill of exchange. Thus Cramoisy in Paris, for example, used to receive more books from Moretus in Antwerp than he sent to Moretus and was thus usually in his debt. But he sent a large number of books to the booksellers of Brussels, especially to Léonard, the father of the Léonard of Paris. Léonard would then transfer to Moretus the money owed to Moretus by Cramoisy. Antwerp and Brussels being neighbouring cities in the same country, there was no longer any problem. Although the system was simple in theory it was complicated in practice, since bills of exchange passed, often many times, from hand to hand. Moreover it seems on occasion to have tempted booksellers, like many other businessmen, to do business on the strength of the bills of exchange they held. This had its dangers. Any interruption of business between countries threatened to paralyse trade because payments were suspended. Bankruptcies then resulted, each one bringing further bankruptcies in its train. Booksellers therefore often preferred, in the interests of their own trade, to re-finance their colleagues when they were threatened with bankruptcy since they were often trading on the strength of their colleague's bills of exchange. This was the standard method of doing business right up to the 18th century.

3
Business Methods at the Time of the Book-Fairs

Thus the creation of a viable commercial network through which to sell a sufficient number of books efficiently and rapidly was a major problem faced by the early printers. The first technique employed to overcome this difficulty was that of the middleman. Early printers soon began to employ men they could trust to canvass sales for them and these agents would visit towns both large and small in search of potential customers. Often they carried a supply of small handbills and posters announcing their business and giving a list of titles they offered. As soon as they arrived in a town these leaflets would be stuck up and distributed. Often they would indicate the name of the inn where the agent stayed and the days on which he did business. This was still evidently a primitive arrangement. However agents were naturally quick to visit towns on the day of a local celebration, when they would be able to reach a larger audience and so do better business. Naturally too they went to those fairs which were attended by merchants from other areas. Such merchants would buy a book or calendar for themselves out of the profits they made. But, more importantly, they would pass on orders from fellow townsmen unable to be at the fair and could provide the means of transport and transfers of money from one place to another. Sometimes some of them were even ready to take on the job of retailing a small number of books in their home town. If an agent found things were going particularly well in a town he would often return and might eventually stay there permanently. He would then start a little stall or a shop either on his own account or on behalf of the printer he worked for. In this way retail bookshops sprung up in a large number of towns, each taking on the job of selling to the public the books printed by the large publishing firms.

From this starting point the book trade soon developed an organisa-tion which covered all Europe. Paris, already well established as a centre of the production and sale of manuscripts, was visited by Peter Schoeffer and his agents as early as 1460–1470. At this time Schoeffer established a permanent agent, Herman Statboen, there. He stocked books of Schoeffer's to the value of 2,425 crowns at the time of his death in 1474. Sweynheym and Pannartz sent agents to Germany from Rome and at the same date printer-booksellers less well established than they contracted with large publishers for them to sell their products or combined to sell their wares themselves. Johannes Rheinardi of Einingen, who printed only one important book, could sell it in the year of its publica-tion, through his contacts with Italian booksellers, in Rome and Perugia, while a group of booksellers in Perugia banded together to publish books and had them sold through their own stalls in Rome, Naples, Siena, Pisa, Bologna, Ferrara and Padua between 1471 and 1476. Similarly, in 1471 Antonius Mathiae and Lambertus of Delft, both printers in business in Genoa, were selling books not only in various Lombard towns, but as far afield as in the kingdom of Naples. We have already seen how Barthélemy Buyer of Lyons had extensive business contacts by 1485, as did Koberger of Nuremberg, and the trade in Venice was also highly organised by then. Some time before his death Nicolas Jenson even gave up printing, it seems, to concentrate on the bookselling side, and for that purpose formed an important partnership with several German merchant book-sellers, the firm 'Nicolas Jenson and Co' ('sociique') which had agents in several Italian towns, notably Rome, Perugia and Naples. After Jenson's death his partners associated themselves for five years with the firm of John of Cologne and Jean Manthen, and the new company had an extensive trading organisation. It is not surprising that with such an increase in retail outlets the size of editions expanded hugely during this period and that at the same time the price of books dropped.[329]

By around 1490 the trade had a good sales organisation across the length and breadth of Europe, retailers were established in most towns selling the books produced by the great publishers and these had agents in a large number of towns. An internal hierarchy now begins to appear within the book trade. Koberger, one of the biggest publishers, had three branch establishments in France – at Paris, Lyons and Toulouse. He was so influential that the Toulouse printer Jean de Paris sent one of his own agents to Spain in 1491 to meet Koberger's men there in order to come to an arrangement. Even earlier, in 1489, Hans Rix, a printer-bookseller from Valencia, is selling books printed by Venetian firms in various parts of Spain. At the same time in France, and to an even greater extent in Germany, the 'colporteur' appears, selling pamphlets and almanacs in town and country. Pedlars like these were an important factor in the spread of the Reformation in the 16th century.

The selling of books at fairs was an established custom from the earliest times, and persisted for centuries, for example in the fairs of the Paris region and in the great fairs at Stourbridge in England.[330] The privileges enjoyed by traders attending a fair made transportation easier, money changers facilitated transactions and the large crowds made it easy to find a buyer. The great fairs became a focus for early printers and booksellers. Other factors helped as well: their regularity made them convenient for balancing accounts and the payment of debts, and for buying equipment from the dye-casters and type engravers who were also to be found there. They were a forum for the discussion of common problems, for announcements of forthcoming publications, and an opportunity to check that other booksellers were not planning to publish the same books; and they made it possible to establish regular business contacts. All these were vital reasons for attendance, and a knowledge of the role of the great European fairs at Leipzig, Lyons, Frankfurt and Medina del Campo is essential to the understanding of the growth of the trade.

The most important book fair was originally at Lyons.[331] From fairly early on this town had been an important centre of the printing industry. Lyons was also the location for some of the great international fairs. From the end of the Hundred Years' War onwards, helped by various concessions and royal privileges, the town devoted its energies to building up the fairs, and, despite numerous vicissitudes, these had become securely established by the end of Louis XI's reign (1483). The

French invasions of Italy actually stimulated trade between Italy and France, especially for Lyons and its fair, which reached its apogee in the first half of the 16th century. Its success was dependent on its favoured position on a commercial crossroads. There was, at that time, a great quantity of goods which was transported on the rivers Saône and Rhône, and in addition Lyons was at the junction of two particularly important overland routes; one crossed over the Guillotière Bridge and reached Italy via the Dauphiné and the Alpine passes, the other rejoined the Loire at Roanne. Lyons was a hive of business activity. As a Venetian, Lippomano, put it: 'Almost on the border of Italy and France, in contact with Germany through Switzerland, it is thus the warehouse of the three richest and most populous countries in Europe'. Its market dealt in all the commodities traded in Europe, particularly spices and silks, and it was from Lyons that rice, almonds, herbs, medicinal plants and dyestuffs from Italy, Portugal and the Levant were distributed throughout France.

The Lyons fair was thus of outstanding commercial importance and it was to encourage its prosperity that the kings of France and the local authorities granted such generous privileges to traders from all countries wishing to attend it. Trade secrets were protected and no merchant was obliged to open his accounts to inspection, moneylending was permitted and foreigners visiting the fair could enter and leave the country unhindered. Traders were exempt from letters of *marque* and reprisal and from the law of *escheat*, and the merchandise they brought to the fair was protected by numerous privileges and exempted from taxes on the transport of goods.

Twice a year, for fifteen days, merchants and traders flocked into the town along with their wagons and, since there was no covered market where businessmen could establish themselves, they set up shop wherever they could find space, on the side streets and the squares, in proper stalls or improvised shelters, even in the inns which they used to store their goods. The centre of it all was the bridges over the Saône and the little streets in the neighbourhood of Saint-Nizier.

When the selling was done, the time came for payment. Business was normally done during the fair on the basis of material credit, and, at the end of the fair, the Exchange would order a stop to all purely commercial transactions. For two or three days letters of credit were 'accepted' by those who had to pay them; i.e. they entered into a formal agreement to pay when due. After that the merchants' representatives would meet to decide the time allowed to meet bills of exchange due at other places and the interest rate until the next fair. Finally, three days later, settlement of the debts that had been recognised was either made in money or, preferably, by exchange of bills. Bankers were of course drawn to Lyons by such dealings and Italians were especially prominent, so that Lyons soon became the financial and banking centre of France.

Printers and booksellers, whose shops were mostly in and around the Rue Mercière, were at the centre of the commercial life of Lyons. Many of them were foreigners. Of the 49 or so booksellers and printers who worked in Lyons before 1500, a minority were French – 20 as against 20 or 22 Germans, 5 Italians, 1 Belgian, 1 Spaniard. Through its geographic position Lyons was the hub of a whole section of the international book trade; it was the booksellers of Lyons who imported Italian books, of such importance at that time, into France, and also German and Swiss – their import business did not hinder them however from imitating and counterfeiting foreign books. Their role in the expansion of the Spanish market was crucial through their branches in Toulouse. Not surprisingly, therefore, major Italian publishers like the Giuntas, the Gabiani or the Portonari soon established branches of their own in Lyons, and these branches tended to become so important that they often then became independent businesses, although remaining in close contact with their former head firm. Thus the Lyons fairs soon became great book fairs, at which books of Italian, German and Swiss origin were imported into France and Spain, while many French editions were exported to Italy, Spain and Germany, notably the famous editions of law books published in Lyons. The fair was also a great gathering place for the ordinary people and vast amounts of their popular reading was sold. Almanacs, prophecies, popular story-books, often illustrated with wood-cuts, were all on sale. Rabelais' *Grandes et Inestimables Cronicques du Grand et Énorme Géant Gargantua* were such a great success there that, according to him, more copies were sold at one Lyons fair than Bibles in ten years.[332]

Another book fair developed during the 16th century and became even more important than those of Lyons: the Frankfurt Fair.[333] When printing started in Mainz, not far away, Frankfurt had long been the site of an important fair, which had become the commercial clearing-house for the whole of the Rhineland, outshining its rivals. Numerous texts which survive from the late 15th and the 16th centuries underline its importance at that time. Drapers came there from England and the Low Countries. Spices from the East, wines from Southern Europe, the manufactures of German cities, were all traded at Frankfurt. Merchants from Lübeck, Vienna, Venice, Lyons, Antwerp and Amsterdam met those from Strasbourg, Basel, Ulm, Nuremberg and Augsburg. Business was done in a variety of commodities: fish, horses, hops and metals from the Hansa towns, Bohemian glass, steel, silver and tin from Styria, copper from Thuringia, linen from Ulm, wine from Alsace, cloth and the work of silver and goldsmiths from Strasbourg, wine from Switzerland, oil and more wine from Italy and products from the East. These were international fairs where an elephant could be seen even before the route to the Indies was known. At these fairs silver was sold as well as merchandise, and to them, from more or less everywhere, the wagon-trains and the merchants made their way, in groups escorted by the soldiers of the Emperor, who was the protector of the fair's privileges.

Printing came comparatively late to Frankfurt: in fact it only really developed from 1530 on when Egenolff started his business there, but the agents of the great booksellers were drawn to the fairs long before. Peter Schoeffer went to them, as did Wenssler and Amerbach in 1478; Amerbach returned frequently and he was soon meeting booksellers from Nuremberg and from Italy there. Koberger regularly brought crates of books to Frankfurt after 1495 – between 1498 and 1500 he never missed a fair. In 1506 the innkeeper at whose inn he used to lodge built him a shop so that his books could be as well displayed there as in Nuremberg and so that he could leave them there from one fair to the next. From his base at the Frankfurt Fair Koberger could do brisk business with the Basel booksellers.

From year to year the booksellers came to the fair from all parts in greater numbers; from Marburg, Leipzig, Wittenberg, Tübingen, Heidelberg and Basel and from foreign lands too. The Venetians have left evidence of their visits after 1498 and the Paris bookseller Jacques Du Puys attended regularly after 1540, as did Robert Estienne soon afterwards. At the last fair for 1557 there were 2 Lyonnese booksellers, 4 Parisians, 2 from Geneva, 5 from Antwerp and others from Utrecht, Amsterdam and Louvain. At the fairs held in 1569 we can trace 87 booksellers, of whom 17 were from Frankfurt, 3 from Venice, 4 from Lyons and 5 from Geneva, and each of whom came with commissions from colleagues who could not be there.

The booksellers' quarter during the fair was in the Büchergasse, 'Book Street', between the river Main and St. Leonard's Church. They had to get to work quickly once the fair started and had little time to rest, unloading wagons, spreading out their books on the stalls, selecting books they wished to purchase for stock from the lists provided by each of the publishers exhibiting, selling their own stock to other booksellers or to individual buyers. They exchanged news with the publishers and booksellers they met, announced their forthcoming publications and took orders for the next fair or for future business. Many copies of a particular work might be bought or sold; Froschauer in a letter dated 10th October 1534 mentions that he brought 2,000 copies of his editions in folio and 8vo of the *Epitome trium terrae partium* and adds that he has sold half of them and that he expects to sell the rest at the next fair.

Frankfurt developed a name also as a market for printing equipment; there printers bought founts and matrices from German typefounders and typecutters and especially from those who were permanently established in the town. Artists in woodcut and copper engraving made their way to the fair to offer their skills. The fairs slowly became the rendezvous for everyone engaged in the book trade, a centre of swarming life, a picturesque scene which writers of the day, such as Henri Estienne, took pleasure in evoking. While booksellers and their assistants leaned from the doorways and windows of their shops and shouted to the passers-by the titles of the new books they had on sale, hawkers passed up and down crying their almanacs, prints and pamphlets containing an account of current events. Authors would be there in the crowd with a manuscript for which they sought a publisher or to watch the sales of their books, and men of letters would gather to seek work suitable to their talent as translators or correctors of the press. In Henri Estienne's words, Frankfurt was the 'new Athens' where you could see celebrated scholars talking and debating amongst themselves in Latin before an astonished public and elbowing aside players who had come to the fair to seek employment from the impresarios who gathered there to form theatrical companies. Shakespeare would have found it a fascinating sight.

Among the most original features of the Frankfurt Fair were the catalogues which were produced of the books available at the fair. These were forerunners of the innumerable bibliographies which are nowadays produced at regular intervals so that one can know the titles of new books as soon as they are published. Catalogues of books for sale and in print were a very early feature of the trade and from at least 1470, if not earlier, agents employed by the big publishers drew up lists, handwritten at first and then later printed, of the books they had for sale. From early on too there were joint catalogues produced by groups of printers, for example the list which the bookseller Albrecht of Memmingen brought out in 1500 contained some 200 titles and was called *Libri venales Venetiis, Nurembergae et Basileae*. In the 16th century the necessity with which publishers were faced of making the titles they produced more widely known led them more and more to print and circulate their list. In 1541 Aldus Manutius the Younger produced a catalogue of this type in Venice, Simon de Colines did one in Paris before 1546, Christopher Froschauer of Zurich followed suit in 1548, Sébastien Gryphe of Lyons and Johann Froben of Basel in 1549, Robert Estienne in 1552 and 1569 and finally Plantin at Antwerp in 1566, 1567, 1575 and 1587.

These catalogues were often distributed at the Frankfurt Fair. After a time it seemed useful to combine the separate catalogues issued into a general catalogue of all the books available there. At Frankfurt, German publishers, and often foreign publishers as well, put on sale for the first time the books that they had recently printed. It soon became evident that only a general catalogue would make it possible for their potential clients to get to know of these new books and for they themselves to obtain the publicity they desired. From 1564 an Augsburg bookseller, Georg Willer, undertook to issue a list of the books for sale at each fair and his catalogue appeared twice a year until 1592. Soon other booksellers – Johann Sauer, Feyerabend and Pieter Schmidt – followed his example. In 1598 the Town Council decided to publish an official catalogue which came out without interruption until the 18th century and served as a source for the first bibliographic studies which were published in Germany in the 17th century.

These catalogues are invaluable first-hand evidence of the titles sold at Frankfurt. From 1564 to 1600 they contain more than 20,000 different titles, of which 14,724 are German, published by 117 firms in 61 towns; 6,112 are foreign and 1,014 are without indication of origin. The catalogues of the 17th century contain still more titles. For the first half of the century there are 18,304 German titles and 17,032 foreign, while in the second half there are 38,662 German and 4,962 foreign. Of the books put on sale many were in German, but for a long time even more were in Latin. In the period 1566 to 1570, of the 329 new books on the market 226 were in Latin, 118 in German; in 1601 to 1605 of the 1,334 new titles 813 were in Latin, 422 in German; in 1631–1635 out of 731 new titles

436 were in Latin, 273 in German. It is not until 1680–1690 that the relationship is reversed and more German than Latin books appear.[334]

The Frankfurt Fair was thus the main market for German books in the second half of the 16th and the first half of the 17th centuries and, at the same time, an international mart for Latin works. Plantin did a lot of business there. He always had a stall at the fair and either went himself or sent a close associate, usually his son-in-law Jean Moretus. There he met representatives of other firms and settled his accounts with them. There too he often bought the printing equipment he required. The Elzeviers were there regularly from the early 17th century, and at least three or four Paris booksellers attended each year along with many others – the English were always present in strength since it was their main source of books printed on the continent. In 1617 the English bookseller John Bill began to reprint the Frankfurt catalogues on a regular basis in London.

The Frankfurt Fair was the international centre for books printed in Latin and particularly for Catholic books. But, in the 16th century especially, it also provided a meeting place for Protestant booksellers. They came from Lyons, Strasbourg, Geneva and Basel to find books by the German Reformers printed in Wittenberg and Leipzig. Genevan printers would often be there and tried to finish printing their polemical Protestant works in time to sell them at the fair. The fair was thus a centre for the distribution of Reformation propaganda, a fact which in the long run could not fail to be disturbing to the Imperial authorities. At the beginning of the 17th century the Imperial Commission on Books began to take action. From then on steps were taken to victimise Protestant booksellers and printers who, as a result, gradually abandoned Frankfurt for Leipzig where they did not encounter the same obstacles.

The Thirty Years War (1618–1648) reduced German book production for a time to virtually nothing and was a terrible blow to the Frankfurt Fair. German publishers had produced 1,511 titles in the year 1610 and 1,780 in 1613. In 1626 they produced only 1,005 and a mere 307 in 1635. Foreign booksellers largely ceased to attend the fair in those latter years and there were hardly any French there after 1620–1625. Even after the war, although business revived, Frankfurt did not recover its position as an international book market and soon even ceased to be the main German mart. There were several reasons for this, but the chief was the changing nature of the German book trade. Up to around 1630–1640 more Catholic than Protestant theological works were published in Germany and the presses in South Germany were more active than in the North. After 1640 this was, as we have seen, no longer the case. The new situation favoured the development of the Leipzig Fair, already for a long time Frankfurt's rival, and was further consolidated by the great increase in the production of Protestant books that followed in the wake of the victories of the Swedish King Gustavus Adolphus.[336]

Printing had come to Leipzig in 1479, much earlier than to Frankfurt, and in 1476 Peter Schoeffer and printers from Basel were already selling books there. Later Koberger, Hans Rynman and various booksellers from Augsburg and Nuremberg did business there. The development of printing in Leipzig was particularly vigorous at the beginning of the 16th century. Some important Protestant printers – like Melchior Lotther – had left Leipzig when George, Elector of Saxony began to persecute them, but the later Protestant Electors practised systematic toleration and allowed Catholic publishers to attend the fair. Then, when, even after the Elector's conversion to Catholicism in 1697, the policy of toleration continued to be practised with regard to the Protestants, the steady growth of the Leipzig Fair was assured. Both the Reformation and the resulting increase in Protestant presses in North Germany assisted in this as did the emergence of the Prussian state in Eastern Europe. In 1600 the first Leipzig trade catalogues were printed and from that date the fair's importance roughly equalled Frankfurt's, eclipsing it after the end of the Thirty Years' War.

The steady growth of Leipzig and the corresponding decline of Frankfurt in the 17th century mark a significant stage in the evolution of the book trade. Frankfurt had been the rendezvous of all the major publishers in Europe. Leipzig on the other hand was first and foremost a centre for German printers, who were joined by Russians, Poles and Dutch. Thus the triumph of the Leipzig Fair around 1630–1640 marks the start of a process of fragmentation in the book trade. After 1640, with fewer and fewer books coming out in Latin, and more and more in the vernacular languages, publishing was ceasing to be an international enterprise.

4
Towards New Business Methods

Commercial publishing and sales methods were slowly changing. Firstly, the question of payment. In the 16th century, as we have seen, barter was the most common method by which printer-booksellers could both distribute the books they produced and obtain, at the same time, the variety of books they needed to sell in their own shops. It amounted to a highly organised system in Germany, and was often used in business deals between publishers in different countries, where it had the advantage that it simplified the task of settling accounts. But it was not without its dangers. Quite often a major publisher was obliged to take books he could not easily sell in exchange for those he provided, so that it was the bigger firms which took the lead in abandoning the procedure in the 17th century. They seem to have gone on making general use of bills of exchange for a time and then later in the 18th century they began to generally employ the credit transfer system. The barter system however continued in Germany for a long time, and, although the Dutch agreed to the continuation of the system in their dealings with German booksellers, they were not willing to exchange their own high quality publications in return for what were often poor quality German books except on the basis of one of their books for three or four German. Not until the end of the 18th century did the booksellers of Leipzig, who specialised in the publication of new works and who were producing work of high quality, succeed, after a long struggle, in putting an end to a practice which disadvantaged them, and which, more generally, hindered the development of the large publishing houses.

The steady growth in output each year made it increasingly hard to know, even in the trade, what was being published, and scholars and the educated reading public could not keep track.[337] The Frankfurt trade catalogues were the equivalent for a long time of contemporary catalogues of books in print, but when that fair began to decline and the book trade began to fragment new reference works were needed. As the 17th century progressed, major publishers increasingly began to put out their own lists, and often they included them at the end of books, but these individual catalogues were inadequate. The German trade had a valuable reference work in its Leipzig catalogues, but elsewhere, in

France and particularly in England, the need was soon felt for periodical lists advertising new publications. In 1648 a bibliographer called Father Jacob began to produce a *Bibliographia Parisiana* and a *Bibliographia Gallica*, lists of new books published in Paris and in France. This was the distant ancestor of the *Bibliographie de la France* and appeared more or less regularly until 1654, then ceased and was not replaced for a long time. In England 'national' bibliographies began at that time. In 1657 there appeared *A Catalogue of the Most Vendible Books in England*, followed by several different works of the same kind. In 1688 John Starkey, a London bookseller, with the assistance of Robert Clavel, began the Term Catalogues, published four times a year under the title of the *Mercurius Librarius*, which came out regularly until 1709 and was succeeded by other similar publications. Using the lists he had made for the Term Catalogues, Clavel brought out four successively revised editions of a general catalogue of books printed in England since 1666, the year of the Great Fire which destroyed so many booksellers' stocks.

Lists of this kind were primarily intended for the trade rather than for scholars and members of the intelligentsia. They had to rely on intelligence coming in from the friends and correspondents that they often had throughout Europe to keep up with current publications which might interest them. In this network of correspondence some learned men who were particularly well placed acted as a kind of central information agency: Peiresc, for example, who was called the 'Procurator General of the Republic of Letters', or Chapelain, or the brothers Dupuy.

By the late 17th century these methods were clearly insufficient to cope with the increase in new publications, and with the advent of the periodical press there appeared a whole series of bibliographical journals some of which were critical while others were not.[338] It was Colbert who took the first initiative of this type. He was concerned to control intellectual life as well as economic and, on the advice of Chapelain, he instructed Dennis de Sallo, a counsellor of the Parlement and a scholar of international repute, to bring out a monthly journal which would publish records of scientific experiments and a review of recent publications: a review evidently intended to influence the opinions of the intelligentsia where necessary. It was called the *Journal des Savants*, the first number being dated 1st January, 1665. Sallo and his collaborators brought together a great deal of information within its pages, but the criticism it contained was too frank for a section of its readership and was felt to be offensive by many authors. Soon Sallo was replaced by the

Abbé Gallois who was somewhat more prudent and left out all criticism of the works summarised in the journal. The *Journal des Savants* was then a great success. It was translated into Italian, German and Latin, and in 1678 its format was reduced by Gallois so that it could be sent abroad and to the provinces through the post, as easily as a letter.

Meanwhile the Royal Society began its *Philosophical Transactions* in 1665, which also came out in a Latin edition at Leipzig from 1675; and the *Journal des Savants* found itself after 1680 rivalled by other journals inspired by different motives, for instance by the *Journal de Trévoux* put out by the Jesuits in the sovereign principality of Dombes in Burgundy between 1712 and 1768, but more typically by the many gazettes which took the field in Holland. The best of these may be mentioned: the *Nouvelles de la République des Lettres* produced by Bayle, which began in 1684; the *Bibliothèque universelle et historique* published by Le Clerc from 1686; and Basnage's *Histoire des ouvrages des savants*. While the *Journal des savants* avoided taking sides, Bayle, Le Clerc and Basnage were critical in their approach and from their base in Holland they first acquainted French readers with English thought and philosophy, notably Locke's. This kind of publication, although in its infancy, exercised from the beginning a profound influence on the evolution of ideas.

Printed books went out of date much more slowly in the 17th century than today. Books in general, and text books in particular, were precious objects, carefully preserved, sometimes resold, which could be expected to have a lengthy useful life. Racine, for instance, made his acquaintance with Greek tragedy through Aldine editions printed in the previous century, 150 years before his time. So the second-hand market was always flourishing and played an important role. Generally it was, of course, in the hands of the 'bouquinistes' and the market stall-holders selling books who were to be found in all the large towns: in Lyons on the Pont de la Saône, in Paris on the bridges and quays of the Seine. But in addition large bookshops were often devoted to the second-hand trade: David Douceur in the late 16th century in Paris turned the pillaging of libraries during the Wars of Religion to good account by accumulating a huge stock of books. In the 17th century Thomas Blaise and later Louis Billaine bought thousands of books abroad, notably in England, and brought out second-hand catalogues to advertise them under the title *Milliaria*. Specialists in second-hand books were often an asset to the world of letters, as when Naudé the librarian searched among the second-hand stalls on the Seine for books looted from Cardinal Mazarin's library during the Fronde (1648–1653) and Camusat, bookseller to the Académie Française, appears to have specialised in the purchase of old books abroad required by the Academicians. Many of the big publisher-booksellers also engaged in this trade.

As in our day, second-hand booksellers stocked up their shops by buying wholesale the libraries of scholars when they died. As this trade developed in the 17th century the book auction became a common commercial practice (and is, indeed, still prevalent today). Henceforth when someone with a well-known library died his collection could be broken up to be sold in lots after a catalogue had been published; very often specialists who sought a particular book, and soon too the bibliophiles, who were already becoming numerous, competed bitterly with the booksellers for the item they coveted. The first sale of this kind known to us is one organised by the Leyden bookseller Poret in 1599 when he sold the library of Marnix de Sainte-Aldegonde. Auctions rapidly thereafter became a very popular method of selling second-hand books in Holland where the Elzeviers presided over many; the practice spread to England and Germany in the second half of the 17th century, and to France at the beginning of the 18th.

The last aspect of the book trade to be reviewed here is street literature. In earliest times, as we have seen, the largest publishers sent out agents to towns where they had no contacts and there they offered, at more or less regular intervals, books for sale. As non-specialist bookshops soon opened in the cities the need for these publishers' agents was reduced, but in small towns and country places where no bookseller could hope to make a steady living, pedlars, from the 15th century onwards, sold simple ephemera to the uneducated and barely literate along with religious statuettes and haberdashery. Their wares consisted mainly of simple ABCs, almanacs, prognostications, Shepherds' Calendars and the like. During the spread of the Reformation pedlars became more and more numerous, escaping the attention of the authorities more easily than the booksellers who were established in one place. They were among the most active agents in the propagation of the new and illicit ideas. They played a particularly important part in Germany in the early stage of the Reformation, distributing everywhere their sometimes Catholic but more usually Protestant pamphlet literature – particularly the polemics directed against the Papacy and Rome which were intended to undermine the prestige and authority of the clergy. Through the hawkers, Protestant propaganda from Geneva was distributed in France in the decade 1540–1550. Regular organised trade networks, which mainly distributed pamphlets and books defending illegal beliefs, and which were forced to varying degrees to operate underground, came into being during the 16th century, first in Germany, then in France and finally throughout Europe.

The consequences of this trade will be dealt with below. Banned books were the more sought after because forbidden. They were passed from hand to hand and commanded high prices. The trade became under such circumstances a highly paid one, and the number of pedlars increased, particularly in France, during the latter half of the 16th century, when many artisans and workers were unemployed. Many women and children figure among the hawkers and pedlars of illicit books as well as many printer's journeymen short of employment whose contacts in the trade meant that they could acquire stocks of forbidden books quite easily and could sometimes even clandestinely print some pamphlets themselves. Despite great efforts to stamp them out, vagrants and 'sturdy beggars' selling contraband literature in pamphlet form along with the copies of official acts and the news-sheets, more and more of which were being published each day that went by, were an everyday feature of the city scene at this time.

When peace returned, great efforts were made to put a stop to this trade. In the large towns the corporations tried to prevent all those who were not registered booksellers from selling books. In vain. Haberdashers were prominent among the many who were prosecuted, while at the same time other attempts to legalise and regulate some types of colportage were made in Paris and other towns. Former journeymen printers who had become unfit for press-work or compositing were authorised to be colporteurs and required to hawk official government publications and acts and were also permitted to sell gazettes and news-sheets by the local government officials. But this system encouraged infringement of the law. Of course the official hawkers and newsvendors carried round a great many more things than those officially sanctioned; always in periods of crisis 'sturdy beggars' multiplied, furtively selling in the most frequented parts of the town the newspapers and pamphlets which could not be openly sold in the booksellers' shops. In the 16th century many street vendors were burned at the stake because they had been caught selling heretical books and in the 17th and 18th centuries in France many more were sent to the Bastille for having sold pamphlets hostile to the royal authority.

Effective repression of colportage was confined to the cities. In the small towns and in the country regulations were almost impossible to enforce and the underground continued in business. Quantities of perfectly legitimate popular literature were distributed by hawkers in the 17th and even more in the 18th centuries. The walls of houses and of simple cottages were commonly adorned with the crude artistic productions of the wood block as a result of their trade. Illustrated Bibles, Shepherds' Calendars, almanacs, and romances read by families in the evening, like *Mélusine* and the *Quatre fils Aymon*, were printed in their thousands by printers who specialised in such productions. The first broadsheets, ancestors of the modern local newspaper, were distributed in this way in the 19th century, along with crude coloured *Images d'Épinal*, the prints celebrating the glory of the Emperor and maintaining his renown in the countryside, and the whole corpus of traditional street literature with its wood-cut illustrations copied from those of the 16th century which, over the course of three centuries, had attained a constantly growing level of popularity. The printing press was thus taking over an area of popular culture which hitherto had been almost exclusively oral.

5
Privilege and Piracy

It would be totally wrong to allow the international character of the booktrade in the period running from the 15th to the 18th century to lead one to conclude that in reality the market in books was without any internal barriers, that the work of publishers was adequately protected by the law and that books could circulate freely. There was no international agreement relating to publishing; there was never anything but imperfect protection against pirated editions; legislation was never anything but local and incomplete; government officials were always both meddlesome and powerless to prevent infringement of the law; and censorship was always exercised by innumerable and often contradictory authorities. Under such conditions there were often many hindrances holding back the development of both the book trade and the exchange of ideas. To tell the history of these restrictive factors would require many volumes and we can do no more than outline that history here.

When a printer brought out a book in the earliest days of the trade there was literally nothing to prevent another printer bringing out the same work if he thought it worth while. Such a situation at first presented few inconveniences. Since classical and medieval texts already well-known in manuscript provided the basis of the market, particularly for early printers, the range of choice among the texts suitable for publication was very large and the need for texts was so pressing that often many separate editions of the same text could appear simultaneously without prejudice to the printers concerned – the market could absorb all that were produced. Publishers in those days had scarcely any interest in doing harm to each other's business and in entering into a competition which they could as easily avoid.

Once the sale of books had been organised the situation changed. Now the most common texts began to be distributed in large numbers, and contemporary writers were increasingly supplying their works to the presses. The competition between publishers became sharper and it became increasingly important to sell at a lower price than one's competitors. There was a growing temptation to reprint a work that had just been brought out by someone else, especially since the pirate did not have to face any of the costs of 'justifying' the layout of the text on the page – he simply copied an edition page for page – and since he escaped the need to pay anything to the author. Moreover he could sell his edition more cheaply than the original if he produced an edition of lower quality or accepted a lower margin of profit. The publications of the humanist publishers were thus frequently counterfeited at the beginning of the 16th century. In Paris the books produced by Joost Bade were often copied by a group of printers and booksellers, and the printer Des Préz even went so far as to have a border cut exactly like one of those used by Bade on the title page of his editions the better to deceive. At Lyons they did not hesitate to pirate Venetian books and publications from Basel. At this time Erasmus and Despautère regularly expressed indignation at seeing unauthorised copies of their works reprinted all over the place.

To some extent this practice inhibited enterprise, since the better printers always feared that if they produced a good quality edition it would promptly be copied in an inferior form at half the price, leaving them with their more expensive product unsold. To circumvent this publishers planning an important book increasingly sought monopolies from government authorities in the publication and sale of a title over a certain period of time.

The demand for copyright, or exclusive right to publish, seems to have originated among Italian publishers, particularly in Milan. We know that as early as 1481 the publisher Andrea de Bosiis was granted a privilege for Jean Simoneta's *Sforziade* which he had printed by Antonio Zarotti; and in 1483 the Duke of Milan granted one for five years to Petrus Justinus of Tolentino to print Francesco Filelfo's *Convivium*. The Venetian Senate soon regularly issued similar privileges and by the early 16th century they are accorded in France, where they could at first be conferred either by the King, or by the Parlements, or even by local courts, and in Germany where both the Emperor and local authorities granted them. In these two countries, the rulers tried to retain for themselves the right to grant the exclusive privilege to print a particular work and sought also to transform these privileges into a means for the closer supervision of the production of the presses. In 1563, Charles IX of France even commanded that a royal licence sealed with the Chancellor's great seal be granted before publication of any book, a device which was intended to make it possible for him to supervise the printer's production. Thereafter he was the only one in France to grant licences.[340] The German Emperor never succeeded in imposing his authority to quite such an extent; although he tried to enforce the same policy on many occasions, local privileges continued to exist side by side with imperial.

The whole system of monopoly and sole rights entailed many disadvantages which a vast mass of often conflicting legislation only made worse. Renewal of privileges and rights in old books (which went on reprinting) were among the most hotly contested issues. In principle privileges could be given for the reprinting of old books as well as for the printing of new ones, and publishers who enjoyed royal favour therefore sought to renew their monopolies indefinitely, while the government at the same time tended to favour the most orthodox and most tractable publishers. When Charles IX and Henri III wanted to set up a powerful publishing syndicate in order to produce works of high (and unexceptionable) quality they did not hesitate to give the monopoly of the publication of the works of the main Church Fathers, and of service books which had been reformed according to the decrees of the Council of Trent, to a group of booksellers who were supporters of the Catholic League. Outside France, Paulus Manutius received similar privileges from the Pope, and Plantin from the King of Spain. While large profits were made from such concessions which could last for up to 30 years, publishers of modern works concentrated on obtaining agreement to an extension of their privileges after the original expiry date.

Most printers and publishers were hurt by the great monopolists and protested vehemently. Generally in France they won the support of the Parlement, which was opposed to any extension of royal prerogative. As a result the monarchy came to exercise its prerogative less and less in the case of the older works, but on the other hand came to be more liberal in the extension of rights in modern works in order better to protect the rights of the publisher who had taken the risk of first publishing the work.

Thus the system of according privileges, even when these were only granted for individual works, made it possible to advantage a particular publisher at the expense of the others. In practice in France it favoured the great Parisian publishers, who were closer to the throne and were more susceptible to pressure and better known than those in the provinces. From the second half of the 17th century on, authors tended to publish their own work exclusively in Paris. Meanwhile provincial printers lacked material for their presses, and when a success came out in Paris they would await with impatience the expiration of the rights in order to publish it in their turn, and would not fail to protest if the rights were renewed in the name of the original printer. Piracy was almost a way of life for them, unavoidable if they were to keep their presses busy, their boldness in breaking the monopolies of the Paris printers encouraged by the weakness and on occasions complicity of the law enforcement machinery.

But even this was not the major disadvantage of the system. Each country and each principality granted monopolies valid only within its jurisdiction, not outside. If France, England or Spain, which were unified states from an early date, could absorb an entire edition within their boundaries, the privileges granted by German or Italian princelings in their territories, or even by the Emperor, did not really offer publishers any tangible security. In these circumstances the great international booksellers were continually in fear of seeing counterfeited the edition they had just produced at great cost.

But printers and booksellers were not ordinarily interested in entering into such conflicts with each other, because, in an age when every big firm had close business contacts with foreign traders, one man's ruin could easily lead to that of many others. Each printer and each town had its own imprints that business propriety and the general interest normally prevented from being counterfeited. If a counterfeit appeared, those who did business with the two parties hurried to intervene in the hope of persuading them to come to an amicable arrangement. Otherwise the victim of the piracy might take reprisals and counterfeit the pirate's own imprints. These wars in which counterfeit edition was pitted against counterfeit edition forced those who did business with the two publishers involved to take sides and degenerated into tests of strength which were to be feared by everyone.

If publishers normally had an interest in avoiding mutual piracy the situation changed when the trade underwent a period of crisis. If in the 16th century, and even in the first half of the 17th century, there were not too many pirated editions, after about 1650 the situation worsened. The period 1640–1660 marks an important change in the history of publishing and even more in the history of the book trade. Book fairs had lost their importance (except in Germany) and the big publishers of every country no longer attended them. The great editions of religious works which were such a feature of the Counter-Reformation and intended as much for export as for home consumption sold fewer copies, fewer works in Latin were published, scholarly works began increasingly to appear in the vernacular, imaginative and popular literature increased and the first newspapers were published. There was a transformation in many areas of the trade during this period of relatively tight credit. Soon there was a crisis in publishing while the book market fragmented into separate national markets. The old fundamental works of theology and apologetics had from that time on a shrinking market, and consequently the publishers of Antwerp, Cologne, Venice and Lyons, who specialised in publishing works such as those of St. Jerome, of Ariaga and of Escobar, could no longer get rid of their monumental editions.[341]

While the publishing business of Antwerp declined day by day, the printers of Cologne, Rouen and Lyons were forced to have recourse to piracy to keep going. A fierce commercial war broke out after about 1650 and lasted for decades. Provincial printers systematically pirated Paris publications if they were at all successful, and efforts were made to bring about the ruin of competitors who were felt to be too large. Thus Berthier, who deserted Lyons to set up a press in Paris and who carried on a successful trade with Spain, was eventually made bankrupt. Cramoisy, Courbé and later Desprez, who were the leading Parisian publishers, were exposed to the same treatment.

The Parisian booksellers of course made efforts to defend themselves. But while the French trade went through a critical stage, the Dutch was expanding. By the late 16th century Amsterdam was, as we have seen, the largest centre, after Paris, for the publication of books in French. Outside French jurisdiction, the Dutch printers could pirate books

printed in France with impunity and could often even export their
pirated editions to Paris without any difficulty. Moreover they could
freely print books banned in France and smuggle them back into France
without running any personal risks, thanks to the absence of any
international law governing copyright and publishing.

6
Censorship and Banned Books

The attempted control and regulation of printing (or rather, the failure
of such attempts) constantly, from the 15th to the 18th century, encouraged the multiplication of pirated editions and, consequently, the
development of a more or less underground book trade. At the same
time the rigours of censorship, combined with the traditional impotence
of the administration when it came to preventing the spread of new ideas,
had a similar effect and also served in many instances to drive the book
trade underground.

The Catholic Church played a critical role in this, especially in the
early stages.[342] As we may recall, when it first appeared printing was
warmly received by many bishops and clergymen who fostered the
establishment of presses. But, as the guardian of orthodoxy, the Church
was at pains to suppress the spread of heretical works. Numerous texts
had been condemned in the Middle Ages, and to read, copy or sell them
had been forbidden. From an early date, and especially when printing was
put into service on behalf of the Reformers, the Church authorities felt
it necessary to prevent the multiplication of pernicious books by the
press. As early as 1475 the University of Cologne received a licence from
the Pope to censor printers, publishers, authors and even readers of
pernicious books. In 1486 Archbishop Berthold of Mainz, though well
disposed towards printing, acted on the strength of a Bull of Innocent
VIII and instructed two priests of his cathedral and two learned doctors
to examine all books. In 1496 he forbade the publication of any book
which had not received the Archbishop's approval, under pain of
excommunication. In 1491, Niccolò Franco, Archbishop of Treviso
and Papal Legate at Venice, drew up a legal code under which no work
treating of the Faith or of the authority of the Church could be printed
unless first authorised by the bishop or vicar-general of the diocese.
Antonio Roselli's treatise on the monarchy and Pico della Mirandola's

writings were condemned at the same time, the last named not being cleared of suspicion of heresy for another six years.

In the 16th century the Church's intervention in censorship matters steadily increased. From 1501 Pope Alexander VI in his Bull *Inter Multiplices* established preventive censorship in Germany, forbidding the printing of any books except with the authorisation of the ecclesiastical powers and appointing the three Archbishop Electors along with the Archbishop of Magdeburg to control the publication of books. In 1515 Pope Leo X at the Lateran Council forbade the printing of any book without the permission of ecclesiastical authority; at Rome this meant the papal vicar or the head of the Holy Office, elsewhere the bishop, the Inquisitor General or their delegates.

It would be pointless and probably impossible to list the judgments and sentences passed down under such edicts, for they increased to an incredible degree in the course of the 16th century. We need merely note that there was such a rapid increase in the number of banned books that it became necessary to compile an *Index Librorum Prohibitorum* which had to be incessantly revised. But the Church could do nothing without help from the secular arm in the enforcement of its decrees. If that help was in fact forthcoming it was because the secular authorities had reasons of their own for suppressing works hostile to the ruler or the government.

The first secular intervention came from the Emperor, who appointed Jacques Oessler of Strasbourg censor and superintendent of printing in the Holy Roman Empire in the early years of the 16th century, and soon afterwards set up an imperial commission to review censorship methods and consider practical ways to ensure the seizure of undesirable books. The commission fell into the hands of the Jesuits and tried at the end of the 16th century to prevent Protestant booksellers from trading in Frankfurt. Despite these efforts, the Emperor's attempts at censorship were largely ineffective: the German princes dealt individually with the regulation of the book trade in their domains. Many of them were opponents of the imperial government and of the Catholic Church, and it was thus natural that among the principal consequences of the severity of the imperial administration was the assistance given to the growth of the Leipzig Fair at the expense of Frankfurt – Leipzig being situated in the territory of the Elector of Saxony.

In France things did not develop in quite the same way. In the first half of the century, while the Sorbonne and the Parlement were stepping up their censorship, their prohibitions and their prosecutions, the King with increasing frequency came to intervene personally in questions relating to the regulation of the press. Charles IX's edict of 1563 requiring every book to be licensed before publication gave him control of all new books. Licences, of course, were only granted in the light of advice from the censors, who were at first the theologians of the Sorbonne and later, in the 17th century, secular officials. Under cover of copyright regulations the King, and those other European monarchs who also adopted this system, kept a close watch on book production, but 'undesirable' books still continued to circulate despite their efforts. We shall see later how French printers went on printing heretical books throughout the period of the Reformation, and how, just outside the French frontiers, important printing businesses specialised in publications of this type. In the 17th and 18th centuries banned books continued to circulate more or less everywhere with the same ease. The number of books liable to incur official displeasure was so great that even the most law-abiding booksellers could always expect to be prosecuted. They could however resign themselves to imprisonment with few qualms, because conviction on such a charge was not generally regarded as disgracing a respectable citizen. In France, Colbert's introduction of a fairly effective police network and his rigid control of the press provoked a crisis. Sentences became harsher. To inhibit the spread of piracies and underground literature, Colbert did not hesitate to limit the number of officially authorised printers and to concentrate them all in the capital. He was disturbed by the trade in banned books entering France from abroad, especially from Holland. Printed outside his jurisdiction, they were often hostile to the Catholic religion and to the French monarchy. He planned measures to prohibit the import of Dutch books into France, but was dissuaded from the idea by Chapelain who pointed out that among the books so prohibited would be works essential for the studies of French scholars.

While the French printing trade, which was soon hit by unfavourable economic conditions in addition to Colbert's regulations, declined, the vacuum created was filled by piracies and unauthorised publications of all kinds. Forbidden tracts and pamphlets were smuggled into France with ease, even into the gaols where the Huguenots were imprisoned. Everywhere underground organisations formed to trade in illegal books. Often the officials of the booksellers' corporations whose job it was to inspect imported crates of books were accomplices in the trade. In practice they took action against smugglers only when they had no choice in the matter. How, in any case, particularly given the administrative limitations of the governments of the period, could one hope to put a stop to the smuggling of books, which were small objects and easily concealed? Consequently the prime outcome of the policy of rigorous official censorship was the establishment, around the French borders in the 18th century, of a series of printing businesses producing pirated editions and editions of banned books in complete freedom. The works of the *philosophes* were printed by these firms. Sometimes indeed the Chancellor had the disagreeable surprise of discovering his coachman bringing pernicious books to Paris concealed in his own carriage. Soon, under Malesherbes' influence, the officials in charge of censorship sought to relax the regulations, granted tacit permission for the publication of certain books and were tolerant in other ways. It is evident that official censorship as it was then understood had proved to be ineffectual.

The Book as a 8
Force for Change

In the last chapter of this study we shall try to draw up a balance-sheet, and to take stock of the distance we have travelled, by delineating the impact of printing on the men of the last decades of the 15th and the first decades of the 16th centuries. We shall attempt, in our study of the printed book over the century following its first appearance, to indicate the role played by the new techniques in the revolutionary changes that took place during the period of the Renaissance and of the Reformation.

I
From Manuscript to Printed Book

In the centuries before the invention of printing those whose job it was to copy books by hand had been able, as we have seen, to adapt their product and their methods of work to changing needs. Workshops capable of turning out dozens if not hundreds of copies of the most popular books at a time existed in many places in the early 15th century, the books most in demand being Books of Hours, works of popular piety and standard elementary text books. Gutenberg's contemporaries may have accepted printing as no more than a device for reproducing mechanically the texts most in demand.

But soon the potential of the new process became obvious, as did its rôle as a force for change as it began to make texts accessible on such a scale as to give them an impact which the manuscript book had never achieved. A few figures will show the extent of the change. Some 30,000–35,000 different editions printed between 1450 and 1500 have survived, representing 10,000–15,000 different texts, and if we were to take into account those which have not survived the figures would perhaps be much larger. Assuming an average print run to be no greater than 500, then about 20 million books were printed *before 1500*,[343] an impressive total even by 20th-century standards, and even more so when we remember that the Europe of that day was far less populous than now. There were certainly fewer than 100 million inhabitants in the countries where printing developed, and of them only a minority could read.

There was obviously a change then, and a swift one. What was the result of it? What kind of books did the public want from its printers and booksellers? To what extent did printing ensure a wider circulation for the traditional medieval texts? How much of that earlier heritage did it preserve? In making a sharp break in the material conditions of intellectual work did the press promote the growth of a new type of literature? Or, on the contrary, did the multiplication of many traditional medieval books by the early presses ensure their unexpected survival for several decades more, as Michelet suggested? These are some of the problems we will now try to answer.

One fact must not be lost sight of: the printer and the bookseller worked above all and from the beginning for profit. The story of the first joint enterprise, Fust and Schoeffer, proves that. Like their modern counterparts, 15th-century publishers only financed the kind of book they felt sure would sell enough copies to show a profit in a reasonable time. We should not therefore be surprised to find that the immediate effect of printing was merely to further increase the circulation of those works which had already enjoyed success in manuscript, and often to consign other less popular texts to oblivion. By multiplying books by the hundred and then thousand, the press achieved both increased volume and at the same time more rigorous selection. If we keep that fact in mind we shall understand better the nature of the printing industry in the 15th century.

A few figures may help at the outset by giving us a general picture of the situation. A high proportion of books printed before 1500 (i.e. of the books referred to as *incunabula*) are in Latin – about 77 per cent. About 7 per cent are in Italian, 4–6 per cent in German, 4–5 per cent in French and just over 1 per cent in Flemish. Religious works are easily predominant among the books of this period, making up 45 per cent of the whole, with classical, medieval and contemporary literatures coming to just over 30 per cent, law just over 10 per cent and books on scientific subjects about 10 per cent.[344]

So the majority, or very nearly, of books were religious and among them of course were many editions of the Scriptures. What subject was more likely in the eyes of printers to sell at a time when most readers were clerics? It is no accident that among the very first major books to issue from the press are two Bibles, the 42-line and the 36-line, and throughout the 15th century editions of the Bible were innumerable. Hain alone lists 109 Latin Bibles, and Copinger 124, with or without commentaries and notes by Walafridus Strabo, Rabanus Maurus, Alcuin or Anselm of Laon. In addition to Latin versions for priests and university students there were translations of the whole Bible: 11 German, 3 Low German, 4 Italian, 1 French and others in Spanish, Flemish and Czech, without counting translations of parts of the Bible, which were even more numerous, especially of the Psalms, the Apocalypse and Job.[345]

Parallel with the sacred texts, and infinitely more numerous, were the indispensable books needed for Church services and for the private prayers of clergy and laity. It would be difficult to suggest a total here, because many books in this category did not survive. Certainly there must have been a huge number of breviaries and missals, the very stuff of the printing trade in smaller places to which, when there was no established press, a printer was often summoned by the local priesthood for the very purpose of printing them. Books of Hours had been in demand, before the printed book, when their manuscripts were copied and illuminated according to standardised procedures. This kind of devotional work kept a great number of presses busy in the 15th century and, as we shall see, even more in the 16th.

Naturally there were far fewer editions of the great classics of medieval philosophy or theology. They were for a more exclusive public, yet an important one, consisting of the lecturers and students at the universities (many thousands at Bologna, Cologne and Paris) for whom the required reading of the syllabus and the essential works of reference were being turned into printed form by the new presses. For example, beside the Bible, there was all the material necessary for its exegesis, there were the *Sententiae* of Peter Lombard and, in even greater numbers, the works of the commentators, Duns Scotus, William of Ockam, Buridanus and Aquinas. The fact that printers specialising in the production of such works were established early in the great commercial towns rather than in the major university towns (Basel, for instance, Venice and Nuremberg) is suggestive. They could send their wares to all points of the compass from a good business centre, even the great unbound folios that had to be carried so cumbrously. Strategic siting of their offices meant more efficient marketing. Of the 16 editions of Lombard's *Sententiae* before 1500, 8 at least came from Basel, 7 from the one firm of Kessler, and not one from Paris, site of the largest university of all at that time. Likewise, Aristotle was published mainly in Venice, Augsburg, Cologne and Leipzig, only one of which was a university town. However, while some of these classic texts were reprinted on a comparatively small number of occasions, the medieval compilations, often in the form of dictionaries and glossaries, ran into many editions: Giovanni Balbi's *Catholicon*, Giovanni Marchesini's *Mammetractatus*, and Pierre Comestor's *Histoire écolâtre* are examples.

Devotional literature found an audience much larger than that of professional theologians, particularly mystical works which by themselves amounted to one-sixth of the entire output: Thomas à Kempis's *Imitation of Christ* began in this period the career which was to make it the most frequently reprinted work of all (after the Bible) down to recent times. Among the Church Fathers it was the mystical rather than the doctrinal works which commanded a large number of editions. Augustine's *City of God* was the most popular, along with the works attributed to him, like the *Meditations* and the *Soliloquies*, the *Dialogues of the Soul with God* and the *Manual*. St. Bernard's works of mysticism were often reprinted too, and to them likewise were added numerous apocryphal works. St. Bonaventura's *Meditationes vitae Christi* and the works of this type traditionally attributed to 'the seraphic doctor' were also popular. The little mystical treatises of Gerson and Pierre d'Ailly were printed and reprinted much more often than their doctrinal works. At the same time there were many editions of the *Fioretti* of St. Francis of Assisi, of Catherine of Siena's *Book of Divine Providence*, and of the *Revelations* of St. Brigid of Sweden. Even more in demand were the writings of those German mystical authors who were to influence so many generations – works like the *Speculum Perfectionis* of Heinrich of Herph, the *Horologium Aeternae Sapientiae* of Heinrich Suso, and many others of the same kind.

The probable reason for the success of such works was that they were not addressed only to the Masters of Arts of the universities but to simple clerks as well and even to the pious laymen for whose edification they were printed in the vernacular.

A large number of works which were intended for the specialised use of priests went into many editions, notably handbooks for the cure of souls: the *Epistola de Miseria Curatorum* (Peddie lists 25 editions); or the *Manipulus Curatorum* by Guy de Montrocher printed about 100 times (Peddie lists 98 editions). Works of everyday use for practising clergymen were equally numerous: collections of sermons, already plentiful in manuscripts, and guides for the confessor – for example the *Confessionale*, generally attributed to St. Antoninus, which was reprinted several hundred times, the *Modus confitendi* of Andreas Escobar which was almost equally successful, Gritsch's *Quadragesimale*, in which the sermons were illustrated with fables (31 editions in Peddie) and, more popular still, the works of Johann Nider.

A whole literature designed to encourage popular piety grew up at the same time. The cult of the Virgin was in full flower during this period and many works celebrating the marvellous life and the virtues of the mother of Christ were printed and reprinted, like Francesco de Insula's *Quodlibeta*, or Cornazzano's *Vita de Nostra Dama* (15 editions according to Peddie). The cult of the saints led to the immense success of Voragine's *Golden Legend* (88 editions in Latin, 18 in French, 5 in English, 2 in German, 2 in Czech, 13 in Flemish, 6 in Italian),[346] and there were countless lives of the saints.

Alongside these books, homiletic and didactic works were in demand, often descending from the tradition of xylograph books and often with illustrations, like the various *Ars Moriendi* which appeared in every language, the various *Vitae Antichristi*, the *Vita Christi* of Ludolphus of Saxony, the illustrated Bibles and the countless other works of the same sort. In face of such a vast number of religious books one is forced to conclude that one of the first effects of the printing press was to multiply the number of works of popular piety generally available; the press thus testifies to the depth of religious feeling among people in the late 15th century.

In the earliest days of the printing press, therefore, among the most important tasks undertaken were those of making the Bible immediately accessible to a greater crowd of readers than ever before, not only in Latin but also in the vernacular; of supplying students and teachers at the universities with the major treatises from the great arsenal of the Schoolmen; of making prayer books for daily prayers and church services, that is to say breviaries and Books of Hours, abundantly available; and, even more important, of making works of practical piety and mysticism generally accessible. The reading public was extended by the sheer numbers of books which reached wider and wider audiences with increasing ease.

Printing also made for a more exact knowledge of the Latin language and of the authors of classical antiquity. Its appearance just preceded the diffusion throughout Europe of the lessons of Italian humanism. All over the place, but especially in Italy, where humanism had already developed long before, interest in the civilisations of antiquity and in the Latin language was growing. Without in any way abandoning traditional courses of study, men like Guillaume Fichet and Johann Heynlin of the Sorbonne were inspiring small groups of men with a love of pure Latinity and, as we have seen, such men were eager to encourage the setting up of presses with a view to making it at last possible to have access to correct texts and to make them widely known. The crucial role of printing in relation to humanist studies up until the last years of the 15th century was not so much to give a wide circulation to those texts which had recently been rediscovered or re-edited free of medieval corruptions by the humanist scholars, as to make generally known, by multiplying the number of copies that were available, those texts which had been most commonly used in the middle ages as an introduction to classical literature.

We must first take notice of the enormous increase in the number of elementary grammars which was brought about by the printing press, above all of copies of the *Doctrinale* of Alexandre de Villedieu, and of Donatus's *De octo partibus linguae latinae*. More than 300 editions of Alexandre de Villedieu's *Doctrinale* have come down to us. This book was the work of a 13th-century grammarian and since that time it had been used by generation after generation of schoolboys. It was a medieval work written in verse, and so revered that Villedieu's successors dared not alter it but merely added glosses and commentaries. Although the humanists often satirised it, Joost Bade considered it worth publishing with additional material, and Erasmus, for his part, listed it among those works to be classed as 'tolerable'. The Donatus was probably reissued as many times as the *Doctrinale*. As we have seen, it may have been the very first book ever printed. It too was a work entirely traditional in outlook, written by a 4th-century grammarian, Jerome's teacher. It had been on the degree syllabus until 1366 and from its pages all medieval schoolboys had learnt their basic Latin.

At the same time we must also note that the Latin classics which were the greatest successes for publishers undoubtedly continued to be those which had been most popular in the Middle Ages, those which had most frequently been adapted and translated into the vernacular. Among them them the most popular were the works of Aesop and Cato, the sources for innumerable popular collections of epigrams and fables in the vernacular and the original models for much that was written in the Middle Ages.

Most schoolboys had begun to read the Latin classics with these two authors after having studied logic and before going on to the moral sciences. Knowledge of Cato's works was still reckoned so important in 1503 that the Rector of the University of Paris waxed indignant when he observed that young graduates were ignorant of Cato because they had spent all their time studying Aristotle. If they were ignorant of the *Disticha*, which Erasmus for example published in an annotated edition, then it was not for lack of printed editions. By 1500 there had been at least 69 editions in Latin, 36 in German and Latin, 9 in Italian and Latin, 2 in Spanish and Latin, not to mention those that appeared only in vernacular translation, of which there were one in Flemish, nine in French and three in German. As for Aesop's *Fables* they were no less popular; before 1500 there were more than 80 Latin editions, mostly printed in Italy, 15 Italian-Latin, 1 Greek and 1 Greek-Latin, 15 German, 1 Low German, 7 French, 3 English, 1 Czech and 2 Flemish, the last two being illustrated and probably meant for non-academic readers.

Thus, when printing first began, the study of Latin still started with the texts which had traditionally provided an introduction to that language. It was these works which the presses first reproduced in quantity, the texts of Aesop and of Cato, but also for example the *Auctores Octo*, a little primer widely used in schools and which the copyists who worked for the mass market had already produced in the hundreds. It contained Cato's *Disticha*, Aesop's *Fables* and some material which was rather more medieval in feeling and outlook: Theodolus, Facetus, Floretus, the *Tobias* of Matthieu de Vendôme, the *Paraboles* of Alain de Lille and a little treatise in rhyming verse, *De contemptu mundi*. At this time too Boethius's *De consolatione philosophiae* enjoyed a great vogue (70 reissues before 1500) – not surprisingly, given that to the great majority of scholars at the end of the 15th century, as indeed for many centuries previously, Boethius represented a perfect blend of classical and medieval thought.

The best Latin style was in fact learnt in those days first and foremost through the reading of the Fathers of the early Church: Jerome, Lactantius and above all Augustine were extraordinarily popular, perhaps partly for this very reason. This knowledge was extended by reading the Latin classics which had been best known and most often copied, translated and adapted in the Middle Ages. Among classical authors, Virgil was particularly often reprinted before 1500, very many editions coming from Italy and intended for scholars, but often too appearing in translation. Ovid, also regarded as a classic throughout the Middle Ages, was as often reprinted as Virgil. He had been many times previously copied by hand, and printed editions were produced for both scholar and layman, both in the original Latin and in verse translations and illustrated adaptations. In the last, more popular form, he went into many editions in the 16th and 17th centuries.

Other classical authors who were popular included Juvenal (61 editions of his *Satires* listed by Hain), Persius (33 editions), Lucian (19) and Plautus (13). Terence, a dramatist held in peculiar esteem during the Middle Ages and whose comedies were so often imitated in the 12th and 13th centuries, went into no fewer than 67 editions. Among the historians Sallust was one of the most popular (57 printings according to Hain). Livy, who had often been summarised and adapted in the Middle Ages, went into 23 editions before 1500, leaving aside the abbreviated editions, and Vegetius went into 99 editions, both according to Hain. Caesar was published in 16 editions according to the *Gesamtkatalog*. Other historians were also widely reprinted.

Of the philosophers, Seneca was still extremely popular (77 editions listed in Hain). It is, however, the immense popularity of the works of Cicero which, among all the editions of classical authors, provides the best evidence for the existence of a new outlook. Cicero was the Latin author who was most frequently reprinted in the course of the 15th century. Not just his philosophical writings but also his speeches and above all his letters were in continuous demand. There were no fewer than 316 editions before 1500, most of them Italian, but many German and even more French. The *De Officiis*, *De Senectute*, and *De Amicitia* – his major works – went into 40 editions, but there were also 38 editions of his speeches and 84 of his Letters, the favourites being the *Epistolae ad familiares*.

This growing interest in classical literature, which had already developed to such a great extent in Italy, was to some people a source of concern, even to some of those who admitted that it was essential to cultivate a better Latin prose style. Already in Italy humanism had introduced paganism into the universities. Were there not Christian authors (the orthodox argument ran) who wrote hexameters comparable with Virgil's, Christian orators the equal of Cicero? Scholars like Dominici in Florence, Wimpfeling in Alsace and even Robert Gaguin in Paris seemed to think so. These Christian authors, moreover, could not be totally neglected, because it was from them that the medieval grammar books which were still in use had drawn their examples. For these reasons many printers were led to publish editions of Christian poets whom they hoped to rescue from oblivion. Thus, writers like Juvencus, Prudentius, Sedulius and Arator were intended to replace Virgil, and the *De Amicitia Christiana* of Peter of Blois was placed on a par with Cicero's *De Amicitia*. Such rescue attempts in the end came to nothing, though it must be admitted that publication by the press gave a new lease of life to some writers whose days of popularity had seemed to have finally come to an end. At the same time, and with greater success, contemporaries who admired classical literature sought to provide schoolboys with Christian texts written in a good Latin style. The work of Baptista Mantuanus (1448–1516), whose poems, notably his *Partheni-cae* and *Bucolicae*, were reprinted more than 100 times between 1488 and 1500 alone, was felt to be suitable, and his popularity continued far into the 16th century. The Italian humanists did not yet reach a large public outside Italy, nor did authors like Tacitus whose works were just being rediscovered. Only with the very last years of the 15th century and the beginning of the 16th century do we find many editions corrected and edited by philologists, and only then do numerous editions of Plato and Homer appear. However the models of Latin composition produced by the humanists had already begun to enjoy great popularity in the 15th century, in particular the works of authors like Andrelini, Beroaldus, Filelfo and Gasparino de Barzizza, whose *Rhetoric* was, as we have seen, the first book printed in Paris. Their popularity is evidence of a change in outlook which only bore fruit in the early 16th century.

Compared with works in Latin, the vernacular works printed were, as we have indicated, very much in the minority – about 22 per cent of the total production of the press in the 15th century. Many texts in modern languages – probably most – were simply translations from Latin, whether of moral tracts, devotional texts, sacred scriptures and commentaries, classical literature or even of medieval literature which had originally been written in Latin. Among the many books printed, there were very few which had originally been written in the vernacular, but some must have found a big audience, especially in Italy. Dante was read and re-read (15 editions are known of his *Divine Comedy*), and Boccaccio was equally popular. His *Decameron* went into 11 Italian editions and was often translated, twice into German, once into French and once into Spanish. Petrarch's *Canzoniere* and the works of Leonardo

Bruni were also reprinted and translated many times.

Courtly love poetry was featured in French printing from the beginning, along with works composed by the writers of the Duke of Burgundy's court. The *Roman de la Rose* went into 8 editions in the 15th century and its popularity did not fade in the 16th. Martin Le Franc's *Champion des dames* was also printed. Among what could be termed the writings of the court circle were Pierre Michault's *Doctrinal de la Court*, and the *Abuzé en cour*, attributed to King René, Jean d'Arras' *Mélusine*, the *Procès de Bélial* and, of course, the works of Christine de Pisan and Alain Chartier. By about 1500, Meschinot's *Lunettes des Princes*, Gringore's *Chasteau de labour*, the *Testaments* of Villon and Jean Michel's *Mystère de la Passion* were entering the period of their greatest popularity.

Some of these titles appear to have been printed only once or twice – the ones most in demand being the *Roman de la Rose*, the *Bélial*, the *Abuzé en cour* and the works of Alain Chartier, Gringore, Meschinot and Villon. Very soon another class of literature begins its printed career. These works had long been popular and their popularity was by no means coming to an end. They were the chivalric romances, especially those celebrating the more or less legendary exploits of the heroes of the Middle Ages. One such, called *Fierabras*, sometimes retitled *The Conquests of Charlemagne*, was printed 13 times in French and twice in Italian. The *Faitz et gestes de Godefroy de Bouillon* came out once in French, once in English, once in German and twice in Flemish. And there were others like *Merlin*, *Pierre de Provence*, *Robert le Diable*, *Lancelot*, *Tristan* and many more. With them should be associated, although they were adaptations and translations from the Latin, the countless Histories of Troy (one called the *Historia destructionis Trojae* was particularly popular) and other works like the *Mer des histoires*, of which more later.

Moralities and improving moralising narratives were among the works most popular with the reading public. Alongside the purely pious tales there were also works displaying a bawdy sense of humour such as the *Cent nouvelles nouvelles*, a collection of tales by courtiers. There were other works, the forerunners of the *plaquettes gothiques* (little books printed in black letter) addressed to the widest possible public of the 16th century. Many of these books which were once, it seems, present in large numbers on the booksellers' stalls have now quite disappeared. There are few of them on the shelves of libraries' rare book collections today and they are rarely referred to. There were, for example, numerous treatments from different points of view of the old theme of the pleasures and pains of marriage, from the *Quinze joies de mariage*, attributed to

Antoine de La Salle to the *Doctrinal des filles mariées* and various works
entitled *Doctrinal des nouveaux mariés*, which often had more serious
advice in them than their titles might suggest. Such works were bought
by the same people to whom the *Faintises du Monde*, attributed to Guillaume Alexis, farces like the *Pathelin*, the many versions of the *Ars
Moriendi* and all the other ephemera which filled the hawker's pack
appealed. These, along with the Shepherds' Calendars, the almanacs, the
calendars and the illustrated popular poems which were designed to be
hung on the wall, must once have been produced in great quantities,
especially in Germany,[347] from the 15th century onwards, but have only
rarely survived to the present day.

Although of course empirical science was scarcely even in its infancy at
this time,[348] in areas that could be called 'scientific' there was quite a
high output, about 3,000 titles, or one-tenth of the total. Especially
often printed were the great medieval compilations in which, as in an
encyclopaedia, the sum total of available knowledge on all subjects was
thought to lie; witness the great success of the *Speculum Mundi* over the
fifty years following the development of printing. This vast work was in
four parts, named respectively the Mirror of Doctrine, the Mirror of
History, the Mirror of Nature and the Mirror of Morality. The first
three parts were the work of the Dominican Vincent de Beauvais, tutor
to St. Louis's children, who had died two hundred years earlier, in 1264.
In the field of natural phenomena the works of 13th-century compilers
were read and re-read, notably the *De proprietatibus rerum* of Pierre de
Crescens, regularly reprinted in many languages. Compilations like
these saved readers the trouble of going back to original sources and were
consulted for their convenience, just as theologians at that time turned to
dictionaries, lexicons and summaries rather than to the original texts.
Finally, of the great scientists and mathematicians of antiquity, Aristotle,
Euclid, Pliny, and Ptolemy were most often published, along with
Avicenna, who was the most admired of the Arab scientists.

The mass of the reading public did not of course frequent those
authors. Even theologians preferred studying the *Auctoritates Aristotelis*
to reading the works of Aristotle, and a book called the *Secret of Secrets*, a
collection of prescriptions often wrongly ascribed to either Aristotle or
Albertus Magnus, which had already been widely circulated in manuscript, was printed over and over again. Such books were read in prefer-

ence to the works we would call truly scientific.

Of course quite a lot of contemporary scientific works were also printed, and these account for about 57 per cent of all scientific incunabula: 255 of them being Italian, 124 German, 46 French, 44 Spanish and 26 from the Low Countries, 21 English or Scottish. But where time had not begun to winnow the wheat from the chaff there was an even higher proportion of valueless work published. The number of authors getting into print on scientific subjects rose each year, but the majority of works were of no lasting scientific interest. Practical astrology was the field to which most of them aspired to make their contribution. In view of the interests of the reading public, we should not be surprised that the account of Marco Polo's travels, the medieval geographical work of the highest value, was only reprinted four times before 1500 and excited much less interest than the fabulous stories told in *The Travels of Sir John Mandeville*. There was thus, from our point of view, a total absence of any objective critical sense, but after all isn't this always the case? We should not be surprised that the picture is no different when we look at the works of mathematics that were published. These came out in print frequently and from an early date: at Treviso the first appeared in 1478, at Venice in 1484, at Barcelona in 1482. Yet the most original treatise on arithmetic and algebra of the second half of the 15th century, the *Triparty* by Nicolas Chuquet (1484), remained in manuscript. Furthermore, the leading contemporary scholar to take an interest in the subject, the famous Regiomontanus, a mathematician and astronomer to whom his patron had given a press with which to print his results, only printed a small fraction of his work, most of which came out after his death, and his *De triangulis*, the first western work on plane and spherical trigonometry, did not reach print until 1533.

So printing does not seem to have played much part in developing scientific theory at the start, though it seems to have helped draw public attention to technical matters. Technical works were printed from an early date, e.g. Alberti's *Ten Books on Architecture* (1485), Pierre de Crescens' *Treatise on Agriculture* (1486). Vulturio of Rimini's *Treatise on Machines* (1472) was reprinted in 1482 and 1483 at Verona, again in 1483 at Bologna, and in 1493 at Venice. These are so many clues to a new outlook which was already apparent in the numerous technical advances made in as many fields in the first half of the 15th century. And printing, after all, was simply the most spectacular.[349]

These then were the main types of book produced in the half-century following the discovery of the printing press. On the basis of what has gone before, what conclusions can we draw as to the consequences of the development of the new technique for reproducing texts?

It is fairly evident at the outset that printing brought about no sudden or radical transformation, and contemporary culture hardly seems at first to have changed, at least as regards its general characteristics. But selection soon became imperative as the decision had to be made as to which of the many thousands of medieval manuscripts were worth printing. As we have seen, booksellers were primarily concerned to make a profit and to sell their products, and consequently they sought out first and foremost those works which were of interest to the largest possible number of their contemporaries. Hence the introduction of printing was in this respect a stage on the road to our present society of mass consumption and of standardisation.

The selection which took place was based on 15th-century standards of excellence and it brought about the final disappearance of works regarded as out-dated. Among the first to go were the encyclopaedias which pre-dated the *Speculum Mundi* and many theological works which pre-dated the exhaustive surveys of the 13th century. Some literary genres also died out with the introduction of printing, like goliardic poetry, of which few printed samples have come down to us and then almost by chance, usually because they were put in at the back of a book to fill a blank page.

Printing at the same time sometimes resurrected long-forgotten writings in which the 15th century seems to have found new interest.[350] It not only brought out classical texts which Italian humanists had been systematically looking for in ancient manuscripts for over a century, and whose popularity in the 16th century we will study below, but also certain medieval works which seemed in the 15th century to have re-newed relevance to contemporary life or renewed practical value. The texts of some Christian poets who wrote in Latin were thus resurrected according to the needs of the moment—but the *Anti-Claudianus* of Alain de Lille and the *Aurora* of Peter of Riga, of which there were so many manuscript copies, were passed over. Above all certain mystical writings of the 12th and 13th century were rescued from oblivion by Lefèvre d'Étaples among others. Time eventually made its own selection among the many products of the press. There were many titles never again reprinted after 1510. On the other hand, between 1450 and 1500 the press failed to print many works, rejecting them as unsuitable, which are now famous, but which, except for those which had the good fortune to be stumbled upon by a 16th-century humanist or some learned Benedictine monk of the 17th or 18th centuries, were not to be resurrected until the advent of modern philological scholarship in the 19th and 20th centuries. Among outstanding works which were temporarily lost were, for example, the *Letters of Héloïse and Abélard*, known to Petrarch, but not in print until 1616; most of John Scotus Erigena and of Roger Bacon, the letters of Loup de Ferrière and Gerbert, the memoirs of Ekkehard of St. Gall, the chronicles and histories of Gervais of Tilbury, Matthew Paris, William of Malmesbury, not to mention, among many other works, those of Hildebert of Lavardin, or the *Chanson de Roland*. The initial process of book selection was thus done by men of the 15th century with 15th-century tastes and priorities.

Although we cannot label the criteria of selection employed by the press with the facile word 'humanist', that is not to say that the press did not assist the humanist movement. It is plain that good editions of the classics in roman type were abundantly available, especially from the Italian presses. The book trade was already sufficiently well organised for these editions to be available throughout Europe. We are approaching the age of Aldus and of his French competitors who followed soon after. At the same time, the exacting nature of the printing process obliged printers, and in due course their readers, to revise their inherited ideas. A desire for typographic accuracy and the constant search for the best manuscript version of a text to provide the basis for a published edition provided an immense stimulus for philological studies. Moreover, while in the Middle Ages authors had had little interest in attaching their name to a work, printers were led to seek out, or have sought out, the true identity of the author of the works they printed – where, that is, they didn't invent it. In the 15th century many works, copied straight from medieval manuscripts, were still printed with apocryphal attributions. But standards soon changed. Contemporary writers who had their names attached to hundreds and thousands of copies of their works became conscious of their individual reputations. This new kind of stimulus was also the sign of a new age when artists began to sign their works, and authorship takes on an altogether new significance. Rapidly, under the mounting flood of new books written for an ever increasing public, the heritage of the Middle Ages lost its hold.

2
Humanism and the Book

The printed book could be said to have 'arrived' between 1500 and 1510. Little by little it displaced the manuscript in library collections, relegating it to second place, and by 1550 the latter was hardly used, except by scholars for special purposes.

A revolution like this is explicable only if we recall the high, and constantly mounting, output of the first presses. As we have seen, the 30,000–35,000 different editions printed before 1500 that have survived represent 15–20 million copies. But there were still more in the 16th century. It is sufficient for our purposes to recall some figures we have previously encountered. In Paris more than 25,000 editions were published in the 16th century; in Lyons, probably 13,000; in Germany about 45,000; in Venice 15,000; in the Low Countries more than 4,200 in the first half of the century; in England, 26,000 in English alone before 1640, of which about 10,000 were of the 16th century.[351] We can deduce from these figures that some 150,000–200,000 different editions could be shown to have been printed between 1500 and 1600. If we assume, for convenience, 1,000 as an average edition, then between 150–200 million copies were published in the 16th century. This is a conservative estimate and probably well below the actual figure. Of course it does not compare with today's output, when in France alone about 15,000 different editions are legally deposited each year, each generally in an edition of between 5,000 and 10,000 copies, not counting pamphlets and periodicals, some of which are printed in editions of 500,000. But the point is that by the 16th century the printed book had been produced in sufficient quantities to make it accessible to anyone who could read. It played a central role in the diffusion of a knowledge of classical literature at the beginning of the century and later in the propagation of Reformation doctrines; it helped to fix the vernacular languages and encouraged the development of national literatures.

First some information about the reading public.[352] It is not surprising if the number of those wanting to start their own private libraries grew in the course of the 16th century, and if the number of books in these private libraries also rose steadily. Catalogues of private libraries included in the inventories of an individual's private possessions which were drawn up before solicitors on the death of their owners give us valuable facts on these libraries in France, particularly those of the more affluent classes.

What kind of people had private libraries? Of 377 such libraries in the late 15th and the 16th centuries of which we have catalogues, 105 belonged to churchmen (53 to ecclesiastical dignitaries, i.e. archbishops, bishops, canons and abbots, 18 to university teachers and students, 35 to parish priests), and a rather larger number (126) were owned by lawyers, of whom 25 were members of the Parlements or of one of the courts of appeal, 6 were local government officials, 45 were barristers, 10 public prosecutors, 15 notaries. As one would expect, the number of lawyers' collections increased steadily in proportion to those of the churchmen:

	Lawyers	*Churchmen*
1480–1500	1	24
1501–1550	54	60
1551–1600	71	21

While churchmen were declining in relative importance as purchasers of books, lawyers, members of an ascending social group, became steadily more important. Their importance as booksellers' clients was especially high in Paris, the seat of government and of the courts of appeal, where the legal profession numbered 10,000. Of 186 Parisian collections listed between 1500 and 1560 no fewer than 109 have been shown to belong to lawyers and royal officials and only 29 to clergymen. Few soldiers or members of the *noblesse d'épée* owned libraries (30 out of the 377), and most of these lived in the provinces. But a surprising number of merchants, tradesmen and artisans owned books, sometimes in large numbers: 66 out of the 377 libraries were owned by haberdashers, weavers, drapers, tanners, grocers, cheesemongers, hawkers, locksmiths, pastrycooks, skinners, dyers, shoemakers and coachbuilders. Of course such collections varied a lot in size, ranging from Canon Guillaud d'Autun's enormous collection of 4,000 books to libraries containing a mere handful of volumes. Despite these variations however, it is apparent that the size of libraries tended to increase steadily throughout the century. The earliest recorded, collected together at the end of the 15th century, were modest affairs, often of 15 or 20 volumes including some manuscripts, but in 1529 a rich merchant of Paris left 170 volumes at his death. From 1525 on one begins to encounter large collections belonging to lawyers and royal officials. Philippe Pot, president of the Parlement's Commissions of Inquiry, owned 309 volumes in 1526 and François de Médulla, a judge in the Parlement, owned 235 in 1529. There was continuous growth; by 1550, collections of 500 are common among judges. In 1550 Baudry, president of the Parlement's Commissions of Inquiry, had a collection of 700 works. In 1554 Lizet, the senior judge in the Parlement, owned 513 books. From this date on there was not a member of Parlement, not a local magistrate, not even a barrister, who did not own a fairly large number of books, as also did a large proportion of chemists, barber-surgeons and public prosecutors.

The owners of such libraries were not the only customers of booksellers of course. Certainly in the 16th century members of the legal profession were an important group among booksellers' customers, but they, together with a few merchants or artisans, were not the only people who bought books. There was always the trade in popular literature. Calendars, lives of the saints, almanacs and Books of Hours sold in large numbers to a much wider public. This was the public Jean Janot catered for, stocking his shops in 1522 with 50,000 religious tracts and other popular matter. It was for sale to this market that Royer acquired the stock of 102,285 Books of Hours and other devotional matter that he owned in 1528, and Guillaume Godard the 271,939 similar works that he held in 1545.[353]

Book production in the first decades of the 16th century shows a clear line of development compared with the earlier period. Religious works were still preponderant, and in fact more were probably printed than in the 15th century, but with the overall increase in production the proportion of religious works decreased markedly, while the constantly growing quantity of classical texts produced is striking. More than 50 per cent of all books printed in Strasbourg in the 15th century were religious while fewer than 10 per cent were by classical authors. From 1500 to 1520, 33 per cent were either Latin or Greek texts or works by contemporary humanists and only 27 per cent were connected with religion.[354] The following table shows an analogous evolution in Paris,[355] although one slower to take effect:

Year	Total production	Religious works	Latin, Greek and Humanist authors
1501	88	53	25
1515	198	105	57
1525	116	56	37
1528	269	93	134
1549	332	56	204

Similar enquiries would produce the same results almost everywhere. There is nothing surprising in this, since these are the years of the triumph of what has come to be called the humanist spirit.

The excellent editions of the classics which came from Italy, from Venice and Milan in particular, had already in the 15th century begun to make better known these writers of antiquity which had not been forgotten by the Middle Ages, as well as introducing, albeit to a still fairly restricted public, those recovered by the efforts of humanist scholars. Here we are at the beginnings of a movement which grew steadily thereafter. In the last years of the 15th and the first years of the 16th centuries, Aldus Manutius was of course the supreme publisher in this field, bringing out numerous learned editions of Greek and Latin authors and making them easier to read by producing them in a small easily managed format. His success was such that competitors soon started up in Basel, Strasbourg and Paris. The story of the struggles and eventual triumph of the humanist printers is a long one which we have already sketched out and will not repeat here. But we must recall some of the achievements of the humanist press. Until about 1500–1510 Italy was the predominant centre of humanist printing. Outside Italy the first development is the publication of little books of verse modelled on the best Latin and composed by emigré Italians such as Andrelini, Beroaldus, Mantuanus or their disciples, by the presses of Mathias Schürer and Jean Schott in Strasbourg and Joost Bade and Gilles de Gourmont in Paris. The *Elegentiae* of Lorenzo Valla became immensely popular. Most important of all, traditional elementary works on Latin prose composition were brought up to date by men like Bade and Erasmus, and sometimes replaced by new grammars, like Despautère's which was an immense success, or Linacre's or Tardif's, or like the *Ars versificatoria* of Ulrich von Hutten, or the *Rudimenta* of Niccolò Perotto. New dictionaries now begin to appear, like Calepin's, or Perotto's *Cornucopiae*, just ahead of Robert Estienne's *Thesaurus Latinus* which was to have a long life.

The audience for the classics was steadily increasing. Those which were already being read in the 15th century became even more widely known. Terence, for example, enjoyed a popularity that continued to grow. The edition prepared by Guy Jouenneaux and Joost Bade and published by Trechsel at Lyons in 1493 was alone reissued 31 times in less than 25 years, up to 1517. The different works of Virgil, printed 161 times in the 15th century, came out 263 times in the 16th, not counting the innumerable translations (of which more later). Slowly all the major Latin literature became generally available. Tacitus, published very infrequently before 1500, went into dozens of editions, and the evidence for a wide readership for such authors is provided by the collections of private citizens of Paris which in the second quarter of the 16th century generally contain a collection of the standard Latin authors, with elegiac poets like Catullus, Tibullus and Propertius being particularly in favour. Horace and above all Persius – there were 15 reissues of Bade's edition of 1499 before 1516 – were the most popular of the satirists. Of the historians, Sallust, Livy, Suetonius, Caesar and, especially, Valerius Maximus were constantly in demand.

The new market for Latin authors was soon followed by a growing demand for Greek literature. Here too Aldus was the main inspiration. With Greek of course there was the technical problem of producing a suitable type, made more difficult by the fact that Greek required more signs than Latin since breathings and accents had to be cast as a single block with the letter for satisfactory results.

Greek[356] was slowly introduced into printed books in the form of quotations, which were especially numerous in Cicero. Most printers at first transcribed them into Latin or left a blank space for the Greek words to be put in by hand. From 1465 more enterprising printers tried to cut a few Greek characters of primitive appearance, sometimes without breathings or accents. Usually they used Roman letters where their shape was not dissimilar to the Greek ones in order to build up a full alphabet, using for example an A for a capital α, c for σ or ς, etc. The first to work this way were Sweynheym and Pannartz at Subiaco (for their edition of Lactantius, 30th October, 1465) and Peter Schoeffer (for his edition of Cicero's *De Officiis*, 1465). Many Italian printers followed their example. There are Greek letters used in quotations in the books of Hahn and Lignamine, produced in Rome in 1470. Wendelin of Speyer at Venice and Zarotto in Milan used them in 1471. Then they occur in 1474 at Ferrara, and in 1476 at Treviso and Vicenza. From 1474 several Italian printers attempted books entirely in Greek or in Greek in one column with a Latin translation in the other. About 1474 Thomas Ferrandus of Brescia printed the *Batrachomyomachia* in Greek and Latin. Dionysius Palavicinus, Bonus Accursius and later Heinrich Scinzenzeler printed or had printed Greek works in Milan from 1476 on, and thereafter Greek works appear in a number of Italian towns especially in Florence, Venice and Milan. At the end of the century they start to appear outside Italy. German and French printers followed the Italian example at first in cutting a few Greek characters for printing quotations. In 1486 Amerbach published in Basel the letters of Filelfo with numerous quotations in Greek. At Deventer, Richard Paffroet (1488) and Jack of

Breda (1496) followed suit. In the notes of an edition of Virgil published by Koberger in 1492 there are some Greek quotations, and a few Greek words crop up in books printed in Paris from 1494 onwards (Gering and Rembolt being the first to use them) and in books printed at Lyons from 1492 onwards (Trechsel taking the lead here). Complete books in Greek do not however appear to have been printed outside Italy until the second decade of the 16th century. Under Tissard's direction, Gilles de Gourmont cast a Greek alphabet with separate breathings and accents in Paris in 1507. This was used to reprint part of the Aldine edition of Theocritus, and it was followed in 1512 by a complete alphabet with breathings and accents incorporated in the letters which Gilles de Gourmont had made. In 1511 Johann Rhau-Grunenberg had the *Εἰσαγωγὴ πρὸς τῶν γραμμάτων ἐλλήνων* printed partly in Greek at Wittenberg and in 1513 he published the text of the *Batrachomyomachia* with Latin translation. From that date progress was swift, and the primitive Greek founts used in these early efforts were replaced by a more elegant design of type. Cardinal Ximenes had a Greek type cut for his Polyglot *New Testament* and *Bible* (1514–1517) and many of the larger publishers, recognising that by then a fairly extensive range of editions of the Latin classics was available, now undertook the publication of Greek texts. New Greek types, mostly in imitation of Aldus's, were coming out in many towns. We find them used in Nuremberg by Conrad Celtes, at Strasbourg by Mathias Schürer, at Augsburg by Johann Miller, at Leipzig by Valentin Schumann, at Cologne by Cervicornus, Soter and Gymnich, and being used by Thomas Anshelm who worked in Pforzheim, Tübingen and Haguenau. Most important of all was Froben, at Basel, who sold Greek founts to printers in France (Paris and Lyons) and Germany. The development of Greek types undertaken by these printers reached its apogee when Francis I of France, anxious to encourage the study of Greek at Paris, had the famous *Grecs du Roi* type cut by Garamond (1541–1550) in imitation of the handwriting of the Cretan calligrapher Vergetus. This fount was later used by the Estiennes and many other Paris printers.

This brief account enables us to see how knowledge of the Greek language could spread and how little by little there could develop a market for the Greek classics in the original language. Aldus, as we have seen, at first concentrated on producing grammars and introductory manuals to facilitate study of the language before he launched into more ambitious publications, while Gilles de Gourmont in Paris and Mathias Schürer at Strasbourg acted similarly, though their types were much more primitive. Thanks to such methodical procedures knowledge of Greek increased, and from about 1525 the study of Greek became, outside Italy, almost a craze. At Oxford and Louvain (1517), at Alcalá (1528), Paris (1529), and in several German towns, it began to be taught officially in the university. In Paris, Bade, followed by Simon de Colines, Antoine Augereau and Christian Wechel and finally by the Estiennes, produced numerous editions of Greek works. In 1530 Clénard wrote that in Paris there had been sold 500 copies of his *Institutiones Linguae Graecae* in the space of a few days, a claim that might appear dubious if we did not know that 40 Greek authors were published in France in the same year, 32 in the original, compared with 33 editions of Latin authors. In 1549, 33 more Greek works came out in Paris compared with 40 in Latin, not counting translations. So in the first half of the 16th century the printing press made first Latin, then Greek and, to some degree, Hebrew literature available to a major public throughout Europe.*

To become a *homo trilinguis*, i.e. to know Greek, Latin and Hebrew, was the aim of many of the humanists, and many of them managed it – Nebrija, Reuchlin, Guidacier, Münster and Clénard, for example. It was also the goal set in France by the Collège Royal, where Vatable taught Hebrew and which was devoted to the three languages. From around 1520–1530 a knowledge of Hebrew became relatively common.[357]

To learn Greek the humanists had turned to the Byzantine scholars who had fled to Italy from the Turks after the Fall of Constantinople in 1453. To learn Hebrew they sought out Jewish scholars, withstanding the suspicions of those who alleged that they wanted to become converts to Judaism and the prejudices of men like the opponents of Reuchlin who denied that Jewish culture was of any importance. The humanists' interest in Hebrew meant that from a fairly early date words and phrases in Hebrew script are to be found quoted in numerous exegetical, theological or linguistic works, just as Greek words and phrases were. But, contrary to what is generally thought, most Jewish printing was done by Jews for Jews. Often humanist printers learnt from Jewish printers, but the books they printed were not always intended for Christian readers. For example the Hebrew Bibles printed by Plantin in editions of 2,500–3,000 copies seem to have been intended not so much for Christian scholars as for Jewish communities.

The invention of printing could not be viewed with indifference by Jews. Hebrew was the language in which their culture found expression.

* The following section on Hebrew books has been based on notes provided by Mr. Moché Catane.

Their reading and writing was in Hebrew. Even the less educated and the women, whose usual language was the vernacular of their Gentile environment, still read and wrote that language in Hebrew script. They were deeply attached to their religion and anxious not to neglect their children's education or the precept which bade them study a part of scripture each day, and so they owned many manuscripts, both sacred and secular. Printing was welcomed by them since it aided the diffusion, at low cost, of the text of works of scholarship, of the prayers, rituals, and ceremonies, and of the religious rules and prescriptions, and moreover it produced books which were carefully corrected without the faults of scribes. Finally for the first time the lay-out of the page made it easy for commentaries to be inserted in the margins of religious texts.

The earliest Hebrew presses belonged to the two most advanced and affluent Jewish communities, those of Spain and Italy, which started printing Hebrew books almost simultaneously. Research carried out in recent decades has shown that Italy was not the only cradle of Jewish printing, although the first dated book, a commentary by Salomon of Troyes (Rachi) on the Pentateuch (Reggio di Calabria, 1475) comes from there. It seems almost certain that other undated works, some of them printed by Conat at Mantua and some believed to be from Rome, although their place of publication is not given, are earlier, while the first Hebrew book from Spain (the same commentary of Salomon of Troyes printed at Montalban) is virtually contemporary with the Italian edition.

The expulsion of the Jews from Spain in 1492 put a savage end to a chapter in the history of Hebrew printing. Portugal, where the Jews had begun printing seven years before the Christians, in 1487, briefly took over as a centre of Hebrew printing, but the Jews of Portugal were forced in 1498 to choose between expulsion or conversion. In these circumstances, Hebrew printing developed above all in Italy. Hebrew presses were set up in a number of places, the best known being at Soncino, near Mantua,[358] whence came the most famous family of Jewish printers, the Soncinos.

There are however a few words printed in Hebrew in occasional humanist works – treatises on exegesis, theology or grammar – printed in Germany, Switzerland, the Low Countries, France and England. The first instance is in Peter Nigri's *Tractatus contra perfidos Judaeos* printed at Essling in 1475, but it was not until 1512 that Thomas Murner published, in Frankfurt, some complete books of Jewish ritual, nor until 1530 that the Jewish printers Hayim Schwartz and David, son of

Jonathan, published a Pentateuch in Silesia. The same Hayim Schwartz printed, with different associates, the inevitable commentary by Salomon of Troyes (at Augsburg in 1533) and then he reappears again at Ichenhausen in Bavaria and at Heddernheim near Frankfurt.[359]

Flourishing centres of Jewish printing were established in Prague (1512) and Cracow, where the Helicz family set up its presses in 1534 and from 1551 onwards produced editions of the texts of congregational prayers for the use of the faithful.[360]

In France, Bernard von Breydenbach's *Peregrinationes* came out at Lyons in 1488, followed by the *Concordance* of Sanctes Pagninus in 1526, while the first book published in Paris that included Hebrew is a grammar by François Tissard published by Gilles de Gourmont, who as we have seen was also the first Paris printer to have cut and use Greek type. In 1520 a little book by David Kimhi was printed by Gourmont, and then parts of the Bible. Gourmont and Wechel in Paris, Céphalon and Gryphe in Lyons all published some Hebrew works and they were followed by Robert Estienne the elder, who printed a Hebrew Bible which is still a famous masterpiece.[361]

Many humanists studied Hebrew in Switzerland and the Low Countries as well as in France. In 1516, Froben published the Psalms in Hebrew at Basel. Some Hebrew letters were in use in Zurich in 1526, but it was not for another 20 years that a book entirely in Hebrew came out there, the epitome of history called *Josippon*. At Louvain and Antwerp only a few manuals with some Hebrew words in them appeared. However, a Christian printer from Antwerp, Daniel Bomberg, who had established himself in Venice in 1517, devoted himself to the publication of Hebrew texts, out of sympathy and personal taste according to his colophons, working with the help of Jewish printers and proof-readers. He was the first to publish the complete Talmud. In placing Salomon of Troyes' commentary and the notes of his disciples (called the *Tossafoth*) in columns on the right and left side of the text he established the form in which this work appeared until the present day; all editions of the Talmud still keep to Bomberg's pagination and lay-out.[362] In all he printed 250 Hebrew books between 1517 and 1549, of which his monumental edition of the Talmud was the masterpiece, and there were some 200 Jewish printers working for him under the direction of the famous Cornelius Adelkind.

It is believed that there were probably 200 Hebrew works printed in the 15th century and 4,000 in the 16th. More than 100 of the surviving incunabula come from Italy; all the rest, except one, come from the

Iberian peninsula (about two-thirds from Spain, one-third from Portugal).[363] Nearly all were traditional texts, only three being contemporary works. The Bible was printed four times in its entirety, parts of it thirty times. There were twenty-seven editions of separate treatises from the Talmud, which was not printed *in toto* until the next century, and two texts of the Mishna were also published. Commentaries on the Bible, particularly on the Pentateuch, are represented by 15 independent volumes, without counting several editions of the text with accompanying commentary. Their authors were generally French or Spanish, with Salomon of Troyes (Rachi) having, as noted, pride of place: five of his works were published in Italy, three in Spain, one in Portugal. Religious laws and works of casuistry were of equal importance. There were twenty-seven of them, including 16 editions in whole or part of the *Arba'a Tourim* of Jacob, son of Aser, 5 of the 'Second Law', the *Mishna Torah* of Maimonides, and 2 of the 'Little Book of Precepts' by Moses of Coucy. Besides these there are 14 prayer books, a commentary on the religious rites and one book which comprises a calendar along with liturgical matter (there are only 2 plain calendars). These then are the devotional works (since Talmudic studies are considered within Judaism as perhaps an even more important religious duty than participation in the rituals of the synagogue) which constitute more than 80 per cent of the total. The remainder can be divided as follows: 6 grammars and dictionaries; 12 volumes of poetry, belles lettres and philosophy; travels, history and medicine (1 volume of each). In the 16th century, besides learned editions of the Bible like the Polyglot of Alcalá on which Nebrija worked, or Plantin's Bible, or Estienne's, there were many elementary grammars and manuals produced under the influence of the humanists. In all, 28 editions of Hebrew grammars came out between 1497 and 1529, the best known being those of Reuchlin, Nebrija, Capiton, Jean Eck, Clénard, Sanctes Pagninus, Eli Levita and Sebastian Munster. All of which goes to prove that the study of Hebrew was held in esteem along with that of Greek.

However scholarly works increasingly came to interest a larger public, one which often had little knowledge of the learned languages, but which had fallen under the influence of the press and had slowly developed a taste for reading. Publishers realised that a restricted market soon became saturated and so had a vested interest in enlarging their readership. In the area with which we are at present concerned this resulted in a sharp increase in the number of translations. Particularly from 1520 onwards, many printers, and amongst them some of the most important, turned their offices into workshops for translators: Jean de Tournes is an example of this in Lyons.[365] Thus the national languages, which were already evolving rapidly, were enriched and purified by contact with the classical languages through the medium of translation.

The movement towards an officially accepted national language began in Italy and was most marked in France. The kings encouraged it as part of their policy of national unification and in 1539 the Ordonnance of Villers-Cotterêts made French the official language in the Courts of Justice. Providing support and encouragement for translators was felt by most rulers to be a useful form of patronage. In France, Louis XII and, in particular, Francis I actively encouraged translations into the vernacular. Louis XII had Claude de Seyssel translate classical works, and these translations Francis I removed from the Royal Library at Fontainebleau for printing. In the reign of Henry of Navarre the production of French translations expanded rapidly, and a growing number were produced at the King's request, often becoming important publishing successes. The most productive translators included a number of illustrious figures: Mellin de Saint-Gelais, for example, who was a contempoary of de Seyssel, and also Guillaume Michel de Tours, Marot, Amyot, de Baïf and Dolet.

Thus the translations of classical authors grew increasingly numerous in France from the beginning of the 16th century. In a country fast becoming rich, populous and unified, publishers could hope for a large enough market for their translations. In Spain and in England a market of this sort was slower to emerge. In England, which had a smaller population than France, booksellers only seem to have found it easy to sell translations in the second half of the century; there were 43 editions of classics in English translation before 1550 and 119 between 1550 and 1600.[366] Naturally there was rather less progress in Germany at the time of the Reformation, and in the Low Countries the linguistic area was too limited to offer much scope for vernacular printing outside the routine chivalric romances or devotional works.

The most frequently translated authors were those whose popularity dated farthest back and was most firmly established. Virgil was tirelessly translated in the 16th century: the 263 Latin editions of his different works were accompanied by 72 Italian translations (as against 6 in the

15th century), 27 French (1 in the 15th century), 11 English (1 in the 15th century), 5 German (none in the 15th century), 5 Spanish (none in the 15th century), 2 in Flemish (none in the 15th).[367] Ovid appears even more often perhaps than Virgil, with innumerable free versions of his poetry and adaptations from the *Metamorphoses*. Meanwhile along with the other major figures, the historians in particular maintain their earlier popularity: Caesar, Suetonius, Josephus, Tacitus, Valerius Maximus, Plutarch, Eusebius, Polybius, Herodian, Xenophon and Thucydides.

Classical antiquity is now brought to the notice of all who can read as a result of the development of the press. Translations often play a more important part than originals in the diffusion of a knowledge of the texts. Plato was not published in France in an unabridged Greek version until 1578, when he was printed with a parallel Latin translation. Until then he was known not so much through extracts from his works printed in Greek as via the Latin translation of Marsilio Ficino, which was reprinted five times in France during the first half of the 16th century, and also through French translations of some of the Dialogues, often reprinted by Gryphe, de Tournes and Vascosan.

The same humanists, philologists, writers and printers who were putting out translations of the classics were also translating Scripture. Naturally the most popular works of the Neo-Latin literature that the humanists had brought into being were translated as well – works like More's *Utopia*, Poggio's *Facetiae*, the poems of Mantuanus, and above all the works of historians like Paolo Emili, Giovio and Guicciardini.

Translations from one modern language into another were a further feature of the age. Italian humanists and poets who had been writing for a long time in their own language exercised a great influence throughout Europe; and, since it was increasingly common to write in the vernacular, there were numerous translations from Italian and Spanish into French, English and German. Petrarch and Boccaccio continued to be widely translated, along with Brandt's *Ship Of Fools*, the popularity of which dated from the previous century. It is impossible to list here all the translations which came out throughout Europe of Italian and also of Spanish authors. The most fashionable and the most popular authors included Sannazaro, Bembo, and Machiavelli, followed later by Ariosto and Tasso. There was also a great vogue in works based, however remotely, on the Platonic theory of love as expounded by Ficino, with works like Caviceo's *Libro del Peregrino*, Judah Abravanel's *Traité de l'Amour* and especially Castiglione's *Libro del Cortegiano*, an idealised portrait of the perfect courtier,[368] to which the *Amadis de Gaula* sought to add further refinements, selling in large numbers. Such an effort by so many translators in every country helped to preserve the homogeneity of European culture at a time when the national vernacular literatures were being born. Sometimes there were more translations than editions of the original work. To mention only a few examples from Spanish literature, the *Libro aureo de Marco Aurelio* by Guevara was published in 1529 and had been reprinted 33 times in Spanish by 1579. It was turned into French in 1530 and English in 1532, then re-issued more than 20 times in French and 5 in English. Likewise the *Carcel de Amor* of Diego de San Pedro, first published in 1492, went into 15 Spanish editions, a dozen French or French-Spanish, 10 Italian and 1 English. The comedy *Calisto y Melibea* (known generally as *Célestine*), by Fernando de Rojas, went into 60 editions in Spanish, 12 in French, 11 in Italian, 3 in German, 3 in Dutch, 2 in Latin, 2 in English and 1 in Catalan.

Latin as the international language did not decline fully until the 17th century. By then the establishment of national literatures everywhere had begun to split up the book market, a process which was encouraged by the development of effective political and religious censorship. Permanent divisions were established between the cultures of the different countries of Europe.

Thus some works by contemporary writers began to reach a very wide public from the 16th century onwards. They included, of course, books of particular importance to our present subject, namely the writings of the leading humanists, whose influence was at that time so extensive.

First we must consider a few bits of evidence relating to the diffusion of the works of some of these authors. Erasmus[369] naturally takes pride of place. His books were in most libraries and private collections during the 16th century. Between 1500 and 1525, 72 editions, reprints and re-editions of the *Adages* in the various stages of their composition were published; from 1525 to 1550, a further 50 or so editions, and from 1550 to 1560 about 40 more. There are 60 known editions of the *Colloquies* published between 1518 and 1526, about 70 from 1526 to 1550, and a further 20 between 1550 and 1600, not counting extracts and translations. In the 50 years between first publication and their eventual inclusion in the *Index Librorum Prohibitorum*, several hundred thousand copies of these two works alone must have been printed.

Rabelais is another example who can be usefully contrasted with

Erasmus, since while the books of the one, written in Latin, circulated throughout Europe, the books of the other formed part of a national literature.[370] His *Pantagruel* appeared in 1533 under the pseudonym Alcofribas Nasier. In addition to the first edition, of which only one copy is known, five other printings were put on sale in the first year (and probably others now lost) and 27 further editions of the two books of *Pantagruel* and of the *Prognostication* came out between 1533 and 1543.

Twelve years after *Pantagruel* Rabelais published his *Tiers Livre*, this time in roman, not black letter as in the case of his earlier works, and no longer using a pseudonym. The book was put out in Paris by Wechel, the humanist printer, and was clearly intended for a more cultivated public. It was re-issued at least 9 times in almost seven years, from 1546 to 1552. His *Quart Livre* appeared in 1548 and was re-issued at least 8 times in the five years after publication, and his *Cinquième Livre* was reprinted 5 times between 1562 and 1565. From 1553 to 1599 the works of Rabelais were re-issued at least 24 times, so that his work must have circulated in the 16th century in several tens of thousands of copies, perhaps as many as 100,000 if we take account of lost editions.

Erasmus and Rabelais had a wide readership, but so did even a man like Budé whose scholarly treatise *De Asse* (*On Money*) went into 20 editions in French and Latin. More's *Utopia* was intended as a more popular work. First published at Antwerp in 1516, it went into 11 re-editions in the course of the 16th century, not counting 12 French, 4 German, 3 English and 3 Italian translations. This kind of evidence, which could be repeated for many other authors, for Vives for instance, proves the existence of a large reading public capable of tackling works of the highest calibre, a public which could only be satisfied by the technology of the printing press. Moreover, the rediscovery of classical literature led to the development of a number of what we can only describe as fashionable fads, which provided the basis for extraordinary publishing triumphs. The fashion for emblems is just one example. Alciat, a legal expert, brought out at Augsburg in 1531 a small collection of moral sayings drawn from antiquity, each illustrated with an engraving. Because of their engravings, Alciat's *Emblems* were an immense success – 39 re-issues have been counted between 1531 and 1550, and 54 between 1551 and 1600. Soon there were imitations by Jean Sambuc, Claude Paradin and Guillaume Guérout, and the vogue for this kind of book went on well into the next century.[371]

In the realm of scientific knowledge the humanists were principally concerned to rescue and restore the texts of the classical theorists, to edit and re-issue them free from the glosses and commentaries of medieval editors. From the 15th century on, the humanists had the main authorities of classical antiquity printed over and over again.[372] In 1499 Aldus published a collection of the basic works of the ancient astronomers, the *Astronomici veteres*, both Greek and Latin. His five folio volume edition of Aristotle in Greek had already appeared (1495–1498), including the *De historia animalium* in volume 3, and the *Historia plantarum* of Theophrastus in volume 4 with the *Problemata* and the *Mechanica*. Ptolemy's *Cosmographia* had already come out in 1475 but without the maps. In 1478 it was published at Rome with copper engraved maps. Herwagen published the first edition of Euclid's *Elements* at Basel in 1533, and in 1544 the first edition of Archimedes' works. Galen was first published by Aldus in 1525 in five small folio volumes, and he published the Greek text of Hippocrates in 1526, an edition having also come out in Rome the previous year. Avicenna came out earlier (1473, 1476 and 1491), but Pliny was published before all the others, being issued by John of Speyer at Venice in 1469, then in 1470, 1473, 1476, 1479 etc. Hence the mechanics, astronomy, geography, physics, natural history and medicine of the ancients were available to everyone capable of appreciating them in new editions and translations replacing the outdated versions of the 12th and 13th centuries. Now it was possible to reinterpret, comment upon, and even add to the teachings of the classical scientists -- or at least this might have been done had they not been so deeply revered. The humanists were in general content simply to reproduce the original text of Ptolemy or Theophrastus or Archimedes, as if all problems were solved by accurate editions of the authorities. Often their interest was as much in the literary qualities of the work as in its scientific value. At the same time they displayed a complete contempt for the medieval authors, and often there seems to have been a conspiracy of silence about the latter, while humanist editors cited classical sources in abundance in order to show off their erudition. Yet some humanist printers had medieval scientific writings systematically copied, and often published them with false attributions.

Alongside the scholastic tradition there thus grew up another separate intellectual tradition based upon the classics. At the same time the printing press encouraged the development of an extensive 'scientific' literature written in the vernacular and intended for a mass market. The bulk of this was made up of summaries, medical remedies, prognostications, and astrological tables. However, printers sometimes hesitated to put out Latin scientific works for a public that must have been very limited. Many texts remained available only in manuscript for a longer period in science than in other field. New treatises of importance often went unpublished or were not printed until after the author's death, like Giorgio Valla's *De expetendis et fugiendis rebus* (1501). Johann Stoeffler, who died in 1531 at nearly 80, printed many astrological tables, but his own *Cosmographicae aliquot descriptiones* only appeared for the first time in 1537 at Marburg. Many similar examples could be quoted.

Works dealing with practical astrology were particularly popular in the 16th century as in the 15th. It was out of interest in astrology that many Paris lawyers and merchants possessed an astrolabe. The conjunction of all the planets under the sign Pisces in February 1524 betokened fearful catastrophes and prompted tracts by no fewer than 56 different authors, among them Stoeffler, Agostino Nifo and Peter Martyr. There is nothing surprising in the importance given to this event: astrology was at that time regarded as a perfectly rational subject. But when Copernicus after much hesitation had the results of his researches published by Joannes Petrejus of Nuremberg in 1543 as *De revolutionibus orbium coelestium libri VI* the public proved to be scarcely interested in a learned work of this kind, and it had to wait 23 years before being re-issued in 1566.

Perhaps early printing rendered its most valuable services to what we might call the descriptive sciences – the natural sciences and anatomy – and that mainly by virtue of its ancillary technique of illustration.[374]

In 1543, the year of Copernicus' *De revolutionibus orbium coelestium*, Vesalius brought out his *De humani corporis fabrica libri septem* published by Oporin at Basel, with fine wood engravings by Jan Stephan von Calcar, a pupil of Titian. These engravings had already been used in 1538 at Venice for the edition of Johannes Gunterus' *Institutiones anatomicae* which Vesalius himself had produced. Vesalius' work was constantly re-issued, copied and imitated, and through the medium of the engravings the human anatomical structure became widely known. At about the same time botanists who had tired of trying to identify their local plant species in the writings of the ancients, to whom they were often unknown, turned to direct observation, and soon the zoologists followed their example. A great deal of work was undertaken in these years. In 1530 there appeared in Strasbourg the first volume of a book which was in effect the prototype of all subsequent works illustrating flora, the remarkable *Herbarum eicones ad naturae imitationem effigiatae* by Otto Brunfels. This was followed in 1542 at Basel by Leonard Fuchs' *Historia stirpium*, and in 1551 at Zurich by Conrad Gessner's four large folio volumes in which he had collected the descriptions of all the animals of which he had found mention in any book whatsoever, placing side by side both real and fabulous creatures. Soon after, Rondelet's book on fishes came out, first in Latin (1551), as was proper to any science, and then French (1558), with excellent wood engravings. At about the same time Pierre Belon of Le Mans published his *Poissons* and *Oiseaux*, and George Agricola, an early mineralogist, brought out his *De ortu et causis subterraneorum* at Basel in 1546, and in 1555 his splendid folio volume *De re metallica*, also published at Basel. All these books had plates to allow easy identification, and wood engravers were at that time turning out thousands of blocks under the direction of naturalists; some 3,000 are still preserved in the Plantin-Moretus Museum. Such sumptuous productions with their magnificent wood blocks found a ready public of enlightened amateurs who were probably often attracted to particular volumes by other than purely scientific reasons.

Although printing certainly helped scholars in some fields, on the whole it could not be said to have hastened the acceptance of new ideas or knowledge. In fact, by popularising long cherished beliefs, strengthening traditional prejudices and giving authority to seductive fallacies, it could even be said to have represented an obstacle to the acceptance of many new views. Even after new discoveries were made they tended to be ignored and reliance continued to be placed in conventional authorities. This is perhaps most strikingly revealed by a study of general attitudes in the 16th century towards the geographical discoveries and the imperial conquests outside Europe which were to have a profound influence on daily life, an influence whose significance and cause the public was slow to appreciate.[375]

For a long time the outcome of the Portuguese voyages of exploration was kept secret; outside an exclusive circle no-one had any knowledge of the new discoveries. In fact, public interest in exploration seems only to have been roused by Christopher Columbus' famous letter in which he describes his first voyage. Without doubt, the news of this voyage provoked quite extensive public interest since this letter was printed simultaneously in Barcelona, Rome, Basel and Paris in 1493, and reprinted at Basel in 1494 and again at Strasbourg in 1497, this time in German. But the curtain only really began to rise in the early 16th century. Peter Martyr's *Libretto*, an account of the first three voyages of Columbus, came out in Venice in 1504, then from 1505 to 1514 a series of documents were published, mainly in Rome, but also in Nuremberg, Cologne and elsewhere, which provided the first printed accounts of the activities of the Portuguese in the East Indies. Many of them were composed in the form of letters addressed to the Pope in the name of the King of Portugal and they were generally printed in Latin, but sometimes also in German. At about the same time another little book came into circulation dealing this time with the New World. This, the *Mundus Novus*, was based on a letter written by Amerigo Vespucci to Lorenzo dei Medici. The book, soon followed by others, proved a great success and was published in several languages after 1504, coming out in Rome, Paris, Vienna and Augsburg. In France it went into 6 French and 1 Latin edition in the first quarter of the 16th century. Then, between 1522 and 1533, three letters of Cortez went into 14 editions in Spain, Italy, France and Germany. By this time, the interest aroused by the conquests, and the encouragement of the kings who supported the publication of books about the new lands, had led to the development in Spain and Portugal of a whole new literature devoted to the New World and its conquest. In Spain, Peter Martyr, whom we have already mentioned, published in 1511 his first *Decades*, which were soon followed by others, and Martin Fernandez de Enciso brought out his *Summa de Geografia* in 1519. In 1526 Fernandez de Oviedo y Valdes began publishing a series of books on the geography and history of the Indies.

All this indicates that the geographic discoveries and the imperial conquests of Spain and Portugal did not pass unnoticed. But let there be no mistake: beyond a comparatively small circle of scholars, merchants and courtiers they were of no great interest outside the Iberian peninsula until about 1550. Moreover, the new experience was not being fully assimilated, and many manuscripts of the greatest importance could not find a printer. Meanwhile it is interesting to note that in France the fabulous tale of Sir John Mandeville's *Travels* was reprinted another 3 times in French in 1530 while the only work of Peter Martyr's to see print before 1550 was an *Extrait . . . des Iles Trouvées* (1533). Moreover Boemius' geography, which does not mention America and which offers only a few new facts about Africa or Asia, was nevertheless reprinted 7 times in French between 1539 and 1558.

Only after 1550 did the situation change. Europe then began to have a clearer understanding of the new geographical horizons. In Spain, Francisco Lopez de Gomara, Cortez's secretary, published the *Historia de las Indias y conquista de Mexico*, and the famous Dominican Father Las Casas published a series of letters in which he defended the Indians. In Portugal the new development was even more marked and a remarkable series of historico-geographical chronicles came out: Juan de Barros' *Decades* began to appear in 1552; in 1551 there began another series, the *Historia do descobrimento e conquista da India pelos Portuguezes*; and in 1557 the *Commentaries* of Albuquerque edited by his son were published. The movement reached its apogee with Camoens' *Lusiads* which had a long lasting vogue. Thus numerous books dealing with the recent discoveries and explorations and especially with the Spanish and Portuguese conquests now began to appear. Some missionaries started to send back regular detailed accounts of their activities. In these circumstances the *Cosmographia Universalis* by Münster, a general description of the known world which came out in Basel in 1544, was an enormous success and went into 46 editions in six languages in the century following its first publication. Whereas only 83 books on geography were published in France before 1550, 48 were published between 1551 and 1560, 70 between 1561 and 1570, 82 between 1571 and 1580, 76 between 1581 and 1590, 54 between 1591 and 1600 (a reduction probably due to the wars), and 112 between 1601 and 1609. The figures would probably be in about the same relative proportions if one took the geographical works published in other languages. Peter Martyr's works had an enormous sale, the chronicles of Castanhedo were translated into Spanish, Latin and French, and Gomara's and Albuquerque's accounts were also in great demand. Among the most popular of the new books were, to name a few at random, the *Historiarum indicarum libri XVI* by the Jesuit Maffei (Venice, 1588–1589), Pigafetta's books on the Congo, and the books about China by Bernardino de Escalante and Gonzales de Mendoza. There were many others, but a special place should be assigned to the *De totius Africae descriptione*, the work of an Arab from Granada who had travelled throughout Africa before being captured by Christian sailors. They handed him over to Pope Leo X, who encouraged him to prepare the work for publication.

After that so many books about the New World came out that it is difficult to keep our bearings. The growing interest the public showed in such works encouraged the publication of great compilations on the subject and these were produced in most of the great publishing centres.

Among the most famous we may note Ramusio's (published in Italy) and above all the work of Hakluyt and Purchas in England. The de Bry family, print dealers in Frankfurt-on-Main, soon began to bring out enormous collections of the major and the lesser voyages, magnificently and meticulously illustrated with etchings. Their publication took 44 years and volumes in the series were frequently reprinted in Latin and German; however the publisher's attempt to bring them out in French had to be abandoned, perhaps through lack of a sufficient number of subscribers willing to stand the cost.

So it is not till after 1560 that the existence of the new worlds was recognised outside of a small circle and regarded as of interest. Only in the closing years of the century does this interest seem to become general. This goes to show how slow public opinion was in the 16th century to take in and assimilate new information which was incompatible with its existing outlook on the world. Moreover one can have doubts as to the extent to which this outlook had, even by the end of the century, changed in its essentials. Atkinson's work on the subject offers evidence which is particularly striking so far as geographical literature in French is concerned. It is very interesting in this respect to see that of the books most read in 16th-century France, Marco Polo's *Travels* do not figure any more than in the previous century, only being published in French once in the whole century (Paris, 1556). The accounts of Jacques Cartier and of Champlain were not to be popular works in their own time either. In the 16th century, the most frequently re-issued geographical works in French were a volume of letters from Japan by the Jesuit Father Frões (19 editions), Villamont's *Travels in Turkey, Syria and Egypt* (13 editions), a work which in our eyes is of little interest, and various works by Louis Le Roy, Postel, Belon and Thevet, which, though original enough in conception, betray a second-hand knowledge of geography and some-times lack both a critical approach and a sufficient quantity of information (Le Roy is perhaps an exception). Boemius, who has already been referred to, went on being published until 1558 and Ortelius was often reprinted, though he was probably esteemed largely for his magnificent engravings. Significantly, all these works seem to have been more popular than the translations of the great Spanish authors, among whom the favourites were Lopez Gomara (6 separate editions in French), Mendoza (5) and Castanheda (5). Nor can it be said that this is because of a general hostility to Spain of political origin, for the works of Father Las Casas attacking Spanish cruelty in the New World were issued in only three editions in French.

Further, if we ask which country attracted most attention some rather interesting facts emerge: the majority of French books on geography and travel were about the region known today as the Near East. There were twice as many books about the Turks, who seem to have had a strong hold on the popular imagination, as about America. Then came a large number on the West Indies and the Portuguese territories, with another almost as large group on Asian Countries such as China and Tartary, and of course on the Holy Land (accounts of journeys to Jerusalem were particularly common). Books on America only came fourth, while Africa and the southern hemisphere hardly seem to have excited any interest. It would seem that French readers in the 16th century had a much greater interest in the nearer parts of the globe than the further, and in regions already well known than in those parts only recently opened up. They turned their gaze on the East rather than the West and, although during the Renaissance their horizons widened, their picture of the world was still distorted.

The cultured reader in the 16th century seems to have been more interested in law than in geography or natural science or even perhaps than in medicine (that is to say scientific medicine, not the popular literature expounding folk remedies). Collections of statutes sold in large numbers, and certain large booksellers in Venice and Lyons specialised in their sale and distribution. More law books were printed in the 16th than in the 15th century. The fact is no surprise to us if we remember that at this time lawyers and jurists formed a large proportion of the book-buying public. More than three-quarters of the French libraries of which we have any knowledge at this time contained a great number of law texts, and many law books belonged to people who might not be expected to have much interest in law – goldsmiths, for example, or millers and apothecaries. Obviously those who were connected with the courts or the legal profession always possessed a large number of their own legal books; in Paris, 42 out of 55 books belonging to a lawyer called Cousinot in 1518 were law books, and so were 318 out of the 513 books which belonged to the Président Lizet in 1531. This proportion was by no means exceptional.

The *Corpus of Civil Law* and the *Corpus of Canon Law* were among the most frequently reprinted of law books and among those most often to be found in libraries. It is impossible to estimate the number of editions of them published since so many have not survived. The same goes for the editions of sections of the *Institutes*, the *Digest*, the *Code* and the *Novellae*, and also of Gratian's *Decretum* and the *Decretals* of Gregory IX. To these might be added the many standard reference works and abstracts like the *Flores Legum*, the *Speculum Juris* and above all the *Modus Legendi Abbreviaturas in Utroque Jure*. These treatises of Roman and Canon Law necessarily formed the basis of any legal library, but works on Common Law and contemporary law were becoming increasingly common, especially in France, and were often reprinted. Such works were commonly to be found in private libraries. However, as royal legislation developed in France, more and more collections of statutes were issued there. Soon specialist printers, appointed by the King, were instructed to print and distribute royal statutes whose text the public needed to know as soon as they were promulgated. The royal example was quickly followed by the Parlements and by the lower courts. Thus increasing numbers of official leaflets and posters were printed to fulfil the role at present played by government gazetteers.

The majority of readers were even more interested in history than in law, and histories, especially those in the vernacular, were often extraordinarily successful. We have noted how of the classical writers the historians were particularly popular and often translated. Herodotus, Thucydides, Tacitus, Suetonius and Valerius Maximus were often published in the 16th century and are to be found in many private collections. Even more common are the works of Livy, Caesar's *Gallic War*, Josephus' *Jewish Antiquities*, Eusebius' *Church History* and Plutarch's *Lives*. Most of these works were regularly translated and sometimes published in illustrated editions. At the same time a great many humanists were producing histories.[376] In their desire to imitate the classics, especially Livy, many of them wrote in Latin. Italy was the pacesetter once again. Leonardo Bruni wrote a history of his own times in the 15th century and Poggio wrote a history of the Florentines, followed by Bembo with a history of the Venetians. Aeneas Sylvius Piccolomini chose to entitle his memoirs *Historia rerum mirabilium sui temporis*. At the end of the 15th century and even more in the 16th century the Italian example was followed throughout Europe: in Spain by Peter Martyr and in France by an Italian, Paolo Emili, who had been appointed historiographer to Charles VIII. He wrote his *De rebus gestis Francorum* at the end of the 15th century. He was followed by Robert Gaguin, a Frenchman, who produced in turn a *Compendium historiae Francorum*. Thereafter works of this sort came out in many places. It is not within our scope to retrace the history of these developments in the writing of history. We must only pause to emphasise the fact – of general significance – that many of these histories were extremely successful and were often translated into the vernacular. Gaguin's *Compendium*, for instance, was reprinted 19 times in Latin between 1494 and 1586 and 7 times in French between 1514 and 1538. Later, the *Historia d'Italia* by Francesco Guicciardini, published in 1561, went into countless Italian editions and numerous French translations, as well as appearing in Spanish, in English and even in Flemish.

The public which was interested in history consisted not only of clerics, humanists and students, but also of lawyers and of courtiers, soldiers, merchants and even simple craftsmen. It was for them that the classical historians and their humanist imitators were translated into the vernacular. But in fact their love of history led more in the direction of the chronicles, which were composed in the medieval manner, and the compilations of annalists and the memoirs of statesmen. Vincent de Beauvais' ancient *Miroir historial* and Rolevinck's *Fasciculus temporum* still had many readers. The *Mer des Histoires* was re-issued and adapted several times during the 16th century, and Hartmann Schedel's *Liber Chronicarum*, better known as the *Nuremberg Chronicle*, was immensely popular, as were other similar works, sometimes printed on one side only so that the leaves could be pasted end to end to form a roll. National histories, annals and chronicles, and even regional ones, were all the fashion: in Spain for example there were the *Cronica de España* by Diego de Valera, and the *De rebus Hispaniae memoralibus* by Lucio Marineo Siculo (6 editions: 5 of them between 1530 and 1539 – 3 being in Castilian and 2 in Latin). In France people were re-reading medieval histories and annals, particularly Gregory of Tours' *Histoire de l'Église de France* or Nicole Gille's *Annales et Chroniques de France*, both of which were reprinted dozens of times in the course of the century. Numerous provincial histories were also produced, some of which, like the *Annales d'Aquitaine* by Jean Bouchet or the *Annales de Bretagne* by d'Argentré, were in constant demand well into the 17th century. Corrozet's *Antiquitez de Paris* (1531) was regularly revised and republished for the rest of the century. Perhaps none of these however was as popular as the *Mémoires* of Philip de Comines and, later, those of Martin Du Bellay, while soon after we have the publication of the *Recherches des Antiquités de la France* by Étienne Pasquier which soon went into countless re-issues. Earlier, 16th-century readers had taken delight in reading the *Illustra-*

tions de la Gaule et singularitez de Troye by Jean Lemaire de Belges. This curious book by a relative of Molinet, which claims to show that the Gauls and Germans derived from a common Trojan ancestry, went into many editions, and its illustrations became a model for tapestries – proof enough that, although the public was interested in 'history', and increasingly in patriotic history, it was still generally unable to distinguish between legend and fact, or perhaps did not care to know the difference.

The same large public which had an insatiable appetite for history, and often preferred legendary histories to objective accounts, the public which, for example, took such an interest in the legend of Troy, was equally fascinated by imaginative literature. The first evidence for this interest that we come across is the fact that the press continues throughout the 16th century to produce numerous editions of medieval stories, and especially of the old stories of chivalry, the fashion for which never faded. While stories printed in the 15th century went on being regularly reprinted, printers were continually on the lookout for unpublished texts to introduce to readers and searched at random through available medieval manuscripts, which they would refurbish according to current taste before publication. Stories which could pass as national epics, like the *Chevalier au Cygne* or *Huon de Bordeaux*, came out along with ancient chivalric romances like *Gérard de Nevers*, *Florimont* and many others. Of the chivalric romances and national epics which appeared in prose, Outrepont has counted 13 national epics that were first published in the 16th century (as against 2 in the 15th) and 8 traditional romances (as against 5 in the previous century). Of the 80 or so medieval stories printed before 1550, the most successful were without any doubt the *Quatre fils Aymon* (18 editions before 1536, about 25 during the whole century), *Fierabras* (about as many) and *Pierre de Provence* (19 editions before 1536). One also sees the taste for the medieval legends of Troy collected together by Raoul Le Fèvre under the title of *Recueil des Histoires de Troyes* continue to develop throughout the 16th century and after, while the *Faits merveilleux de Virgile* continued to cast Virgil in the role of a medieval wizard. The legends of Baudoin of Flanders, Huon of Bordeaux, Ogier the Dane, Perceforest and the stories of the Knights of the Round Table, of King Arthur, Lancelot of the Lake, Merlin, Sir Perceval, and Tristan were all also undiminished in their popularity. Even all these works could not quench the thirst of the 16th-century public for fiction. So the *Roman de la Rose* had to be reprinted 14 more times during the first forty years of the century. Boccaccio's *Fiammetta* was so popular partly because it appealed to this aspect of popular taste, and the classical novels, for example such as Apuleius' *The Golden Ass* and Heliodorus' *Aethiopica*, were also extraordinarily in demand, and were often translated and reprinted.

At the same time there developed throughout Europe a number of literary forms which were more or less closely related to the fictional novel or story. This relationship accounts for much of their popular appeal and undoubtedly contributed to the success of More's *Utopia* and of Rabelais' work. But the two countries in which, in the 16th century, fictional works were most often written were without doubt Spain and Italy. In Spain chivalric romances had an enormous popular appeal. It was there that at the beginning of the 16th century there was published a chivalric romance whose origins are now obscure, but which was to be without question the most successful best seller of its day, the *Amadís de Gaula*. In the 16th century there were more than 60 Spanish editions of this book and of its sequels, along with a mass of French and Italian translations, and an edition in English, one in German and one in Dutch. Its success was such that there grew up in the course of the century a whole cycle of *Amadis* stories. The exploits of Esplandián, son of Amadis and stories of Amadis of England, of Palmerin of Oliva, of Palmerin of England and so on were intended to profit from the success of Amadis of Gaul.

While new editions of *Amadís de Gaula* continued to appear on the market, new works of fiction, of very different types, were produced in great numbers. In Spain sentimental novels were very popular: the *Carcel de Amor*, for instance, by Diego de San Pedro (partly based on Boccaccio's *Fiammetta* whose popularity we have already noticed) or the *Tratado de Amores de Arnalte y Lucenda* (3 Spanish editions between 1522 and 1527; 17 French, the first in 1537; and 4 English), the *Historia de Grisel y Mirabella* by Juan de Flores (8 Spanish, 9 Italian and 19 French editions) and the anonymous *Questions d'Amour* (about 15 editions). This tradition ultimately led to the pastoral and sentimental novel with Montemayor's *Diana*, and later, in France, with Honoré d'Urfé's *Astrée*, a 17th century work. This literary form thus developed from Boccaccio's *Fiammetta*, while on the other hand in Italy works of a different kind, especially the Arthurian and Carolingian cycles, tales of chivalry which were of French origin, led to the creation of a series of chivalric epics. These, without doubt, owed their success to their fictional character. Pulci's *Morgante* and Boiardo's *Orlando Innamorato* were followed by

Ariosto's *Orlando Furioso* which was a great success. At the same time, traditional tales of knights and stories like *Petit Jean de Saintré*, written to beguile the leisure hours of Burgundian nobles, joined the Shepherds' Calendars in the chapmen's packs. Here we see at work a process of evolution still apparent in our own day by which a masterpiece originally addressed to an elite audience is revised by later generations for a wider and wider public. Those who go to the cinema, read the comic-strips in the newspapers or watch television enter through these new intermediaries into contact with Victor Hugo, Stendhal, de Maupassant, and such classic writers – or at least with what purports to be their work.

3
The Book and the Reformation

Traditional moral and religious works were of course still being published, while the book-buying public grew, while the presses published the Latin and Greek classics in the original and in translation, and while new literary forms developed. The *Imitation of Christ* by Thomas à Kempis, the *Golden Legend* and the lives of saints were as popular as ever at the beginning of the 16th century, as were the *Mirror of Redemption*, Cato's moral tales, and the various lives of Antichrist. Authors like Heinrich Suso, Gerson and Nider were widely read, and so were the mystics who had been so popular in the 15th century, as well as the standard collections of sermons, to which could be added the writings of new preachers. Similarly, the Church Fathers, particularly Augstine and St. Bernard were still selling in large numbers. The monuments of scholastic theology like Ockham, Pierre de la Palud, Guillaume Durand, Duns Scotus and Buridanus sold as well as they had before, and more recent thinkers like Jean Mair, Tateret and Bricot shared in their popularity and were printed in vast numbers by the presses of Paris up until about 1520. At the same time, in the early years of the century, a completely new theological literature was created by men like Erasmus, Lefèvre d'Etaples and their circle, based on the study of the Scriptures. Thus religious works continued to be printed in large numbers at the beginning of the 16th century – perhaps in even larger numbers than in the 15th century. But they represented a smaller percentage, as have seen, of the total – constantly growing – output of the presses than they had before.[377] All in all, it seems that they, unlike the majority of secular works, did not reach a larger public than they had in the previous century. It is true that the works of Lefèvre d'Étaples – for example his translation of the Epistles of St. Paul – and, even more, some of the works of Erasmus, appear to have been in great demand. The number of reprints of such works shows just how wide a circulation scholarly works could at that time attain. But, in general, religious works scarcely circulated outside the relatively restricted circles of educated clerics and of humanists until about 1520.

This state of affairs changed abruptly in 1517 in Germany, a little later and more gradually elsewhere. Religious issues swiftly became questions of the foremost importance and unleashed the strongest passions. For the first time in history there developed a propaganda campaign conducted through the medium of the press. The capacity of the press to serve the interests of those who wished to influence thought and mould public opinion was revealed.

We must, of course, be careful not to ascribe to the book or even to the preacher too important a role in the birth and development of the Reformation. It would be wrong to regard propaganda and propagandists as the main cause of such developments. It is not part of our intention to revive the ridiculous thesis that the Reformation was the child of the printing press. It is perhaps the case that a book on its own has never been sufficient to change anybody's mind. But if it does not succeed in convincing, the printed book is at least tangible evidence of convictions held because it embodies and symbolises them; it furnishes arguments to those who are already converts, lets them develop and refine their faith, offers them points which will help them to triumph in debate, and encourages the hesitant. For all these reasons books played a critical part in the development of Protestantism in the 16th century. Before then the Church had detected many heresies but had always triumphed over them, in the West at least. One is justifiably inclined to wonder, as Henri Hauser did, what might have happened if some of the earlier heresies (the Hussite, for example) had had the power of the press at their disposal – power that Luther and Calvin used with great skill, first in the attack on Rome and then in the diffusion of their new doctrines. Central to their campaigns was the systematic attempt to place within reach of everyone and in the vernacular the Holy Writ which provided the basis of the reformed and restored religion. Hauser has emphasised that it was with good reason that: 'The Reformers likened in the frontispieces of their books the press which enabled them to distribute their spiritual beverage to a changed people, to a winepress from which a noble vintage gushed'.[378]

Printing had already indeed been long prepared for this new role, firstly through the manufacture in vast quantities of pious pictures, which dated back to the days of xylographic reproduction, then through the production, also in vast quantities, of books of simple piety, especially Books of Hours, and finally through the production of numerous copies of the sacred Scriptures, often in the vernacular. There were after all 19 editions of the Bible in High German before Luther, 24 editions of the Old Testament (or at least parts of it) in the old French translation of the illustrated Bibles before Lefèvre d'Étaples' version. Moreover while the press was facilitating and encouraging the renewal of scriptural studies it was also turning out thousands of handbills, posters and broadsheets intended for the general public. The first literature of information, the ancestor of the modern newspaper, was developing. It is hard for us to envisage now because so little of it survives, but its importance cannot be overestimated. The poster and the placard are probably older than the printed book, and many of them provided information about current events. At the same time, and more and more often as the 15th century went by, reports announcing occurrences of all kinds, such as the passage of a comet, or describing a festival or the ceremonial entry of a king into a city, or narrating the outcome of a battle, were printed by the thousand. Handbills of this type informed the French of their king's exploits in Italy and of their army's victories, or the Germans of the vicissitudes of the election of the Emperor, preparing the way for the countless *Flugschriften* printed during the Reformation.[379]

It was often through such ephemeral leaflets and tracts that the public was informed of the activities of the Reformers, of the controversies in which they were engaged, of the progress of heresy and of the measures taken to oppose it. One has only to think, if one wishes to measure the influence of the printing press, of the role played in the progress of the Reformation by posters. Before every big event in the Reformation there was a poster to advertise it, a poster which served to give the event general importance. When Luther began his attack on Indulgences, the act which marked that step was not so much the words of his sermon as the poster which he affixed to the door of the Augustinian chapel at Wittenberg on the 31st October, 1517. His Theses, translated into German and summarised, were printed as flysheets and distributed throughout Germany. Within 15 days they had been seen in every part of the country. A few years later, when Luther was summoned before the Imperial Diet at Worms in 1521, he crossed through Germany preceded by the Emperor's herald and he was upset to find in every town he passed through, Emperor Charles V's Edict stuck up on the walls commanding that his books should be burned. It was, one suspects, through such posters that ordinary people learnt of the existence of condemned or proscribed books, which they must often have then hastened to acquire. Such condemnations moreover were often met with replies which were also placarded on the walls of the town. For instance, a kind of poster warfare broke out in Meaux in 1524–1525: bills were posted denouncing Briçonnet as a Lutheran and when he riposted in December 1524 by putting up on the gates of the town and the walls of the Cathedral the pardon granted him by Clement VII, the Papal Bulls were taken down and replaced by more notices denouncing the Pope as Antichrist. Soon – the ultimate insult – someone posted on 13th January 1528 a faked Bull of Clement VII which 'permitted and enjoined the reading, re-reading and dissemination of Luther's works'. This little war led finally in 1534 to the 'affaire des placards', the crisis brought about by the famous posters denouncing the mass, which were printed by Pierre de Vingle in Neuchâtel and were found even on the doors of the King's apartments. The repression which followed this provocative act and the policy then enacted by Francis I towards the press are well known.

Notices like these were simply the outward and visible sign of the growing struggle. They were discovered on walls, on Church doors, or hanging from gateways. Some were posted clandestinely at night and attacked the mass or the Pope, others were official notices announcing the measures that were being taken to combat heresy, denouncing 'pernicious books' and ordering them to be delivered up. Naturally the public read all these with interest and followed the course of the argument, the blows and counter-blows, while behind this literature of the streets stood the great mass of books classed as 'ill-favoured' or 'heretical' or 'scandalous'. It is with their production and distribution at this time that we must now concern ourselves.

The eager demand for copies of Luther's propositions on Indulgences surprised their author and showed him that Germany was waiting only for a sign, for a leader, to assert her secret feelings publicly. This signal the press sent out. Ulrich von Hutten, weary of addressing his works only to a restricted circle of learned theologians, translated his dialogues *Febris Prima* and *Febris Secunda* into German (1519–1520),[380] and Luther wrote his appeal *To the Christian Nobility of the German Nation* (1520) in German, for it was intended for the widest possible audience, although Luther's replies to the orthodox theologians continued to be in Latin. Thousands of copies of his sermons, of his edifying tracts and of his vigorous polemics, all in the common tongue, streamed from the presses of Wittenberg. They were immediately reprinted throughout Germany, slight, easily-transported tracts which were, however, well-printed, with clear, bold titles within beautiful borders decorated in the German style. There was neither place of publication nor date on them, but the resounding name Martin Luther at the front, often with his portrait, which let readers become familiar with his likeness.[381]

All Germany caught fire. Pamphlets filled with the thunder of violent prose came out on all sides. No fewer than 630 *Flugschriften* (as they are aptly called in German) survive from the years between 1520 and 1530. Every device, not only of the printer's art, but also of illustration and even of caricature, was brought into service. To ridicule the Pope and the monks, pamphlets entitled *Pope Donkey* and *Cow Monk* were produced. Murner, a friar, and author of *The Lutheran Madman*, has a name which is like the German word for tomcat, and so naturally he appears in caricature as a monk with a cat's head. The proportion of books printed in German rose sharply: in Magdeburg, Rostock, Hamburg, Wittenberg and Cologne, 70 works in Low German were published from 1501 to 1510 and 98 from 1511 to 1520, but 284 (of which 232 were about religion and Church affairs) from 1521 to 1530 and 244 from 1531 to 1540 (180 of them on religion). Luther's works were prominent among them, of course, and it has been estimated that they represented more than one-third of the total number of German books sold between 1518 and 1525.[382] Some of them were enormously popular: the sermon *Von Ablasz und Gnade* was reprinted more than twenty times between 1518 and 1520. Of the sermon *Von der Betrachtung Heiligen Leidens Christi* (1519) about 20 editions are known. A letter of Beatus Rhenanus dated 24th May, 1519 tells us that his *Theology* and his *Explanation of the Lord's Prayer* 'were not so much sold as seized'. The famous pamphlet *To the Christian Nobility of the German Nation* came out on the 18th August 1520 and had to be reprinted on the 25th. In three weeks 4,000 copies were distributed and within two years there had been 13 editions. Some 18 reprints of the tract *On Liberty* are known, dating from before 1526, and figures for Luther's three most famous works of the year 1522 reveal the extent of the almost desperate eagerness to read everything he wrote shown by his audience: the *Von Menschenlehre zu Meiden* was printed 13 times, the *Booklet on Marriage* eleven times, and the *Betbüchlein* 25 times before 1545.

Thereafter German presses were mainly kept busy with the publications of the Reformers. Like much of the bourgeoisie of the time, printers were often not particularly fond of the old Church and the contacts many of them had with humanists and men of culture put them in touch with new ideas. Often they refused to print Catholic pamphlets but devoted painstaking care to printing the works of Luther, Hutten and Melanchthon, and even if it was not always from conviction that they behaved like this it was at least from self-interest. Everything revolved around Luther at this time. His adversaries' attacks on him had no success. Murner's *Lutheran Madman* sold feebly, and meanwhile the works which had previously been most sought after, those of Erasmus in particular, were bought by an ever diminishing readership. Luther, on the other hand, made the fortunes of his printers. Melchior Lotther and Hans Lufft were among the richest and most substantial citizens of Wittenberg where Lufft became Burgomaster. In Strasbourg, Knobloch, once renowned for his generosity towards Catholic institutions, turned his office into a centre of Lutheran propaganda. Of some 70 German printers studied by Goetze,[383] at least 45 worked for Luther, including of course all of the printers at Wittenberg, six out of eight of the printers in Strasbourg, and nine of those at Augsburg, as against three who were Catholics. Even in towns where the secular authority remained faithful to Rome, Reformation works were printed – usually with impunity, although some precautions were necessary. At Haguenau, Setzer, who is remembered for his association with Melanchthon, printed the latter's works along with those of Luther and pamphlets by Bugenhagen, Brenz, Johann Agricola and Urbanus Rhegius. The Imperial Chancellery reacted in 1524 and 1526, but its reaction was feeble and timid as long as Setzer published books in Latin intended for export, even when he prefaced some of the works with eloquent Latin denunciations of 'The synagogue of Antichrist', meaning Rome. Only when he issued an Anabaptist booklet in German in 1531 was the work seized, but even this did not prevent him from printing Servetus' *De Trinitatis Erroribus* in 1537.[384]

Such leniency was not to be found everywhere. In 1527, for example, in Nuremberg, Hans Guldenrund was proceeded against for printing a work against the Papacy. Above all it was the Elector George of Saxony who would not tolerate rebellious printers in his domain. Leipzig was abandoned by several printers, for the publication of Catholic works, which were the only ones permitted, was not a source of profit. This is perhaps why Jacob Thanner, who stayed in Leipzig, was imprisoned for debt, while Wolfgang Stöckel showed more business sense and set up a printing office outside the Catholic Elector's territory so that he could recover his losses by printing Lutheran tracts. Hawkers undertook the task of importing these into those states where they were forbidden and of distributing them in rural areas. However, in states where the Reformation had been accepted, the Protestant authorities were often stricter and more energetic than their Catholic counterparts in enforcing their interpretation of the decisions of the Diet of Worms which, although originally directed against Luther, in explicit terms only banned the publication of defamatory works. The Protestants could thus use them to act against printers who issued Catholic pamphlets. Sigmund Grim was arrested in 1526 in Augsburg for publishing the *Missa est Sacrificium* by Jean Eck. Grüninger, who was the only Strasbourg printer to remain loyal to the old faith, and went on bravely putting out works by Eck, Erasmus and Murner, had his *Lutheran Madman* confiscated by the magistrates in 1522. In Germany as a whole, books defending the Catholic faith were few in number in comparison to the flood-tide of works hostile to Rome. Until 1522 some few printers published both Lutheran and Catholic material; as did Adam Dyon in Breslau, Hans Knapps in Magdeburg and Hans Schoeffer in Mainz. Not until 1526–1528 did the Catholic counter-attack develop. It was based on Leipzig, where it had the support of George of Saxony; on Fribourg in Switzerland; on Ingolstadt, an ancient centre of Papal support where Alexander of Weissenhorn, a printer who had come from Augsburg, joined up with Eck, Cochlaeus and the theologians of the university and printed their works; and on Lucerne where Murner set up a press in 1526 to publish his own works. Elsewhere, printers who were not working on behalf of the Reformation restricted themselves normally to issuing works of scholarship or theology which had no direct connection with the momentous events of the time.

Reformation propaganda in the form of pamphlets and tracts began to filter into the countryside through the activities of the colporteurs, and there is little doubt that printing played its part in fomenting the Peasants' Revolt. Some printers, moreover, seem to have been sincere converts to radical politics and religion. Hetzer, a reader for Silvan Otmar and one of the Baptists in Augsburg, wrote some tracts himself and Conrad

Kerner, a printer of Strasbourg and Rottenburg, was condemned to pay a heavy fine and was held to be a dangerous troublemaker after the incidents which took place in the last named town, while in 1527 in Nuremberg a well known Anabaptist printer was burned. Thus the Anabaptists under Carlstadt and later the peasant leaders found printers prepared, either by conviction or from hope of profits, to support them.

The Peasants' Revolt and its suppression marked one of the decisive turning points in the history of the Lutheran Reformation. Thereafter pamphlets were not so plentiful and even Luther himself published fewer polemics, though he continued with his translation of the Bible which was a great success. The first edition of his *New Testament*, printed by Melchior Lotther at Wittenberg on three presses working flat out, appeared in September 1522 and was sold out in about ten weeks despite its comparatively high price. In two years, between 1522 and 1524, 14 reprints of the *New Testament* came out at Wittenberg and 66 others at Augsburg, Basel, Strasbourg and Leipzig. Adam Petri at Basel produced as many as seven editions of it. Cochlaeus lamented, 'Everyone is reading this translation and knows it by heart'. The *Old Testament* translation began to appear in 1523 and was equally successful. The Scriptures were henceforth in everyone's hands and the passions roused by religious controversy were such that even those who were illiterate had the text read and explained to them by better educated friends. Thus Zwingli could testify when the Peasants' Revolt had begun that the home of every peasant had become a school where he studied both Old and New Testaments.

This development continued unchecked. Luther progressed with his translation of the Old Testament, consulting Melanchthon and his associates at every step, and published it book by book. In all, 87 editions of his New Testament in High German and 19 in Low German came out between 1519 and 1535. The translations which he printed separately of the various individual books of the Old Testament were promptly pirated by Frederick Peypus of Nuremberg, Froschauer of Zurich, and Peter Schoeffer of Worms, among many others. In all, 430 editions in whole or in part came out between 1522 and 1546 and some of the editions contained exceptionally large numbers of copies. Hans Hergot, for example, put out in 1526 a pirated edition without the author's name on it, which ran to 3,000 copies. Luther's translation of the Bible was thus printed in enormous and unprecedented numbers and production scarcely declined during the second half of the century, for Hans Lufft issued 37 editions of the Old Testament between 1546 and 1580. This suggests that Crellius may not have been exaggerating when he said that Lufft alone was responsible for printing 100,000 copies of the Bible between 1534 and 1574. At Frankfurt 24 editions of the entire Bible were printed in the same period without counting partial editions. The grand total of copies printed must have reached one million during the first half of the 16th century and more than that in the second. The Bible was thus a bestseller even in the terms of our own day. When we consider that the translation of the Bible was only part of Luther's work, and that in addition he wrote sermons, polemics such as *To the Christian Nobility of Germany*, and catechisms which, cheaper and easier to understand, were produced in even greater numbers, then we can see that we have here for the first time a truly mass readership and a popular literature within everybody's reach.[385]

Just as one of the things that Luther required of the printing press was that it should place the Scriptures in the vernacular within the reach of all, so too, at almost the same time, this was one of the goals of the French Reformers. When Lefèvre d'Étaples was summoned to Meaux by Briçonnet, a reforming bishop, in 1521 he gave up his scholarly studies to begin a translation of the Bible into French for the ordinary reader. In 1523 the Gospels, the Epistles and the Acts of the Apostles were printed by Simon de Colines, and they were followed in 1524 by the Psalms and finally in 1525 by the *Épitres et Évangiles pour les cinquante-deux semaines de l' an* (*Epistles and Gospels for the Fifty-Two Weeks of the Year*), a devotional manual intended to bring the elementary and everyday truths of Christianity home to the average reader. In this way the Scriptures were placed in the hands of Frenchmen in a convenient form, in 8vo or 16mo, at about the same time as they came out in Germany. In the summer of 1524 Briçonnet arranged public readings which were in a more homely style than sermons. For an hour each morning the preacher read from the Bible and commented on it in front of a congregation of the common people, while for the more educated he interpreted the Psalms. Soon, after the first experiments proved successful, the meetings multiplied and four 'Readers' were given the job of visiting the larger towns. To complete the instruction of the more educated among the faithful, the bishop had copies of the Gospels in French distributed, urging that their recipients should bring them with them to divine service. One of his followers was so encouraged by this that he determined to establish a press at Meaux and took steps to obtain the necessary equipment.

As a result of this action the ordinary people of Meaux and the surrounding region, the weavers and carders and other humble artisans, were won over to the Gospel by means of methods which were to become those of the Huguenot reformers. Circles were formed of people who gathered together to read and to study the Bible and to sing the canticles (which were more readily grasped by the non-readers amongst them). Out of such circles Protestant Churches often developed in France as in Germany. The passion roused by religious issues was so strong at the time that the translations of Lefèvre spread with a speed which astonishes us now. Soon they were in circulation not only in Meaux and in Paris, but also in Lyons, Normandy and Champagne, and copies were to be found as far afield as in Provence and among the Valdensians of Dauphiné and Piedmont. At the same time the first collections of prayers in French were being printed in Paris.

At this time too, France came into contact with Luther's works. The international character of the book trade makes it easy to imagine how these should have quickly become available in France. Printers and booksellers from Paris and Lyons came into contact with those of Leipzig and Wittenberg during the Frankfurt Fairs and doubtless often brought back a few copies of the books which were making such a stir in Germany. Very early on, moreover, some foreign booksellers arranged to distribute in France editions specially printed for the purpose. Froben for instance, in a letter to Luther dated 14th February 1519, says he has reprinted some of his works and exported 600 copies of them to France, as well as others to England, Spain, Italy and Brabant. Even in Paris Conrad Resch at the sign of the *Écu de Bâle* used equipment he had acquired in Basel to turn out a series of polemical religious tracts, among them the one in which Luther set out the reasons which had led him to burn at Wittenberg the Papal Bull which condemned him. From about 1520 Luther was read and discussed in Parisian colleges, and his writings soon penetrated as far as Lyons and Meaux. The reactions of the authorities to the spread of heretical works are well known. After the Bull of 15th June 1520, came condemnation by the University of Paris on 15th April 1521. This seems to have unleashed a real press campaign, with the publication of numerous pamphlets and songs. Melanchthon's reply

Adversus furiosum Parisiensium theologastrorum decretum was on sale in Paris in Latin and French by that July. Already on 18th March 1521 a royal command in response to the instructions of the Papal Bull had ordered the Parlement to bring before the courts printers and booksellers and to ensure that no new work that did not bear the *imprimatur* of the University could be published and especially none which concerned Holy Scripture. On 13th June 1521 the Parlement issued an embargo, which was to become infamous, on the printing or sale of writings on Scripture that had not first been scrutinised by the Doctors of the Faculty of Theology in Paris. Renewed on the 22nd March 1522, the ban instituted a new principle, that of preliminary authorisation, and at the Council of Paris the bishops of the province of Sens were already compiling an inventory of banned works. Briçonnet and his associates were soon also under suspicion and the group at Meaux disbanded, Lefèvre being forced to take refuge for a time in Strasbourg. He was recalled by the King in 1526 and given the post of Royal Librarian at Blois and charged with the task of creating an educational system for French children, though he was not permitted to publish his translations in France. It was at Antwerp, and then anonymously, that his *Nouveau Testament* came out in 1528 and the *Sainte Bible*, the Bible in French, in 1530.

Thus an outright policy of repression (sometimes contrary to the King's wishes) was adopted by the Faculty of Theology of the University of Paris and by the Parlement, and their activities were closely co-ordinated by Noël Beda and Pierre Lizet. Printers and booksellers now had to take care not to distribute the more suspect works too openly. However before the 'affaire des placards' of 1534, they were seriously investigated only rarely, though they were fairly closely watched and often harassed, at least in Paris. Despite some bold attempts to print banned literature, notably by Simon Dubois, Marguerite of Navarre's printer, whose presses were turning out quantities of Lutheran tracts first in Paris and later at Alençon, it was difficult under the circumstances to print all the polemical works necessary to ensure the diffusion of the new ideas.[388]

Foreign printers and booksellers naturally tried to supply the French market with such works and already the first French Reformers were planning to set up a printing business over which they would have full control. In 1523, Lambert, a Franciscan from Avignon who had left his order to join Luther at Wittenberg, was planning to start a printing press in Hamburg to publish Luther's works in French, and at the same time Coct and Farel harboured similar schemes. Farel put these plans into effect at Neuchâtel in 1533 and Geneva in 1536. Meanwhile French refugees turned to German printers for help. Soon along the French frontier, at Antwerp, Strasbourg and Basel, presses were producing propaganda intended for clandestine export to France. Strasbourg was perhaps the main centre of this activity, and French refugees received a hearty welcome in that city which had been won over to the cause of the Reformers at an early date. There were many well known names amongst them. Lambert, back from Wittenberg, stayed from 1524 to 1526. Lefèvre d'Étaples, who had fled from Meaux in October 1525, arrived with Roussel and stayed with Capiton, a leader of the Reformation in Strasbourg. Near them lived Michel d'Arande and Farel. Later still Strasbourg took in Servetus, and Calvin married there and published the second Latin edition of his *Institutes of the Christian Religion* in 1539. Alongside these famous refugees there were the vast numbers who flooded into the town with each new wave of persecution. By 1538 they were numerous enough for Calvin to establish a French parish in the town and were to be 15,000 strong in 1576 after St. Bartholomew's Eve.

Thus Strasbourg naturally became a propaganda centre for the dissemination of the new ideas in France. For a long time its printers avoided running into difficulties with the authorities by not publishing works in French, except on rare occasions, and with the persistent exception of Jean Prüss; their mission was in fact different, and the service they rendered to French Protestantism between 1520 and 1540 was that of making available in France Luther's Latin works and of producing Latin translations of his German works, the translations being made by organised groups. A number of important printers devoted themselves to this task, men like Jean Schott, Herwagen, Rizhel and Setzer. Their massive output was sold in France to the intense chagrin of French Catholics who could not denounce Strasbourg enough in their anger. At Antwerp meanwhile, a group of printers was specialising in the production of polemical tracts in French. Vorstermann and especially Martin de Keyseren (in French, Martin Lempereur) were the most energetic in this field, the latter taking upon himself, in 1528 and 1530, the task of putting out the translations of the Bible which Lefèvre was unable to print in France. De Keyseren also published a translation of Erasmus' *Enchiridion* in French, believed to have been the work of Berquin. Above all, along with Simon Dubois, he specialised in the printing of the little devotional manuals which were circulating in France before 1530 and were perhaps the most effective vehicles of Lutheran theology. Thus the whole range of Protestant propaganda was produced in Antwerp, doubtless as a result of the efforts of the French refugees, and from there it could easily be smuggled into France by merchants and pedlars. The Spanish authorities perhaps initially pretended not to notice these publications intended for the export market, and in fact Lefèvre's Bible had obtained the approval of the theologians of Louvain, but they were eventually roused into action. On the 14th November 1529 they ordered that no more New Testaments were to be published in Antwerp, 'nor the gospels, epistles, prophets, nor any other books in French or Low German which contain prefaces or prologues, marginalia or glosses containing or suggesting any evil doctrines or theological error'. This ban, renewed in 1531, appears to have made the printers of Antwerp a little more prudent and there is a tendency thereafter for them to seek out rather less compromising texts to be printed in French.

Froben at Basel decided, at Erasmus' request, to print no more Lutheran works but his colleague Adam Petri made no such act of self-denial and profited by his persistence. Part of his output was meant for France. French refugees were numerous in Basel and were perhaps more influential than in Strasbourg, and so there too they encouraged the publication of Protestant propaganda and helped with the task of getting it into France. Thomas Wolff, a Basel printer, seems to have had especially close connections with them. Like Martin Lempereur at Antwerp he printed works in French. In 1523 he produced the *Somme de l'Escriture Sainte* and in the following year the famous satire against the decision of the University of Paris, which was given the name of Murmau. He was also responsible, for example, for an edition of Lefèvre's *New Testament* in 1525 which was decorated with wood-cuts copied from those designed by Cranach for the first edition of Luther's Bible. At the same time, like Herwagen of Strasbourg, he brought out many Latin translations of Luther's German works.

Such books printed just beyond the borders of France, often at the instigation of Frenchmen, entered France in large numbers and with ease. There is abundant evidence for this, especially from the lists of books seized in the houses of heretics, which were often produced in trials for heresy. But how did the books enter France with so little difficulty? Merchants returning from business trips and hawkers have often been put forward as an explanation. And of course they did import some books. But the underground organisations based in Geneva were especially important. They developed from about 1540 or 1550 and distributed the books printed in the city of Calvin. Before then, the colporteurs were certainly very active, and afterwards it was still they who set out from the large towns distributing banned literature secretly, often through the local bookseller, in the small towns and villages. But it is reasonable to assume that a large part of the trade in subversive books was carried on underground as if it was an ordinary business, and indeed a business run on a very large scale. French booksellers and printers thus played the major part in the trade. Many of them were sympathetic to the new ideas, especially in Lyons, and many joined the Protestant Church. Through their constant business dealings with their colleagues abroad they often helped introduce forbidden books into France, and they also took the risk of printing dangerous works. Many had friendly relations with exiled leaders of the Reformation and rendered them assistance in all sorts of ways, sometimes acting as their bankers, more often as informers and intermediaries. They did this without running too many risks because they knew how to take precautions and to secure themselves the necessary protection. There was no police force, legal procedures were very complicated and the King himself was not always inclined to act harshly. This is evident from a study of, for example, the activities of the group of booksellers, all relatives or business partners of each other, who acted in strict concert throughout the period of the Reformation, keeping shops in Paris and Lyons at the sign of the *Écu de Bâle* and of the *Écu de Cologne*, and representing the interests of Basel booksellers in France.[389]

The founder of the enterprise was Johann Schabler (written as Cabiller in French) better known as Wattenschnee, originally from Swabia. He settled in Lyons in 1483 with a compatriot, the printer Matthew Husz, who he seems to have financed. In 1485 he set up on his own. Rather than being a publisher or local bookseller, he was somewhat like Barthélemy Buyer, a broker in books and a bookseller who specialised in doing business at the book fairs. He quickly became the principal representative of the booksellers of Basel in Lyons and obtained the citizenship of Basel in 1495. By 1504 he showed signs of wanting to extend his business and handed over direction of his shop in Lyons to one of his employees, Pierre Parmentier, with whom he placed in partnership, some time between 1521 and 1524, his first cousin once removed, Jean Vaugris. The two partners were assigned to well defined areas. Parmentier covered the towns in the South of France, Italy and Spain, while Vaugris was in charge of Strasbourg, Basel, Geneva and Flanders.

In 1536 or thereabouts, Parmentier set up two branches, one at Avignon and the other at Toulouse.

Schabler, after toying with the idea of setting up in Nantes, quite probably to establish a staging post on the route to Spain for publishers in Basel and Lyons, seems to have become involved around 1504 in publishing in Paris, where he is found in business with Kerver and Petit bringing out a monumental edition of Canon law. He may already have had a shop there, but in any case his nephew, Conrad Resch, was established in 1516 at the sign of the *Écu de Bâle* in the Rue St. Jacques. During the Lyons Fair, letters and packets flooded in to Michel Parmentier who would see that they reached their destination. Alciat, Rabelais, Jean Du Bellay and the Amerbach family relied on his good offices as did many others, including the Reformers. Schabler, who had retired to Basel by 1516 at the latest, maintained good relations with Farel and Coct, and Vaugris, his agent in Frankfurt and Strasbourg, seems to have been in close liaison with the Reform movement. He wrote to Amerbach on the 22nd of November 1520, 'If you have the Luther in German, send it to me at Lyons for there are some good journeymen who wish to read it'. He is often the first with news of events as a result of his travels and connections. Requested to send on some money to Boniface Amerbach who was studying at Avignon, he tells him in an accompanying letter of Hutten's death, and adds some news of Erasmus. In 1524 we see him intervening to hasten publication of a treatise of Farel's, the *De Oratione Dominica*, at Basel, and on 20th August of the same year he sends a letter to Farel, then at Montbéliard, which tells us a lot about the role he was playing. A few lines from that letter, written in a French full of the most extraordinary spellings, are worth reproducing here:

'William, my worthy brother and friend, the grace and peace of God be upon you. I have had your letters in which you tell me that some money was to be delivered to M. le Chevalier [Anémond de Coct]. I have sent him 10 écus by way of my uncle Conrat [Conrad Resch]. Item, I have had your books bound, for as soon as they were brought to me, straightaway I dropped everything else in order to attend to your affairs. Item, I am sending the books to you in a consignment addressed to the Chevalier along with 200 *Paters* [i.e. Farel's *Exposition Familière de l'Oraison Dominicale et des Articles du Credo*] and 50 *Epistolae* [probably a work by Farel now lost], but I do not know how you intend to sell them or have them sold. . . . I have expressed my gratitude to my agents, so that they may become eager to sell books and by this means they will be sold little by little and at the same time some profit will be made. Item, if it is possible I think you should have a translation of the New Testament done, on the basis of M[artin] L[uther]'s version, by someone who would be able to do it well, for it would be a great benefit for the countries of France, Burgundy, Savoy etc. If need be I can send a French scholar from Lyons or Paris, and if there is someone at Basel who would be suitable, then so much the better. Item, I leave Basel for Frankfurt today. From Basel, 19th August, 1524.'

Without question then, Vaugris played a crucial part in the distribution of Reformation propaganda. In his shops in Paris and Châlons there must certainly have been a plentiful supply of heretical books printed by the Basel publishers whose representative he was – Schabler, Froben, Cratander, Curion. So when he died suddenly in June 1527 at Nettancourt in Lorraine, on his way back from a business trip to Paris, where he was planning to open another shop, the chapter of St.-Benoît-le-Bétourné alerted the Parlement to seize the stocks of books he had stored in the new shop he had just set up in an office of the house of the Unicorn, where Kerver had his workshop. The Bishop of Châlons took similar measures. The Basel booksellers were concerned at this and alerted the City Council which expressed anger and intervened. The Parlement was unwilling to stir up trouble with the Swiss and the enquiries seem to have stopped. This, however, did not prevent the bookseller Andreas Weingartner, a relative of Vaugris' wife and also a citizen of Basel, from being harassed by the authorities in Paris in 1529.

Like Vaugris, Conrad Resch, whose shop was at the sign of the *Écu de Bâle* in Paris, was completely dedicated to the Reformation and it was he who produced, as we have seen, the earliest surviving French translation of Luther. Resch was deeply interested in the religious controversies of the time and, significantly, the two printers he employed, Pierre Vidoue and Simon Dubois, were equally committed. In 1523 he had Pierre Vidoue print Erasmus' *Paraphrases* on the Epistles, a work which seems to have aroused the hostility of the University of Paris.

In 1526 Conrad Resch followed Schabler and Vaugris to Basel, probably in order to be able to act more freely. Like his two relatives he stayed in the book business, regularly attending the fairs, and maintaining his business interests in France. He seems at this time to have been in constant communication with Farel and Calvin, and in 1538 Louis du Tillet, in Paris, offered to send some funds to Calvin, then in Basel, as a result of the activities of Resch as an intermediary. While Resch was in

Basel, Christian Wechel, a former agent of Resch's now at the Paris *Écu de Bâle*, showed himself to be as strong in his support for the Reformation as his former boss. He came originally from Brabant, and maintained close links with Germany and often published works by German authors, particularly Dürer's theoretical treatises. Among his publications were many heretical works, but he was very prudent and avoided undue risks to such an extent that, for example, he obtained a royal privilege to bring out, in 1528 and 1530, an apparently inoffensive tract called *Livre de parfaite oraison*, part of which was actually an adaptation of some passages from Luther's *Betbüchlein*. In 1530 he published the *Prières et Oraisons de la Bible*, a translation of the *Precationes biblicae* by Otto Brunfels, a little book which made known a selection of Biblical texts which would have been forbidden if translated openly but which, because of its harmless appearance, was not put on the Index until 1551. Thanks to such devious methods Wechel does not seem to have ever been seriously troubled by the authorities and died peacefully in Paris. His son, however, who only escaped the Massacre of St. Bartholomew because of the help he was given by his tenant, Hubert Languet, a minister from Saxony who was staying in Paris, went to settle in Frankfurt the following year.

Another establishment grew up alongside the *Écu de Bâle*. It too had links with the printers of Basel and with the Reformation. It was started by Jean and François Frellon, sons of a Paris bookseller, who began at the sign of the *Écu de Cologne* in Lyons. Jean, the elder of the two, after working for Conrad Resch, went, it seems, to Basel either to complete his training or to get away from Paris where his religious views may have made it dangerous for him to stay. On his return he settled not in Paris, where however he continued to own a shop, but in Lyons, which was a more tolerant city. Soon afterwards he went into partnership with his brother François and in 1542 he turned publisher. Out of prudence no doubt, he claimed to be a Catholic, but his real convictions can scarcely be questioned. He certainly introduced into France many heretical works printed by his friends the printers of Basel. He was, along with Conrad Resch, their Paris agent. So close were his relations with Basel that on the 3rd May 1538, when the City Council learnt that Francis I had just issued an edict forbidding the sale of books *Lutheranae farinae*, it renewed the initiative it had taken in 1527 when Vaugris' stock was seized on his death, and sent a letter to the chief prosecutor for the Paris region recommending to him their two fellow citizens (*cives nostros*) Resch and Frellon, *bibliopolas*, and asking him to take no notice of the false accusations directed against them. False accusations? It is unlikely, for Frellon like Resch was in correspondence with Farel and Calvin, and Servetus worked for a time as a press reader for him. Frellon was the intermediary in the correspondence between Servetus and Calvin, and when Servetus published his *Christianissimi Restitutis* at Vienne in Dauphiné, Frellon agreed to help with its distribution. While the books he published certainly appear to be similar to those intended to be used in Catholic worship, very often they were in fact a vehicle for Protestant doctrines. Such is the case for example with two booklets he published in 1545, the *Precationes christianae ad imitationem psalmorum compositae* and the *Precationes biblicae . . . Veteris et Novi Testamenti*. Again in 1553 in his *New Testament* the Devil of Temptation is represented as a monk with cloven hooves. His connection with Antoine Vincent, a publisher of Lyons and Geneva who, as we shall see, was deeply dedicated to the Protestant cause, leaves no doubt as to Frellon's real sympathies or as to the nature of his activities.

So, under cover of Basel citizenship, an organised group of booksellers, supporters of the Reformation, could throughout the first half of the 16th century maintain in France almost without hindrance shops filled with heretical literature and could even manage on occasion to print Protestant works in Paris and Lyons. They acted as agents for the booksellers of Basel, and as couriers and sometimes as bankers for Farel, Calvin and their friends. In view of their activities there is no cause to be surprised that banned books circulated in France in ever greater numbers despite all the regulations forbidding them. Nor were the *Écu de Bâle* and the *Écu de Cologne* the only headquarters for such activities. Far from it.

To sell forbidden books, to violate the prohibitions of the Sorbonne, of the Parlement, of even the King himself, this in fact became increasingly a purely commercial necessity for many booksellers. Already in 1521 the ban on Luther's books, which aroused such strong interest and so of course always sold in great numbers, must have seemed to many to be a serious restriction on their business activities. The impossibility of openly publishing Ulrich von Hutten's pamphlets, especially when his literary works were selling so well, must have similarly seemed a threat to trade. In this period when humanism and the Reformation were still bound up together, when the works of the humanists were so extraordinarily in demand, publishers saw works written by the authors who were most desired banned one after the other. After the ban on Lefèvre's translation of the Bible in 1525, Erasmus, some of whose works were to be found in every bookshop, was next to suffer. Then Marot came under suspicion. While Lefèvre's new Bible was coming out in Antwerp and Basel, the booksellers of Paris and Lyons had in theory to settle for reprinting the old illustrated version which indeed sold well and was repeatedly reprinted, so great was the desire to read the sacred book. Yet how much more would this have been true of Lefèvre's version! In May and June, 1525, the Faculty of Theology condemned four of Erasmus' works: the *Déclaration des louanges de mariage*, the *Brièeve admonition de la manière de prier*, the *Symbole des Apôtres* and the *Complainte de la paix*. In May 1562, they forbade the reading of his *Colloquies*, especially by young people. As this was a title of which many Parisian booksellers must have possessed copies in their bookshops, we can imagine the reaction of the trade. Even when they wanted to publish the most widely read treatises of the Church Fathers they had to secure authorisation, and so suspect was Erasmus in the eyes of the Sorbonne that even an edition of Jerome based on Erasmus' text was viewed with reservations when Chevallon brought it out. The Sorbonne did not fail to express its disapproval, issuing a stern warning, and so Chevallon, having learnt his lesson, submitted to the Sorbonne's inspection, on 15th February 1530, the edition of St. Augustine which he was preparing for the press.

The proceedings brought against Berquin at this time, and the tortures he was subjected to, must have made more than one bookseller tremble. But it was really in 1530 that the harassment of booksellers and printers began to be common practice. In April 1530 the Sorbonne condemned the view that it was necessary to study Greek and Hebrew if one was to understand the Bible properly. On the 2nd of March 1531 the same authority censored a whole series of books, among them the *Unio dissidentium*, the *Oraison de Jésus-Christ qui est le Pater Noster*, the *Credo avec les Dix Commandements de la Loi, le tout en Français*, and at its instigation the High Court of Parlement delegated to two of its members on 12th July 1531 the duty of inspecting (together with two representatives of the Faculty of Theology) all books on sale in Paris and of seizing any containing 'false doctrine'. This decree, renewed on 17th May 1532, allowed the theologians to search bookshops, a privilege which they appear to have taken advantage of to such an extent that the Parlement had to forbid them to search premises or ban books except in the presence of the Parlement's representatives. Finally, the affair of the royal lecturers broke out at the beginning of 1534. On reading the notices announcing that Agathas Guidacerius, Jean Vatable and Pierre Danès proposed to expound the Scriptures and Aristotle, both the Parlement and the Sorbonne exploded. The Parlement forbade the reading and expounding of the Scriptures without the permission of the Faculty of Theology. It is clear that the premises of the booksellers officially appointed as agents to the royal lecturers were searched at the same time – Wechel, Jérôme de Gourmont and Augereau were named in the notices that had been at the origin of the whole business. Augereau, we know, spent a period in gaol.[391]

Subject to the authority of the University, and often on friendly terms with members of the Faculty of Theology and with officers of the Parlement, the twin bastions of orthodoxy, most Paris booksellers and printers were perhaps much less inclined than their counterparts elsewhere to give their support to the new ideology. But they still had a clientele to satisfy, so that in the end they could not but be exasperated by the restrictions placed upon their commercial activities. One incident in particular illustrates this. In 1545, after the Parlement had ratified the condemnation of a long list of works drawn up by the Faculty of Theology, the 24 booksellers licensed by the University agreed to protest that this measure would quite possibly bankrupt them, since it meant that stocks already in their shops had to be written off as a total loss and printing orders then in train had to be cancelled. In view of these circumstances they petitioned for authorisation to sell the offending works if they were accompanied by a slip listing the censured passages so that the public would not be led astray. The request was of course refused.[392]

In face of such measures the trade was of course tempted to evade the law, especially since the enforcement of the law was ill-administered and, in addition, particularly up until 1534, the party in favour of toleration was strong at Court, thanks to the influence of Marguerite of Navarre and of Jean and Guillaume Du Bellay, and was willing to intervene in defence of those who fell foul of the religious authorities. It was well known, moreover, that the King wanted to see the fervour of the theologians and magistrates somewhat moderated. At this point in time, in any case, the exact demarcation between heresy and orthodoxy was still blurred. It is important not to forget that it was then that the King intervened in favour of Berquin, and of Marot when he tried to defend Erasmus against the attacks of the Sorbonne; that Lefèvre d'Étaples found asylum in the King's service; that royal privileges were granted to books condemned by the Sorbonne as heretical; and that the King's sister herself was under suspicion and one of her books was attacked.

Later still, at the height of the storm in the last years of his reign, Francis I granted his protection against the Sorbonne to Robert Estienne, his printer, and in 1545 he granted a privilege to Rabelais and allowed him to have Wechel print his *Tiers livre*, although his *Gargantua* and his *Pantagruel* were already on the Index drawn up by the Sorbonne and the Parlement.

Ignoring the royal licence, the Sorbonne speedily condemned that book, too, and Rabelais thought it wise to flee to Metz despite royal protection, although even condemnation by the Sorbonne did not prevent the King renewing the privilege granted in 1545 for another ten years from 1550. It was a strange epoch when the bookseller Jean André, printer to the Parlement and agent for the Président Lizet, whose press actually printed the editions of the Index in which some of Marot's works were included, printed on the same press in 1544 a collection of verse in honour of Marot's memory – of Marot who was both a heretic and the King's Poet.

In conditions like these it is hardly surprising that censorship was ineffectual, that more and more heretical books were produced, and that Protestantism won over a steady stream of converts. The truth is that French booksellers were able in many cases to go on selling and printing heterodox literature in response to the demands of their eager clients without running any serious risk, so long as they acted prudently and adopted a few elementary subterfuges. Of course they could not openly publish a work which had just been banned, but they could always adopt the dodge which Rabelais' publishers adopted each time his books were condemned – simply drop their address from the title page. There was nothing in any case to prevent them printing refutations of heresy by authors like Jean Eck or John Fisher or Béda except when the King expressly forbade it. The danger was similarly no more than minimal in bringing out a book with every appearance of orthodoxy yet with daring propositions cunningly inserted into the argument. There were in fact many ways of beating the theologians and throwing the Parlement off the scent.

Thus editions of doubtful orthodoxy multiplied despite all the condemnations. Those produced abroad might be more open in their attacks, those produced in France might dissimulate the audacity of their arguments, but religious propaganda could be successfully carried on in either way, as can be seen from a study of the publishing history of a number of works.

Let us look for instance at the *Heures de Nostre Dame*. Translated by the poet Gringore, under the pseudonym 'Mère Sotte', in 1525, the French text was different in important respects from the original Latin. Moreover, as a rather tasteless joke, the poet seems to have had himself drawn as Christ being mocked, wearing a clerical overcoat and a mortarboard. The illustration seems to have gone unnoticed, but the text made the Parlement uneasy and they decided to consult the Sorbonne. The book was duly condemned by the Sorbonne on 26th August 1525, and the Parlement forbade its publication. But its publisher, Jean Petit, did not lose hope of re-using the wood-cuts he had had made at great expense for the book or of reprinting the same text. He waited three years before publishing a second edition in 1528 when he presumably thought the affair would have been forgotten, and out of prudence he substituted in a number of copies a less compromising block for the grotesque one used in the original. The *Heures de Nostre Dame* was reprinted again in 1533 and about 1540, once again with the same grotesque illustration. Perhaps this work was not really all that subversive, but even Luther's works seem to have been published and sold in France without meeting with much greater difficulties. The *Betbüchlein* is one example: first published in 1522 it was translated into Latin in 1525 and published by Herwagen in Strasbourg. As we saw, Wechel published in 1528 and 1530, under cover of a royal licence, a little devotional manual called *Livre de vraie et parfaite Oraision* whose table of contents offered no hint of heresy, but which in fact contained a partial translation of Luther's book. By that time, however, the Inquisitors of the Sorbonne had learnt to be suspicious of appearances and on 2nd March 1531 they condemned the volume. This made little difference, for Martin Lempereur took over the printing at Antwerp in 1534. Then, after a suitable lapse of time, Jean de Brie's widow reprinted it openly in Paris in 1540, and her edition was followed by that of Jacques Regnault and Eustache Foucault, also printed in Paris, in 1543. Guillaume Vissmaken, at Antwerp in 1545, and Olivier Arnoullet at an unspecified date in Lyons, put out further impressions. Several thousands of copies of Luther's text in a translation which may have been partly Berquin's work were thus printed in six different editions without booksellers or printers being punished.[393]

Many works of the Reformers were issued in those days on the same huge scale. The *Unio Dissidentium*, signed by Hermann Bodius (Martin Bucer's pseudonym), was printed in Latin at Cologne in 1527, then at Antwerp in 1531, and at Lyons in 1531, 1532, 1533 and 1534. It was printed in French on Martin Lempereur's press in 1528 and 1532, with further impressions from Geneva in 1539 and 1551. The *De disciplina et institutione puerorum* by Otto Brunfels, which was to be condemned by the Sorbonne in 1533 and which had been first published in 1525, was issued before its condemnation by Robert Estienne in 1527 in Paris, then in 1538 by Gryphe in Lyons, and again in Paris in 1541 and 1542, now bound with another work, Hegendorff's *Institutio*. In 1558 Robert Granjon published a French translation of it at Lyons. Brunfels' *Precationes biblicae* were however a still greater success. Emigré French Protestants who were seeking to bring out, as a substitute for editions of the New Testament, short tracts packed with quotations from the Bible, got hold of this work and translated it. Under the title of *Prières et Oraisons de la Bible* the French version enjoyed a success all the greater for the fact that it was not censored until 1550 at Louvain, and until 1551 at Paris. Vorstermann printed it at Antwerp in 1529 and Martin Lempereur reprinted it there in 1533. It was Wechel who put out a Paris edition in 1530, and Dolet printed it in 1542, and Jean de Tournes in 1543.

Until 1534 printers and booksellers who dealt in such books could evidently count on immunity, and it was rare for anyone to be seriously harassed before that date. After the 'affaire des placards' it was no longer so. The savage reaction of the King is well known.[394] Penitential processions were staged on the 22nd, 23rd and 24th October 1534, and Parlement had it announced in the palace that: 'If anybody lays information against the person or persons who put up the aforesaid notices and his information proves to be correct, he will be rewarded with the sum of 100 écus by the court. On the other hand, anyone found to be harbouring such persons will be burned.' After that, denunciations flooded in to Paris. In Tours searches were made at the home of printers and booksellers, and they figured largely among the suspects who were arrested. November 1534 saw the first series of spectacular executions. On the 10th it was a printer who was burned, for having printed and bound the 'false works' of Luther, and on the 19th it was the turn of a bookseller. On the 24th December Antoine Augereau, one of the printers of the *Miroir de l'âme pécheresse*, who had already suffered imprisonment at the time of the case involving the royal lecturers, was sent to the stake. Then, on 21st January 1535, in the day-time there was a penitential procession in which the King took part through the streets of Paris, and in the evening, in the streets through which the procession had passed, six heretics were burned at the stake. To complete the symbolism, three large sacks of books found in their possession were added to the pyres before the execution.

The large number of handbills recovered and the many suspected books seized during the enquiries must certainly have surprised the King, who seems to have suddenly understood the importance of the book in the propagation of heresy. Books, moreover, provided the sole tangible proof of a suspect's guilt, materialising as it were his private heretical opinions. Resolved upon the extirpation of heresy, François I took extreme measures and on 13th January 1535 forbade any book to be printed within the kingdom on pain of death by hanging. It was an extraordinary decree, impossible to enforce, and in any case unlikely to settle anything – the offending notices, the origin of all these measures, had after all been printed by Pierre de Vingle outside France, at Neuchâtel where he was safe from reach. Budé and Jean Du Bellay objected to the decree and it was finally revoked. On 23rd February the King announced that he would suspend final judgment and meanwhile 12 Parisian printers were to be appointed. 'They and none besides' were to publish 'those books which are necessary and approved for the public good', and they were forbidden to print any new books.

The decree was very like those issued by English sovereigns in the same period, but it was never enforced. In fact French printers seem to have carried on working uninterruptedly, and they printed as many books in 1535 as in any other year. But henceforth they were certainly subject to a more rigorous supervision. On 25th January 1535, the names of seven men who worked in the book trade appeared in the list of suspected heretics. On the run, they were summoned to the accompaniment of trumpet calls. Thereafter printers and booksellers were often arrested and some were sent to the stake. To put a stop to the production and sale of increasing numbers of forbidden books, a trade which naturally grew at the same rate as the support for heretical beliefs, a whole body of legislation developed and was made steadily more precise and rigorous. When copies of Calvin's *Institution Chrétienne* were seized in 1542 Parlement took the opportunity to reaffirm the ban on the sale of books of any kind which had not first been examined by censors delegated by the theologians of the Sorbonne. The first French Index came out, as we have seen, in 1545, the product of a series of searches carried out over the preceding years in the bookshops of Paris. In April 1547 the King took the initiative and issued an edict at Fontainebleau banning yet again the printing and sale of works relating to Scripture, along with the sale of any books which came from Geneva or Germany, unless they had been submitted to prior scrutiny by the Faculty of Theology. Finally in 1551 the King in an edict issued at Châteaubriant confirmed, consolidated and systematised all previous measures and in doing so specifically forbade the import of any books from Geneva or heretical countries.

In short then, there came into being a mass of draconian legislation, precise enough to meet all eventualities, and yet generally ignored. In fact these regulations only serve to reflect in the process of their elaboration the progress of support for Protestantism and the growing trade in banned books. After 1540, and even more so after 1550, the French printers and booksellers became steadily bolder. Secret presses came into operation all over the place, colporteurs were everywhere with their packs, and heretical tracts without imprints or with false imprints appeared in ever greater numbers. At the same time innocuous titles were increasingly used to mask heretical material. An extensive literature developed which in outward appearance was unimpeachably orthodox but was in reality a vehicle for heretical propaganda. It took on all the forms taken by popular literature, and so even appeared under the guise of alphabets or almanacs. For example, the *Figures de l'Apocalypse* which was published in 1552 and bore the imprint of Étienne Groulleau, successor to Denys Janot who was one of the largest Parisian publishers of popular booklets, was heretical. So too was the *Alphabet ou Instruction chrétienne pour les petits enfants* which was repeatedly censured yet was openly printed by Pierre Estiard at Lyons in 1558, before he left for Strasbourg. So too was the *Miroir du Pénitent*, a small volume of devotions published just as openly by Jean de Tournes at Lyons in 1559.[395]

What did the elegant regulations formulated by lawyers matter? What did it matter, under these circumstances, that a printer here or there was arrested, or even burnt? To be effective the repression would have to have been much more severe, and even then it might still have failed. Most of those arrested or burnt were colporteurs, or occasionally small booksellers and boy assistants. Among the real victims of the repression there cannot be found a single name belonging to one of the great printing dynasties that dominated the trade. Imbart de la Tour, noting this fact, claims that the wealthy booksellers and the printers who owned their own premises took no risks and that heretical books were generally printed on clandestine presses. There may be some truth in this insofar as Paris is concerned. But above all, the big publishers had too many connections and more than enough sources of protection. When danger threatened there were too many friends who sought to save them, to warn them, to hold up the enquiries. If things came to the worst, men like Conrad Bade and Robert Estienne had plenty of time in which to prepare for flight.

In Lyons especially, printers and booksellers carried on their trade in almost complete freedom. After 1542 the old illustrated Bible was no longer printed, and Olivétan's version was printed instead, dressed up to impart an air of orthodoxy. None of the printers involved – Arnoullet, Frellon, de Tournes, Guillaume Rouillé, Payen, Pidier, Bacquenois, the Beringens – got into any trouble as a result. Later, from 1558 onwards, Robert Granjon, son-in-law of the painter Bernard Salomon (himself Jean de Tournes' son-in-law) used a type fount called *Civilité*, although it was instantly identifiable as his, to print a small series of devotional manuals which were heretical through and through. This however did not prevent him later from going to Rome to cut type for the Vatican. During this period the most famous of the printers and booksellers of Lyons were inclined towards Protestantism and many were in contact with Farel, Calvin and Geneva. Jean de Tournes lived in constant contact with Protestant associates and Sébastien Gryphe welcomed Dolet on his release from prison in Toulouse, and did not hesitate to print works that had been condemned by the Sorbonne. The Sennetons, who were influential publishers, were converts to the new religion and so was Frellon. Balthasar Arnoullet nominally practised the Catholic religion, but he was in partnership with Guillaume Guéroult who later turns up in Geneva. He enjoyed close relations with Calvin and employed Servetus as a corrector. In 1553 he allowed Guéroult secretly to publish the *Christiana Restitutio* in Vienne. It was necessary for Calvin, who was hostile to Servetus, to denounce Arnoullet before he was put in prison. But even then he was soon released, took up his craft as a printer again and was reconciled with Calvin. In this kind of climate it is not surprising that heretical books were available in great numbers. Was there not Antoine Vincent, with his two offices, one in Geneva and one in Lyons, to provide the capital and to organise production and sale, on a scale previously unattained in Paris, Metz, Lyons or Geneva?

The project that Lambert, Coct and Farel had nurtured for so long, that of providing for the French Reformation a haven for refugees and a propaganda base analogous to Luther's at Wittenberg, was finally realised when, with the support of a section of the town's merchants, Farel entered Neuchâtel in 1530 and, on the 4th of November, expelled the priests and abolished the Mass.

Neuchâtel now became both a meeting place for French emigrés and the main centre of evangelical propaganda. Farel, being a hard-headed man of action, was fully aware of the power of the press and quickly set about persuading a printer, Pierre de Vingle[396] to come to Neuchâtel. Pierre was himself the son of a printer, Jean de Vingle, and came from Picardy. He had worked as a foreman for Claude Nourry from 1525 to 1531. Nourry, whose workshop was in Lyons, was something of a specialist in the publication of popular literature and Pierre married his daughter. When he converted to the Reformed Church he put himself at Farel's disposal and, from 1525 onwards, made use of Nourry's press to turn out Protestant works under false imprints. In 1531 he printed in his own name that little tract we have already mentioned more than once, the *Unio Dissidentium*, condemned by the Sorbonne on 2nd March of the same year. Pierre was soon afterwards hounded out of Lyons for, by his own account, printing French New Testaments. He obtained a letter of introduction from the Bernese so that he could set up a business in Geneva, but the situation there was too unstable at that time and Farel advised him to go on to Manosque, in an area which was in the process of going over to Protestantism, and one in which Farel, who came from Gap, had relatives. There he sold works of Protestant propaganda and simple ephemera like Shepherds' Calendars. However, in October 1532 the Waldensians asked Farel to have a Bible and the *Union de plusieurs passages de l'Écriture sainte*, a translation by Saulnier from Bucer's original in Latin, printed for the evangelisation of the valleys they inhabited in Dauphiné and Piedmont. Pierre de Vingle was just the man for the job. In December 1532 Martin Gonin, the poet, was in Geneva waiting for de Vingle's arrival, with 500 gold écus collected from the Waldensians to pay for the project. De Vingle, with his letter of introduction from the Bernese, arrived a little later and set up his press in a house next door to one occupied by a rich merchant called Jean Chautemps, who seems to have helped out with his own money and whose children had Olivétan, Calvin's cousin, as their tutor. At Chautemps' request the city magistrates gave de Vingle leave to print and sell an edition of the Bible based on the Antwerp edition of Lefèvre d'Étaples' translation. But on the 13th of April they forbade publication of the *Union*, which nevertheless came out, but secretly, under the false imprint 'Printed at Antwerp by Pierre Du Pont'. The

New Testament, though not the whole Bible, came from de Vingle's press in April. He continued with another work, Olivétan's *Instruction des enfants*, and then in August he went to set up shop in Neuchâtel, where he worked unmolested and, helped by Marcourt, a local minister, and by Thomas Malingre, a former Dominican, produced an enormous number of books. In 1533 he brought out Farel's liturgy and a collection of evangelical hymns. Next year came the *Sommaire* and then a number of pamphlets, the *Livre des Marchands* and the famous placards attacking the Mass. In 1535 he produced Olivétan's Bible and many other works whose provenance has only recently been established. All his output was directed first and foremost at readers in France, and came out either with no imprint or with one of a number of false imprints: 'Printed in Corinth', or 'Printed in Paris by Pierre de Vignolle, Rue de la Sorbonne', or simply 'Printed in Paris'.

From Neuchâtel Farel pursued the attack on Geneva. On the 10th of August, 1535 the Council of Two Hundred abolished the Mass, and eleven months later Calvin made his entry into the city. With the occupation of Geneva there was an open road to Lyons. France was cut off from the Catholic states of Germany by an uninterrupted line of Protestant communities stretching from Strasbourg to Geneva. She was now surrounded by Protestant cities whose presses produced a continuous stream of heretical books. Henceforward Farel's emissaries were constantly on the road from Frankfurt and Strasbourg to Basel and Geneva, from Geneva to Lyons and Paris. France was now inundated with books printed in Geneva.

When Farel and Calvin went back to Geneva the city had only a few presses, restricted to ordinary jobbing work, like Wiegand Kœln's, which printed notices and almanacs in black letter. Farel set out at once to remedy the situation. It was presumably at his request that Jean Gérard from Suze set up a press in 1536 and in that year printed the New Testament in French, followed by the Psalms of David and the *Instruction des enfants*, after which came a host of propaganda pamphlets. From 1540 Gérard's productivity went up even higher, reaching a peak in 1545. He produced many works by Viret, and even more by Calvin, whose official printer he was.

Other presses began to work as well in the new Protestant stronghold. From 1538 to 1544 Jean Michel worked there, using equipment from the press in Neuchâtel, and Michel Du Bois was active there from 1537 to

1541. Jean Crespin, the son of a Paris lawyer, and himself a lawyer, arrived in 1548 and turned printer, and in 1549 and 1550 came two famous Paris printers, Conrad Bade and Robert Estienne. From that date Geneva had many large printing offices within the city. With the large influx of refugees came more printers and booksellers: from 1550 to 1560 more than 130 arrived. Between 1533 and 1540 only 42 books had been printed; between 1540 and 1550 there were 193 books produced, and between 1550 and 1564 there were 527. By then about forty presses were working, most of them in the hands of a small group of big publishers who had effective control of the book trade: Jean Crespin, Robert Estienne and, even more powerful, Antoine Vincent and Laurent de Normandie, who between the two of them seem to have controlled all the traffic in books for France.[397]

Apart from Estienne, the Genevan printers were almost exclusively concerned with the publication of religious works, as a sample will show. There are 59 surviving editions of either the Bible or the New Testament in French from the period 1550 to 1564, not counting the Latin, Greek, Italian and Spanish editions. There were also numerous editions of the Psalms, as we shall see later. Then there were scurrilous pamphlets attacking the Pope as the antithesis of Jesus, like the *Comédie du Pape malade et tirant à sa fin*. But even more common, intended to enable every believer to conduct a theological argument and to spread the new doctrines as far as possible throughout every social class, were little theological treatises in the vernacular, such as the *Abrégé de la doctrine évangélique et papistique* by Viret, Bullinger's *Brief sommaire de la doctrine évangélique* and the *Bouclier de la foi mis en dialogue* by Barthélemy Causse. Yet more numerous than all these works were the writings of Calvin. Between 1550 and 1564, 256 impressions of his works were issued, 160 of them in Geneva. The *Institution Chrétienne* alone went into 25 impressions during that period, 9 in Latin, 16 in French, most of which came from Genevan presses, and more popular still perhaps were the *Catéchisme par demandes et réponses* of 1541 and the translation of the Bible that Calvin produced in 1551. With such a rate of production the penetration of the new orthodoxy was assured.

The financing and marketing of a publication programme on this scale brought many problems. Genevan booksellers and printers naturally sent their wares to the Frankfurt fair, where booksellers from Protestant countries could stock up freely, and French booksellers, who would also be present, could work out ways and means to avoid the ban on the imports of heretical works, and to get them into France. From 1542, however, an organised attack on books coming from Geneva began in France, and in 1548 a general ban on anything at all printed there was introduced, so that thereafter they had to be sold clandestinely by hawker and packman. Every Genevan printer had his own network of colporteurs, each of whom undertook to sell his books in the area assigned to him. In this hazardous business booksellers were jointly responsible with their travelling salesmen for any losses, and a final reckoning was made when the books were sold. Soon these networks were duplicated by those formed by the preachers who were sent into France from Geneva, some of them previously involved in the book trade – Conrad Bade, for example, who shut up his shop in 1562 to go and preach the gospel in the Orléans region and died there of the plague. Via Collonges, St.-Jean-de-Losne, Langres and St.-Dizier if they came from Germany, via Gex, Savoy, the Chablais and thence via Lyons if they came from Geneva, heretical books poured into France. Not simply in a few isolated copies, but in hundreds at a time in packing cases, in the baggage of a merchant or the wagon of a colporteur. As there was no effective police force the risks of being caught on the road were few, except perhaps by watchmen at the city gates. But how were watchmen to find the crate or crates of books among all the other crates of legitimate merchandise, especially if, as a further precaution, the books were concealed under other goods? Thus the books arrived at their destination without difficulty, often going first to Paris or Lyons, and from there being distributed around the provinces. They nearly always ended up on sale in a bookshop. Booksellers were quite willing to act as receivers, as we know they did in Tours, Poitiers, Angers, Périgueux and Baugé. Sometimes when circumstances were propitious, when a particular region was for the moment fairly tolerant towards heresy, they would risk slipping a heretical book on to their open shelves along with the orthodox volumes. They could do this without too much risk if the book, as often happened, carried a false imprint and appeared, to anyone who was not already familiar with it, to be a perfectly orthodox devotional work. But in general, compromising books would be hidden in the cellar or in some store-room for sale to initiates only. Often too the colporteurs who worked the area would sell ABCs, almanacs and Psalters which served to convey heretical ideas. Thus heretical books made their way everywhere, even into monasteries and seminaries. And they could be easily concealed if danger threatened since their format was usually small, 8vo or 16mo.[398] At Toulon an apothecary, finding himself under suspicion, buried his library in his garden, and many copies of these little books and tracts have come to light over the years concealed in all kinds of hiding places.

It is not easy to assess the real extent of this underground trade. How many editions have disappeared in the interval? There seems little doubt that business was carried on on a very big scale. We have evidence to that effect, in the case for example of Laurent de Normandie.[199] A friend of Calvin, and like him coming originally from Noyon, he was active in Geneva as a lawyer, but his main energy went into publishing and book-selling and he was in control of an extensive underground network. He had four presses working in 1563 at Perrin's, the printer's, and we can be sure there were others besides. When he died in 1569 there were 34,912 books in his shops. In order to distribute them he was in direct contact with a great number of booksellers: Luc Josse and Claude Bocheron in Metz, Sébastien Martin in Sisteron, Loys de Hu in Rheims, and many others. But he specialised in recruiting colporteurs from among the refugees who came from all parts of France and who often developed some connection with the trade. Take, for example, Jacques Bernard and Antoine Valleau, to whom he sent 17 crates and 4 bales of books on 6th December, 1653 for onward transmission and distribution in France, or Lavaudo, a native of Havre-de-Grâce, to whom he sent on the 15th of the same month books for sale in France. Nicolas Ballon, who took refuge in Geneva in 1555, bought religious books from Laurent de Normandie which he went and hawked in France. He was arrested in Poitiers in 1556, condemned to death, escaped, was re-arrested in Châlons-sur-Marne and burned in Paris in 1558. And there are many other similar examples. Quite evidently the authorities had little success in their policy of repression and failed to curb the spread of heretical doctrines through the book trade. The action of the Parlement in passing the Decree of 1542 was designed to re-order the book trade after the seizure of copies of Calvin's *Institution Chrétienne*. The copies taken were burnt. The colporteur responsible for their distribution, Antoine Lenoir, who had come into France from Geneva by way of Antwerp, had to make a public recantation on the steps of Notre-Dame and at St. Quentin. But his subsequent banishment had no effect on the underground movement, any more than the symbolic burning of a copy of the *Institution Chrétienne* in front of Notre-Dame in 1544. Though the book-trade was restricted by ever more decrees and regulations, though heretic colporteurs were hunted down and it became common-place between 1556 and 1560 for them to be sent to the stake, nothing could impede the invasion of France by forbidden literature.

The editions of the Psalms published on the eve of the wars of religion in France give us the opportunity to measure the extent of this invasion.[400] The importance given to the singing of Psalms by the Reformed Church is well known. Translated by Marot and Theodore Beza, they were sung by the early groups of Reformers when they met at Pré-aux-Clercs or in the barn at Wassy. They were sung by heretics when they went to the stake and by Protestant soldiers going into battle during the wars of religion. Marot's rendering had been banned several times in France, although François I liked and read them, and Henri II sang them and had them sung at Court, where each nobleman adopted his own Psalm which had often been assigned to him by the King. So it is no surprise that at the conclusion of the Poissy Conference, Catherine de Medici agreed at the request of Theodore Beza, who had just completed their translation, to grant a licence authorising Antoine Vincent, the Lyons bookseller, to publish the new French version. Margaret of Parma, who also favoured toleration, granted Christopher Plantin a similar licence at about the same time.

Antoine Vincent then mounted the most gigantic enterprise ever undertaken in publishing until then, his aim being to provide every French Protestant with his own personal copy of the Psalms. Vincent was a bookseller in Lyons, where he was in partnership with the brothers Frellon, but he also ran a publishing house in Geneva, where he personally owned four presses as well as being able to get other printers to work for him. All the presses in Geneva, either at his instigation or on their own initiative, then set to work publishing the Psalms. In a few months 27,400 copies were ready. At Lyons too the presses were put to work on the same project. Vincent further took advantage of his licence to draw up agreements with printers in Metz, Poitiers, St. Lô and Paris. He signed a contract with 19 important Paris printers and publishers for them to issue the Psalms, under the terms of which 8 per cent of the profits were to go to poor members of the Reformed Church in Paris. Tens of thousands of copies of the Psalms were thus printed in the space of a few months. Such mass production of a book intended to be bought by heretics in the period just before the Wars of Religion in France was bound to provoke swift and violent reaction. A number of the important Parisian publishers who had contracted with Vincent were thrown into gaol, men like Guillaume Le Noir, Le Preux and Oudin Petit. The time had come when it was necessary to choose between orthodoxy and flight, and while the Haultin family, who held an outstanding position among Protestant printers, moved to La Rochelle, André Wechel fled to

Frankfurt, and Jean Le Preux and Jean Petit the Third left for Lausanne and Geneva. At the same time further campaigns of pamphlets and manifestos began, produced on the outbreak of the Civil Wars for which the busy printing presses had prepared the ground. But they are part of another story.

4
Printing and Language

Just as printing favoured the growth of the Reformation, so it helped mould our modern European languages. Until the beginning of the 16th century the national languages of Western Europe, which had developed as written languages at different dates in different countries, had continued to evolve, following closely the development of the spoken language. For this reason, the French of the *Chansons de Geste*, for example, in the 12th century differs greatly from that written by Villon in the 15th.[401] In the 16th century such developments began to cease to take place, and by the 17th century languages in Europe had generally assumed their modern forms. At the same time, some written languages of the Middle Ages disappeared or were henceforth used more and more rarely for written as opposed to spoken communication. Provençal is one instance, Irish another. Finally, Latin was used less frequently and little by little it became a dead language.[402]

There thus took place a process of unification and consolidation which established fairly large territories throughout which a single language was written. Within these territories the languages which are still today the languages of each nation more or less rapidly attained their definitive development. Spelling also became fixed. It came to correspond less and less with pronunciation and was sometimes complicated by the influence exercised upon it by the classical languages.[402] Printing was not the only factor which acted to bring about this evolution. The Chancelleries had long made attempts to obtain general acceptance for usages which in many cases became those of the literary language. The emergence or strengthening of centralising national monarchies in the 16th century favoured the trend towards a unified national language. The policies of the Kings of France and Spain were particularly clearly directed towards this end. But printing certainly exercised a far profounder influence on the development of the national languages than any other factor, as Meillet and Ferdinand Brunot have both emphasised. Publishers in their search for the largest possible market naturally tended to encourage the growing use of the vernacular for new purposes. Moreover the press gave the book a permanent and unchanging text. Books 'now escaped the tendency peculiar to scribes, partly conscious and partly unconscious. to modernise the text they were copying as they went along' (A. Meillet). When they took over from the scribes printers began to eliminate the whims of spelling and the phrases of dialect which would have made their books less readily understood by a wide public.

Despite the Renaissance in classical studies, Latin began to lose ground during the 16th century. From 1530 onwards, this process becomes increasingly unmistakeable. We need scarcely be surprised. The book-reading public became from then on, as we have seen, increasingly a lay public – made up in large part of women and of merchants, many of whom had hardly any knowledge of Latin. The leaders of the Reformation had this general public in mind when they wrote their works of propaganda in the vernacular, and the humanists did not hesitate to use the same vehicle to express their ideas whenever they sought a large audience. In Italy indeed this had already been the case for some centuries. Petrarch had used Italian long before and he was a good enough model to persuade them to overcome their scruples. Budé, who was so proud of his ability to translate, in the presence of the King, a letter in Greek which he had received from his friend Lascaris, came at the end of his life to write his *Institution du Prince* in French. In an odd way the revival of classical learning helped to make Latin a dead language. As Ferdinand Brunot has emphasised, Ciceronianism, the taste for pure Latinity, while it got rid of solecisms and of the barbarisms which had come into general usage, forced writers into using awkward circumlocutions, and the need to render new ideas aptly began to make writers turn away from the stiffness of Latin.[403]

We should not be surprised if the figures suggest that an increasing proportion of books were published in the vernacular in the course of the 16th century. On this subject no overall statistics can be obtained. But one can regard as significant, for example, the fact that of 2,254 books published in Antwerp from 1500 to 1540, 787 had been in Flemish, 148 in French, 88 in English and about 20 in Danish, in Spanish or in Italian – nearly half the total.[404] The customers of the booksellers of

Antwerp, a great commercial centre, were of course, in part at least, merchants who had only recently become wealthy and were not yet very cultivated, but the same trend towards the vernacular is observable generally. In Aragon from 1501 to 1510 some 25 books were published in Latin as against 15 in Spanish, but in the next 30 years, 115 were printed in Latin against no more than 5 in Spanish, and then from 1541 to 1550 only 14 were printed in Latin and 72 in Spanish.[405] Still we must not jump to hasty conclusions on the basis of such evidence, any more than on the basis of the bibliographies which suggest that books printed in England in the 16th century were printed primarily in English. The printing trade in both England and Spain fulfilled, as it were, a supplementary function inasmuch as the Latin books required were imported from France, Germany and the Low Countries. If we look at book production in Paris, however, the progress made by the modern languages appears indisputable. In 1501 there were only 8 books in French out of the 88 produced, and only 38 out of 269 in 1528. But by 1530 there were already 121 French works and 10 German among the 456 editions produced in the whole of present-day France (including Alsace). In 1549, of 332 books printed in Paris, 70 were in French, and in 1575, 245 out of 445, the majority in fact. Many of these were pamphlets and leaflets, but nevertheless, even once the Wars of Religion were over, most works printed in Paris were in French.[406]

The decline of Latin took place in Germany to a precocious extent during Luther's life-time, but the progress made by the national language was not kept up. Weiler's bibliography, which is however far from complete, lists 4,000 works printed in various German dialects between 1501 and 1525. From 1520, thanks to Luther, the tide was running particularly strongly. Whereas in 1519 there were still only 40 titles in German, there were 211 in 1521; in 1522, 347; in 1525, 498, among which there were 198 editions of Luther's various works.[407] During the whole period of the Reformation, books produced were predominantly in German. But later Latin made a recovery. As we have seen, by the late 16th century Latin works were clearly in the majority at the Frankfurt fair. Of course many German books for the local market would not appear in the fair catalogues, but it does seem as if, with the Catholics gaining ground, their presses were printing more Latin works. German finally triumphed: but it did so later than the other modern languages, and not until the 17th century, when the Leipzig fair took the place of Frankfurt's.

The unifying process which was brought about by printing in the formation of a literary language was particularly marked in Germany.[408] Certainly a long time before the arrival of the printing press a common language had begun to be developed in the various Chancelleries, the work of expert draughtsmen who strove for the utmost clarity and precision. In the second half of the 15th century, before the full impact of printing could begin to be felt, a style and an orthography had begun to emerge which were accepted as the proper form for a written language by an important section of the German intelligentsia and which became the basis of modern German.[409]

But Luther, with the aid of the press, played a decisive role in the development of the German language. Wishing, as he said, 'to be understood at the same time by the people of both Upper and Lower Germany', he tried to impose on the language he was forging a set of principles which would enable him to attain this goal. The wide diffusion of his works, and in particular of his Bible, made it possible for him to become the legislator of the German language. He did not achieve this reformation of the language at a stroke, however, and indeed at the beginning he failed to see the difficulties which would derive from the differences between the various dialects of Germany. At first he worked rather at random and he did not develop a methodical procedure until 1524 when he set about simplifying the spelling by suppressing, for example, the use of twin consonants (nn, tt).

The standardisation of grammar and vocabulary is even more important than spelling in establishing a language that can be readily understood by one and all, and Luther made efforts to rid himself of his own native dialect, that of Lower Saxony. Having lived most of his life in Thuringia and Saxony, the language as refined in the Chancellery of Saxony naturally appealed to him as the most perfect model and provided much of his inspiration. For a long time, however, traces of the local dialect were to be found in his grammar, traces of which he only freed himself by dint of much patient effort. But it was vocabulary which chiefly interested him. He looked for the most precise word to convey his meaning, but at the same time he would try and choose from among a number of synonyms the word most used by ordinary people. With this end in view he drew on the popular speech of Middle and Lower Germany, but Thuringia and Saxony gave him his essential vocabulary.

Thus Luther fashioned a language which was in all respects closer to modern German than the language of most of his contemporaries. The literary qualities of his works, their massive sales and the almost sacred character which was given to his translation of the Old and New Testaments by the faithful, all tended to make his language a model which was generally adopted. Immediately comprehensible to all readers who spoke High German, it may at first have taken aback Bavarians or Swabians, but, in the end, in almost every case where a number of synonyms existed, the word used by Luther ended up being generally employed, and many words which had previously been confined to Middle Germany were eventually used throughout the German-speaking area as a result of his influence. His vocabulary imposed itself so imperiously that few printers dared to alter it in the smallest detail. Some printers in Basel, Augsburg, Nuremberg and Strasbourg allowed themselves to modify his spelling here and there. But the vocabulary was never altered, and when it seemed that Luther's terms would be incomprehensible to the local population they contented themselves with the addition of a glossary to the work.

High German was thus established in a pre-eminent position while printing made more and more works in that language available, so that it came increasingly to seem to be the national literary language. Luther's example soon appeared insufficient, however, and grammars were felt to be needed in order to provide a more methodical way to learn the language. Starting in the second quarter of the century, grammars of the German language, a subject which had previously been scarcely studied at all, began to appear. At first they were written in Latin, the most famous being the *Grammatica Germanicae linguae . . . ex bibliis Lutheri Germanicis et aliis eius libris collecta*, published by Johann Çlajus at Leipzig in 1578, and from that date on the language, whose essential characteristics had been determined by Luther, spread through Protestant circles and eventually, despite the resistance they put up, overwhelmed the Catholics too.

By encouraging the multiplication of the number of texts available in the vernacular the printing press everywhere favoured, as it had done in Germany, the development and the systematisation of the literary language of the nation. In England[410] the effect of the Reformation was to encourage the publication of translations of Scripture and of religious works, and their language was to be as influential on the development of English as Luther's in Germany. First Tyndale, then Coverdale translated the Scriptures, and their pioneer work was followed by succeeding versions culminating in one of the supreme achievements of English prose, the *Authorised Version* of 1611. Already in 1549, however, there had appeared a work which more than any other gave the English nation a feeling for the dignity of their language, the *Booke of the Common Prayer and Administration of the Sacramentes*, to which the *Whole Booke of Psalmes* was added in 1567, in the metrical version of Sternhold and Hopkins. These works were in a vocabulary all the more readily understood by virtue of the fact that it was very restricted, amounting only to 6,500 words (Shakespeare's runs to 21,000) and many of the phrases, as with those of Luther in Germany, were soon in current usage. Printing, in producing tens of thousands of copies of these works, fixed the language. At this time there was a busy book trade in England, but much of it, especially up to 1540, was based on the import of books from the continent, from France and Spain in particular. Many of these were translated and soon in addition the Latin and Greek classics were also translated into English. It was often thanks to this process of translation and publication that the English language, at the same time as it took on its final form, became enriched with numerous Spanish, French and Latin expressions. These foreign additions to the language were so numerous that at the end of the century there was a violent reaction against their use – a sign of a real crisis in the development of the national language. While English grammars were printed in increasing numbers, spelling was slowly being stabilised by printers who sometimes systematically eliminated the more cumbersome orthographical peculiarities in the manuscripts given them by authors to be used for copy. This effort to introduce a measure of uniformity becomes clear when a surviving original manuscript and its printed version can be compared. The following examples come from such a comparison carried out in the case of Harington's translation of Ariosto:[411]

Manuscript	*Printed Text*
bee	be
on	one
greef	grief
thease	these
swoord	sword
noorse	nurse
skolding	scolding
servaunt	servant

If printing helped raise national languages to a level at which they could provide a means of expression for a national literature, and helped at the same time to establish standardised conventions in respect of spelling, grammar and vocabulary, printers were to draw back later, once a basic regularity had been attained. They resisted more systematic attempts at codification on the part of revolutionary innovators. They felt this was going too far and their reluctance comes out most strongly over the question of spelling. It was in this field, as we have seen, that Luther's influence in German had been least decisive. Printers in England did away with the most peculiar spellings where they served as an irritant to readers but still left many other oddities untouched. The reactions of French printers to problems of spelling deserves however the closest attention, if only because such inhibitions were there most clearly visible. In the 16th century, in France as elsewhere, the ordinary spoken language became the secure basis of the national literary language, while at the same time numerous efforts were made to enrich and codify this language.[412] By then the written language had already attained a certain degree of uniformity, mainly due to the tradition developed over the centuries within the Royal Chancellery and in the courts of justice by the legal profession, as well as through the determined efforts of a relatively strong central monarchy. As a result, the majority of French printers appeared – a few innovators excepted – to be relatively conservative. In order to prevent their stocks from becoming obsolete, and their work from being made complicated, they had in fact a strong interest in preventing radical changes, in encouraging the survival of traditional conventions and in avoiding the application of unduly rigid rules, especially when it came to spelling; in short in favouring a slow consolidation of the literary language so that it came to conform to the best established practices. However one should not be surprised that just when the use of roman and italic type was becoming generalised in France, especially around 1530, some humanist printers showed more daring and appeared in the first rank of those struggling to reform the language. Among them was Geoffroy Tory, a former professor at the du Plessis College who had lived a long time in Italy and who was skilled in the art of engraving blocks, taking his inspiration from Italian models. He wanted his native tongue to be as regulated and as polished as Greek or Latin, and in his famous work, *Champ fleury*, his interest in design also finds expression. In that work, published in 1529, he expounds a rather surprising theory according to which the rules for the design of roman capital letters can be established on the basis of the proportions of the human body. In it he sang the praises of the French language, twenty years before Du Bellay, and above all he studied the letters of the language from every point of view; he demonstrated their pronunciation in Latin, Greek and French and showed how each separate region of France pronounced them. At the same time he proposed the principles on which a reform of French spelling should be carried out, calling in particular for the use of accents, the cedilla and the apostrophe. He put his reforms into practice in the *Adolescence clémentine* and in the *Briesve doctrine pour deuement escriptre selon la propriété du langaige françois*, both of which came out in 1533. Thereafter the whole question of spelling reform became a matter of public debate. After Dubois in 1529 published a *Très utile et compendieux traicté de l'art et science dorthographie Gallicane* in which he advocates a number of simplifications, Étienne Dolet, like Tory both a humanist and a printer, published a work in 1540 with a significant title: the *Manière de bien tracduire d'une langue en aultre. D'advantage de la punctuation de la langue françoise plus Des accents d'ycelle*, most of the contents of which however are lifted from the *Briesve doctrine*. Spelling became something of an obsession with almost everyone concerned with making French a cultivated language, and in 1535 Olivétan, the translator of the Bible, expressed the hope 'that some lasting ruling will be issued on this question'. Louis Meigret attempted to issue this ruling in 1542 in his *Traité touchant le commun usage de l'escriture Françoise* and in later writings. He was an exponent of radical spelling reform and tackled the problem as a whole, advocating the dropping of unnecessary letters (writing *un* for example instead of *ung*, *autre* instead of *aultre*, *renars* instead of *renards*), substituting one letter for another (*ombre* instead of *umbre*, *maintenant* instead of *meintenant*, *manger* instead of *manjer*) and adding further qualifications to letters (*o* meaning an open 'o', thus 'mort' being written 'mǫrt').

It is no part of our subject to go into the details of the controversies stirred up by Meigret's work, but it is necessary to emphasise that, in spite of the support they received from the most celebrated writers of the day, the initiatives of the innovators achieved little, largely because, as a general rule, in matters of language any revolutionary reform is always eventually blocked by the inertia of habit. But, more particularly, the failure of the reformers was due to the fact that the printers had the final say in the matter and the great majority of them preferred to leave well alone. Grammarians like Peletier du Mans or Honorat Rambaud, who thought the best plan was to devise an entirely new alphabet, did find some printers who were willing to support the idea, but such men found little support among their colleagues. Charles Beaulieux, who has made a careful study of the books published by Arnoul Langelier, one of the great Paris publishers, and in particular has compared closely the two editions of the *Deffence et illustration* which he published in 1549 and 1557, has shown that conventions varied even within a single firm. 'Y' was a letter much less esteemed in 1557 than in 1549, and the 'é' which was sometimes used in 1549 was often dropped in 1557, while the cedilla, which is used earlier in the publications of Geoffroy Tory and of Antoine Augereau, was beginning to come into use at Langelier's by then.

Spelling long remained subject to the whims of foremen and compositors: authors might complain but they could not prevent it. Little by little however standards were fixed, not so much by *a priori* principles invented by innovating theoreticians as by the slow changing of habits. In fact the man who did most to stabilise French orthography in the 16th century was Robert Estienne, a humanist printer, but one who had a singularly conservative approach to the subject. His influence derived not from his theories but from the dictionaries he published.

Born in 1503, the son of the printer Henri Estienne I, Robert had been able to take full advantage of the new humanist scholarship of the Renaissance. Guillaume Budé was a close friend of his, and often collaborated with him on editions. His main concern was always the publication of correct Scriptural texts. He worked tirelessly at this problem, but also did a tremendous amount of work in the field of lexicography. When invited to revise and reprint Calepin's Latin dictionary, a work of prime importance, he preferred to start from scratch on an entirely new work, the *Thesaurus Linguae Latinae*, which appeared in 1531–1532 and in a new enlarged edition in 1536. In 1538 he brought out for students his *Dictionnaire Latino-Gallicum*, whose long-lasting success we have already had cause to note, and finally in 1539–1540 came his *Dictionnaire Français-Latin*, which reappeared half as big again in its 2nd edition of 1549. In addition he compiled two lexicons, based on his two major dictionaries, for class use (1542 and 1544).

In compiling such dictionaries, Estienne was naturally deeply involved in questions of French spelling. He had consulted the grammars of Meigret and Dubois, but strove above all to conform to the spelling adopted by the Royal Chancellery, the Treasury and the Parlement. Moreover, quite naturally since he was linking French words to their Latin equivalents, he adopted in doubtful cases a spelling which conformed with the Latin form. The work was not at all revolutionary but it was a convenient reference work which won support from both printers and the legal profession. As a result the dictionaries quickly became the accepted authority on questions of orthography.

But fanciful spelling by no means disappeared. That didn't happen for a long time – not until the 17th century, the century of Vaugelas, Ménage and the *Dictionnaire de l'Académie Française*. Gradually however spelling became standardised. In this process the influence of Dutch and Flemish printers like Plantin and the Elzeviers should not be under-estimated. As large-scale publishers of French works they came up against tricky problems, since their journeymen had to set texts in French when they only had a rudimentary knowledge of the language. In order to avoid unacceptable errors they were therefore led in certain cases to advocate a series of systematic simplifications. Plantin, who was inter-ested in problems relating to language and who must have found in a city as cosmopolitan as Antwerp ample material for reflection, was the first to realise how useful it would be for Flemish publishers to adopt a simplified system of French orthography. In his very first books, and consistently thereafter, he made use of the letter 'j', and dropped the final 'x' and a large number of superfluous median letters which he replaced with accents, as Ronsard had done. In the preface to the *Trésor de Amadis* (1560) he published a kind of manifesto and announced that he would print 'êt' for 'est' (*prêt* for *preste*), '*outre*' for '*oultre*', and '*mieux*' for '*mieulx*'. He gave up some of his innovations later, probably to avoid any repercussions on the sale of his books in France, but he still used a form of spelling that was very simple for its time in his Franco-Flemish dictionaries. His example was followed by other printers in the Low Countries, for example by Waesberghe, a specialist publisher of dic-tionaries, and above all by the Elzeviers who systematically utilised the 'j' and the 'v' and helped to bring into general usage. So foreign printers played a big part in standardising the spelling of French words through the thousands of copies of their publications that they marketed in France, copies which, in view of the high standard of their typography, were highly approved of by French scholars.

Whatever the attitude of printers to spelling reform, there is no doubt that printing generally favoured the development of literature written in the vernacular. Printing thus helped to render the national languages increasingly sophisticated as modes of expression, and in the 16th century they established, on an unquestionable basis, their claim to be languages with an independent literature. At the same time there was a fairly general movement to produce grammars for these languages.

In 1493 Antonio de Nebrija published his *Grammatica Castellana* which, although criticised in the 16th century by Juan Valdes, nevertheless played an important role in the creation of modern Spanish, and facilitated the adoption throughout Spain of Castilian linguistic conventions. It was in large part as a result of its influence that Aragonese printers and writers could take a significant step towards the elimination from their publications of the regional peculiarities which marked them previously.⁴¹³ There were a great number of grammarians in 16th-century France, and theoreticians of language and style like Du Bellay were even more numerous. We have seen how Luther's writings served as a model for grammarians seeking to codify practice in literary German during the last quarter of the 16th century. In England theorists like Thomas Smith (1560), John Hart (1570) and William Bullokar (1580) noted the growing divergence between the pronunciation and the spelling of English since spelling had become stabilised under the influence of the press, and they proposed radical reforms. At the same time, grammars and dictionaries began to appear in Italy, where as early as 1304–1306 Dante had written his *De vulgari eloquentia*. Machiavelli, Bembo, Trissino and many others were studying the native language and trying to establish its grammar. Meanwhile Sperone Speroni invented, in order to demonstrate the pre-eminence of Italian, a set of arguments which Du Bellay would turn to his own purposes in his *Défense et illustration de la langue française*. But the debate about the primacy of one or other of the various Italian dialects was a hindrance to any theoretical progress. Lacking any centralising political authority which might have imposed an official view, or anyone with a personal authority to compare to Luther's, the Italians went on debating for a considerable time to come whether Tuscan should simply be adopted as the literary language or whether, in order to establish such a language, it was necessary to create a synthesis of several of the Italian dialects.

The fate of Latin was by now sealed, but it resisted the inevitable for a long time.* It had the advantage of being universally understood, and successfully maintained its position for a long time, especially in the world of scholarship, even on occasion winning back lost ground. It is true that in the 16th century scholarly works which had originally been written in Latin were on occasion translated or adapted – this was the case in France for example with Budé's *De asse* and with Charles Estienne's *Anatomy*. Moreover, at this time Belon, and later Paré and

---

* Most of what follows is based on information given to us by M. André Stegmann, whom we would like to thank.

Palissy, were writing in French. But this was unusual and the Faculty of Medicine at Paris expressed indignation that Paré should have chosen not to write in Latin. The Catholic Church, which, unlike the Reformed Church, was opposed to the use and development of the vernacular, supported Latin in its attempt to survive. Often it approved new works announcing scientific advances as long as they were in Latin, but condemned them when scholars started to popularise their ideas in a language intelligible to the average reader. The scholars often preferred Latin which had the double advantage of being understood by their peers and of shielding them from prosecution.

When the Counter-Reformation triumphed over a large area of Europe, the Jesuits through their colleges disseminated the knowledge of Latin among the most intellectually active sections of society and encouraged the development of a whole new literature in Latin which they tried to enliven even through the medium of drama. The Latin theatre enjoyed a great vogue at this time and all Europe knew and discussed Grotius' Latin tragedies or those of Vernulz, who succeeded Justus Lipsius at the University of Louvain. Latin, noblest of languages, was used for that most noble of poetic forms, the epic, and countless epic poems in Latin were put into print during the 17th century. A royal marriage, a birth, a victory, even if they were the subject of an epic poem of no more than fifteen lines, had to be praised in Latin. When La Rochelle was captured, the epic poems in praise of Louis XIII which came from the pens of Italians, Flemings, Germans and even Frenchmen were almost all in Latin. Malherbe, who composed an ode in French for the occasion, was an exception, but under his influence we see more and more odes written in French. Thus Latin lost ground only very slowly. Probably the final blow was stuck at Latin with the decline of the Frankfurt fair around 1630 and the fragmentation of the book-trade. But, in a number of areas, it was not entirely displaced by the modern vernaculars until the end of the 17th and even the beginning of the 18th centuries.

Several reasons may account for its stubborn survival. First of all it remained the most widely used language of international communication. In countries whose national languages were rarely learnt by foreigners there was a greater tendency to write in Latin. This was the case in Flanders and even in Germany, where the huge team of jurists associated with Courinus in the years 1640 to 1660 published their works in Latin. The same was true in England. Shakespeare and the Tudor drama were more or less unknown on the continent at this time, while Camden,

Hobbes, Barclay and even John Owen the epigrammatist, enjoyed a popularity equal to that of any other European writer because they wrote in Latin. In Spain, Italy and France, Latin was perhaps rather less used, but it was still essential to write in Latin when addressing a European public, especially when engaging in disputations on questions whose interest extended beyond the confines of a single country, whether they were questions of religion, politics, literature or law. It was the intended audience above all that determined the choice of language used by the writer. Thus Fitzherbert, the Jesuit Rector of the English College at Rome, writes in English when he issues a theological tract for the conversion of Anglicans at home, but when he attacks Machiavelli for the benefit of a European audience he writes in Latin. When Filesac, Rector of the University of Paris and a theologian, rules on a matter of canon law of interest in France he writes in French (1606). Ten years later he uses Latin when writing two little tracts on the question of the limits of royal authority – so vigorously debated at that time – in order that his comments might find an audience beyond the borders of France. The same is true of Richelieu's propagandists, of Father Sirmond for example who replies in Latin to attacks by Father Endemon Joannes over the Italian War and the alliance of the Most Christian King with the Reformers. The war in Flanders and the Low Countries also led to the publication of numerous pamphlets. Several of the histories of this war were originally composed in the vernacular and were translated into Latin, often in Germany, in the towns which held book fairs, in order to obtain a wider public for them. Many literary works, especially tragedies and epics, were likewise rendered into Latin after they had been successful in the vernacular.

Latin no doubt also owed its survival to its precision and clarity. In the face of modern languages which were constantly developing it had the advantage of possessing a fixed vocabulary whose meaning was easy to determine by reference to well-known and authoritative texts. It must have partly been for this reason that it continued to be the language of diplomacy, science and philosophy in the 17th century. Its use in medicine became steadily rarer, but it went on being the language of mathematics and astronomy.

Descartes wrote the *Discours de la Méthode* in French, but his correspondence, like Pascal's, was very often in Latin. The authoritative text of the *Meditations* is the Latin : it is to that, rather than the French, that it is still necessary to have recourse if one wants to elucidate a difficult point. Even Chapelain, who composed his great epic, *La Pucelle*, in French, still found in 1665 that a scientific work reached a much larger public if it was published in Latin. Not until the time of Fontenelle did the *Mémoires de l'Académie des Sciences* come out in French, and Leibnitz, along with many Germans of his age, normally wrote in Latin. In short it was not until the late 17th century that Latin was finally overthrown and replaced by the other national languages and by French as the natural language of philosophy, science and diplomacy. Every educated European then had to know French, books in French were published and sold all over Europe by emigré booksellers of French or Walloon extraction and men like Bayle, Basnage, Le Clerc and their imitators were editing scholarly journals in French for an international audience.

Literature and learning were still international in the 16th century despite the decline of Latin. The books published in the various national languages could expect to be translated into many languages, as we have seen, if they were worthy of interest. But little by little the fragmentation of the world of letters began to take effect. What did the French know about Shakespeare in the 17th century? Or about contemporary German writing in the 18th century? In 1630 in France, Chapelain complained that, as a result of the decline of the Frankfurt Fair, he did not know what was being published in Germany. At the end of the 17th century and in the early 18th century it was only through the medium of Dutch journals that English culture penetrated France. French was pre-eminent in the 18th century as an international language but it could never fully occupy the place left permanently vacant by the disappearance of Latin. So, by encouraging publication in the national languages for economic reasons, the book trade was in the end fostering the development of those languages – and bringing about the decline of Latin. This was to be a fateful development. It marked, it is true, the origin of a culture belonging to the masses, but its consequences, once set in motion were incalculable. The unified Latin culture of Europe was finally dissolved by the rise of the vernacular languages which was consolidated by the printing press.

Notes

1   W. Wattenbach, *Das Schriftwesen im Mittelalter*, 3rd edition, Leipzig, 1896;
    J. W. Thompson, *The Medieval Library*, Chicago, 1939 (Bibliography);
    Mgr Lesne, *Les Livres: scriptoria et bibliothèques du début du VIII à la fin du
    XI Siècle*, in Vol. 4 of the *Histoire de la Propriété Ecclésiastique*, Lille, 1938.

2   Douet D'Arcq, *Comptes de l'Hôtel des Rois de France aux XIV et XV Siècles*,
    Paris, 1865 (*Société de l'Histoire de France*, pp. 64, 67, 97, 101ff., 151, 160,
    162, 183, 224, 231, 233, 332 and 334.

3   J. W. Thompson, op. cit.

4   Douet D'Arcq, op. cit.

5   J. de la Lande, *L'Art de faire le parchemin*, Paris, 1761.

6   A. Ruppel, *Johannes Gutenberg, sein Leben und sein Werk*, Berlin, 1947, p. 141.

7   On this, see Mgr Lesne, op. cit., and J. W. Thompson, op. cit.

8   R. R. Root, 'Publication before Printing', in *Publications of the Modern
    Language Association* (PMLA), XXVIII, 1913, p. 417.

9   P. Delalain, *Étude sur le Libraire Parisien du XIII au XV Siècle*, Paris, 1891.

10 Ibid.; and *Chartularium Universitatis Parisiensis*, ed. H. Denifle and E.
    Chatelain, Vol. 1 (1889), Vol. 2 (1891), Paris, 1889–97, 4 vols.

11 J. Destrez, *La 'Pecia' dans les Manuscrits Universitaires du XIII et du XIV
    Siècle*, Paris, 1935.

12 D. A. Callus, 'Introduction of Aristotelian Learning to Oxford', in
    Proceedings of the British Academy, Vol. XXIX, 1943. St. Bernard com-
    plained about the popularity of Abelard's ideas, altogether too hasty in
    his view. When Abelard was expelled from the university, students paid
    for private lessons from him. Cf. *Patres Latini*, CLXXXII.

13 L. Delisle, *Recherches sur la Librairie de Charles V*, Paris, 1907, 3 volumes,
    one of plates.

14 E. Faral, *Les Jongleurs en France au Moyen Age*, Paris, 1910, (*Bibliothèque de
    l'École des Hautes Études. Sciences Historiques et Philologiques*, fascicule 187).

15 R. R. Root, loc. cit.

16 L. Delaissé, 'Les Chroniques de Hainault et l'Atelier de Jean Wauquelin
    à Mons', in the *Bulletin des Musées Royaux des Beaux-Arts*, Brussels, 1955.

17 L. Delisle, *Le Cabinet des Manuscrits*, Paris, 1868–1881, 3 Vols. Vol. 1,
    p. 102.

18 On royal patronage in the 15th century, see Doutrepont, *La Littérature
    Française à la Cour des Ducs de Bourgogne*, Paris, 1909, and A. Coville, *La Vie
    Intellectuelle dans la Domaine d'Anjou-Provence de 1380 à 1435*, Paris, 1941.

19 Nicole Oresme, *Le Livre des Éthiques d'Aristote*, published from the text

of MS. 2902 in the Belgian Royal Library, by A. D. Menut, New York, 1940.

20   H. Loomis, 'The Auchinleck Manuscript and a possible London bookshop of 1330–1340', in *Publications of the Modern Language Association*, LVIII, 1942, p. 595–627.

21   J. J. Guiffrey, *Inventaires de Jean, Duc de Berry, 1401–1416*, Paris, 1894–96; M. Thomas, 'Recherches sur un Groupe de Manuscrits à Peinture du Début du XV Siècle', in *Bulletin Bibliographique de la Société Internationale Arthurienne*, 4, 1952, p. 81–89.

22   H. Martin, *Les Miniaturistes Français*, Paris, 1906.

23   L. Delisle, *Le Cabinet des Manuscrits*, passim.

24   On illuminators' workshops in the early part of the 15th century, see the catalogue of the exhibition, *Manuscrits à Peinture du XIII au XVI Siècle*, Paris, Bibliothèque Nationale, 1955. Reviews of this have been compiled by Jean Porcher, with an extensive bibliography.

25   The Tenth Congress, Rome, 4–11 September, 1955, in *Atti*, Florence, 1955, p. 152 ff. On imposition, see below, p. ooo.

26   H. S. Bennett, 'The Author and his Public in the 14th and 15th Century', in *Essays and Studies by Members of the English Association*, XXIII, 1938, p. 7 ff.

27   We do not deal here with the question how papermaking spread from Asia to Europe. There is no doubt that Spanish mills were the first in Europe, and paper made there was used elsewhere; but the industry as such started in Italy and from there spread to the rest of Europe. On this see T. F. Carter, *The Invention of Printing in China and its Spread Westward*, revised by L. Carrington Goodrich, 2nd edition, New York, 1955.

28   A. Blum, *Les Origines du Papier, de l'Imprimerie et de la Gravure*, Paris, 1935, p. 22. (English edition, *On the Origin of Paper*, New York, 1934, translated by H. M. Lydenberg.)

29   On the water mill and medieval technology, see M. Bloch, 'Avènement et Conquêtes du Moulin à Eau', in *Annales d'Histoire Économique et Sociale*, VII, 1935; R. Gilles, 'Lents Progres de la Technique', in *Revue de Synthèse*, XXXII, 1953. On the paper mill, see C. M. Briquet, *Opuscula*, 1955.

30   See A. Zonghi, *Zonghi's Watermarks*, Hilversum, 1953, and C. M. Briquet, op. cit.

31   C. M. Briquet, *Les Filigranes: dictionnaire historique des marques de papier*, Paris, 1907, 4 Vols. (reissued 1927), nos. 65–71.

32   A. Zonghi, op. cit., p. 27; A. Blanchet, *Essai sur l'Histoire du Papier et de sa Fabrication*, Part 1, Paris, 1900, p. 61 ff.

33   Archives Nationales, JJ, 76 (1340–1348).

34   On Champagne as a papermaking region, see L. Le Clert, *Le Papier; recherches et notes pour servir à l'histoire du papier, principalement à Troyes et aux environs, depuis le XIV siècle*, Paris, 1926, 2 Vols.

35   Gerson, *De Laude Scriptorum*.

36   See the article, *Papier* in Diderot and d'Alembert's *Encyclopédie Française*, 1751–1772.

37   C. M. Briquet, *Opuscula*, p. 20; J. M. Janot, *Les Moulins à Papier de la Région Vosgienne*, Paris, 1952, 2 Vols. Vol. 1, p. 60.

38 Nowadays sizing is done in vats. In hard (i.e. calcareous) water the paper does not precipitate easily. Since sizing was formerly done in the open air they did not have to think about these problems, but chalky water must have made sizing difficult.

39 E. Blanchard, 'L'Industrie du Papier dans la France du Sud-Est', in the *Bulletin de la Société Scientifique du Dauphiné*, XLVI, 1925, p. 279–460.

40 R. Corraze, 'L'Industrie du Papier à Toulouse', in *Contribution à l'Histoire de la Papeterie en France*, II, 1934, p. 95 ff.

41 Cf. L. Le Clert, op. cit., and A. Nicolaï, *Histoire des Moulins à Papier du Sud-Ouest de la France (1300–1800)*, Bordeaux, 1935, 2 Vols.

42 A. Blanchet, op. cit., p. 60, 101–102, 108; C. M. Briquet, op. cit., p. 70 ff., and p. 182 ff.

43 L. Le Clert, op. cit., Vol. 1.

44 E. Crevaux, 'L'Évolution de l'Industrie Papetière au XVIII Siècle', in *Le Papier*, March, 1938, p. 193–197, and April, 1938, p. 289–298.

45 H. Chobaut, 'Les Débuts de l'Industrie du Papier dans le Comtat Venaissin', in *Le Bibliographe Moderne*, XXIV, 1928/29, p. 157–215.

46 A. Blanchet, op. cit., p. 72–76.

47 L. Le Clert, op. cit.; H. Stein, 'La Papeterie d'Essones', in *Annales de la Société Historique et Archéologique du Gâtinais*, XII, 1894, p. 334–364; 'La Papeterie de Saint-Cloud', a supplement to *Le Bibliographe Moderne*, VIII, 1904.

48 C. M. Briquet, *Les Filigranes*, nos. 345 ff.

49 Cf. H. J. Martin, 'Quelques Aspects de l'Édition Parisienne au XVII Siècle', in *Annales*, 7th Year, 1953, p. 314 ff.

50 Antoine Vitré, *Ce que les Presses qui Travaillent à Présent dans Paris consomment de Papier*, Mémoire in the Bibliothêque Nationale, MS. fr. (French) 16746, leaves 402 ff.

51 Cf. p. 42 and note 71.

52 L. Le Clert, op. cit., Vol. 2, p. 351 ff, and E. Howe, 'The Le Bé Family', in *Signature*, (8), 1938.

53 F. Ritter, *Histoire de l'Imprimerie à Strasbourg aux XV et XVI Siècles*, Paris, 1955, p. 467.

54 C. M. Briquet, op. cit., nos. 873–881.

55 R. Gandhilon, 'Imprimeurs et Papetiers du Midi de la France', in *Contribution à l'Histoire de la Papeterie en France*, Vol. 2, 1934, p. 91 ff.

56 Cf. P. Baud, *L'Industrie Chimique en France. Étude Historique et Géographique*, Paris, 1932, p. 195 ff. (An essential work.)

57 C. M. Briquet, *Opuscula*, p. 269 ff.

58 C. M. Briquet, *Les Filigranes*, passim; A. Schute, 'Die Ältesten Papiermühlen der Rheinlande', in the *Gutenberg-Jahrbuch*, 1932, p. 44–52, and 'Papiermühlen und Wasserzeichenforschung', in the *Gutenberg-Jahrbuch*, 1934, p. 9–27.

59 R. Rooses, *Christophe Plantin*, 2nd edition, Antwerp, 1892, p. 116 and 123. For his dedication copies, Plantin secured paper of much better quality from Lyons and Italy.

60 R. Lebègue, *Les Correspondants de Peiresc dans les Anciens Pays-Bas*, Brussels, 1943, p. 61.

61   C. Mortet, *Les Origines et les Débuts de l'Imprimerie d'après les Recherches les plus Récentes*, Paris, 1922, p. 8 ff.; A. Blum, *Les Origines de la Gravure en France*, Paris, 1927, p. 12 ff.; H. Bouchot, *Les Deux Cents Incunables Xylographiques du Département des Estampes*, Paris, 1903, p. 40–49.

62   C. Mortet, op. cit., p. 18 ff.

63   Cf. p. 50 ff.

64   C. Mortet, op. cit., p. 18, 20 ff.; H. Bouchot, op. cit., p. 55.

65   C. Mortet, op. cit., p. 11; A. Blum, op. cit., p. 35 ff., 52 ff.

66   C. Mortet, op. cit., p. 22 ff.

67   Ibid., p. 28 ff.

68   Ibid., p. 31.

69   Marius Audin, 'La Metallographie et le Problème du Livre', in the *Gutenberg-Jahrbuch*, 1930, p. 11–52; 'Typographie et Stereographie', in the *Gutenberg-Jahrbuch*, 1931, p. 28–37; and Vol. 1 of the *Somme Typographique*, Paris, 1948.

70   De Laborde, *Débuts de l'Imprimerie à Strasbourg*, Paris, 1840; C. Mortet, op. cit., p. 35–37; A. Ruppel, *Johannes Gutenberg, sein Leben und sein Werk*, Berlin, 1941; for a more recent discussion see H. Lufing, 'Neue Literatur zur Geschichte des Buchwesens', in *Archiv für Kulturgeschichte*, XXXVII, fascicule 2, 1955, p. 244–263.

71   André Heilmann owned a paper mill near Strasbourg; cf. F. Ritter, op. cit., p. 67 and 487.

72   H. Requin, 'Documents inédits sur les Origines de la Typographie', in *Bulletin Historique et Philologique du Comité des Travaux Historiques et Scientifiques*, 1890, p. 288 ff., p. 328–350; and his *L'Imprimerie à Avignon en 1444*, Paris, 1890.

73   In Marius Audin, *Somme Typographique*, Vol. 1.

74   C. Mortet, op. cit., p. 37.

75   The most important of these studies are listed in Victor Scholderer's bibliography, 'The Invention of Printing', in *The Library*, XXI, June, 1940, p. 1–25.

76   Cf. C. Mortet, op. cit., p. 39, and V. Scholderer, op. cit., p. 2.

77   Cf. note 75.

78   C. Mortet, op. cit., p. 51 ff.; R. Blum, *Der Prozess Fust gegen Gutenberg*, Wiesbaden, 1954.

79   The essential source on Gutenberg is Ruppel, *Gutenberg*. On Gutenberg's residence in Bamberg, see A. Dresler, 'Hat Gutenberg in Bamberg Gedruckt?' in *Das Antiquaria*, 1955, p. 197–200, and p. 229 ff.; discussed in H. Lufing, *Neue Literatur zur Geschichte des Buchwesens*, loc. cit.

80   Seymour de Ricci, *Catalogue Raisonné des Premières Impressions de Mayence*, Mainz, 1911.

81   Cf. A. Gieeseke, 'Das Schriftmetall Gutenbergs', in the *Gutenberg-Jahrbuch*, 1944–49, p. 63 ff.; V. Scholderer, 'The Shape of Early Types', in the *Gutenberg-Jahrbuch*, 1927, p. 24 ff.

82   A. Firmin-Didot, *Alde Manuce et l'Hellénisme à Venise*, Paris, 1875, p. 99 ff.

83   On the types recovered from the River Saône, see Marius Audin, 'A propos des premières Techniques Typographiques', in *Bibliothèque d'Humanisme et Renaissance*, Vol. XVIII, 1956, p. 161–170; and M. Audin,

Les Types Lyonnais Primitifs Conservés au Département des Imprimés, Biblio-thèque Nationale, Paris, 1955.

84 P. S. Fournier, *Manuel Typographique*, Paris, 1764–66, 2 Vols. Vol. 1, p. 109 ff. (English edition, *Fournier on Typefounding*, London, 1930, translated by Harry Carter.)

85 On this see K. Haebler, 'Schriftguss und Schrifthandel in der Frühdruck-zeit', in *Zentralblatt für Bibliothekswesen*, 1924, p. 81–104; H. Harisse, *Les Premiers Incunables Bâlois et Leurs Dérivés: Toulouse, Lyon, Vienne en Dauphiné, Spire, Eltville, etc, 1471–1484*, Paris, 1902, 2nd edition.

86 Fournier, in his *Manuel Typographique*, includes an interesting table of European foundries operating in 1766. The Imprimerie Royale, whose collection of punches is now the finest in the world and includes the 'Grecs du Roi' cut by Garamond; Fournier Senior, the author's brother, who succeeded the Le Bé family (includes the matrices and punches of Guillaume Le Bé I, the famous 16th century punch cutter, Garamond's and Simon de Colines's, etc.); Sanlecque (created by Jacques de Sanlecque, Guillaume Le Bé's pupil in 1596, since when they have remained in the family) and five other, more recent, foundries. Fournier also cites two Lyons foundries. He lists 23 German foundries, the best known being Lotther in Frankfurt and Breitkopf in Leipzig. In Holland, three in Amsterdam, including Jean Bus, Van Dijck's famous successor, one in Haarlem, Wetstein's, taken over by Enschedé, still working today, and which possesses lead matrices dating from the 16th century, and four others. In Antwerp, Plantin-Moretus, of course, now the Plantin Museum. In England, only four foundries, but all well-equipped: Cottrell in Oxford, James Watson in Edinburgh, and above all, Caslon in London and Baskerville in Birmingham (Beaumarchais bought back the latter's types to print his complete edition of Voltaire at Kehl). Only a few foundries in Italy, the most famous being at the Vatican, started by Granjon in 1578 after being summoned to Rome by Pope Gregory XIII; it has Oriental types with which the Tipografia della Propaganda printed books for missionaries going out East. Finally, there are two in Spain, one in Sweden, one in Copenhagen, one in Lisbon, one in Warsaw, two or three in Russia. In all, some sixty foundries supplied Europe's needs.

87 Ibid., Vol. I, p. 125.

88 Pierre Didot explains his system for the first time in his *Essai de Fables Nouvelles*, Paris, 1786; on the system propounded by P. S. Fournier, see his *Manuel Typographique*, Vol. I, p. 129 ff., Paris, 1764–1766, 2 vols.

89 On the problems of the printer's case, see P. S. Fournier, op. cit., Vol. 2, p. 119–142, and D. Fertel, *La Science Pratique de l'Imprimerie*, Amiens, 1723.

90 D. Fertel, op. cit., p. 11 ff.

91 See A. F. Momoro, *Traité Élémentaire de l'Imprimerie*, Paris, 1793; and the article 'Imprimerie' in the *Encyclopédie Française*.

92 Marius Audin, *Somme Typographique*, Vol. 2, p. 124 ff.

93 On the hand press, see P. Dietrichs, 'Die Buchdruckerpresse von Johannes Gutenberg bis Friedrich König', in *Jahresbericht der Gutenberg Gesellschaft*, Mainz, 1930; J. W. Enschedé, 'Houten hand presen in de zestiende eeuw', in *Tijdschrift voor Boek en Bibliotheeksvezen*, 1906, p. 195–208 and p. 262–277;

D. Fertel, op. cit.; J. Moxon, *Mechanick Exercises, or The Doctrine of Handy-Works*, London, 1683; L. Neipp, *Les Machines à Imprimer depuis Gutenberg*, Paris, 1951.

94   In France, at any rate, Cf. D. Fertel, op. cit., p. 231. It was not perhaps true of some big centres of printing. In England there were joiners who specialised in the making of printing presses.

95   On this see M. Audin's works. He thought the holes, in the final analysis, were tricks of the trade to permit printing in two colours, and were drilled in certain letters only, not only in the entire fount. Cf. Marius Audin, *Les Types Lyonnais Primitifs*. Bibliothèque Nationale, Dépt. des Imprimés, p. 21.

96   Marius Audin, 'A propos des Premières Techniques Typographiques', *loc. cit.*, p. 165–170.

97   K. Haebler, *The Study of Incunabula*, New York, 1933, p. 79–82.

98   J. W. Enschedé, loc. cit.

99   Cf. p. 131.

100   Marius Audin, *Somme Typographique*, Vol. 2, p. 94 ff.

101   See especially, C. Mortet, *Le Format des Livres. Notions Pratiques suivies de Recherches Historiques*, Paris, 1925; K. Haebler, op. cit.

102   C. Samaran, 'Contribution à l'Histoire du Livre Manuscrit du Moyen Age. Manuscrits Imposés et Manuscrits non "Coupés",' in *Comitato Internazionale di Scienze Storiche*, Fifth International Congress, Florence, 1957, p. 88 ff.

103   On the route by which paper came from China to Europe, see T. F. Carter, *The Invention of Printing in China and its Spread Westward*, rev. by L. Carrington Goodrich, 2nd edition, New York, 1955.

104   Edouard Chavannes, *Les Documents Chinois Decouverts par Aurel Stein dans les Sables du Turkestan Oriental*, Oxford, 1913.

105   E. Chavannes, 'Les Livres Chinois avant l'Invention du Papier', in *Journal Asiatique*, V, 1905, p. 5–75.

106   Aurel Stein, *Serindia. Detailed Report of Explorations in Central Asia and Westernmost Asia*, Oxford, 1921, Vol. 2, p. 669–677.

107   J. Von Wiesner, 'Über die ältesten bis jetzt aufgefundenen Hadernpapiere', *Sitzungsberichte der Königliche Akademie der Wissenschaften: Philosophical and Historical Series*, CLXVIII, Part 5, Vienna, 1911.

108   Paul Pelliot, *Les Débuts de l'Imprimerie en Chine*, Paris, 1953. (Oeuvres Posthumes de P. Pelliot, Vol. 4.); K. T. Wu, 'The Development of Printing in China', in *T'ien Hsia*, III, September, 1936, pl 137–160.

109   Kim Won-Young, *Early Moveable Type in Korea*, Seoul, 1954. (36 pages of Korean text, 15 pages of English text, and 26 plates. National Museum of Korea, Series A, Vol. 1).

110   C. Beaulieux, 'Manuscrits et Imprimés en France, XV–XVI Siècle', in *Mélanges Offerts à Émile Chatelain*, Paris, 1910; C. Mortet, 'Observations sur les Influences qui ont Diversifié les Caractères Employés par les Imprimeurs du XV Siècle', in *Gutenberg-Festschrift*, 1926, p. 210–213.

111   L. S. Olschki, *Incunables Illustrés Imitant les Manuscrits. Le Passage du Manuscrit au Livre Imprimé*, Florence, 1914.

112   Jacques Guignard, 'Du Manuscrit au Livre', in *La France Graphique*, 9th

Year, February, 1955, p. 8–16, and the titles referred to in notes 110 and 111; on the various manuscript hands and the origins of Humanistic script, see B. Bischoff, G. J. Lieftinck and G. Battelli, *Nomenclature des Écritures Livresques du IX au XVI Siècle*, Paris, 1954. See also, S. Morison, 'Early Humanistic Script and the First Roman Type', in *The Library*, XXVI, 1943, p. 1–30.

113   G. Lepreux, *Gallia Typographica. Province de Normandie*, Vol. 1, p. 276, Paris, 1912, 2 vols.

114   H. Harisse, *Les Premiers Incunables Bâlois et leurs Dérivés: Toulouse, Lyon . . .*, Paris, 1902, 2nd edition.

115   C. Perrat, 'Barthélemy Buyer et les Débuts de l'Imprimerie à Lyon', in *Humanisme et Renaissance*, Vol. 2, 1935, p. 103–121 and p. 349–387.

116   Cf. T. B. Reed, *A History of the Old English Type Foundries*, ed. A. F. Johnson, London, 1937.

117   E. P. Goldschmidt, *The Printed Books of the Renaissance*, Cambridge, 1950, p. 3.

118   Ibid., p. 5 ff.

119   On the history of type faces, essential reading is A. F. Johnson. *Type Designs, Their History and Development*, London, 1934; D. B. Updike, *Printing Types, Their History, Forms and Use*, 2nd edition, Cambridge, 1952, 2 Vols.

120   For the history of Italic type and its beginnings, see S. Morison, 'Towards an Ideal Type', in *The Fleuron*, II, 1924, p. 57–76; 'On Script Types', in *The Fleuron*, IV, 1925, p. 1–42; 'The Chancery Types of Italy and France', in *The Fleuron*, III, 1925, p. 53–60. The practice of using italic for quotations seems to have been begun by Froben at Basle, in 1510–1520.

121   E. P. Goldschmidt, op. cit., p. 24.

122   D. B. Updike, op. cit., Vol. 1, p. 139 ff.

123   Cf. p. 199 ff.

124   K. Haebler, *The Study of Incunabula*, New York, 1953.

125   A. F. Johnson, *German Renaissance Title Borders*, Oxford, 1929; J. Von Pflug-Hartung, *Rahmen Deutscher Buchtitel im 16.* Jahrhundert, Stuttgart, 1909; A. F. Johnson, 'The Title Borders of Hans Holbein', in the *Gutenberg-Jahrbuch*, 1937, p. 115–120.

126   See the previous note, and A. F. Johnson, *A Catalogue of Engraved and Etched English Title-pages*, Oxford, 1934; 'A Catalogue of Italian Engraved Title-pages in the 16th Century', in *Bibliographical Society Supplement*, 1936, p. i–xi and 1–27; R. Brun, *Le Livre Français*, Paris, 1948, p. 44 ff.

127   Cf. L. Voet in Bibliothèque Nationale. *Anvers, Ville de Plantin et de Rubens*. (Catalogue of an exhibition), Paris, 1951, p. 56 ff.

128   P. Hofer, *Baroque Book Illustration*, Cambridge, 1951; Bibliothèque Nationale. *L'Art du Livre à l'Imprimerie Nationale*, Paris, 1951, p. 56 ff.

129   G. Duplessis, *Essai sur les Différentes Éditions des "Icones Veteris Testamenti" de Holbein*, Paris, 1884; *Essai Bibliographique sur les Différentes Éditions des Oeuvres d'Ovide Ornées de Planches, Publiées au XV et au XVI Siècle*, Paris 1889.

130   Cf. below, and G. Duplessis, *Les Emblèmes d'Alciat*, Paris, 1884.

131   A. W. Pollard, *Fine Books*, London, 1912, p. 96.

132   M. Sander, *Le Livre à Figures Italien depuis 1467 jusqu'à 1530*, Milan, 1942, 6 Vols. There is an excellent historical introduction to Volume 4.

133   J. Macfarlane, 'Antoine Vérard', in *Transactions of the Bibliographical Society of London*, Vol. 4, 1896.

134   M. Sander, op. cit., Vol. 4.

135   This practice was followed currently at Lyon where Trechsel published a Latin and a French version of Terence simultaneously, each illustrated with the same wood blocks, attributed to Perréal. Cf. A. Martin, *Le Livre Illustré en France au XV Siècle*, Paris, 1931, p. 167.

136   A. Martin, op. cit., p. 141.

137   A. F. Johnson, 'Basle Ornaments on Paris Books, 1519–1536', in *The Library*, 1927/28, p. 355–360.

138   On the *Biblia Pauperum* and the *Speculum Humanae Salvationis*, see A. Mâle, *L'Art Religieux de la Fin du Moyen Age*, Paris, 1922, p. 232 ff.; and especially J. Lutz and P. Perdrizet, *"Speculum Humanae Salvationis"*. *Les Sources et l'Influence Iconographiques*, Mulhouse, 1909, 2 Vols. On the influence of mural painting, see M. Hébert, 'Gravures d'Illustration et Peintures Murales à la fin du Moyen Age', in *Association des Bibliothèques Français. Bulletin d'Information*, no. 20, June, 1956, p. 69 ff. We wish to thank Mlle Hébert for help on the question of book illustration. On enamels, see Marquet de Vasselot, 'Une planche des "Grandes Heures" de Vostre, copiée par deux emailleurs limousins', in *Bibliographe Moderne*, Vol. 16 (1912–13), and 'Une Suite d'Émaux Limousins à Sujets Tirés de l'*Enéide*', in *Bulletin de la Société de l'Histoire de l'Art Français*, 1st fascicule, 1912. On Bernard Salomon's influence on wood engraving, see E. A. Standen, 'A Picture for Every Story', in *The Metropolitan Museum of Art Bulletin*, April 1957, p. 165–175; C. Damiron, *La Faïence de Lyon*, Lyons, 1926. On tapestries, R. A. Weigart, *La Tapisserie Française*, 1957, and Marguerite Sartor, *Les Tapisseries, Toiles Peintes et Broderies de Reims*, Reims, 1912. On the influence of lace designs on decorated borders, S. Morison and Francis Meynell, 'Printers' flowers and Arabesques', in *The Fleuron*, no. 1, 1923, p. 1–43.

139   On French illustrated books in the 16th century, see R. Brun, *Le Livre Illustré en France au XVI Siècle*, and *Le Livre Français*, p. 39–63. For Germany, see especially R. Muther, *Die deutsche Bücherillustration der Gotik und Frührenaissance (1460–1530)*, Munich, 1884.

140   On this, see A. M. Hind and S. Colvin, *Catalogue of Early Italian Engravings Preserved in the Department of Prints and Drawings in the British Museum*, London, 1909–10, 2 Vols.; M. Pittaluga, *L'Incisione Italiana nel Cinquecento*, Milan, n.d.; L. Rosenthal, *La Gravure*, 2nd edition, Paris, 1939.

141   R. Brun, *Le Livre Illustré . . .* p. 126 ff.

142   Bibliothèque Nationale. *Anvers, Ville de Plantin et de Rubens*, (Catalogue of an exhibition), p. 106 ff., 201 ff., 257 ff., Paris, n.d.

143   E. Bouvy, *La Gravure en France au XVII Siècle: la gravure de portrait et d'allégorie*, Paris, 1927.

144   F. Courboin, *Graveurs et Marchands d'Estampes au XVIII Siècle*, Paris, 1914; H. Cohen, *Guide de l'Amateur de Livres à Gravures du XVIII Siècle*, Paris, 1912.

145   See R. Brun, 'Manuel de l'Amateur de Reliure Ancienne', in *Bulletin du Bibliophile*, 1935–37; and E. Ph. Goldschmidt, *Gothic and Renaissance Bookbinding*, London, 1928, 2 Vols.

146   E. Ph. Goldschmidt, op. cit., Vol. 1, p. 54 ff.

147   L. M. Michon, *La Reliure Française* . . . Paris, 1951, p. 53 ff.

148   Ibid., p. 39 ff.

149   Ibid., p. 86 ff.

150   E. Coyecque, 'Cinq Libraires Parisiens sous François I (1521–1529)', and 'La Librairie de Didier Maheu en 1520', in *Mémoires de la Société de L'Histoire de Paris et de l'Ile de France*, Vol. 21, 1894, p. 53–136, and p. 197–205; and same author, *Recueil d'Actes Notariés Relatifs à l'Histoire de Paris au XVI Siècle*, Paris, 1905–1929, 2 Vols.

151   E. Coyecque, 'Cinq Libraires Parisiens', loc. cit.

152   E. Coyecque, 'La Librairie de Didier Maheu', loc. cit.

153   The name 'Bourgeois' was given to the gothic *bastarda* types used to print books for the bourgeoisie (romances of chivalry and prayer books).

154   H. Stein, *Wolfgang Hopyl, Imprimeur-Libraire Parisien du XV Siècle. Note sur son Atelier Typographique*, Fontainebleau, 1891; 'Nouveaux Documents sur Wolfgang Hopyl, Imprimeur à Paris', in *Bibliographe Moderne*, Vol. 9, 1905, p. 178–193.

155   E. Coyecque, *Recueil d'Actes Notariés Relatifs à l'Histoire de Paris*, nos. 2029, 2854, 2875, 3312, 3390, 4132, 4227, and 4610.

156   Ibid., no. 15.

157   Ibid., nos. 2975 and 2997.

158   Ibid., no. 544.

159   Ibid., no. 533.

160   Ibid., no. 435.

161   P. Renouard, *Bibliographie des Impressions et des Oeuvres de Josse Bade Ascensius*, Paris, 1909, 3 Vols. Vol. 1, p. 58 ff.

162   E. Coyecque, *Recueil d'Actes Notariés* . . . no. 37.

163   Ibid., no. 465.

164   Ibid., no. 500.

165   Ibid., no. 645.

166   H. Hauser, *Ouvriers du Temps Passé*, Paris, 1917, p. 185.

167   E. Coyecque, op. cit., no. 1262.

168   Ibid., no. 2975.

169   R. Fulin, 'Documenti per Servire alla Storia della Tipografia Veneziana', from the Venice Archives, Vol. 23, Part 1, p. 2. A 'quinternion' is a quire of five leaves.

170   Cf. H. F. Brown, *The Venetian Printing Press*, London, 1891, p. 17 ff.

171   V. Fineschi, *Notizie Storiche sopra la Stamperia di Ripoli*, Florence, 1781.

172   P. Pansier, *Histoire du Livre et de l'Imprimerie à Avignon du XIV au XVI Siècle*, Avignon, 1922, p. 142 ff.

173   A. de la Bouralière, *L'Imprimerie et la Librairie à Poitiers pendant le XVI Siècle*, Paris, 1900, p. 367 ff.

174   Archives Nationales. Central registry of Paris notaries.

175   P. Mellotée, *Histoire Économique de l'Imprimerie*, Vol. 1 (the only one to appear), Paris, 1905, p. 448 ff.

176 Ibid., p. 449–452. To this we may add the production costs of three works:
   1. Colombat's *Almanach*. 72,000 copies printed annually at the beginning of the 18th century:

	£
Paper	2,000
Printing (Presswork)	540
Composition and Correcting	2,500
Total	5,040

(Cf. *Mémoire sur les Vexations qu'exercent les Libraires et Imprimeurs de Paris*, published by Lucien Faucou, Paris, 1879, p. 31.)
   2. Moreri's *Dictionary*. An edition of 2,000 copies each of 6 volumes in folio, early 18th century:

	£
Paper	54,000
Composition	12,000
Presswork	12,750
Wear and tear of types, ink, candles, correcting and other expenses	15,000
Total	93,750

(Cf. *Mémoire sur les Vexations* . . . p. 35.)
   3. Third edition of Gibbon's *Decline and Fall* (1775): 1,000 copies.

	£	s
Paper	171	
Printing	117	
Correction	5	5
Various expenses	16	15
Total	310	

(Cf. Mumby, *Publishing and Bookselling*, London, 1949, p. 197.)

177 H. Harisse, *Les Premiers Incunables Bâlois et Leurs Dérivés: Toulouse, Lyon, Vienne en Dauphiné, Spire, Eltville, etc., 1471–1484*, Paris, 1902, 2nd edition.

178 A. Hanauer, *Les Imprimeurs de Haguenau*, Strasbourg, 1904; F. Ritter, *Histoire de l'Imprimerie Alsacienne aux XV et XVI Siècles*, Paris–Strasbourg, 1955, p. 369–410.

179 C. Perrat, 'Barthélemy Buyer et les Débuts de L'Imprimerie à Lyon', in *Humanisme et Renaissance*, Vol. 2, 1935, p. 103–121 and p. 349–387.

180 J. Macfarlane, *Antoine Vérard*, London, 1899; A. Claudin, *Histoire de l'Imprimerie en France*, Paris, 1900–1905, 4 Vols. Vol. 2, p. 385–506; J. Guignard, 'Recherches pour Servir à l'Histoire du Livre à Tours . . .', in École des Chartes. *Positions des Thèses*, 1938, p. 36–44.

181 P. Renouard, 'Quelques Documents sur les Petit, Libraires Parisiens, et Leur Famille (XV et XVI Siècles)', in *Bulletin de la Société de l'Histoire de Paris et de l'Ile de France*, Vol. 23, 1896, p. 133–153.

182   P. Renouard, *Bibliographie des Impressions et des Oeuvres de Josse Bade Ascensius*, Vol. 1, p. 19 ff., Paris, 1909, 3 Vols.

183   A. A. Renouard, *Annales de l'Imprimerie des Alde . . .* 3rd edition, Paris, 1834, 3 Vols. Appendix on the Giuntas at the end of Vol. 3.

184   O. von Hase, *Die Koberger*, Leipzig, 1885.

185   M. Rooses, *Christophe Plantin*, 2nd edition, Antwerp, 1896–98.

186   H.-J. Martin, 'Sébastien Cramoisy et le Grand Commerce du Livre au XVII Siècle', in the *Gutenberg-Jahrbuch*, 1957, p. 179–188.

187   G. Lepreux, *Gallia Typographica*. Paris Series, Vol. 1: *Livre d'Or des Imprimeurs du Roi*, p. 34 ff.

188   H. Hauser, *Ouvriers du Temps Passé*, Paris, 1917, p. 231.

189   L. Morin, *Les Apprentis-Imprimeurs du Temps Passé*, Lyon, 1898. Colourful background on the lives of apprentices and 'compagnons' can be found in Restif de la Bretonne's *Monsieur Nicolas*.

190   Cf. p. 170 ff.

191   Cf. p. 191 ff.

192   P. Chaix, *Recherches sur l'Imprimerie à Genève de 1550 à 1564*, Geneva, 1954, p. 3 ff.

193   M. Sabbe, *L'Oeuvre de Christophe Plantin et de ses Successeurs*, Brussels, 1937, p. 188 ff.

194   H. Hauser, op. cit.

195   Bibliothèque Nationale, MS fr. (French) 22064, sheet no. 19.

196   H. Hauser, op. cit., p. 218 ff.; L. M. Michon, 'A propos des Grèves d'Imprimeurs à Paris et à Lyon au XVI Siècle', in *Fédération des Sociétés Historiques et Archéologiques de Paris et de l'Ile-de-France. Mémoires*, 1953, p. 103–115; K. Pallmann, 'Frankfurts Buchdruckerordnungen', in *Archiv für Geschichte des Deutschen Buchhandels*, 1881, p. 261–273; Bibliothèque Nationale, MS fr. (French) 22064, sheets 45–47.

197   H. Hauser, op. cit., p. 34, 94 and 104; M. Rooses, op. cit., p. 240, no. 1; P. Chaix, op. cit., p. 39 ff.

198   Bibliothèque Nationale, MS fr. (French) 22064, sheets 45–47.

199   M. Sabbe, op. cit., p. 159 ff.

200   H. Hauser, op. cit., p. 177 ff. And see Marius Audin, 'Les Grèves dans l'Imprimerie à Lyon au XVI Siècle', in the *Gutenberg-Jahrbuch*, 1935, p. 172–189, and L. M. Michon, 'A Propos des Grèves d'Imprimeurs à Paris et à Lyon au XVI Siècle', loc. cit. An unpublished article rounding off H. Hauser's work.

201   M. Rooses, op. cit., p. 241.

202   K. Pallmann, 'Ein Buchdruckerstreik zu Frankfurt-am-Main im Jahre 1597', in *Archiv für Geschichte des Deutschen Buchhandels*, 1883, p. 11–21.

203   P. Chaix, op. cit., p. 25 ff.

204   Bibliothèque Nationale, MS, fr. (French) 22064, sheets no. 52, 56 and 60, and Decree of the Council of State, dated 19 June 1702.

205   Plantin-Moretus Archives, no. 526, the Anisson dossier, 28 November 1671.

206   E. de Broglie, *Mabillon et la Société de Saint-German-des-Prés au XVIII Siècle*, Paris, 1888, 2 Vols. Vol. 1, p. 374 and 422; Vol. 2, p. 363. See also J. B. Vanel, *Les Bénédictins de Saint-Germain-des-Prés et les Savants Lyonnais*,

Paris-Lyons, 1894.

207   P. Mellotée, *Histoire Économique de l'Imprimerie*, p. 142 ff.

208   E. von Biena, *Les Huguetan de Mercur et de Vrijhoeven*, The Hague, 1918.

209   A. Cartier, M. Audin and E. Vial, *Bibliographie des Éditions des de Tournes*, Paris, 1937.

210   P. Ducourtieux, *Les Barbou, Imprimeurs, Lyon, Limoges, Paris (1524–1820)*, Limoges, 1895–98.

211   E. Pasquier and V. Dauphin, *Imprimeurs et Libraires de l'Anjou, Angers, 1932*, and M. M. Kleerkooper and W. P. van Stockum, *De Boekhandel te Amsterdam*, The Hague, 1914.

212   *Amerbachkorrespondenz*, edited by Alfred Hartmann, Basle, 1942–47, 3 Vols. Cf. L. Febvre, *Au Coeur du XVI Siècle Religieux*, Paris, 1957.

213   See notably A. A. Renouard, *Annales de l'Imprimerie des Alde*, 3rd edition, Paris, 1834, 3 Vols.; A. Firmin-Didot, *Alde Manuce et l'Hellénisme à Venise*, Paris, 1875.

214   P. Renouard, *Bibliographie des Impressions et des Oeuvres de Josse Badius Ascensius*.

215   Cf. p. 122.

216   E. Armstrong, *Robert Estienne, Royal Printer*, Cambridge, 1954.

217   A. J. Bernard, *Geoffroy Tory*, 2nd edition, Paris, 1865.

218   J. Baudrier, *Bibliographie Lyonnaise*, Vol. 8, Lyons, 1895–1921, 12 Vols. Revised by George Tricou, Paris, 1963.

219   F. Ritter, *Histoire de l'Imprimerie Alsacienne*, p. 377–387, Paris, Strasbourg, 1955.

220   L. Febvre, 'Dolet, Propagateur de l'Évangile', in *Bibliothèque d'Humanisme et Renaissance*, Vol. 8, 1945, p. 98–170.

221   H. J. Martin, 'Sébastien Cramoisy et le Grand Commerce du Livre à Paris au XVII Siècle', in the *Gutenberg-Jahrbuch*, 1957, p. 179–188.

222   J. Chapelain, *Correspondance*, edited by Tamizey de Larroque, Paris, 1880–83.

223   Cf. p. 138–139.

224   M. H. Clément-Janin, *Recherches sur les Imprimeurs Dijonnais*, p. 30–43.

225   P. J. H. Baudet, *Leven en Werken van W. J. Blaeu*, Utrecht, 1871.

226   H. J. Martin, *Sébastien Cramoisy*, loc. cit.

227   F. Lachêvre, *Le Libertinage devant le Parlement de Paris. Le Procès de Théophile de Viau*, Paris, 1909, 2 Vols.

228   H. J. Martin, *Guillaume Desprez, Imprimeur de Pascal et Port-Royal*, loc. cit.

229   G. Mongrédien, *La Vie Quotidienne sous Louis XIV*, Paris, 1948, p. 175.

230   The Ducal Museum (Bouillon). *Le Journal Encyclopédique et la Société Typographique*. An exhibition in honour of Pierre Rousseau (1716–1785) and Charles-Auguste de Weissenbruch (1744–1826), Bouillon, 1955.

231   Cf. p. 197.

232   Voltaire, *Lettres inédites à son Imprimeur, Gabriel Cramer*, Geneva, 1952 (edited by Gagnebin).

233   W. Bennett, *John Baskerville, the Birmingham Printer*, Birmingham, 1931; J. H. Benton, *John Baskerville, Typefounder and Printer, 1706–1775*, Boston, 1914.

234   R. Bertieri, *L'Arte di Giambattista Bodoni*, Milan, 1913.

235   L. de Peluson, 'Les Didot', in *Arts et Métiers Graphiques*, 1929–30, p. 779–789.

236   Cf. p. 185 and 211.

237   J. Hoyoux, 'Les Moyens d'Existence d'Érasme', in *Bibliothèque d'Humanisme et Renaissance*, Vol. 6, 1944, p. 7–59.

238   M. Rooses, *Christophe Plantin*, 2nd edition, p. 257, Antwerp, 1892.

239   H. J. Martin, 'Quelques aspects de l'Édition Parisienne au XVII Siècle', in *Annales*, 7th Year, 1952, p. 309–319.

240   G. Mongrédien, *La Vie Littéraire au XVII Siècle*, Paris, 1947, p. 257.

241   Ibid., p. 275 ff.

242   H. J. Martin, loc. cit.

243   L. Kirschbaum, 'Author's Copyright in England before 1640', in *Papers of the Bibliographical Society of America*, 1946, p. 43–80; H. Falk, *Les Privilèges de Librairie sous l'Ancien Régime*, Paris, 1906; F. Milkau, *Handbuch des Bibliothekswissenschaft*, Vol. 1, p. 905 ff., Wiesbaden, 1952–1961, 4 vols.

244   W. W. Greg, *Some Aspects of London Publishing between 1550 and 1650*, Oxford, 1956.

245   M. Pelisson, *Les Hommes de Lettres au XVIII Siècle*, Paris, 1911.

246   R. Bouvier and E. Maynial, *Les Comptes Dramatiques de Balzac*, Paris, 1938.

247   On Jenson's possible mission, see A. Claudin, *Histoire de l'Imprimerie en France*, Vol. 1, p. 11, no. 2; J. Guignard in *Bulletin de la Société des Antiquaires de France*, 1945–47, p. 39.

248   Cf. the map on pp. 184–185.

249   K. Haebler, *Die Deutschen Buchdrucker des XV Jahrhunderts im Auslande*, Munich, 1924.

250   A. Claudin, *Les Origines de l'Imprimerie à Albi en Languedoc (1480–1484). Les Pérégrinations de J. Neumeister, Compagnon de Gutenberg en Allemagne, en Italie at en France (1483–1484)*, Paris, 1880; L. Charles-Bellet, 'Les Deux Séjours à Albi d'un Compagnon de Gutenberg', in *Revue du Tarn*, 1881, p. 81–91.

251   J. Marchand, *Une Enquête sur l'Imprimerie et la Librairie en Guyenne, Mars 1701*, Bordeaux, 1939.

252   A. Claudin, *Les Imprimeries Particulières en France au XV Siècle*, Paris, 1897; A. de la Borderie, *L'Imprimerie en Bretagne au XV Siècle*, Nantes, 1878.

253   M. Langlois, *Le Missel de Chartres Imprimé en 1482*, Chartres, 1904.

254   J. Janssen, *L'Allemagne et la Réforme*, Paris, 1887–1914, 9 Vols., Vol. 1, p. 7 ff.

255   L. Delisle, *Livres Imprimés à Cluny au XV Siècle*, Paris, 1897.

256   M. H. Clément-Janin, *Recherches sur les Imprimeurs Dijonnais et sur les Imprimeurs de la Côte-d'Or*, Dijon, 1883, p. 1 ff.

257   J. Janssen, op. cit., p. 14 ff.

258   Ibid.

259   V. Fineschi, *Notizie Storiche sopra la Stamperia di Ripoli*, Florence, 1781; G. Galli, 'Gli Ultimi Mesi della Stamperia di Ripoli e la Stampa del Platone', in *Studi e Richerche sulla Storia della Stampa del Quattrocento*, Milan, 1942, p. 159–184.

260   A. Renaudet, *Préréforme et Humanisme à Paris pendant les Premières Guerres*

d'Italie (1494–1517), Paris, 1953, passim; A. Claudin, *Origines de l'Imprimerie à Paris. La Première Presse à la Sorbonne*, Paris, 1899; J. Monfrin, 'Les Lectures de Guillaume Fichet et de Jean Heylin d'après les Registres de Prêt de la Bibliothèque de la Sorbonne', in *Bibliothèque d'Humanisme et Renaissance*, Vol. 17, 1955, p. 7 and 23.

261 A. Willems, *Les Elzevier*, Brussels, 1880.

262 E. Pasquier and V. Dauphin, *Imprimeurs et Libraires de l'Anjou*, Angers, 1932.

263 G. Pepreux, *Gallia Typographica. Province de Normandie*, Vol. 1; A. de la Bouralière. *L'Imprimerie et la Librairie à Poitiers pendant le XVI Siècle*, Paris, 1900; E. F. Kossman, *De Boekhandelte's Gravenhage*, The Hague, 1937.

264 E. Pasquier and V. Dauphin, op. cit.

265 Cf. p. 117 ff.

266 Cf. p. 126 ff.

267 Cf. the map on p. 184. The date on which printing began in a town is a hotly debated matter and we do not pretend to have settled it. We have simply accepted the dates currently agreed by scholars.

268 A. Claudin, *Histoire de l'Imprimerie en France*, Vol. 1, p. 67 ff.; H. Lehmann-Haupt, *Peter Schoeffer of Gernsheim and Mainz*, Rochester, New York, 1900.

269 P. Pansier, *Histoire du Livre et de l'Imprimerie à Avignon du XIV au XVI Siècle*, p. 129 ff., Avignon, 1922, 3 Vols.

270 Cf. p. 167–168.

271 These figures are intended only to give an idea of the scale of operations. They are based on an annotated copy of K. Burger, *The Printers and the Publishers of the XV Century with Lists of their Works*, London, 1902.

272 Cf. p. 248 ff.

273 Bibliothèque Nationale. *Anvers, Ville de Plantin et de Rubens* (Exhibition Catalogue), p. 95 ff.

274 F. Ritter, *Histoire de l'Imprimerie Alsacienne aux XV et XVI Siècles*.

275 On German publishing in the 16th century, see F. Milkau, *Handbuch der Bibliothekswissenschaft*, 2nd edition by Georg Leyn, Vol. 1: *Schrift und Buch*, Wiesbaden, 1952, p. 490 ff.; J. Benzing, *Buchdrucker-lexicon des 16.Jahrhunderts: Deutsches Sprachgebiet*, Frankfurt, 1952.

276 G. Lepreux, 'Introduction de l'Imprimerie dans les Villes de France', in *Supplement au Bulletin Officiel de l'Union des Maîtres Imprimeurs*, Special Number, December, 1925, p. 9 ff.

277 P. Renouard, *L'Édition Française en 1530*, Paris, 1931.

278 C. Perez Pastor, *Bibliografia Madrilena*, Madrid, 1891–1907, 3 Vols. According to this bibliography, 769 works were printed at Madrid between 1566 and 1600, and 1,471 between 1601 and 1626.

279 H. S. Bennett, *English Books and Readers, 1475 to 1557*, Cambridge, 1952; M. Plant, *The English Book Trade*, London, 1939; F. A. Mumby, *Publishing and Bookselling*, London, 1949.

280 Cf. p. 290 ff.

281 Cf. p. 287 ff.

282 Cf. p. 314 ff.

283 Cf. p. 228 ff.

284 P. J. H. Baudet, *Leven en Werk van W. J. Blaeu*, Utrecht, 1871.

285 H. J. Martin, 'Quelques Aspects de l'Édition Parisienne au XVII Siècle', in *Annales*, 7th Year, 1952, p. 309–319.

286 P. Mellotée, *Histoire Économique de l'Imprimerie*, p. 458 ff., Paris, 1905.

287 The basic work is M. Kleerkooper and W. P. van Stockum, *De Boekhandel te Amsterdam, voornamelijk in de 17 Eeuw*, The Hague, 1914, 5 Vols. It has an excellent selection of documents.

288 Cf. *Lettres inédites de Jean-Jacques Rousseau à Marc-Michel Rey*, edited by J. Bosscha, Amsterdam and Paris, 1858.

289 See H. Lehmann-Haupt, *The Book in America*, 2nd edition, New York, 1951.

290 K. Haebler, *The Study of Incunabula*, New York, 1933, p. 171 ff.

291 O. von Hase, *Die Koberger*, 2nd edition, Leipzig, 1885.

292 P. Renouard, *Bibliographie des Impressions et des Oeuvres de Josse Bade*, Vol. 1, p. 57–59; Vol. 2, p. 155.

293 E. Coyecque, *Recueil d'Actes Notariés Relatifs à l'Histoire de Paris*, Vol. 1, no. 866.

294 Ibid, no. 1262.

295 P. Pansier, *Histoire du Livre et de l'Imprimerie à Avignon du XIV au XVI Siècle*, Avignon, 1922, p. 85 ff. and 100 ff.

296 A. Hanauer, *Les Imprimeurs de Haguenau*, p. 23, Strasbourg, 1904.

297 P. Renouard, *Bibliographie des Éditions de Simon de Colines*, p. 96 ff. and p. 461, Paris, 1894. See also the *Bibliotheca Belgica*, 2nd Series, E.466, Brussels, 1964.

298 P. Renouard, *Bibliographie des Éditions de Simon de Colines*, p. 23.

299 Cf. p. 296 ff.

300 M. Rooses, *Christophe Plantin*, 2nd edition.

301 In 1587 the size of an edition was limited by the Stationers' Company to ensure work. Only certain categories of books could exceed 1250–1500 copies in one edition: grammars, prayer books, catechisms, Statutes and Proclamations, calendars, almanacs and prognostications. In fact the limit set does not seem to have inhibited the Master Printers, and Shakespeare's plays in the quarto edition do not appear to have exceeded 1000 copies. The limits were abolished in 1637. Cf. E. Boswell and W. W. Greg, *Records of the Court of the Stationers' Company, 1576–1602, Register B*, London, 1930, p. xliii ff.; and M. Plant, *The English Book Trade*, London, 1939.

302 Bibliothèque Nationale, MS fr. (French) 22074, sheet no. 2.

303 G. Mongrédien, *La Vie Littéraire au XVII Siècle*, p. 272.

304 Bibliothèque Nationale, MS fr. (French) 21856, f. 40.

305 Ibid.

306 Kleerkooper, (Daniel Elzevier Betrekkingen met Engeland', in *Tijdschrift voor Boek en Bibliotheekvezen*, 1910.

307 G. Cohen, *Écrivains Français en Hollande dans la première partie du XVII Siècle*, Paris, 1920.

308 P. Delalain, *Les Libraires et Imprimeurs de l'Académie Française de 1634 à 1793*, Paris, 1907, p. 57.

309 Ibid.

310 Council decree of 17 October 1704.

311 Plantin-Moretus Archives, 296, leaves 680–682.

312 M. M. Kleerkooper and W. van Stockum, *De Boekhandel te Amsterdam* ...
The Hague, 1914, the article on 'Halma'.
313 Ibid.
314 H. J. Martin, *Guillaume Desprez*, loc. cit.
315 Bibliothèque Nationale, MS fr. (French) 22127, sheet no. 52.
316 Lyons city archives, HH 101.
317 Bibliothèque Nationale MS lat. (Latin) 11915.
318 *Mémoire sur les Vexations qu'Exercent les Libraires et Imprimeurs de Paris*,
Lucien Faucou, Paris, 1879.
319 Ibid.
320 P. Mellotée, *Histoire Économique de l'Imprimerie*, Vol. 1, *L'Ancien Régime*,
p. 449–452.
321 Ducal Museum (Bouillon). *Le Journal Encyclopédique et la Société Typographique*.
322 On this see Introduction to Voltaire's *Lettres Inédites à son Imprimeur
Gabriel Cramer*, edited by Gagnebin, Geneva, 1952; G. Bengesco,
Bibliographie Voltaire, Vol. 1, p. 342 (Voltaire's letter of 28 December,
1751), Paris, 1882–1890, 4 Vols. Likewise in England the usual edition
was 2000, sometimes rising to 10,000. Cf. M. Plant, *The English Book Trade*,
London, 1939, p. 94.
323 M. Plant, op. cit., p. 257.
324 Plantin-Moretus archives, 148, leaves 163–164. Some of the books
ordered came from Fouet's stock and had been printed 20 years previously,
which shows how slow sales were.
325 Bibliothèque Nationale, MS fr. (French) 21856, f. 40.
326 Voltaire, *Lettres inédites à son Imprimeur Gabriel Cramer*, Introduction.
327 We have fairly detailed information about the role of a town like Nantes
as a staging post, thanks to the Ruiz archives. They were Spanish merchant
bankers who acted as middlemen between France and Spain. André and
Simon Ruiz undertook delivery of French paper to Spain in the latter part
of the 16th century. André Ruiz worked in close contact with the papermakers of Thiers where there were Spanish agents. In 1552 he sent 2041
bales of paper to Spain, each bale containing between 18 and 24 reams of
500 sheets. In 1553 he despatched 826 bales; in 1554, 383 bales; in 1555,
436 bales. Between 1557 and 1564 he despatched 1057 bales of books, 919
from Lyons and 103 from Paris (most of the Paris consignment was
ordered from Lyons). The business extended as far afield as Burgos,
Valladolid and Salamanca, but the heart of the trade was Medina del
Campo. Seeneton and Pesnot were among the Lyons booksellers (Charles
Pesnot, nephew of the firm's proprietor, was first an agent for his company
at Medina before returning to Lyons to take over direction of the firm).
Then come the Giuntas, the Rouille-Portonari and the Millis, all with
agents at Medina del Campo. In 1574 André Ruiz arranged delivery of
126 bales of church service-books from Antwerp to Spain, and he and
Francisco de la Presa tried to set up a large establishment to supply Spain
with service-books, in 1578. They failed, but the archives reveal that there
were fifty bishops in Spain each requiring 1500 breviaries. In all, 40
presses could operate in Castille turning out 40,000 missals and 40,000

breviaries. Cf. H. Lapeyre, *Une Famille de Marchands, les Ruys*, Paris, 1955, p. 566 ff. Nantes' value as a staging post is explained by its position at the mouth of the Loire, transport by river being cheaper than by land, as is shown by the following tables, one taken from Lapeyre (op. cit.) the other from E. Trocmé and M. Delafosse, *Le Commerce Rochelais de la Fin du XV Siècle au Début du XVII Siècle*, Paris, 1952, p. 95.

Cost of transporting books from Lyons to Spain and Portugal via La Rochelle in 1563:

Carriage from Lyons–La Rochelle (Overland)	5–6 livres
La Rochelle–Bilbao	14–16 sols (one-eighth the above)
La Rochelle–Lisbon	20 sols (one-sixth)
La Rochelle–Seville	1 livre 10 sols (one-quarter)

Consignment of 21 volumes (less than a normal load) from Lyons to Medina del Campo, via Nantes:

Lyons–Nantes (overland, then via the Loire)	1 livre 7 sols . . . 563 mrs
Marine insurance	4 per cent: 365 mrs
Bilbao–Medina	488 mrs

Thus a simple comparison shows us why the Lyons–La Rochelle route was rarely used, and why booksellers preferred to transport their merchandise via the Loire and Nantes.

328 It must be emphasised throughout that we mean bartering books for books, although many booksellers did barter books in exchange for other products; nearly all of them acquired paper in this way. Booksellers in smaller towns traded for local products, hence Nicolas of Grenoble, a very rich banker and a dealer in leather, sent gloves and chamois leather to Paris and Lyons, and so paid booksellers there for his books.

329 A. Claudin, *Histoire de l'Imprimerie*, Vol. 1, p. 67 ff.; F. Milkau, *Handbuch der Bibliothekswissenschaft*, Vol. 1, p. 875 ff.

330 M. Plant, *The English Book Trade*, p. 262 ff.

331 H. Brésard, *Les Foires de Lyon au XV et au XVI Siècle*, Lyons, 1914.

332 J. Guignard, 'Les Premiers Éditeurs de Rabelais', in *Association des Bibliothécaires Français. Bulletin d'Information*, no. 13, March, 1954, p. 13 ff.

333 F. Milkau, op. cit., Vol. 1, p. 879 ff.; Fr. Kapp and J. Goldfriedrich, *Geshchichte des Deutschen Buchhandels*, Leipzig, 1886; H. Estienne, *The Frankfurt Book Fair*, translated and with an introduction by J. W. Thompson, Chicago, 1911.

334 See Kapp and Goldfriedrich, op. cit., Vol. 1; H. Estienne, op. cit. And see A. Dietz, *Zur Geschichte der Frankfurter Büchermesse, 1462–1792*, Frankfurt, 1921.

335 A. Growoll, *Three Centuries of English Book Trade Bibliography*, New York, 1903.

336 F. Milkau, op. cit., p. 894.

337 A. Growoll, op. cit., and the works cited in note 334.

338 G. Weill, *Le Journal, Origine, Évolution de la Presse Périodique*, Paris, 1934

(Vol. 95 of *L'Évolution de L'Humanité*), p. 19 ff.

339 P. Renouard, *Bibliographie des Impressions et des Oeuvres de Josse Bade Ascensius* (Introduction).

340 H. Falk, *Les Privilèges de Librairie sous l'Ancien Régime*, Paris, 1906.

341 *Briefwisseling van de Gebroeders Verdussen,1669–1672*, edited by M. Sabbe, Antwerp–The Hague, 1936, 2 Vols.; H. J. Martin, 'L'Édition Parisienne au XVII Siècle', in *Annales*, 7th Year, 1952, p. 309–319.

342 G. H. Putnam, *Books and Their Makers during the Middle Ages*, London, 1896–1897, 2 vols.

343 Of course we mean only to indicate some idea of scale. According to Vladimir Loublinsky, production would be somewhere between 12 and 20 million copies. Cf. the review of the first edition of the present book in *Vestnik Istorii Mirovoi Kultury*, Moscow, 1959, no. 4.

344 *Encyclopédie Française*, Vol. 18, *La Civilisation Écrite*, Paris, 1939; R. Steele, 'What Fifteenth Century Books Are About', in *The Library*, New Series, Vol. 5, 1903–07; J. M. Lehnart, *Pre-Reformation Printed Books: a study in statistical and applied bibliography*, New York, 1935.

345 W. A. Copinger, *Incunabula Biblica, or, The First Half Century of the Latin Bible*, London, 1892. In an appendix the author quotes 437 editions of the Bible in the 16th century. (See *Gesamtkatalog* under 'Bible'). The examples given are taken from various sources, and are only an indication, not meant to be definitive.

346 M. Pellechet, 'Jacques de Voragine. Liste des Editions de ses Ouvrages Publiées au XV Siècle' (from the *Revue des Bibliothèques*, April, 1895).

347 See particularly B. Woledge, *Bibliographie des Romans et Nouvelles en Prose Antérieurs à 1500*, Geneva, 1954.

348 On scientific publications in the 15th century, see G. Sarton, 'Scientific literature transmitted through incunabula', in *Osiris*, Vol. 5, 1938, p. 41–245.

349 B. Gilles, 'Lents Progrès de la Technique', in *Revue de Synthèse*, 32, 1953, p. 69–88.

350 E. P. Goldschmidt, *Medieval Texts and their First Appearance in Print*, Oxford, 1943.

351 The examples given are from notes prepared by P. Renouard for the *Bibliographie des Impressions Parisiennes au XVI Siècle*. For Lyons see *Bibliographie Lyonnaise* by J. Baudrier. For England, the *Short Title Catalogue of Books Printed before 1640*, edited by Pollard and Redgrave, London, 1926. For Germany and Venice, see J. Benzing, *Die Buchdrucker des 16 und 17 Jahrhunderts im Deutschen Sprachgebiet*, Wiesbaden, 1965.

352 The figures are taken from Mlle Nicole Bourdel's thesis at the École des Chartes. See also R. Doucet, *Les Bibliothèques Parisiennes au XVI Siècle*, Paris, 1956, and A. H. Schutz, *Vernacular Books in Parisian Private Libraries of the Sixteenth Century*, Chapel Hill, North Carolina, 1958.

353 Cf. R. Doucet, op. cit.

354 P. Ritter, *Histoire de l'Imprimerie Alsacienne au XV et XVI Siècle*, p. 463 ff.

355 P. Renouard's notes.

356 R. Proctor, *The Printing of Greek in the Fifteenth Century*, Oxford, 1900; British Museum. *Greek Printing Types, 1465–1927*, (Catalogue of an exhibi-

tion), London, 1927.

357 Paul Colomies, *Gallia Orientalis*, The Hague, 1665; by the same author, *Italia et Hispania Orientalis*, The Hague, 1730; Wilhelm Bacher, *Die Hebräische Sprachwissenschaft vom 10 bis zum 16 Jahrhundert*, Treves, 1892; Bernhard Walde, *Christliche Hebraisten Deutschlands am Ausgang des Mittelalters*, Münster-in-Westfallen, 1916; *Encyclopedia Judaica*, see 'Hebräische Sprache (Christliche Hebraisten)'; Daniel Mierowski, *Hebrew Grammar and Grammarians Throughout the Ages*, Johannesburg, 1955 (doctorate thesis); L. Kukenheim, *Contribution à l'Histoire de la Grammaire Grecque, Latine et Hébraïque à l'Époque de la Renaissance*, Leyden, 1951. For the previous period, refer to J. Soury, *Des Études Hebraïques et Exégétiques chez les Chrétiens d'Occident*, Paris, 1867; Samuel Berger, *Quem Notitiam Linguae Hebraicae Habuerint Christiani Medii Aevi Temporibus in Gallia*, Nancy, 1893.

358 D. W. Amram, *The Makers of Hebrew Books in Italy*, Philadelphia, 1909; C. B. Friedberg, *Toledoth Ha-defous Ha-ivri Bi-medinoth Italya, Aspanya-Portugalya, Togarma We-arstoth Hakedem*. (History of Printing in Italy, Spain, Portugal, Turkey and the West), Antwerp, 1934. On the Soncino family, see Giacomo Manzoni, *Annali Tipografici dei Soncini*, Bologna, 1883–86. Vols. 1 and 2 the only ones to appear.

359 C. B. Friedberg, *Toledoth Ha-defous Ha-ivri Be-arim Ha-ele Chebe-Erope Ha-tikhona: Augsburg, Offenbach*. (History of Hebrew printing in the following Towns in Central Europe: Augsburg, Offenbach), Antwerp, 1935; K. Haebler, 'Die Deutschen Buchdrucker des XV Jahrhunderts' (a chapter from *Die Hebräische Drucker, 1475–1500*, Munich, 1924.)

360 C. B. Friedberg, *Toledoth Ha-defous Ha-ivri be Polonye* (History of Hebrew printing in Poland), Antwerp, 1933.

361 See, H. Ormont, 'Alphabets Grecs et Hébreux Publiés à Paris au XVI Siècle' (from *Bulletin de la Société de l'Histoire de Paris et de l'Ile-de-France*, 1885); same author, 'Spécimens de Caractères Hébreux Gravés à Paris et à Venise par Guillaume Le Bé (1546–1574)' (from *Mémoires de la Société de l'Histoire de Paris*, 1887), and 'Spécimens de Caractères Hébreux, Grecs, Latins et de Musique, Gravés à Venise et à Paris par Guillaume Le Bé (1545–1592)' (from the same *Mémoires*, 1889). See also E. Howe, 'An Introduction to Hebrew Typography', and 'The Le Bé Family', in *Signature*, 5, 1937, and 8, 1938.

362 R. N. Rabbinowitz, *Maamar 'al Hadpassath Ha-Talmoud* (The printing of the Talmud), Munich, 1877; 2nd edition, Jerusalem, 1940.

363 Alexander Marx, 'The Choice of Books by the Printers of Hebrew Incunables' reprinted from *To Doctor R*, Philadelphia, 1948.

364 After their expulsion from Spain and Portugal, Jewish printers set up presses in Turkey where they were well received, and pioneered printing there. Turkey was thus a cradle of Hebrew printing, and the Book of the Four Generations of Jacob appeared there in the years 1493–1503. By 1503 several Jewish printers were at work in the Turkish Empire. The celebrated Gerson de Soncino, after wandering from town to town and working in eight Italian towns between 1489 and 1534, discouraged by piracies of his work and competitors, ended up in Turkey where his imprint appears in Salonica and Constantinople, (cf. G. Manzoni, *Annali*

Tipografici dei Soncini, and A. M. Habermann, *Ha-madpissim bene Soncino* (The printers of the Soncino family), Vienna, 1933. So successful was this sojourn that in 1586 Nicola de Nicolay in his *Discours et Histoires Véritables des Navigations, Pérégrinations et Voyages Faits en Turquie* says, with some exaggeration, that the Jews 'set up printing presses in Constantinople never seen before in those regions, and produced books in a good letter in various languages, Greek, Latin, Italian, Spanish, and those spoken in the Levant'. Cf. A. Blum, 'L'Hellénisme à Constantinople après la Conquête Turque', in *Revue des Deux-Mondes*, May 1943, p. 98 ff., and C. Roth, 'Jewish Printers of Non-Jewish Books in the 15th and 16th century', in *Journal of Jewish Studies*, IV, 3, 1953.

365   F. Brunot, *Histoire de la Langue Française*, Vol. 2: 16th Century, p. 3, Paris, 1905–1953, 13 Vols.

366   H. B. Lathrop, *Translations from the Classics into English from Caxton to Chapman (1477–1620)*, Madison, Wisconsin, 1933.

367   G. Mambelli, *Gli Annali delle Edizioni Virgiliane*, Florence, 1954.

368   A. J. Festigiere, *La Philosophie de l'Amour de Marsile Ficin et son Influence sur la Littérature Française du XVI Siècle*, 2nd edition, Paris, 1944.

369   *Bibliotheca Belgica*, 2nd Series, Vols. 6–14.

370   Cf. P. P. Plan, *Les Éditions de Rabelais de 1532 à 1711*, Paris, 1904.

371   G. Duplessis, *Les Emblèmes d'Alciat*, Paris, 1884; M. Praz, *Studies in Seventeenth Century Imagery*, London, 1939, 2 Vols.

372   L. Febvre, *Le Problème de l'Incroyance au XVI Siècle: la religion de Rabelais*, Paris, 1968 (reprint); L. Thorndike, *Science and Thought in the 15th Century*, New York, 1929. Here we confine discussion to a brief review of the question, with the help of these two works. We would also mention a very valuable guide: George Sarton, *The Appreciation of Ancient and Medieval Science during the Renaissance*, Philadelphia, 1955.

373   L. Febvre, *ibid.* p. 358–9.

374   On the evolution of illustration from the early fabulous pictures to accurate observation of nature, see Sarton, op. cit., p. 89 ff.

375   B. Penrose, *Travel and Discovery in the Renaissance*, Cambridge, 1952; G. Atkinson, *Les Nouveaux Horizons de la Renaissance Française*, Paris, 1935.

376   Van Tieghem, 'La Littérature Latine de la Renaissance', in *Bibliothèque d'Humanisme et Renaissance*, VI, 1944, p. 177–409.

377   Cf. p. 371.

378   H. Hauser, *La Naissance du Protestantisme*, Paris, 1940, and *Études sur la Réforme Française*, Paris, 1909, p. 86 ff., and p. 255 ff.

379   See particularly J. P. Seguin, 'L'Information à la fin du XV Siècle en France', in *Arts et Traditions Populaires*, October/December 1956, no. 4, and 1957, nos. 1 and 2.

380   On the widespread influence of Ulrich von Hutten's works, see J. Benzing, *Ulrich von Hutten end seine Drucker*, Wiesbaden, 1956.

381   L. Febvre, *Un Destin: Martin Luther*, Paris, 1928.

382   M. Gravier, *Luther et l'Opinion Publique*, Paris, 1942.

383   A. Goetze, *Die Hochdeutschen Drucker der Reformationszeit*, Strasbourg, 1905.

384   C. Ritter, *Histoire de l'Imprimerie Alsacienne au XV et au XVI Siècle*,

p. 384–396.

385 On this see the Weimar Edition. And see O. Clemen, *Die Lutherische Reformation und der Buchdruck*, Leipzig, 1939.

386 P. Imbart de la Tour, *Les Origines de la Réforme*, Paris, 1914, Vol. 3.

387 See W. G. Moore, *La Réforme Allemande et la Littérature Francaise. Recherches sur la Notoriété de Luther en France*, Strasbourg, 1930.

388 A. Tricard, 'La Propagande Évangélique en France: l'Imprimeur Simon Dubois (1526–1534)', in *Aspects de la Propagande Religieuse*, Geneva, 1957, p. 1–37.

389 J. Baudrier, *Bibliographie Lyonnaise*, Vol. 8; J. Plattard, 'L'Écu de Bâle', in *Revue du XVI Siècle*, Vol. 13, 1926, p. 282–285; P. Renouard, *Imprimeurs Parisiens, Libraires et Fondeurs de Caractères*, op. cit., articles on Cabiller, Resch, and Vidoue; E. Hubert, 'Chrétien Wechel, Imprimeur à Paris', in the *Gutenberg-Jahrbuch*, 1954, p. 181–187.

390 L. Delisle, 'Notice sur un Registre des Procès-Verbaux de la Faculté de Théologie de Paris pendant les Années 1505–1533' (offprint of an article in *Notices et Extraits des Manuscrits de la Bibliothèque Nationale et Autres Bibliothèques*, Vol. 36, 1899, p. 17–27. Cf. J. Guignard, 'Imprimeurs et Libraires Parisiens, 1525–1536', in *Bulletin de l'Association Guillaume Bude*, 3rd Series, no. 2, June, 1953, p. 74.

391 J. Veyrin-Forrer, 'Antoine Augereau, Graveur de Lettres et Imprimeur Parisien (vers 1485–1534)', in *Paris et Ile-de-France. Mémoires Publiés par la Fédération des Sociétés Historiques . . . de Paris et de l'Ile-de-France*, 1957.

392 N. Weiss, *Jean Du Bellay, les Protestants et la Sorbonne (1529–1535)*, Paris, 1904.

393 W. G. Moore, *La Réforme Allemande et la Littérature Francaise*, p. 446 ff. and passim.

394 N. Weiss, and V. L. Bourilly, 'Jean Du Bellay, les Protestants et la Sorbonne', in *Bulletin de la Société de l'Histoire du Protestantisme Français*, Vol. 53, 1904, p. 97–143; L. Febvre, 'L'origine des Placards de 1534', in *Bibliothèque d'Humanisme et Renaissance*, Vol. 7, 1945, p. 62–75; R. Hari, 'Les Placards de 1534' in *Aspects de la Propagande Religieuse*, Geneva, Droz, 1957, p. 79–142. The articles in the last mentioned work are of outstanding merit.

395 H. Hauser, *Études sur la Réforme Française*, p. 255–298.

396 T. Dufour, 'Notice Bibliographique sur le Catéchisme et la Confession de Foi de Calvin (1537) et sur les Autres Livres Imprimés à Genève et à Neuchâtel dans les Premiers Temps de la Réforme (1533–1540)', p. ccx–cclxxxviii of *Le Catéchisme Français de Calvin*, Geneva, 1878; J. Guignard, *L'Introduction de l'Imprimerie à Neuchâtel et Pierre de Vingle*, Neuchâtel, 1933; H. Delarue, 'Olivétan et Pierre de Vingle à Genève, 1532–1553', in *Bibliothèque d'Humanisme et Renaissance*, Vol. 8, 1946, p. 105–118; E. Droz, 'Pierre de Vingle, l'Imprimeur de Farel', and G. Berthoud, 'Livres pseudo-Catholiques de Contenu Protestant', in *Aspects de la Propagande Religieuse*, p. 38–78, and p. 143–166.

397 See P. Chaix, *Recherches sur l'Imprimerie à Genève de 1550 à 1564*, Geneva, 1954, and M. Kingdom, *Geneva and the Coming of the Wars of Religion in France, 1555–1563*, Geneva, 1956.

398 P. Imbart de la Tour, *Les Origines de la Réforme*, Paris, 1935, Vol. 4, p. 292–299.

399 H. L. Schlaepfer, 'Laurent de Normandie', in *Aspects de la Propagande Religieuse*, p. 176–230.

400 E. Droz, 'Antoine Vincent. La Propagande Protestante par le Psautier', in *Aspects de la Propagande Religieuse*, p. 276–293.

401 Cf. A. Meillet, *Les Langues dans L'Europe Nouvelle*, Paris, 1928, p. 16.

402 Ibid., p. 160.

403 F. Brunot, *Histoire de la Langue Française*, Vol. 2: *Le XVI Siècle*, p. 2 ff.

404 Bibliothèque Nationale. *Anvers au Temps de Plantin et de Rubens*, (Catalogue of an exhibition), p. 95.

405 J. M. Sanchez, *Bibliografia Aragonesa del Siglo XVI*, Madrid, 1913, 2 Vols.

406 Information from the papers of P. Renouard.

407 E. Weiler, *Repertorium Typographicum. Die Deutsche Literatur im ersten Viertel des Sechzehnten Jahrhunderts*, Nordlingen, 1864; F. Milkau, *Handbuch der Bibliothekswissenschaft*, Vol. 1, p. 516 ff.; B. Clausse, 'Niederdeutsche Drucke im XVI Jahrhundert', in *Zeitschrift für Bibliothekswesen*, 29, 1912, p. 201 ff.

408 E. Tonnelat, *Histoire de la Langue Allemande*, Paris, 1927, p. 127–145.

409 Cf. E. Tonnelat, op. cit., p. 125.

410 F. Mossé, *Esquisse d'une Histoire de la Langue Anglaise*, Lyons, 1947, p. 105 ff.

411 Quoted in Mossé.

412 F. Brunot, *Histoire de la Langue Française*, Vol. 2: *Le XVI Siècle*, Paris, 1931; C. Beaulieux, *Histoire de l'Orthographie Française*, Paris, 1927, 2 Vols.

413 R. Menendez Pidal, 'El Lenguaje del Siglo XVI', in *Cruz y Raya*, 6th and 15th September 1933, p. 7–63.

Index